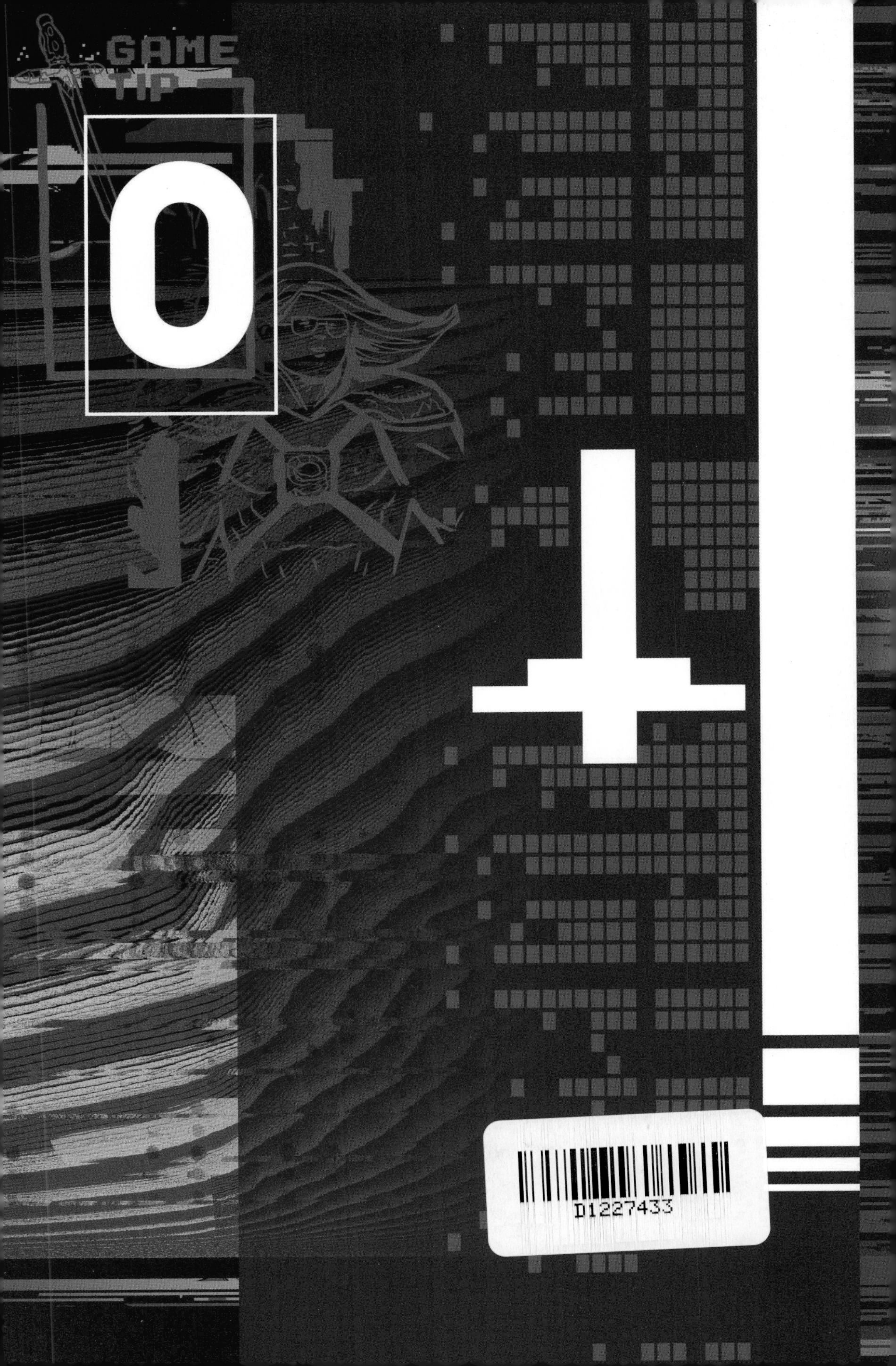
GAME
TIP
0

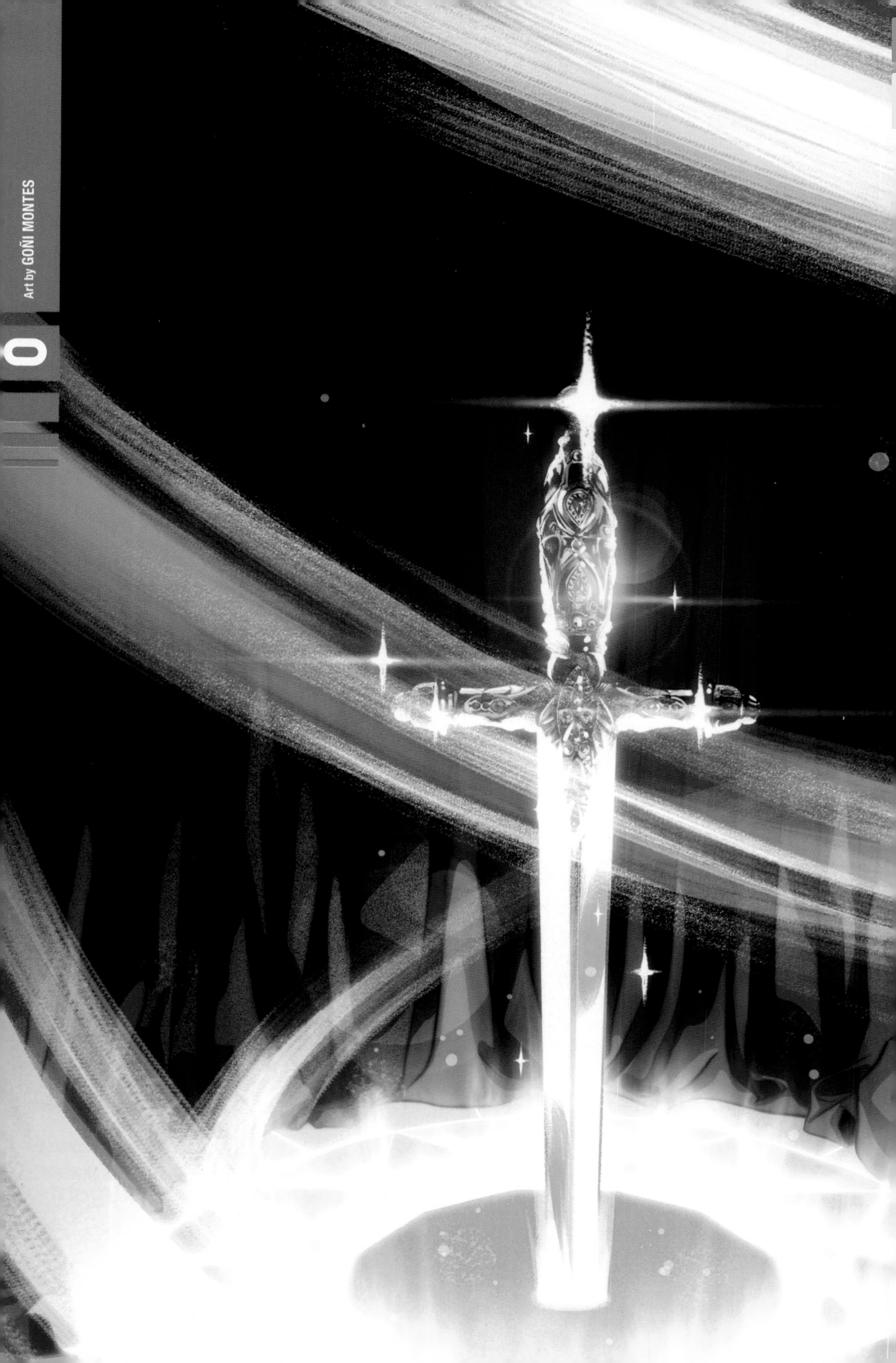

Art by GOÑI MONTES

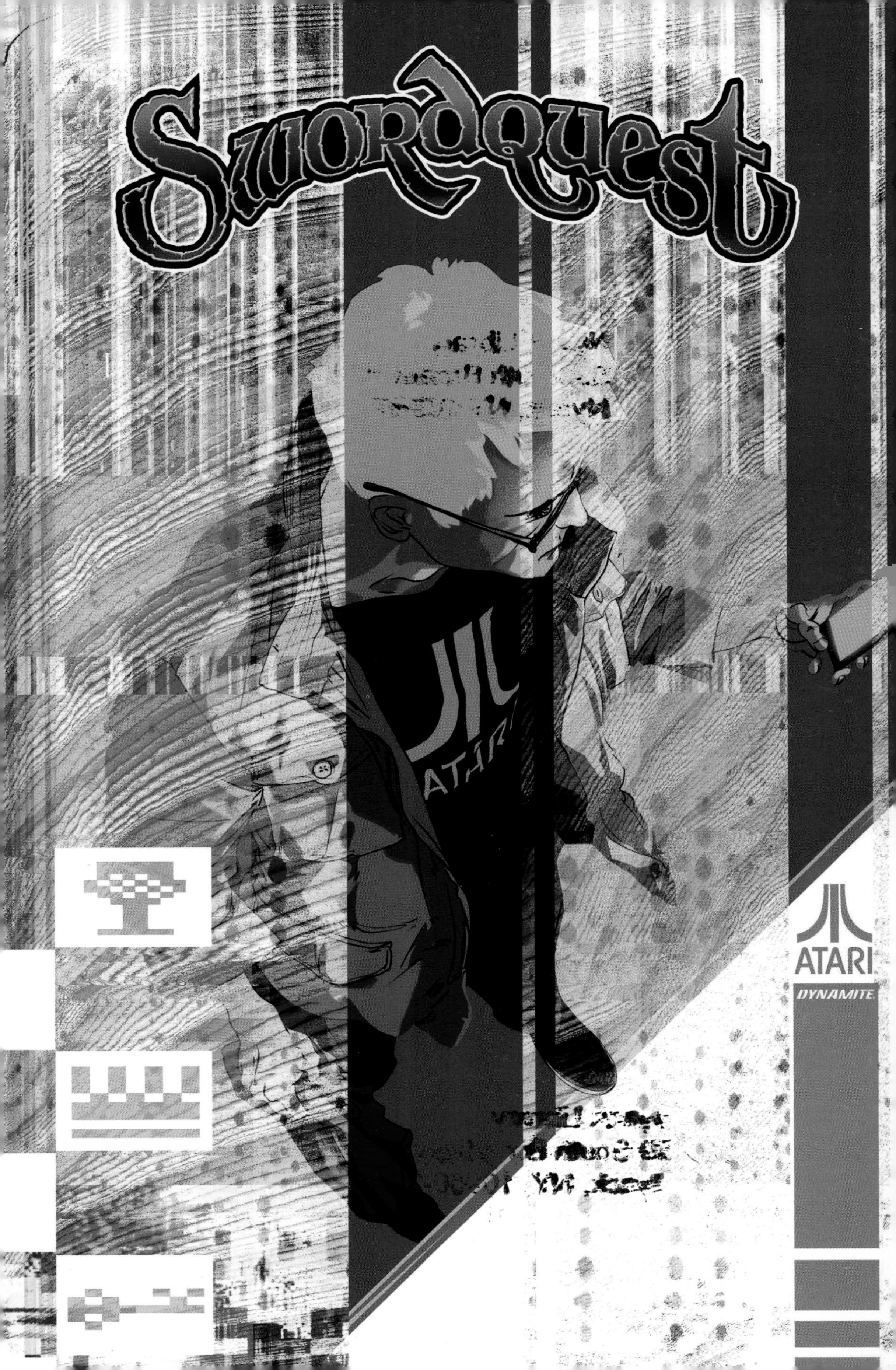
Swordquest™
ATARI
DYNAMITE

WRITTEN BY
chad bowers & chris sims

ART BY
ghostwriter x

ISSUE 0-2 & 4-5 COLORS BY
ghostwriter x

ISSUE 3 COLORS BY
chris o'halloran

ISSUE 0-2 COLOR FLATS BY
karl fan

ISSUE 4-5 COLOR FLATS BY
ellie wright

LETTERS BY
josh krach

COLLECTION COVER BY
goñi montes

EDITED BY
kevin ketner

COLLECTION DESIGN BY
cathleen heard

DYNAMITE.

Online at www.DYNAMITE.com
On Facebook /Dynamitecomics
On Instagram /Dynamitecomics

On Tumblr dynamitecomics.tumblr.com
On Twitter @dynamitecomics
On YouTube /Dynamitecomics

Nick Barrucci, CEO / Publisher
Juan Collado, President / COO

Joe Rybandt, Executive Editor
Matt Idelson, Senior Editor
Anthony Marques, Associate Editor
Kevin Ketner, Assistant Editor

Jason Ullmeyer, Art Director
Geoff Harkins, Senior Graphic Designer
Cathleen Heard, Graphic Designer
Alexis Persson, Graphic Designer

Chris Caniano, Digital Associate
Rachel Kilbury, Digital Assistant

Brandon Dante Primavera, V.P. of IT and Operations
Rich Young, Director of Business Development

Alan Payne, V.P. of Sales and Marketing
Janie Mackenzie, Marketing Coordinator
Pat O'Connell, Sales Manager

Paperback:
ISBN-13: 978-1-5241-0488-7

First Printing
10 9 8 7 6 5 4 3 2 1

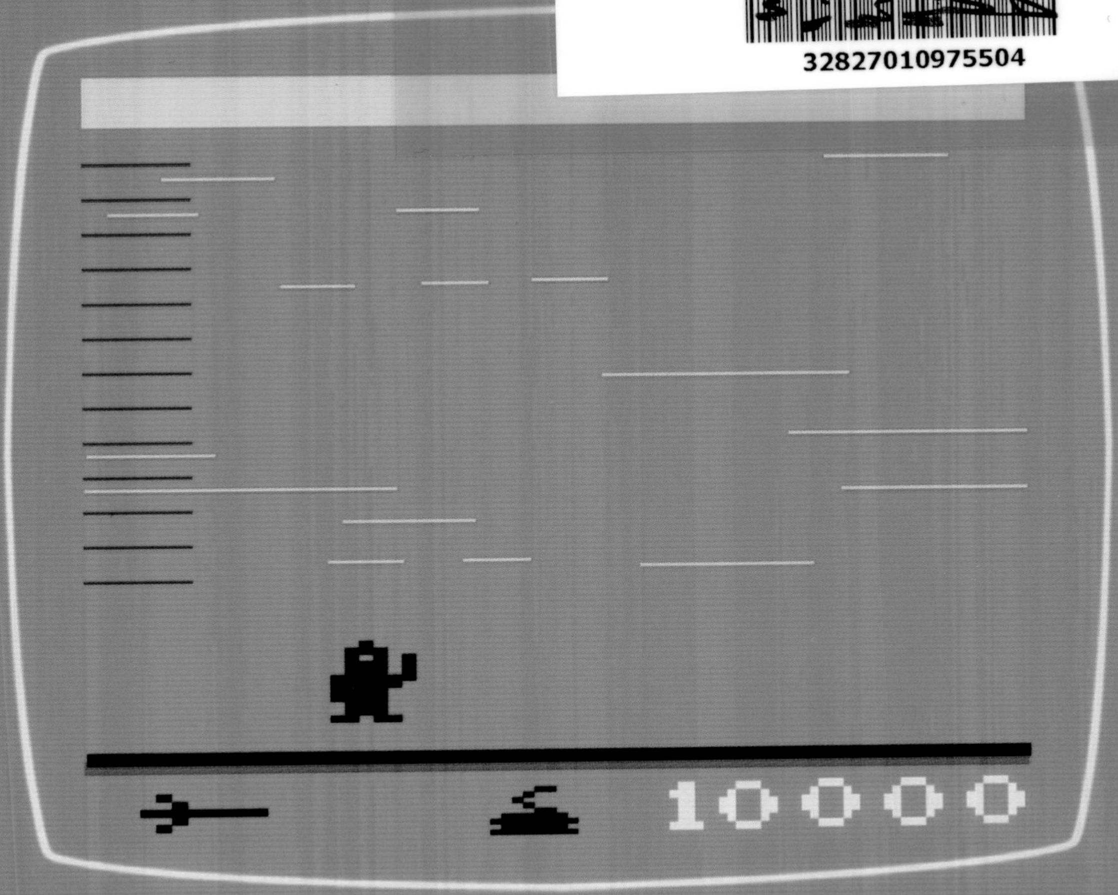
10000

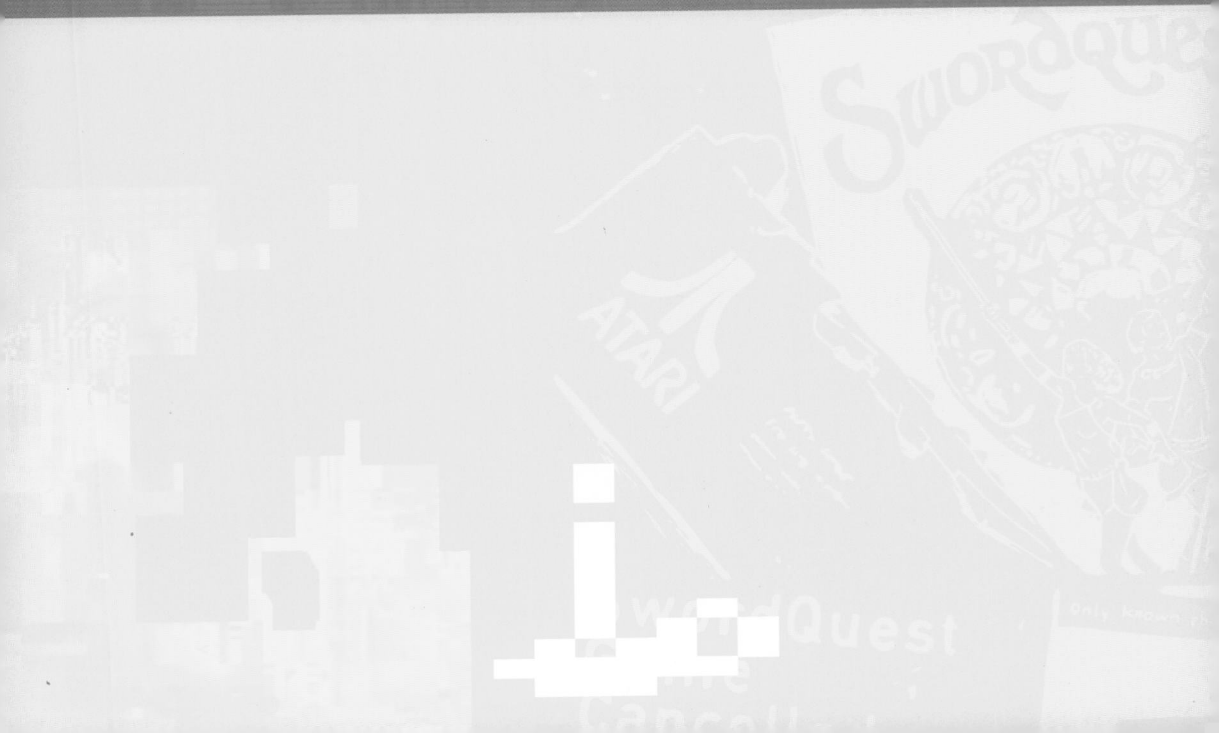
Swordque
ATARI
rdQuest

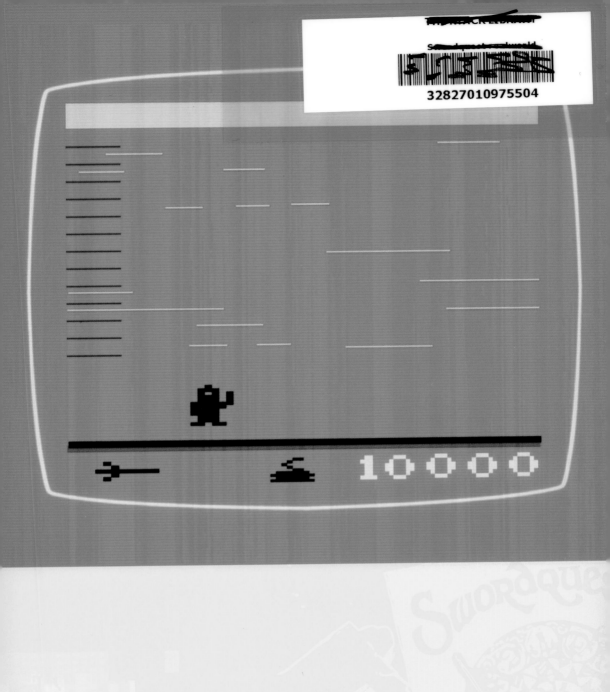

REALWORLD

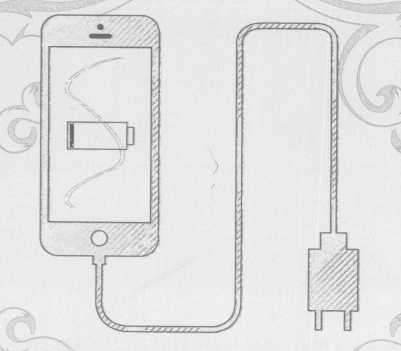

The child Peter Case and the Twins Perez,
Quested they did, through Earth, Fire, and Water.
But the World of Air never did arrive,
Leading their hopes and dreams to slaughter.
Adults they find themselves, worse for wear,
Back on the Quest, for the Sword they must steal.
Beware of enemies, gird their loins, they must,
Because ~~this~~ is about to get Real.

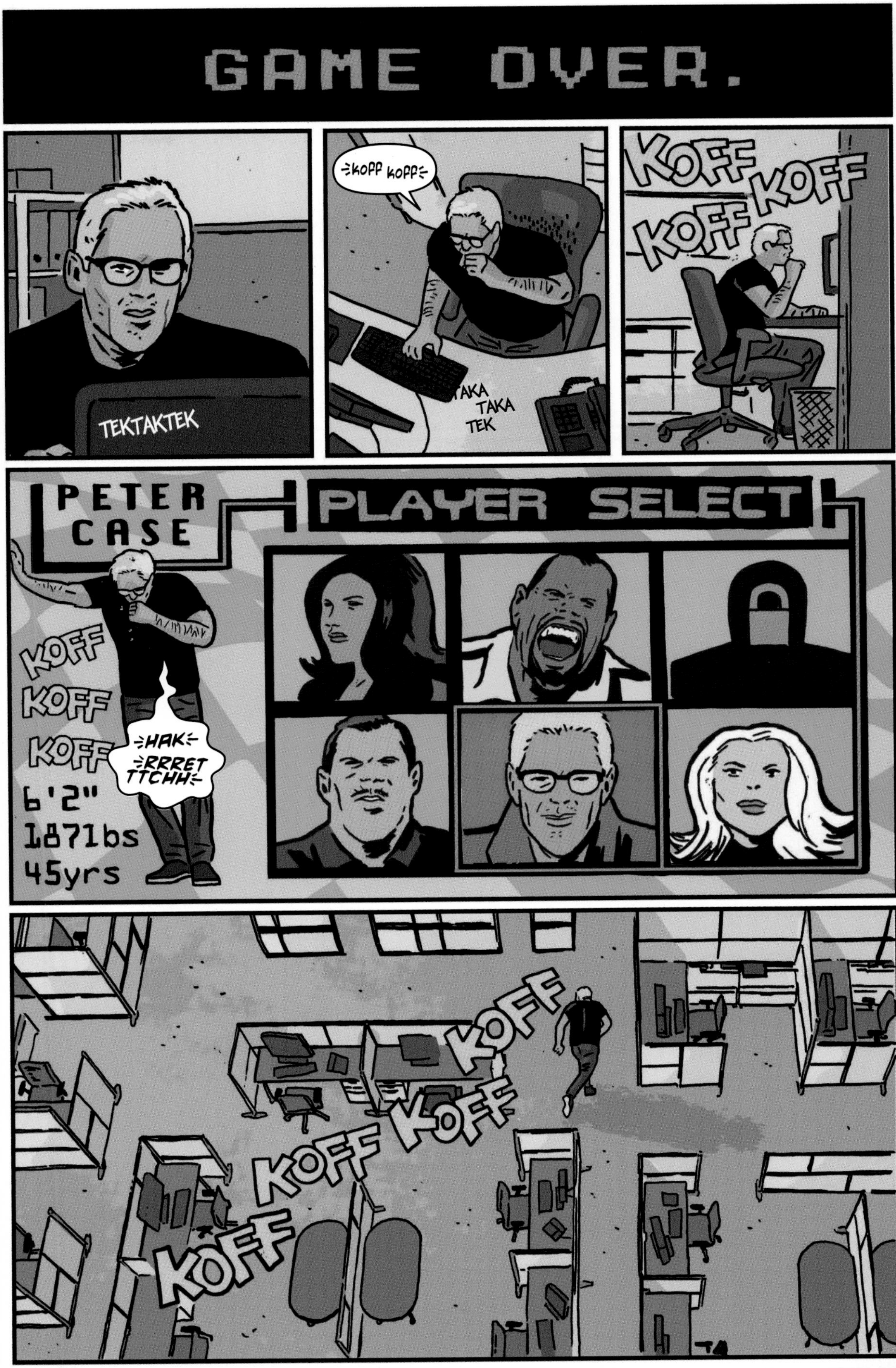
GAME OVER.
TEKTAKTEK
KOFF KOFF
TAKA TAKA TEK
KOFF KOFF KOFF
PETER CASE
PLAYER SELECT
KOFF
KOFF
KOFF
HAK RRRET TTCHH
6'2"
187lbs
45yrs
KOFF KOFF KOFF KOFF

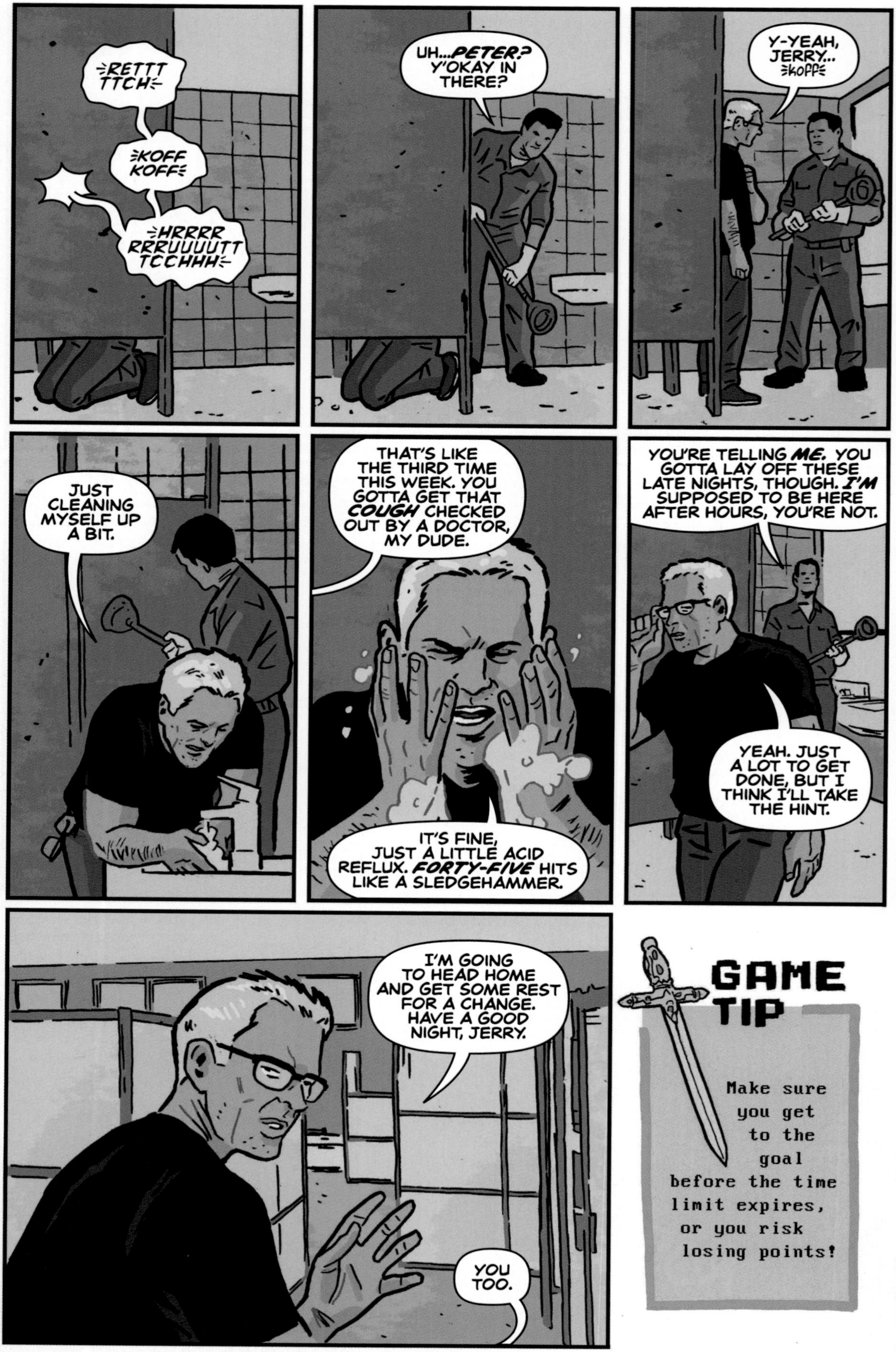
RETTT TTCH
KOFF KOFF
HRRRR RRRUUUUTT TCCHHH
UH...PETER? Y'OKAY IN THERE?
Y-YEAH, JERRY... KOFF
JUST CLEANING MYSELF UP A BIT.
THAT'S LIKE THE THIRD TIME THIS WEEK. YOU GOTTA GET THAT COUGH CHECKED OUT BY A DOCTOR, MY DUDE.
IT'S FINE, JUST A LITTLE ACID REFLUX. FORTY-FIVE HITS LIKE A SLEDGEHAMMER.
YOU'RE TELLING ME. YOU GOTTA LAY OFF THESE LATE NIGHTS, THOUGH. I'M SUPPOSED TO BE HERE AFTER HOURS, YOU'RE NOT.
YEAH. JUST A LOT TO GET DONE, BUT I THINK I'LL TAKE THE HINT.
I'M GOING TO HEAD HOME AND GET SOME REST FOR A CHANGE. HAVE A GOOD NIGHT, JERRY.
YOU TOO.
GAME TIP
Make sure you get to the goal before the time limit expires, or you risk losing points!

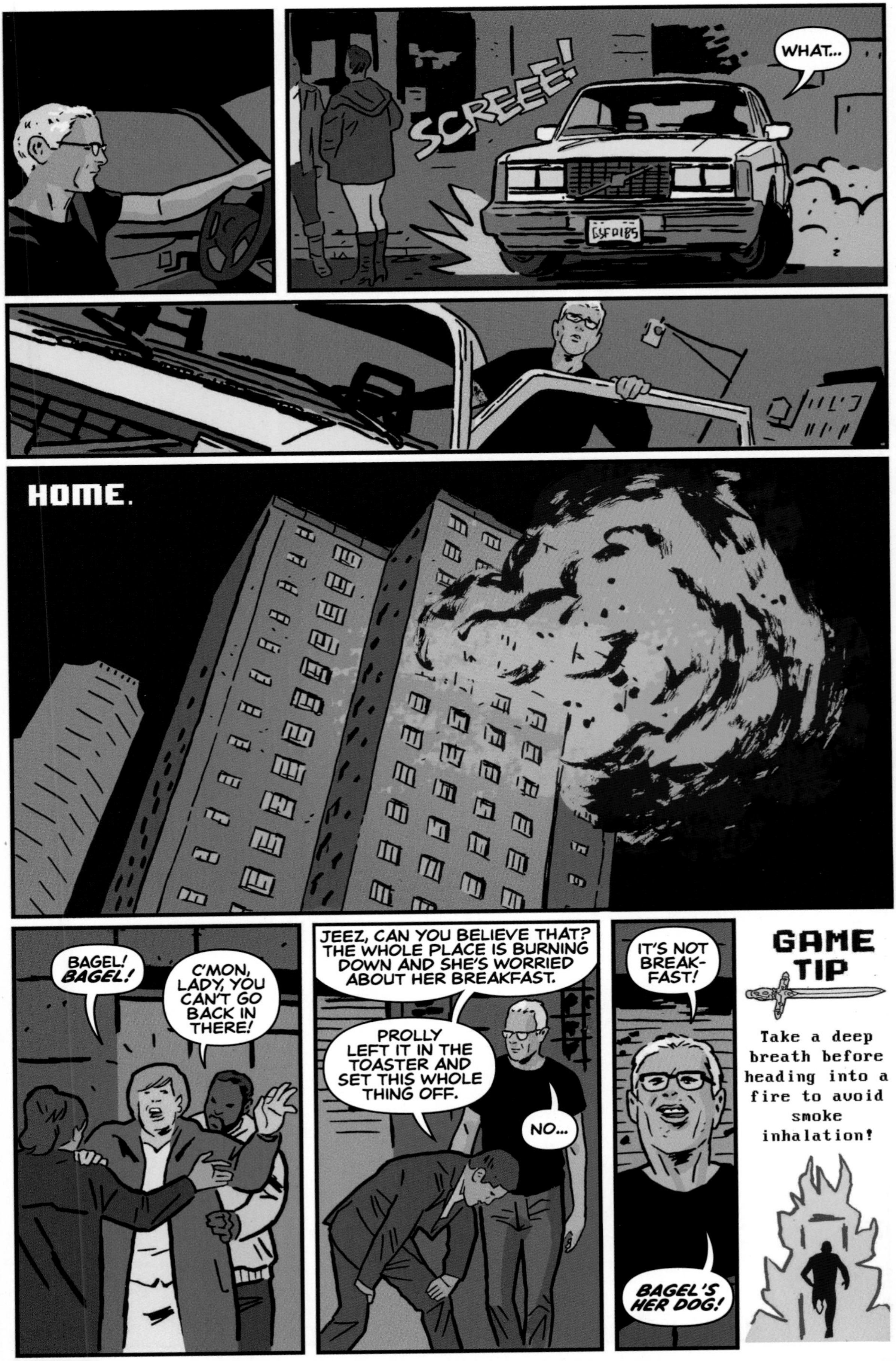
SCREEEE!
WHAT...
GSF0185
HOME.
BAGEL! BAGEL!
C'MON, LADY, YOU CAN'T GO BACK IN THERE!
JEEZ, CAN YOU BELIEVE THAT? THE WHOLE PLACE IS BURNING DOWN AND SHE'S WORRIED ABOUT HER BREAKFAST.
PROLLY LEFT IT IN THE TOASTER AND SET THIS WHOLE THING OFF.
NO...
IT'S NOT BREAK-FAST!
BAGEL'S HER DOG!
GAME TIP
Take a deep breath before heading into a fire to avoid smoke inhalation!

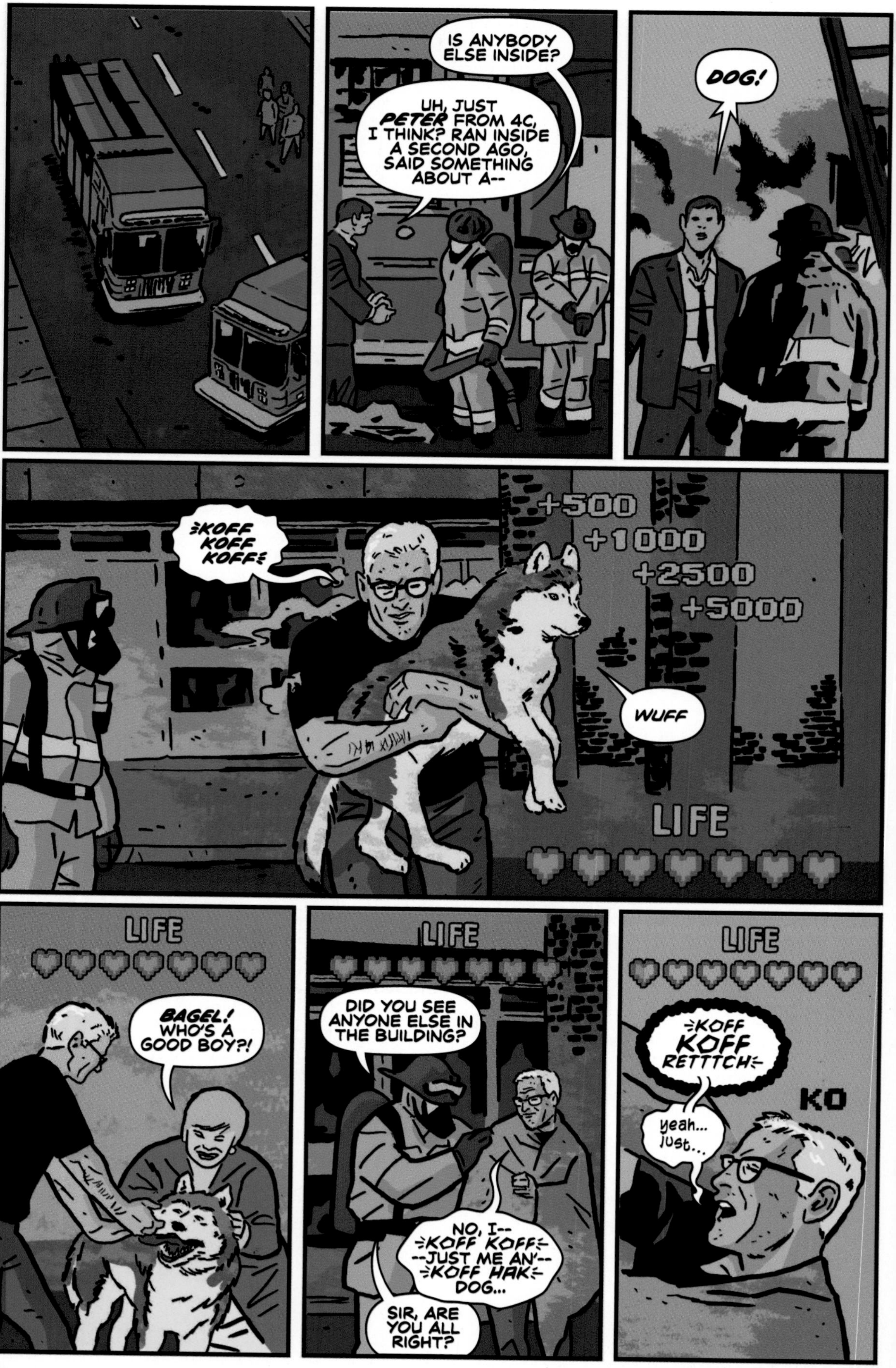
IS ANYBODY ELSE INSIDE?
UH, JUST PETER FROM 4C, I THINK? RAN INSIDE A SECOND AGO, SAID SOMETHING ABOUT A--
DOG!
KOFF KOFF KOFF
+500
+1000
+2500
+5000
WUFF
LIFE
LIFE
BAGEL! WHO'S A GOOD BOY?!
LIFE
DID YOU SEE ANYONE ELSE IN THE BUILDING?
NO, I-- KOFF KOFF --JUST ME AN'-- KOFF HAK DOG...
SIR, ARE YOU ALL RIGHT?
LIFE
KOFF KOFF RETTTCH
KO
yeah... just...

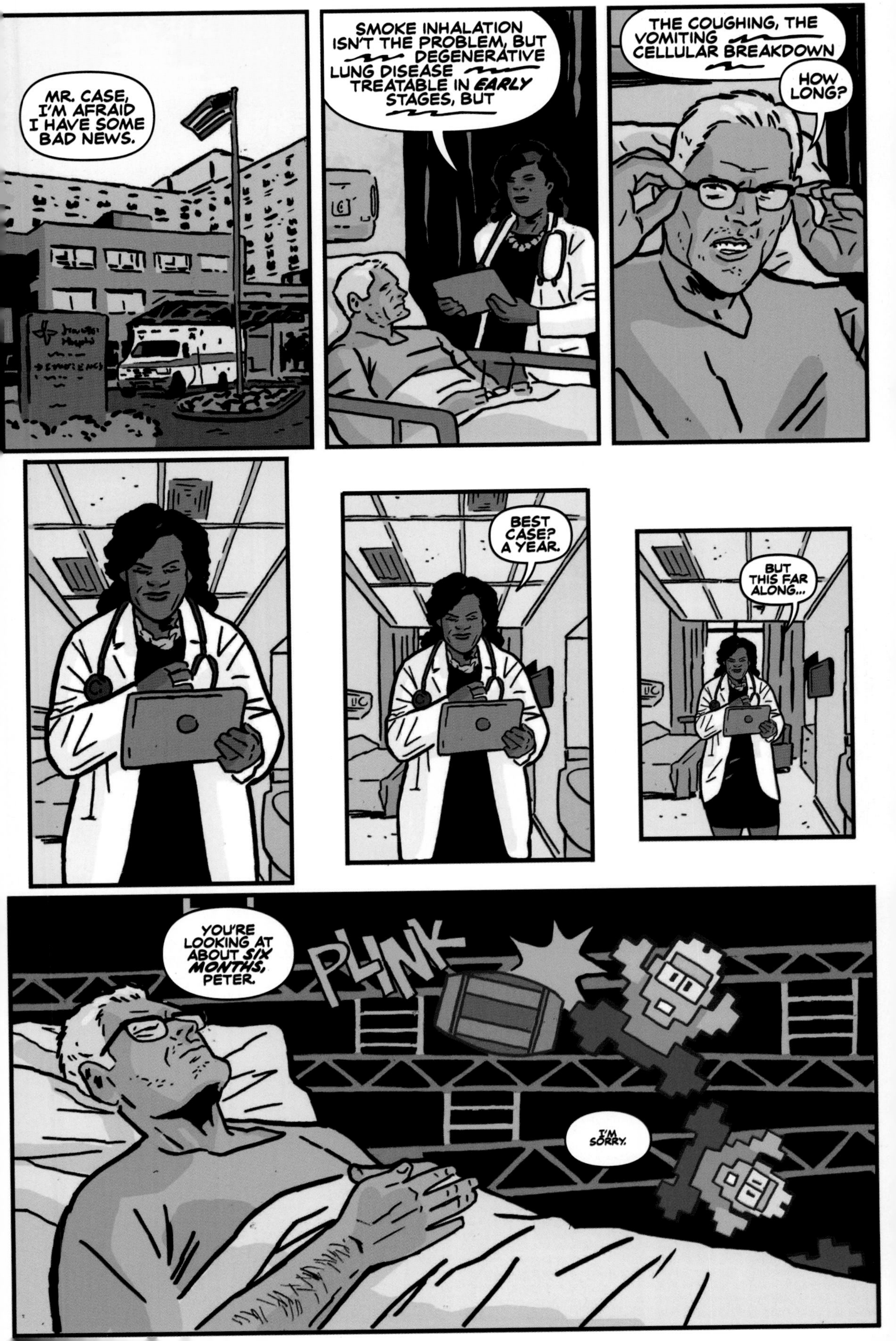
MR. CASE, I'M AFRAID I HAVE SOME BAD NEWS.
SMOKE INHALATION ISN'T THE PROBLEM, BUT DEGENERATIVE LUNG DISEASE TREATABLE IN EARLY STAGES, BUT
THE COUGHING, THE VOMITING CELLULAR BREAKDOWN
HOW LONG?
BEST CASE? A YEAR.
BUT THIS FAR ALONG...
YOU'RE LOOKING AT ABOUT SIX MONTHS, PETER.
PLINK
I'M SORRY.

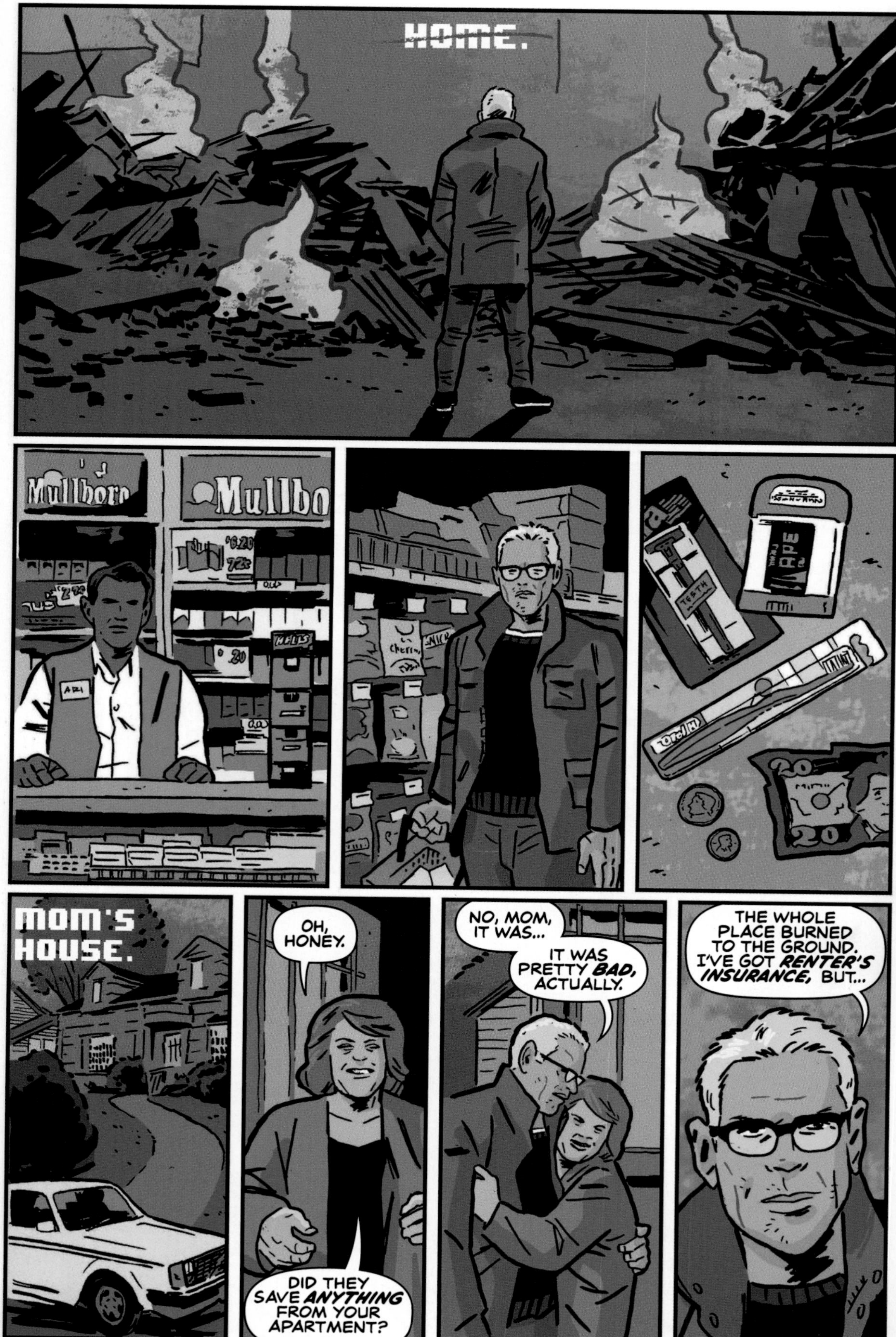
HOME.
Mullboro
Mullbo
ARI
MOM'S HOUSE.
OH, HONEY.
DID THEY SAVE ANYTHING FROM YOUR APARTMENT?
NO, MOM, IT WAS...
IT WAS PRETTY BAD, ACTUALLY.
THE WHOLE PLACE BURNED TO THE GROUND. I'VE GOT RENTER'S INSURANCE, BUT...

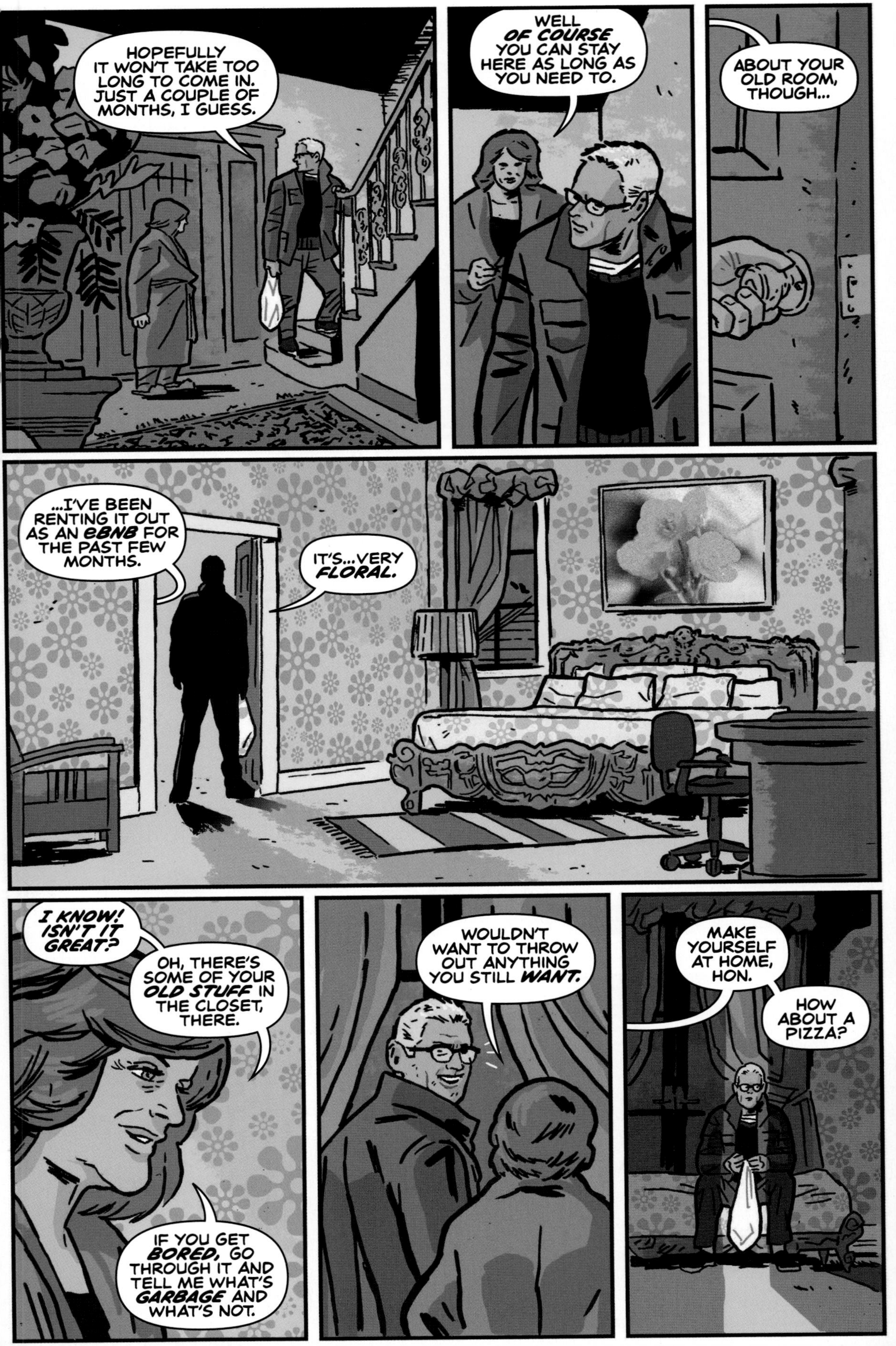
HOPEFULLY IT WON'T TAKE TOO LONG TO COME IN. JUST A COUPLE OF MONTHS, I GUESS.
WELL OF COURSE YOU CAN STAY HERE AS LONG AS YOU NEED TO.
ABOUT YOUR OLD ROOM, THOUGH...
...I'VE BEEN RENTING IT OUT AS AN eBNB FOR THE PAST FEW MONTHS.
IT'S...VERY FLORAL.
I KNOW! ISN'T IT GREAT?
OH, THERE'S SOME OF YOUR OLD STUFF IN THE CLOSET, THERE.
IF YOU GET BORED, GO THROUGH IT AND TELL ME WHAT'S GARBAGE AND WHAT'S NOT.
WOULDN'T WANT TO THROW OUT ANYTHING YOU STILL WANT.
MAKE YOURSELF AT HOME, HON.
HOW ABOUT A PIZZA?

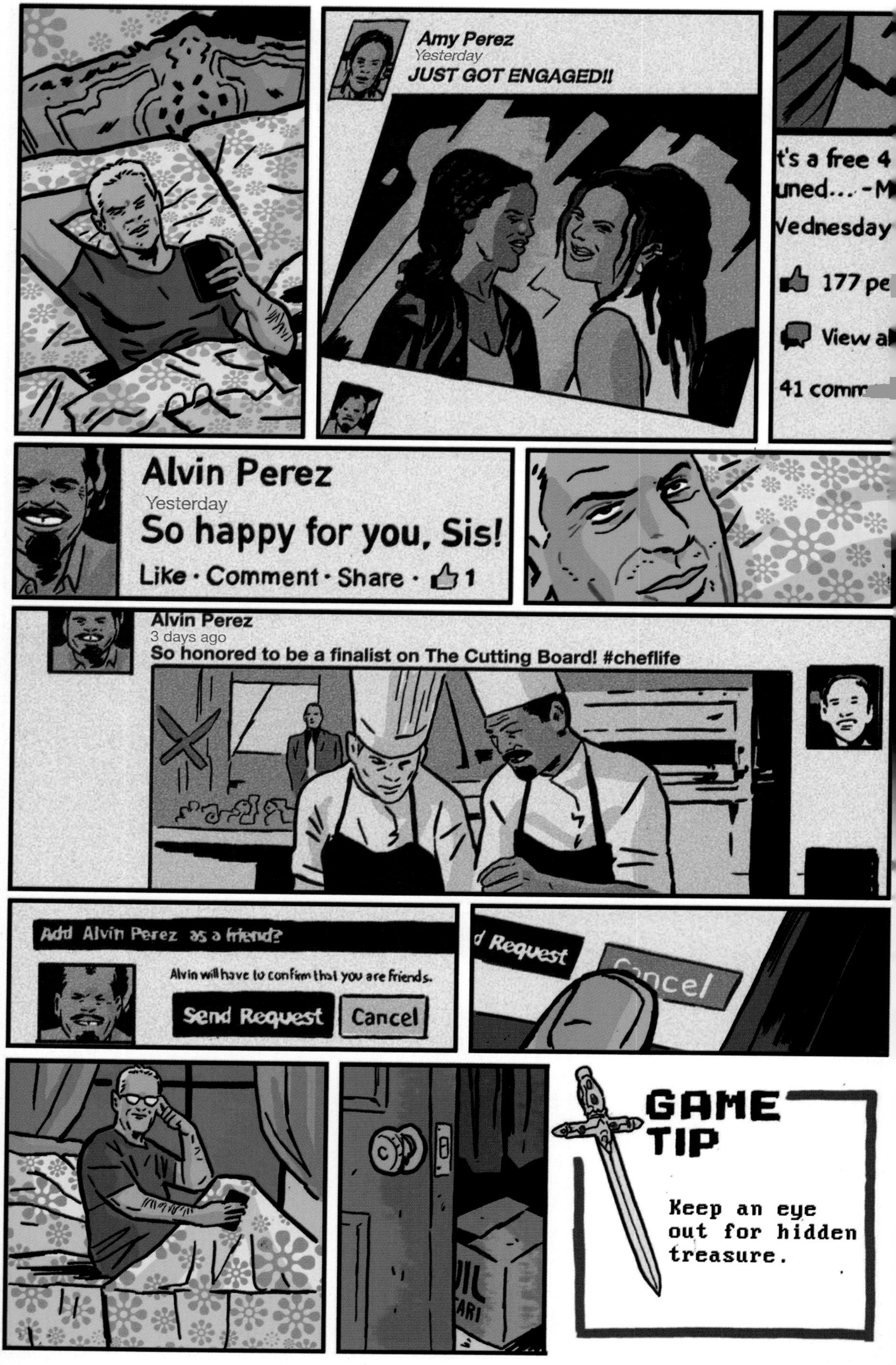
Amy Perez
Yesterday
JUST GOT ENGAGED!!
t's a free 4
uned... -M
Vednesday
177 pe
View al
41 comm
Alvin Perez
Yesterday
So happy for you, Sis!
Like · Comment · Share · 1
Alvin Perez
3 days ago
So honored to be a finalist on The Cutting Board! #cheflife
Add Alvin Perez as a friend?
Alvin will have to confirm that you are friends.
Send Request
Cancel
d Request
ncel
GAME TIP
Keep an eye out for hidden treasure.

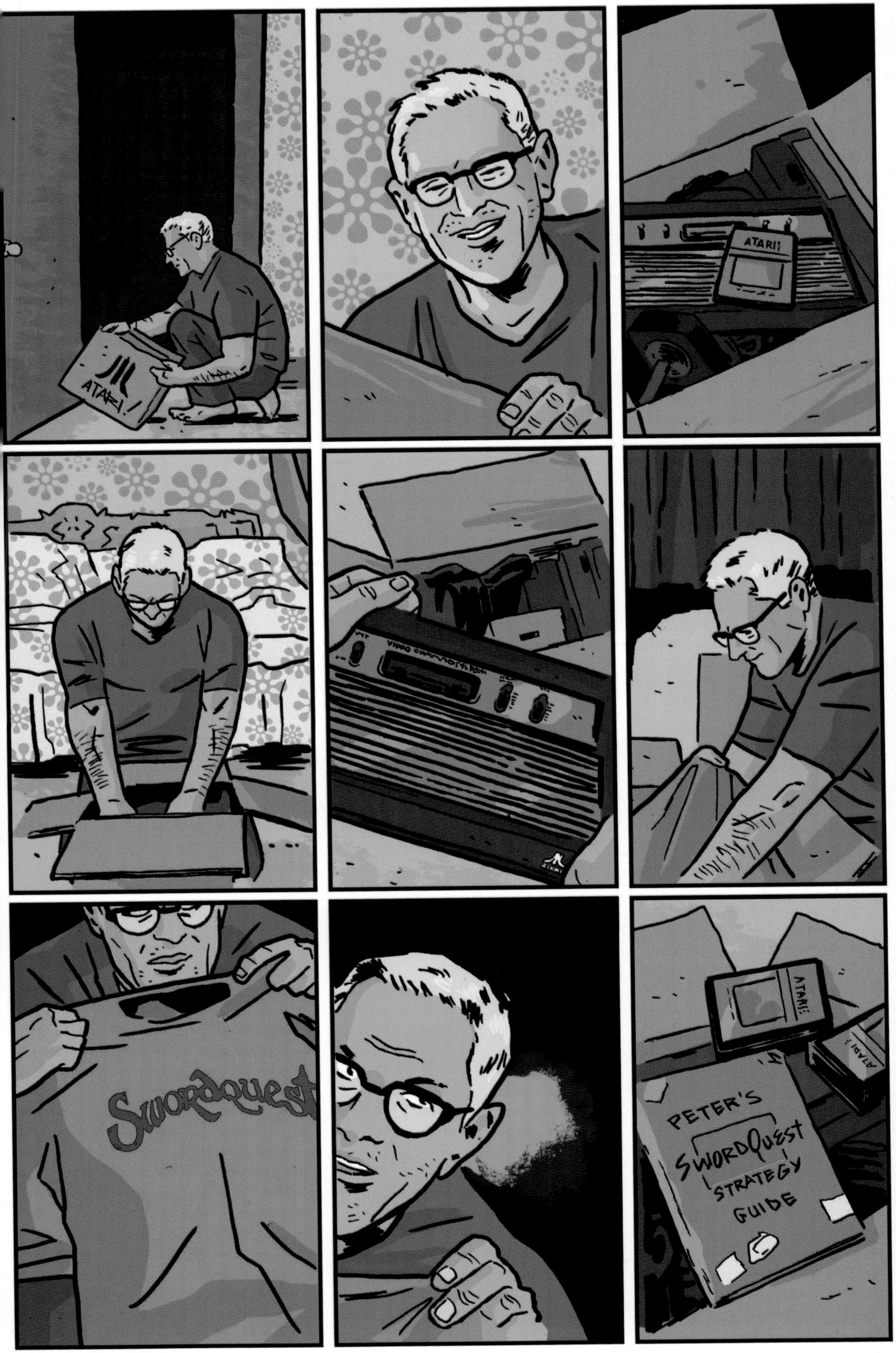
ATARI
ATARI
ATARI
SWORDQUEST
ATARI
ATARI
PETER'S
SWORDQUEST
STRATEGY
GUIDE

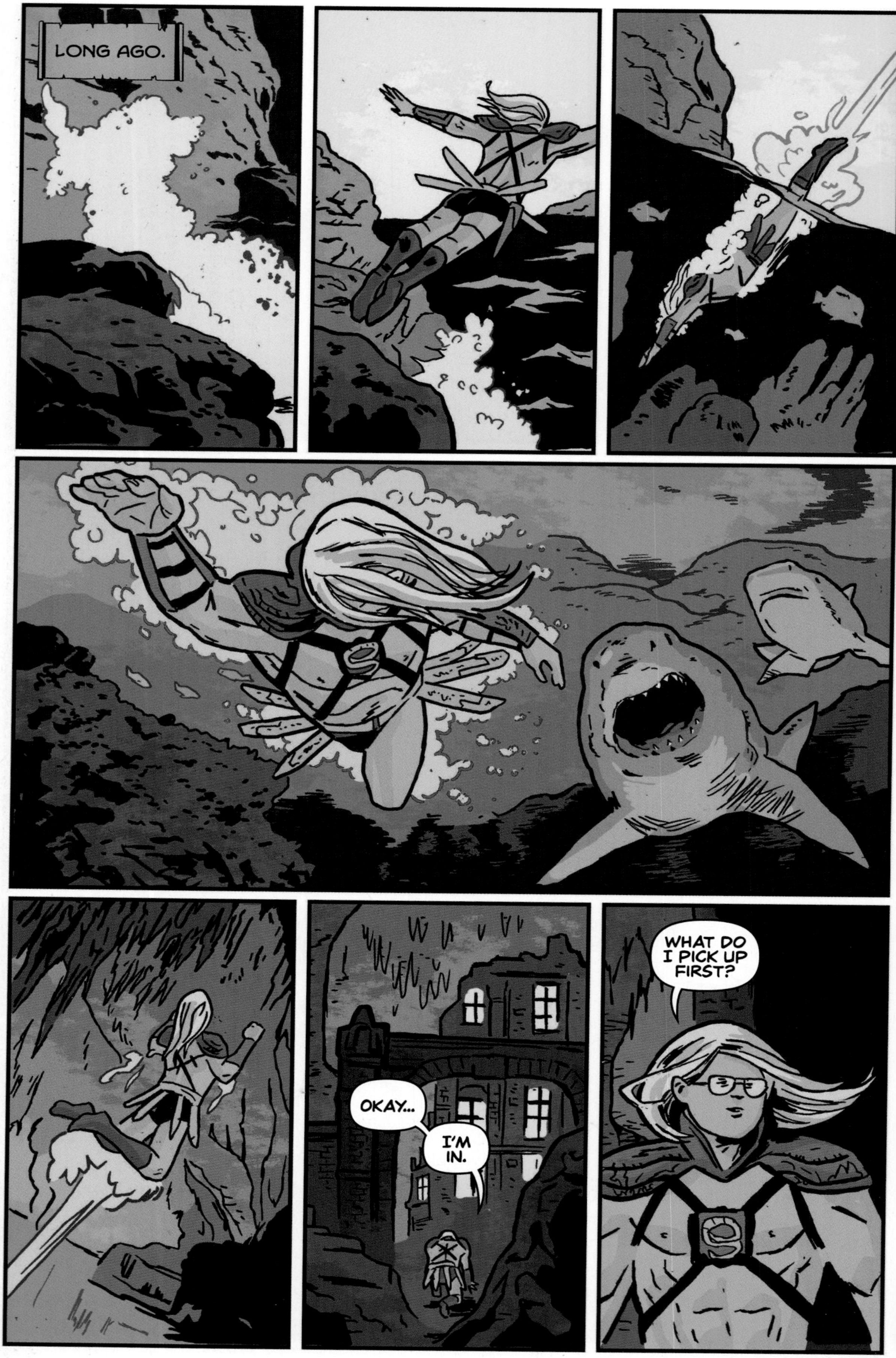
LONG AGO.
OKAY...
I'M IN.
WHAT DO I PICK UP FIRST?

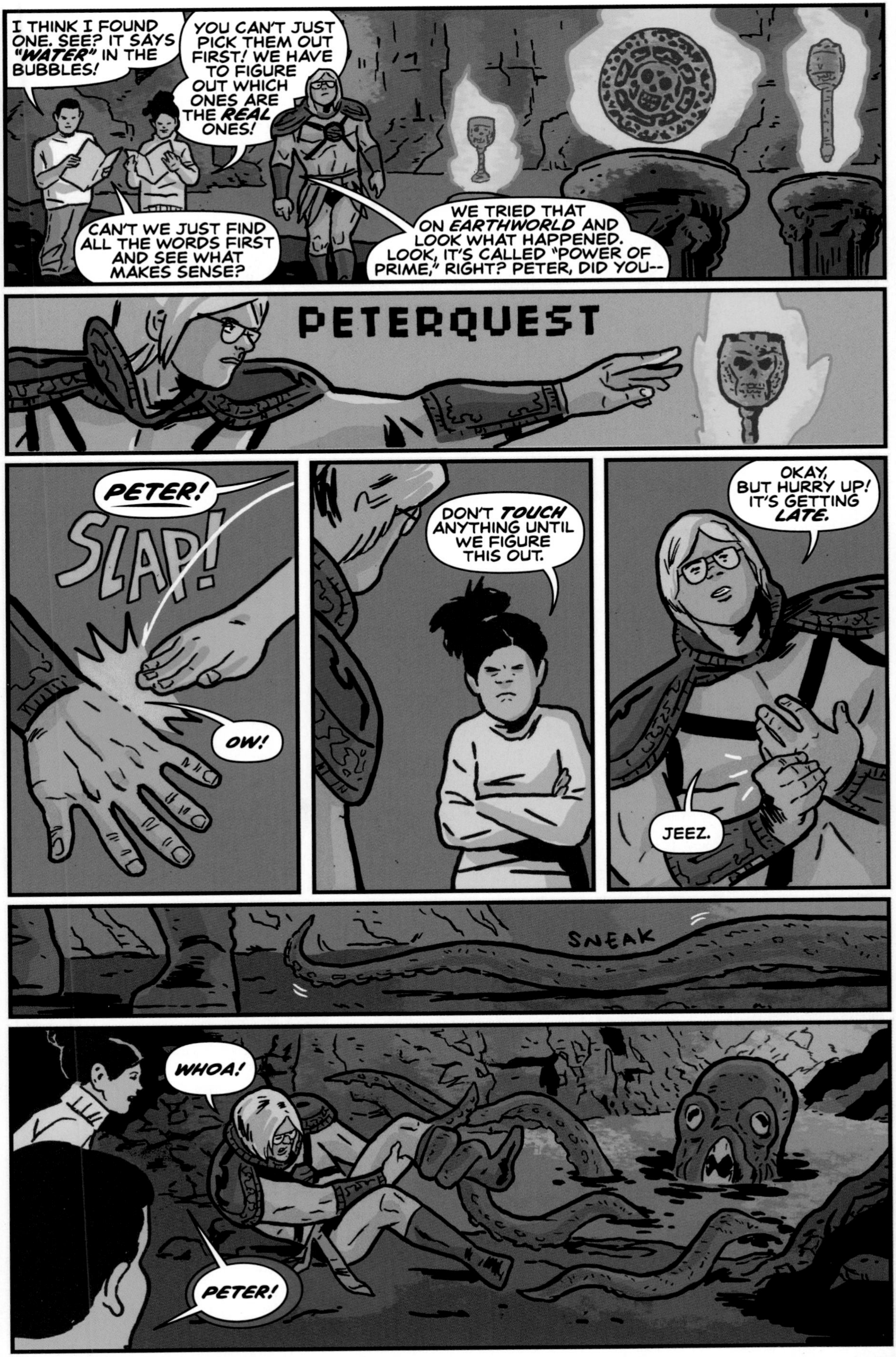
I THINK I FOUND ONE. SEE? IT SAYS "WATER" IN THE BUBBLES!
YOU CAN'T JUST PICK THEM OUT FIRST! WE HAVE TO FIGURE OUT WHICH ONES ARE THE REAL ONES!
CAN'T WE JUST FIND ALL THE WORDS FIRST AND SEE WHAT MAKES SENSE?
WE TRIED THAT ON EARTHWORLD AND LOOK WHAT HAPPENED. LOOK, IT'S CALLED "POWER OF PRIME," RIGHT? PETER, DID YOU--
PETERQUEST
PETER!
SLAP!
OW!
DON'T TOUCH ANYTHING UNTIL WE FIGURE THIS OUT.
OKAY, BUT HURRY UP! IT'S GETTING LATE.
JEEZ.
SNEAK
WHOA!
PETER!

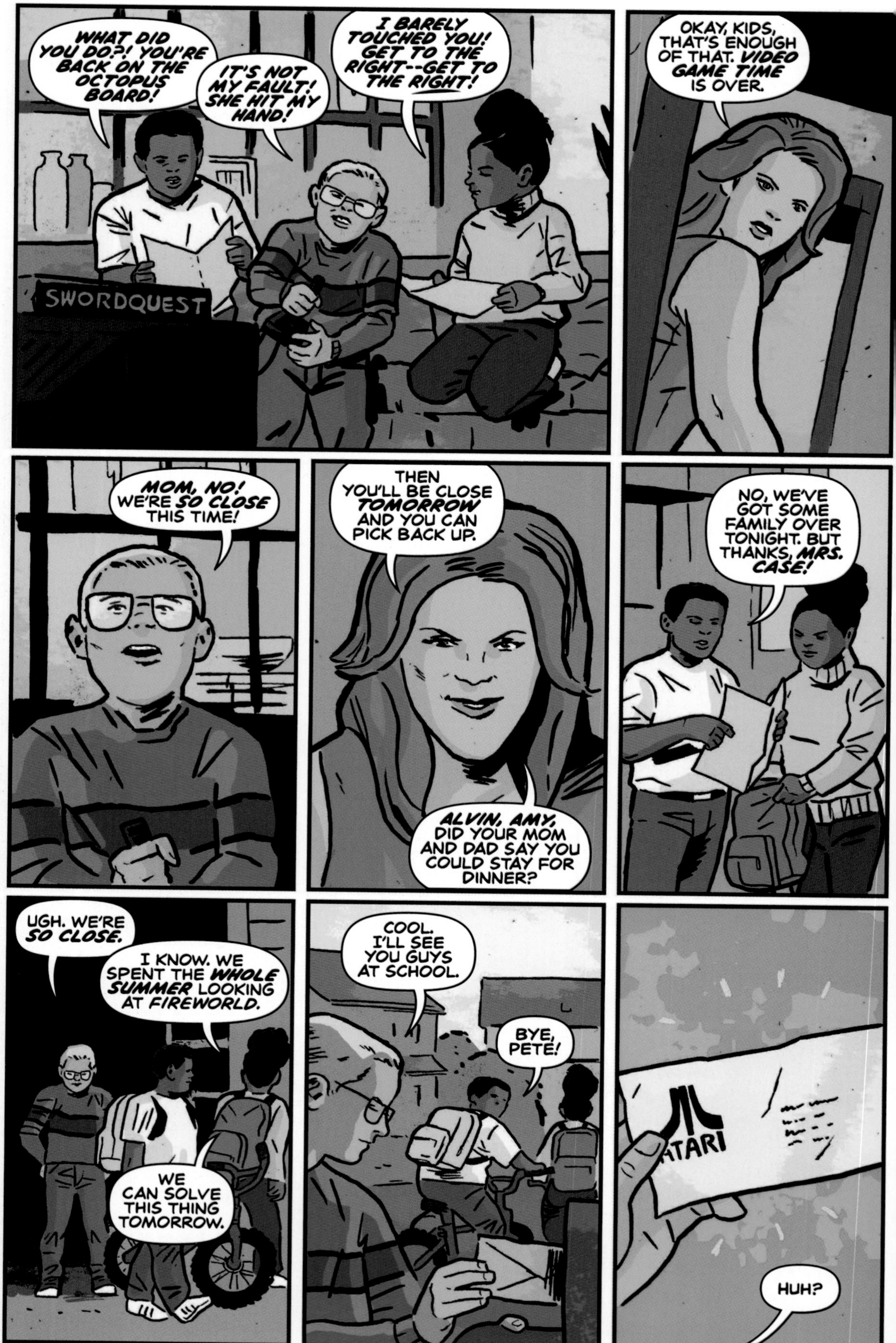
WHAT DID YOU DO?! YOU'RE BACK ON THE OCTOPUS BOARD!
IT'S NOT MY FAULT! SHE HIT MY HAND!
I BARELY TOUCHED YOU! GET TO THE RIGHT--GET TO THE RIGHT!
SWORDQUEST
OKAY, KIDS, THAT'S ENOUGH OF THAT. VIDEO GAME TIME IS OVER.
MOM, NO! WE'RE SO CLOSE THIS TIME!
THEN YOU'LL BE CLOSE TOMORROW AND YOU CAN PICK BACK UP.
ALVIN, AMY, DID YOUR MOM AND DAD SAY YOU COULD STAY FOR DINNER?
NO, WE'VE GOT SOME FAMILY OVER TONIGHT. BUT THANKS, MRS. CASE!
UGH. WE'RE SO CLOSE.
I KNOW. WE SPENT THE WHOLE SUMMER LOOKING AT FIREWORLD.
WE CAN SOLVE THIS THING TOMORROW.
COOL. I'LL SEE YOU GUYS AT SCHOOL.
BYE, PETE!
ATARI
HUH?

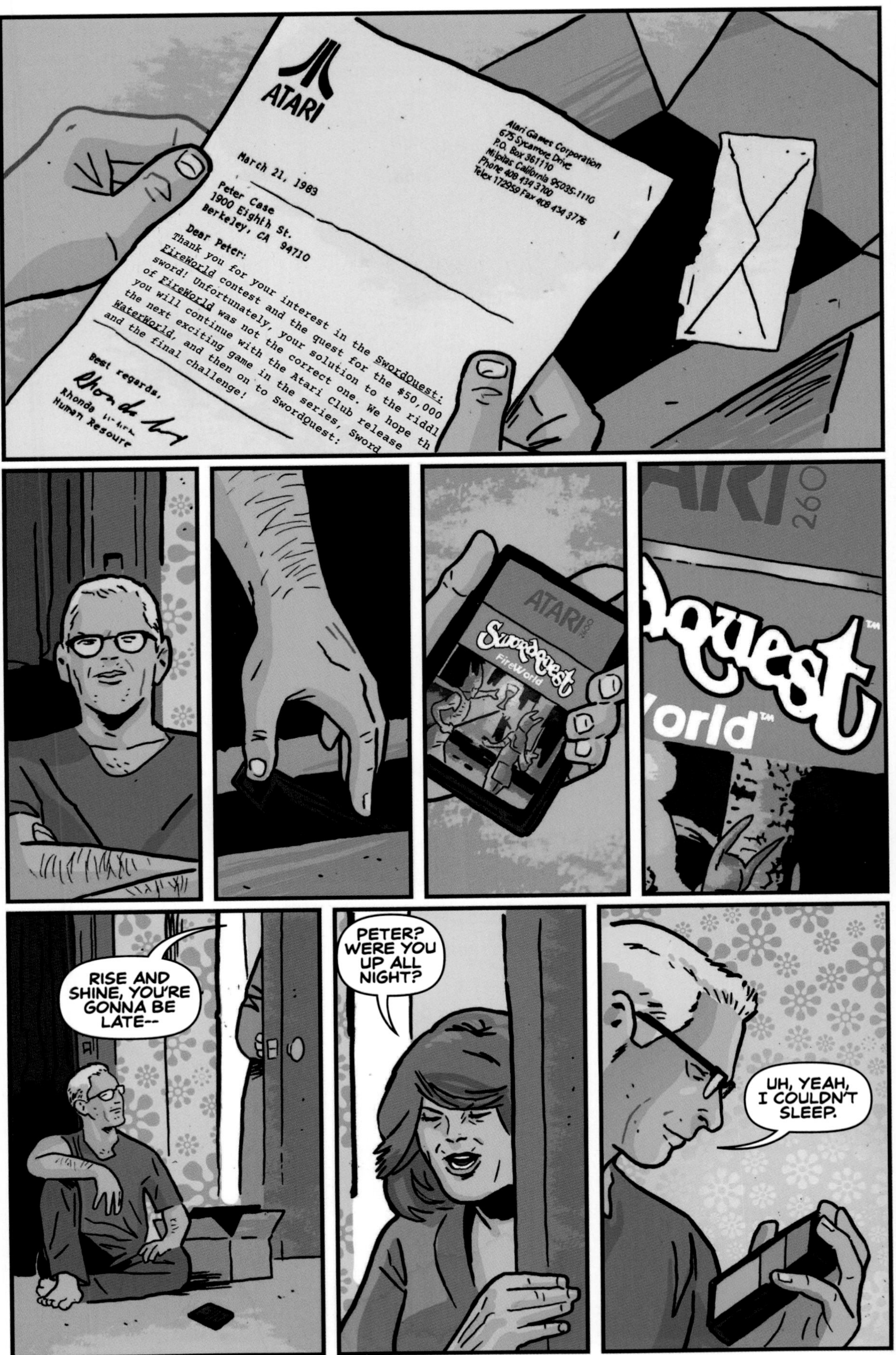
ATARI
Atari Games Corporation
675 Sycamore Drive
P.O. Box 361110
Milpitas California 95035-1110
Phone 408 434 3700
Telex 172959 Fax 408 434 3776
March 21, 1983
Peter Case
1900 Eighth St.
Berkeley, CA 94710
Dear Peter:
Thank you for your interest in the SwordQuest:
FireWorld contest and the quest for the $50,000
sword! Unfortunately, your solution to the riddl
of FireWorld was not the correct one. We hope th
you will continue with the Atari Club release
the next exciting game in the series, Sword
WaterWorld, and then on to SwordQuest:
and the final challenge!
Best regards,
Rhonda
Human Resour
ATARI
SwordQuest
FireWorld
RISE AND SHINE, YOU'RE GONNA BE LATE--
PETER? WERE YOU UP ALL NIGHT?
UH, YEAH, I COULDN'T SLEEP.

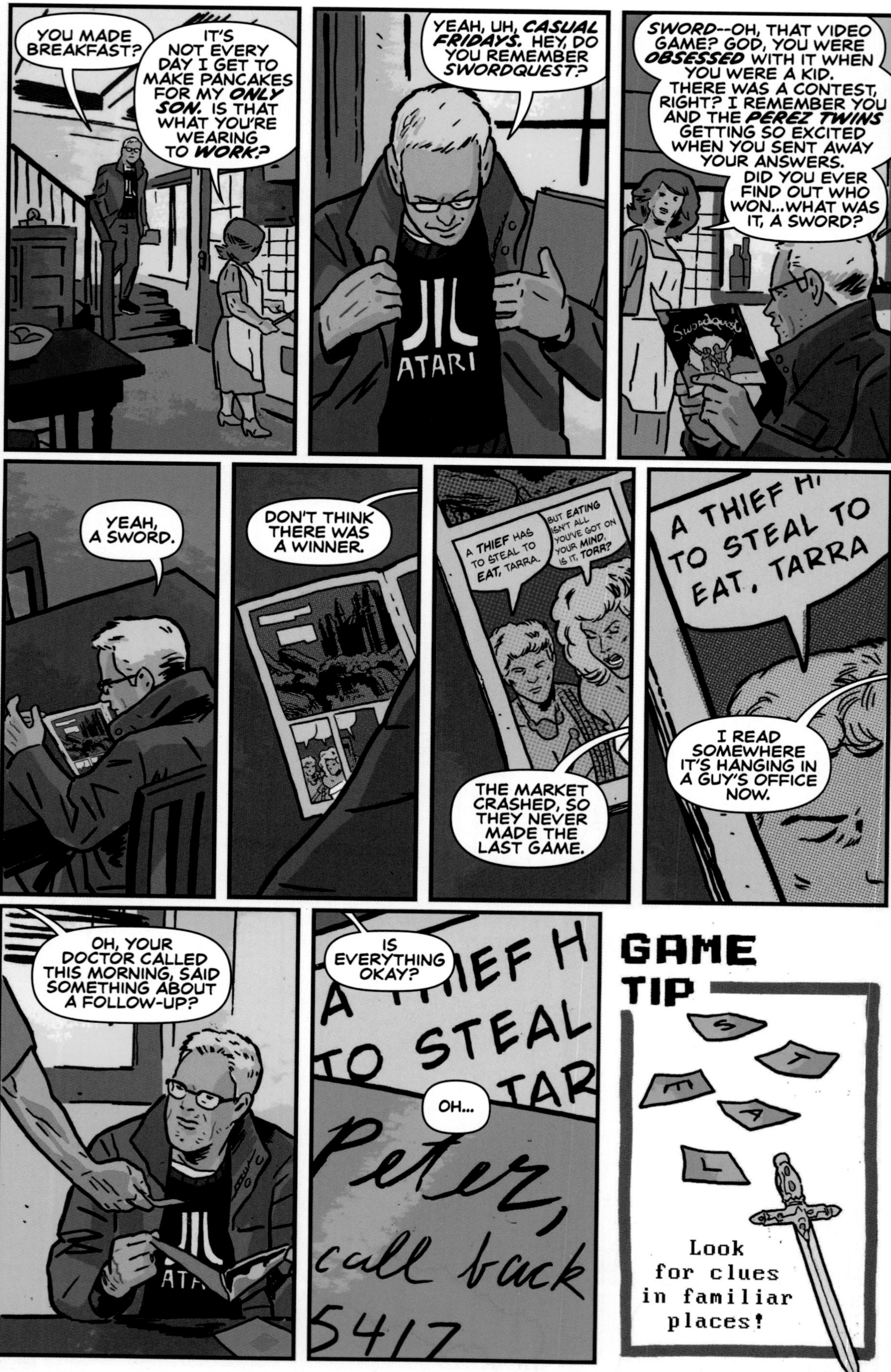
YOU MADE BREAKFAST?
IT'S NOT EVERY DAY I GET TO MAKE PANCAKES FOR MY ONLY SON. IS THAT WHAT YOU'RE WEARING TO WORK?
YEAH, UH, CASUAL FRIDAYS. HEY, DO YOU REMEMBER SWORDQUEST?
ATARI
SWORD--OH, THAT VIDEO GAME? GOD, YOU WERE OBSESSED WITH IT WHEN YOU WERE A KID. THERE WAS A CONTEST, RIGHT? I REMEMBER YOU AND THE PEREZ TWINS GETTING SO EXCITED WHEN YOU SENT AWAY YOUR ANSWERS.
DID YOU EVER FIND OUT WHO WON...WHAT WAS IT, A SWORD?
YEAH, A SWORD.
DON'T THINK THERE WAS A WINNER.
A THIEF HAS TO STEAL TO EAT, TARRA.
BUT EATING ISN'T ALL YOU'VE GOT ON YOUR MIND, IS IT, TORR?
THE MARKET CRASHED, SO THEY NEVER MADE THE LAST GAME.
A THIEF H TO STEAL TO EAT, TARRA
I READ SOMEWHERE IT'S HANGING IN A GUY'S OFFICE NOW.
OH, YOUR DOCTOR CALLED THIS MORNING, SAID SOMETHING ABOUT A FOLLOW-UP?
IS EVERYTHING OKAY?
A THIEF H TO STEAL TAR
OH...
Peter, call back 5417
GAME TIP
S T M A L
Look for clues in familiar places!

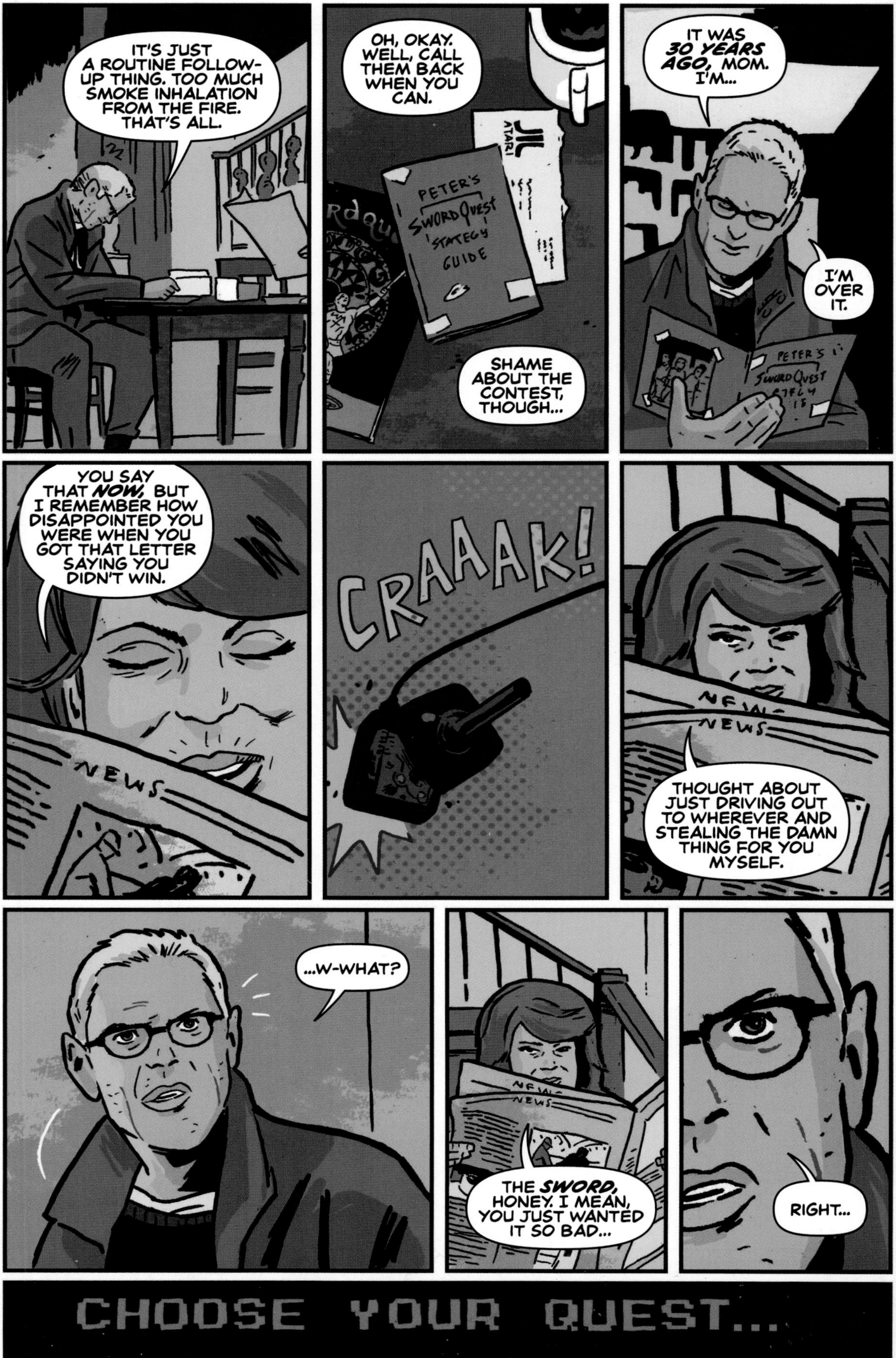
IT'S JUST A ROUTINE FOLLOW-UP THING. TOO MUCH SMOKE INHALATION FROM THE FIRE. THAT'S ALL.
OH, OKAY. WELL, CALL THEM BACK WHEN YOU CAN.
ATARI
PETER'S SWORDQUEST STATEGY GUIDE
SHAME ABOUT THE CONTEST, THOUGH...
IT WAS *30 YEARS AGO*, MOM. I'M...
I'M OVER IT.
YOU SAY THAT *NOW,* BUT I REMEMBER HOW DISAPPOINTED YOU WERE WHEN YOU GOT THAT LETTER SAYING YOU DIDN'T WIN.
NEWS
CRAAAK!
NEWS
THOUGHT ABOUT JUST DRIVING OUT TO WHEREVER AND STEALING THE DAMN THING FOR YOU MYSELF.
...W-WHAT?
NEWS
THE *SWORD,* HONEY. I MEAN, YOU JUST WANTED IT SO BAD...
RIGHT...
CHOOSE YOUR QUEST...

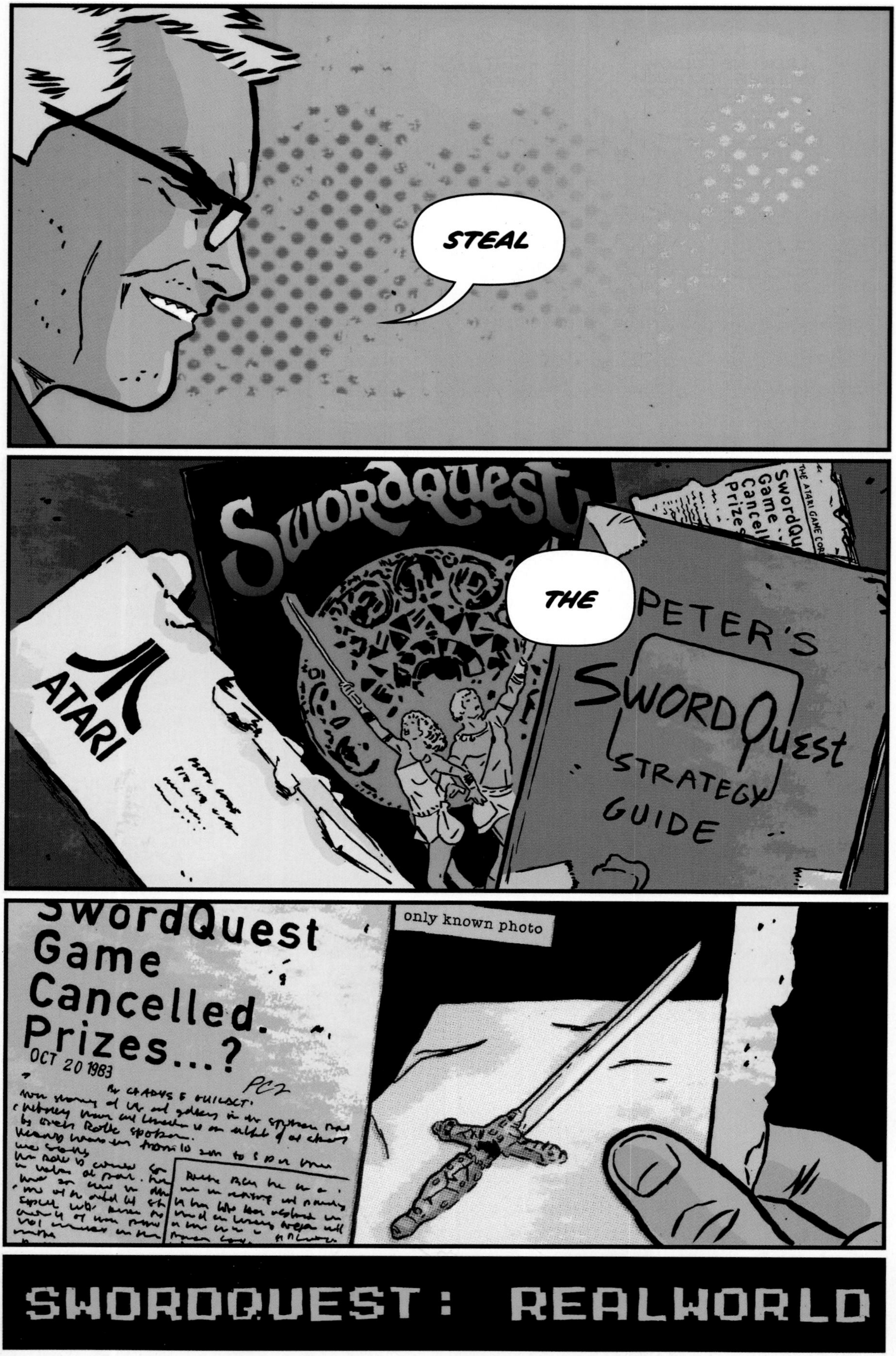
STEAL
SwordQuest
ATARI
THE
PETER'S SWORDQUEST STRATEGY GUIDE
SwordQuest Game Cancelled. Prizes...?
OCT 20 1983
only known photo
SWORDQUEST: REALWORLD

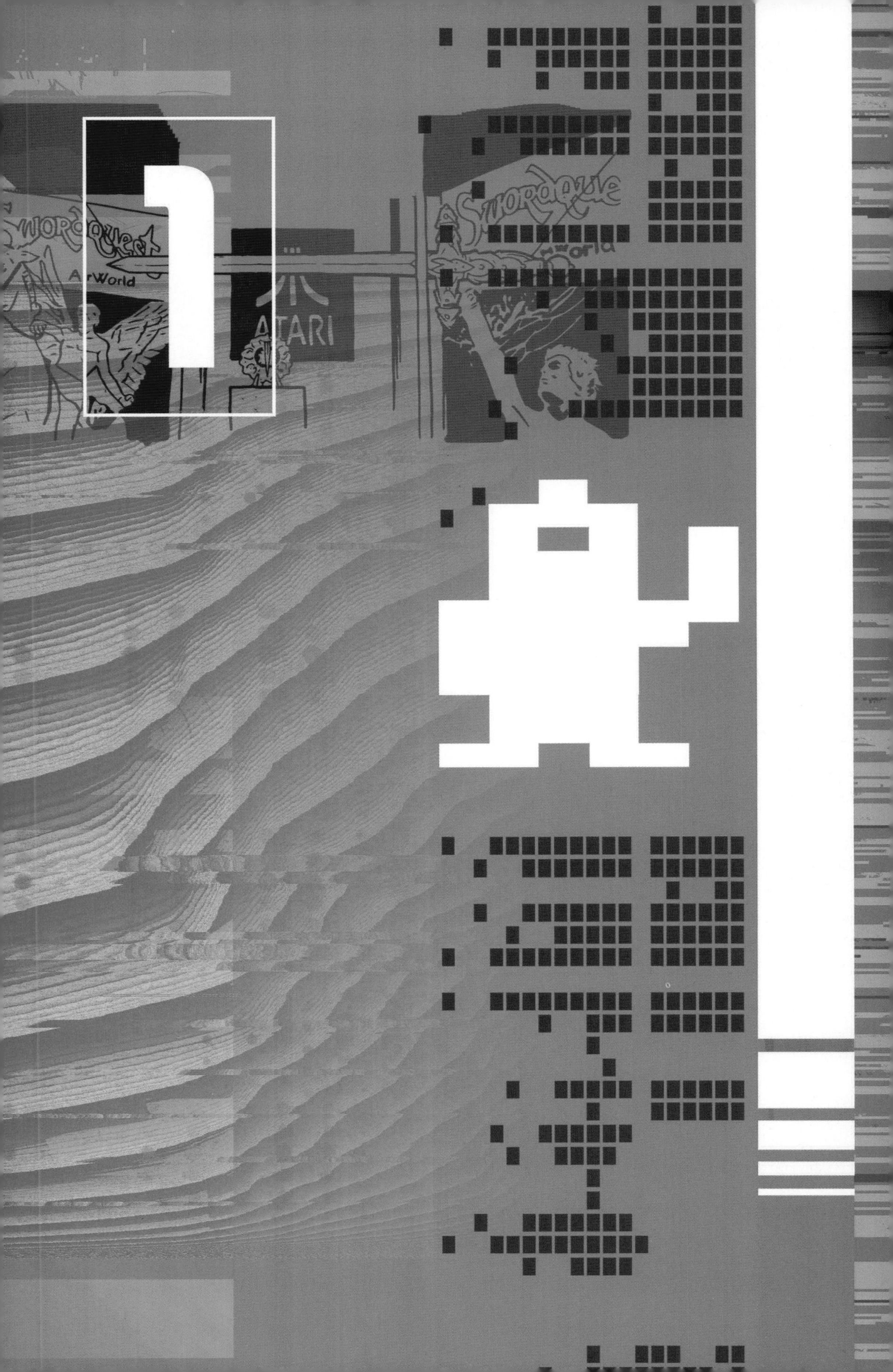
1
ATARI

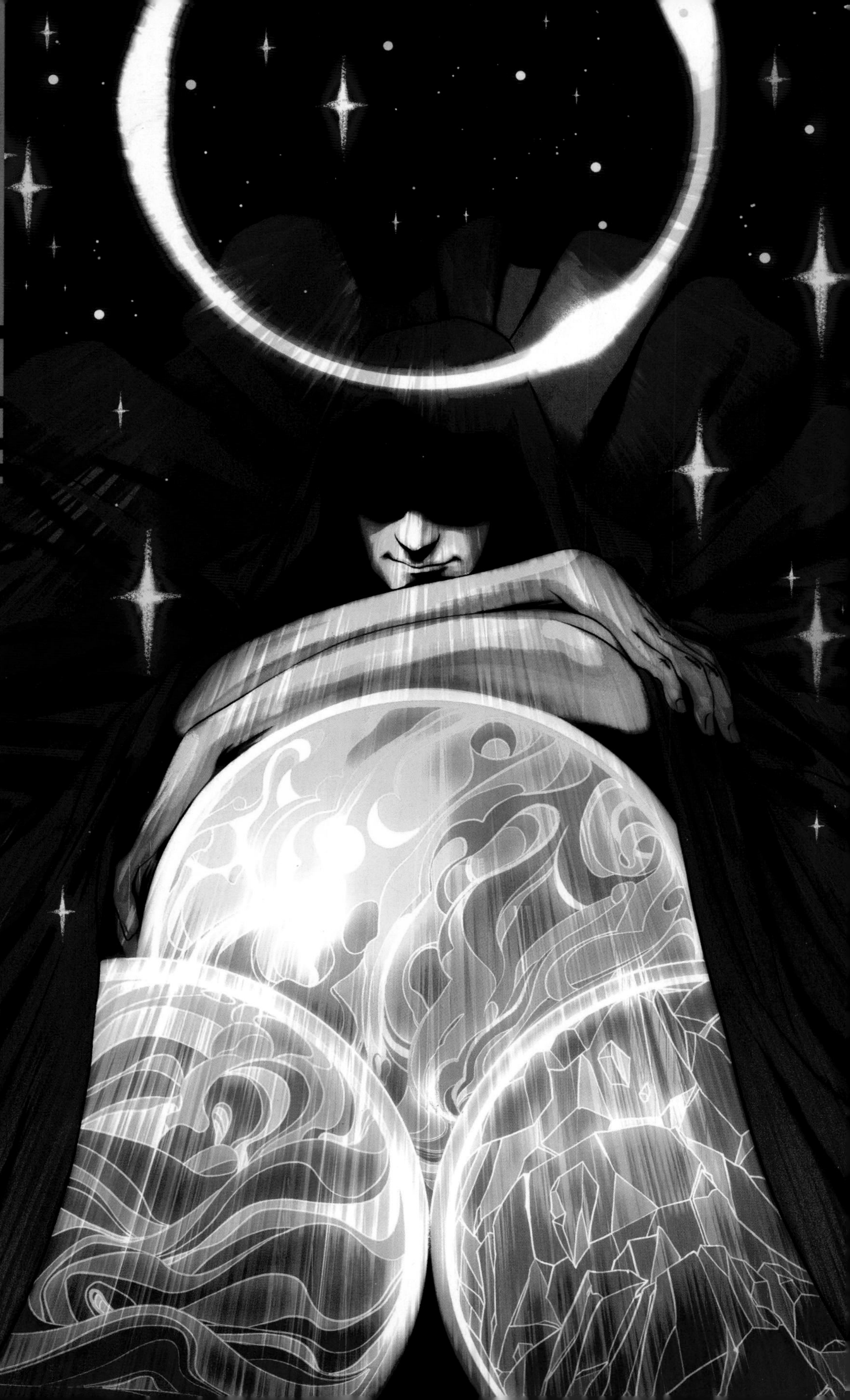
Art by GOÑI MONTES

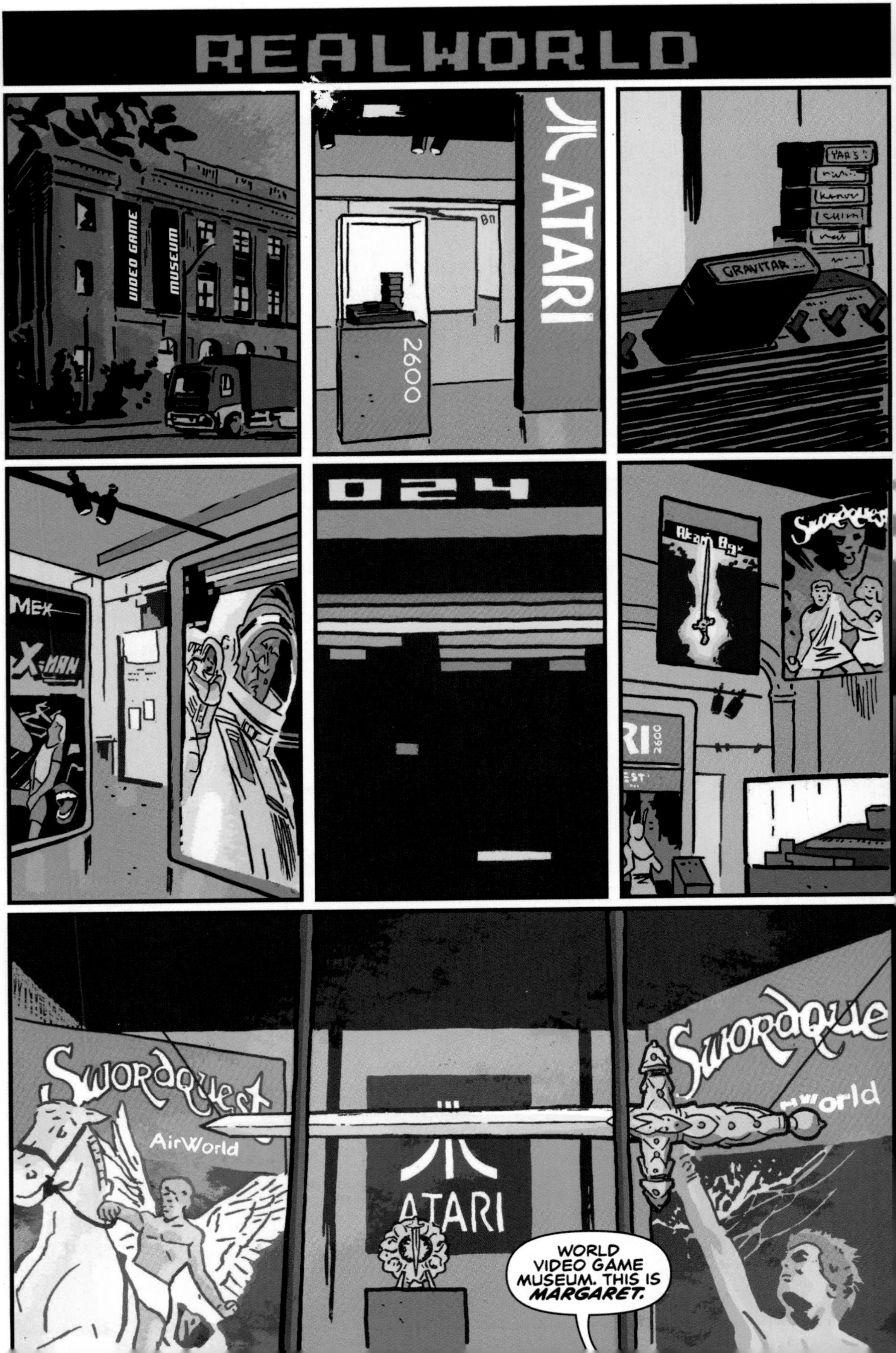
REALWORLD
VIDEO GAME
MUSEUM
ATARI
2600
GRAVITAR
YAR'S
024
X-MAN
Swordquest
Swordquest
AirWorld
ATARI
Swordque
WORLD VIDEO GAME MUSEUM. THIS IS *MARGARET.*

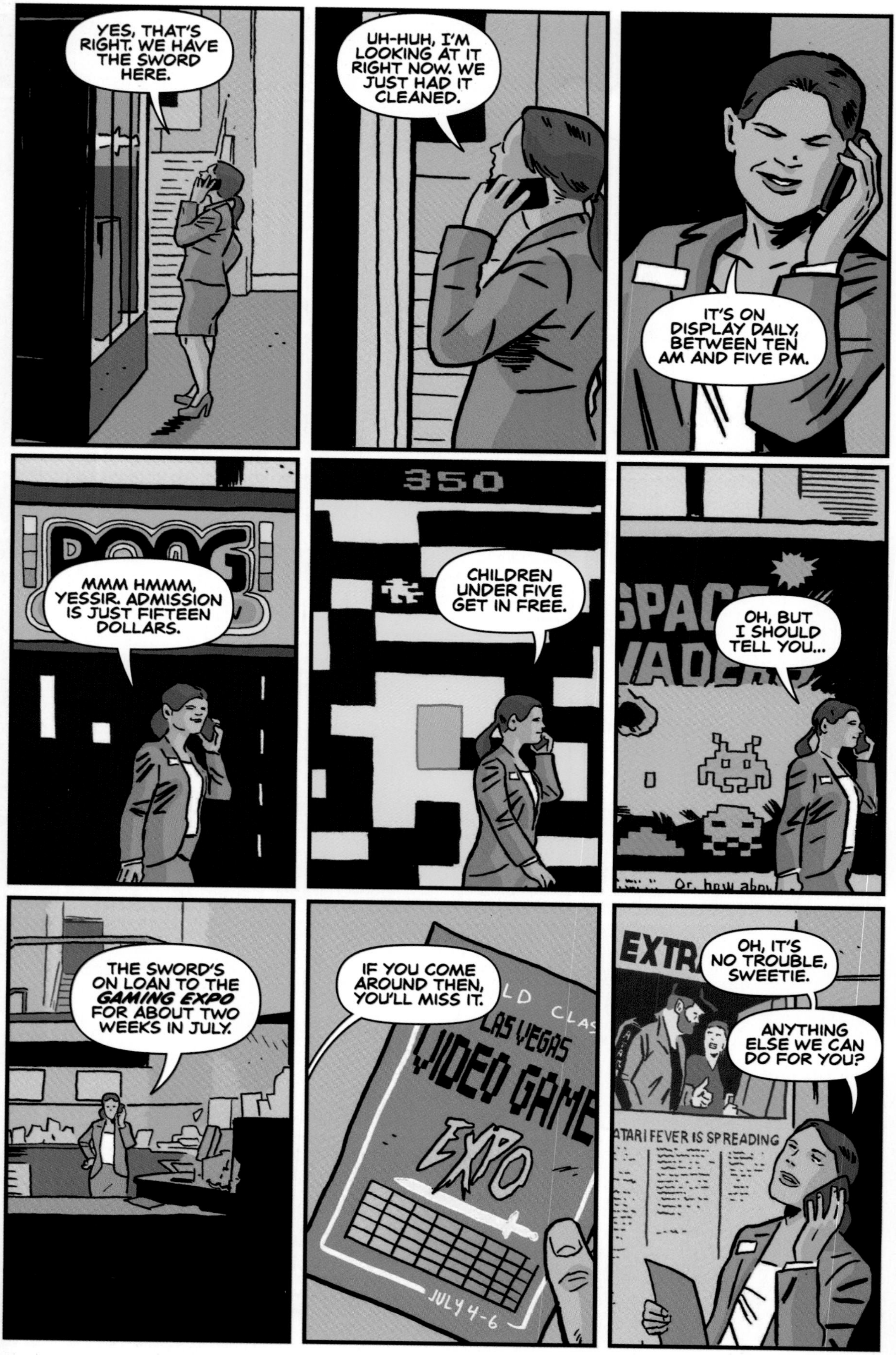
YES, THAT'S RIGHT. WE HAVE THE SWORD HERE.
UH-HUH, I'M LOOKING AT IT RIGHT NOW. WE JUST HAD IT CLEANED.
IT'S ON DISPLAY DAILY, BETWEEN TEN AM AND FIVE PM.
MMM HMMM, YESSIR. ADMISSION IS JUST FIFTEEN DOLLARS.
350
CHILDREN UNDER FIVE GET IN FREE.
OH, BUT I SHOULD TELL YOU...
THE SWORD'S ON LOAN TO THE *GAMING EXPO* FOR ABOUT TWO WEEKS IN JULY.
IF YOU COME AROUND THEN, YOU'LL MISS IT.
LAS VEGAS VIDEO GAME EXPO
JULY 4-6
OH, IT'S NO TROUBLE, SWEETIE.
ANYTHING ELSE WE CAN DO FOR YOU?
ATARI FEVER IS SPREADING

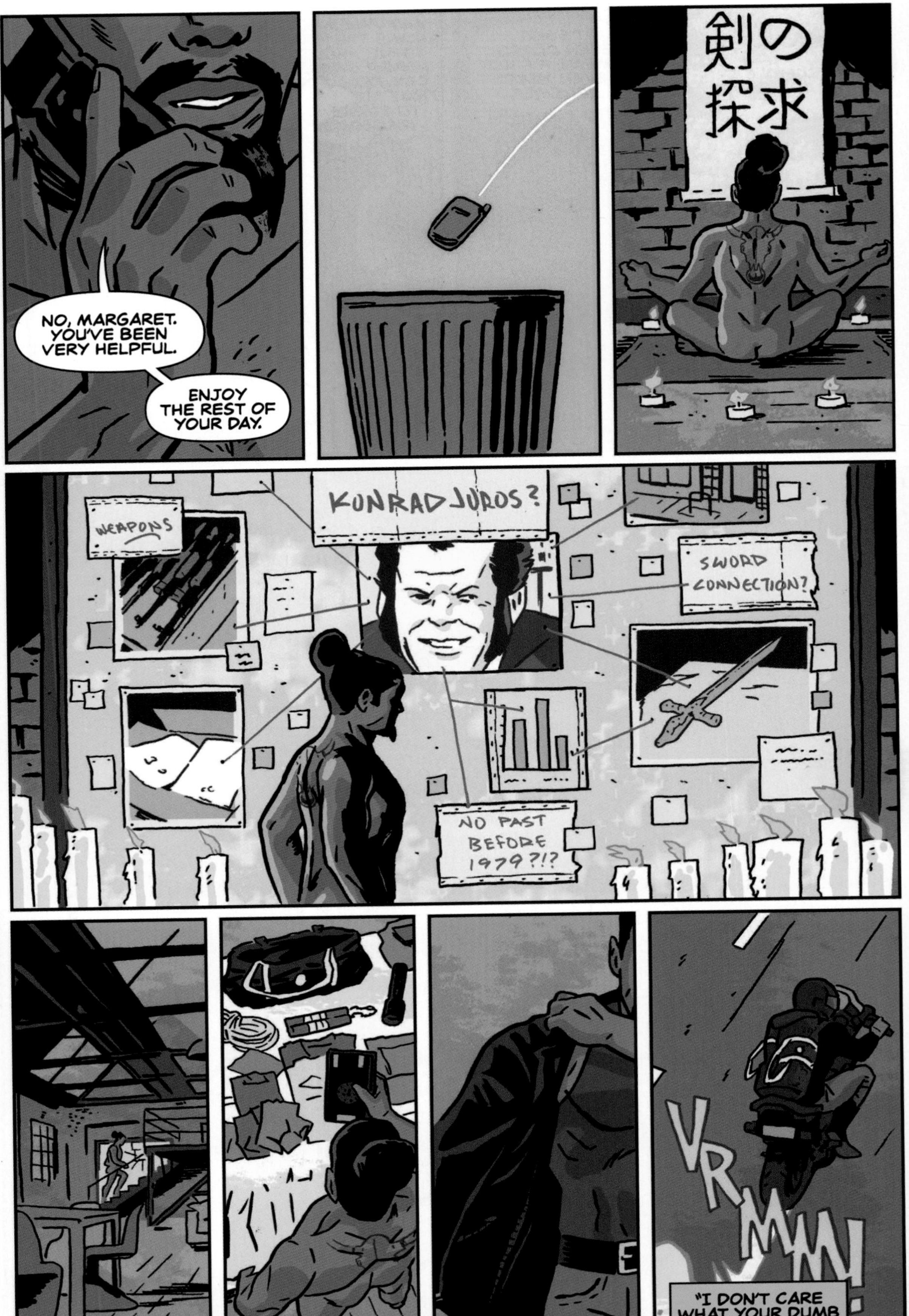
NO, MARGARET. YOU'VE BEEN VERY HELPFUL.
ENJOY THE REST OF YOUR DAY.
剣の探求
KONRAD JUROS?
WEAPONS
SWORD CONNECTION?
NO PAST BEFORE 1979?!?
VRMMM!
"I DON'T CARE WHAT YOUR DUMB BOOK SAYS--

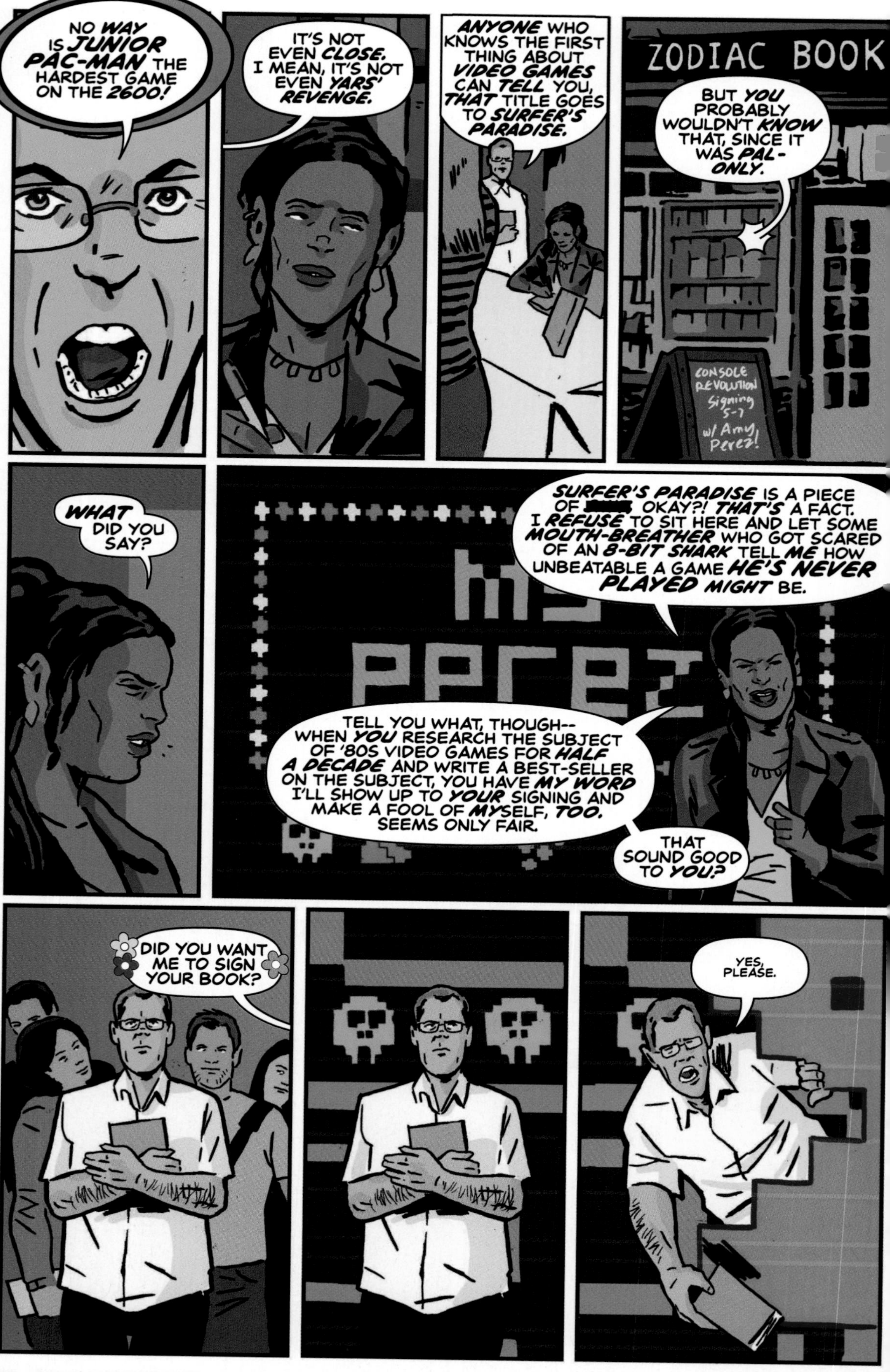
NO WAY IS JUNIOR PAC-MAN THE HARDEST GAME ON THE 2600!
IT'S NOT EVEN CLOSE. I MEAN, IT'S NOT EVEN YARS' REVENGE.
ANYONE WHO KNOWS THE FIRST THING ABOUT VIDEO GAMES CAN TELL YOU, THAT TITLE GOES TO SURFER'S PARADISE.
ZODIAC BOOK
BUT YOU PROBABLY WOULDN'T KNOW THAT, SINCE IT WAS PAL-ONLY.
CONSOLE REVOLUTION Signing 5-7 w/ Amy Perez!
WHAT DID YOU SAY?
SURFER'S PARADISE IS A PIECE OF [redacted], OKAY?! THAT'S A FACT. I REFUSE TO SIT HERE AND LET SOME MOUTH-BREATHER WHO GOT SCARED OF AN 8-BIT SHARK TELL ME HOW UNBEATABLE A GAME HE'S NEVER PLAYED MIGHT BE.
TELL YOU WHAT, THOUGH-- WHEN YOU RESEARCH THE SUBJECT OF '80S VIDEO GAMES FOR HALF A DECADE AND WRITE A BEST-SELLER ON THE SUBJECT, YOU HAVE MY WORD I'LL SHOW UP TO YOUR SIGNING AND MAKE A FOOL OF MYSELF, TOO. SEEMS ONLY FAIR.
THAT SOUND GOOD TO YOU?
DID YOU WANT ME TO SIGN YOUR BOOK?
YES, PLEASE.

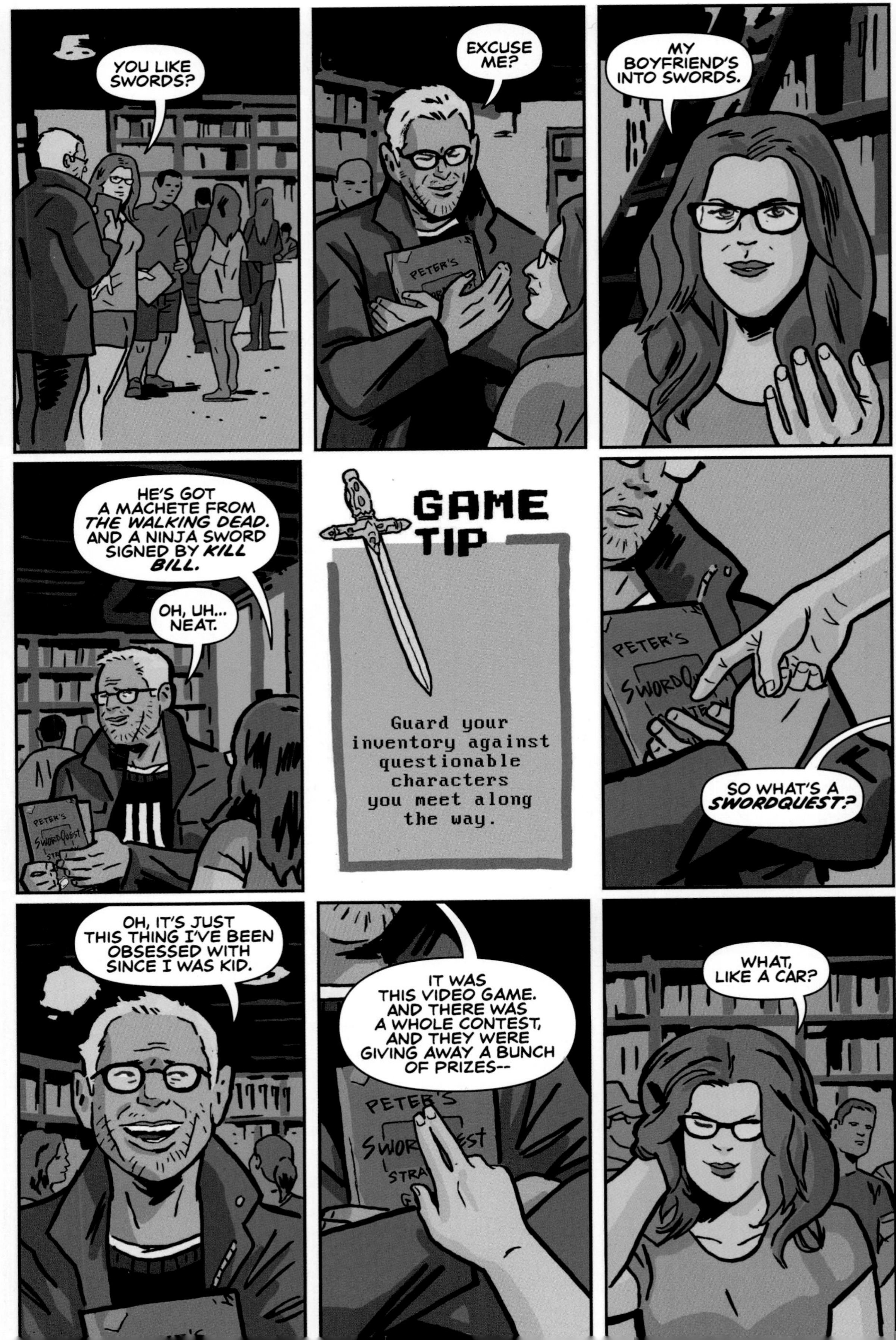

YOU LIKE SWORDS?
EXCUSE ME?
MY BOYFRIEND'S INTO SWORDS.
HE'S GOT A MACHETE FROM *THE WALKING DEAD*. AND A NINJA SWORD SIGNED BY *KILL BILL*.
OH, UH... NEAT.
PETER'S SWORDQUEST STRA
GAME TIP
Guard your inventory against questionable characters you meet along the way.
PETER'S SWORDQ
SO WHAT'S A *SWORDQUEST?*
OH, IT'S JUST THIS THING I'VE BEEN OBSESSED WITH SINCE I WAS KID.
IT WAS THIS VIDEO GAME. AND THERE WAS A WHOLE CONTEST, AND THEY WERE GIVING AWAY A BUNCH OF PRIZES--
WHAT, LIKE A CAR?

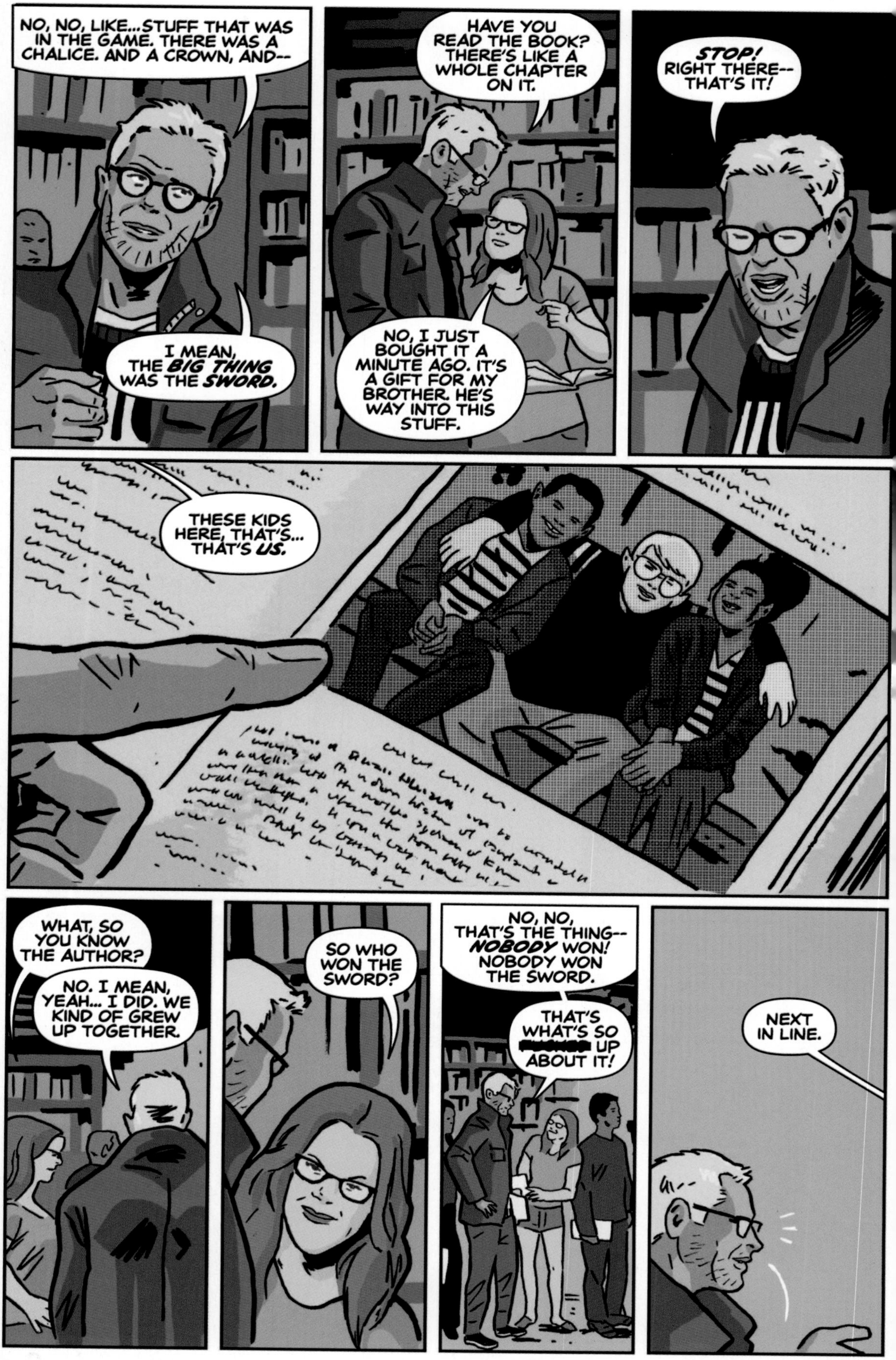
NO, NO, LIKE...STUFF THAT WAS IN THE GAME. THERE WAS A CHALICE. AND A CROWN, AND--
I MEAN, THE *BIG THING* WAS THE *SWORD.*
HAVE YOU READ THE BOOK? THERE'S LIKE A WHOLE CHAPTER ON IT.
NO, I JUST BOUGHT IT A MINUTE AGO. IT'S A GIFT FOR MY BROTHER. HE'S WAY INTO THIS STUFF.
STOP! RIGHT THERE-- THAT'S IT!
THESE KIDS HERE, THAT'S... THAT'S *US.*
WHAT, SO YOU KNOW THE AUTHOR?
NO. I MEAN, YEAH... I DID. WE KIND OF GREW UP TOGETHER.
SO WHO WON THE SWORD?
NO, NO, THAT'S THE THING-- *NOBODY* WON! NOBODY WON THE SWORD.
THAT'S WHAT'S SO [redacted] UP ABOUT IT!
NEXT IN LINE.

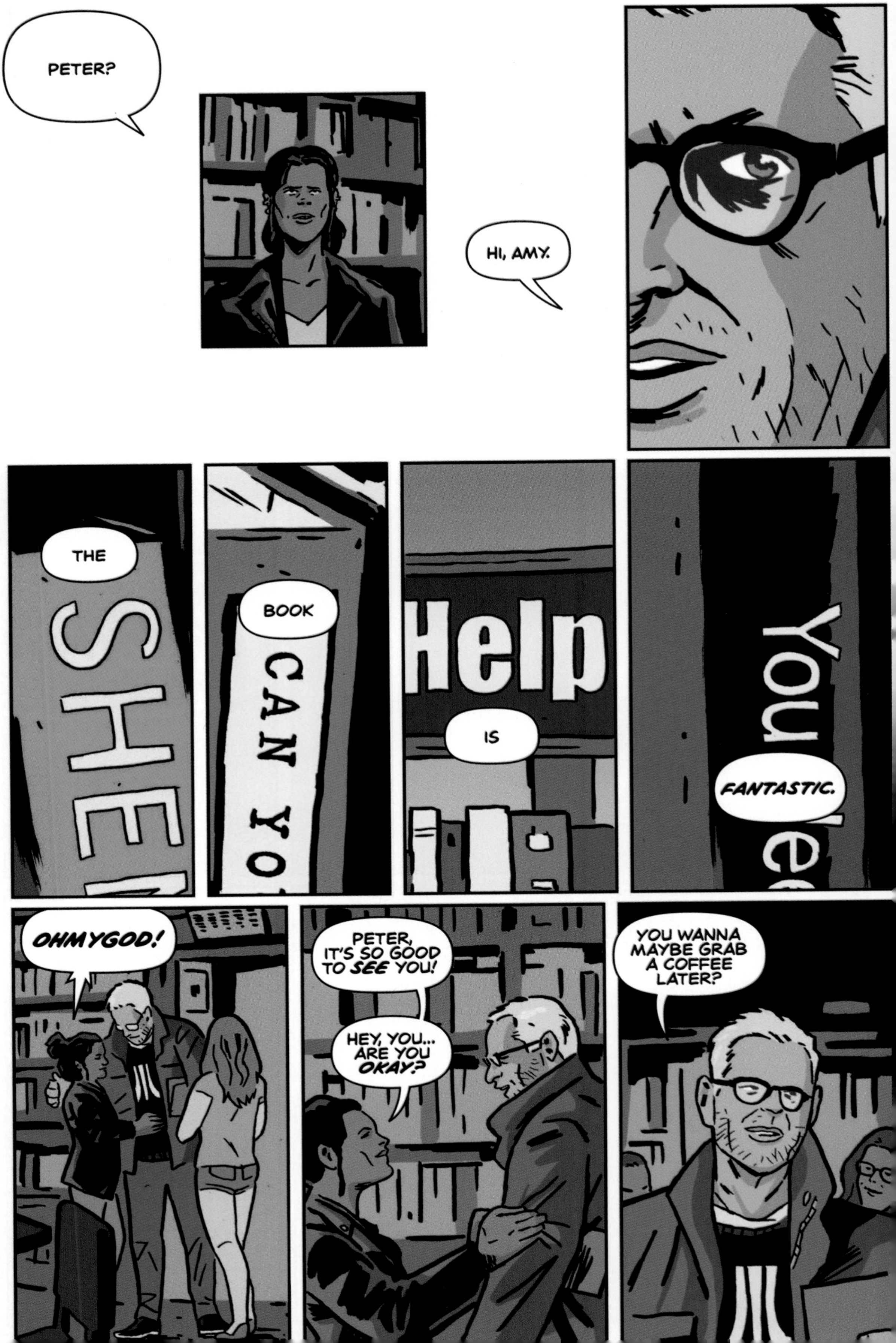
PETER?
HI, AMY.
THE
BOOK
Help
IS
You
FANTASTIC.
OHMYGOD!
PETER, IT'S SO GOOD TO SEE YOU!
HEY, YOU... ARE YOU OKAY?
YOU WANNA MAYBE GRAB A COFFEE LATER?

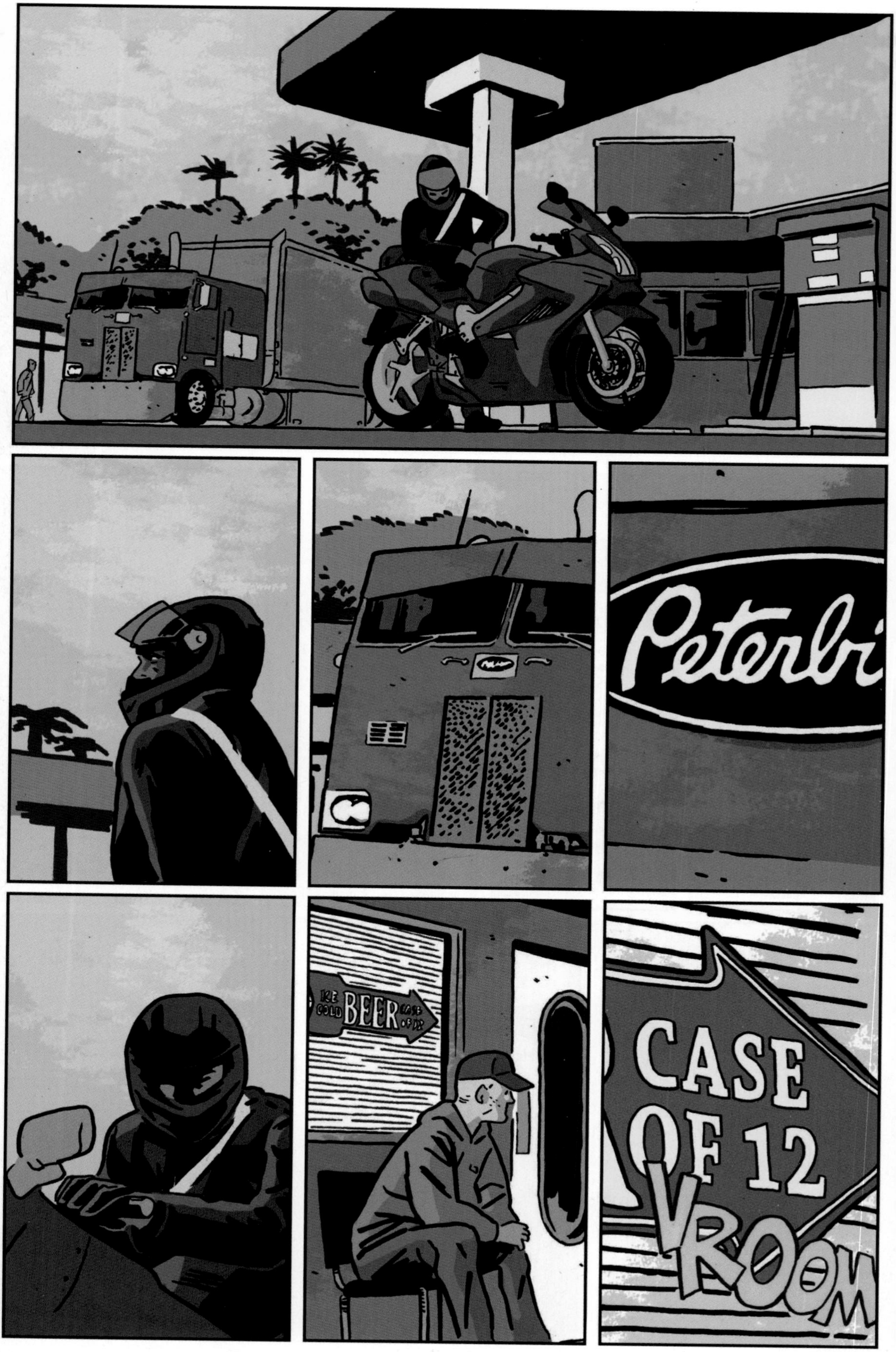
Peterbi
ICE COLD BEER CASE OF 12
CASE OF 12
VROOM

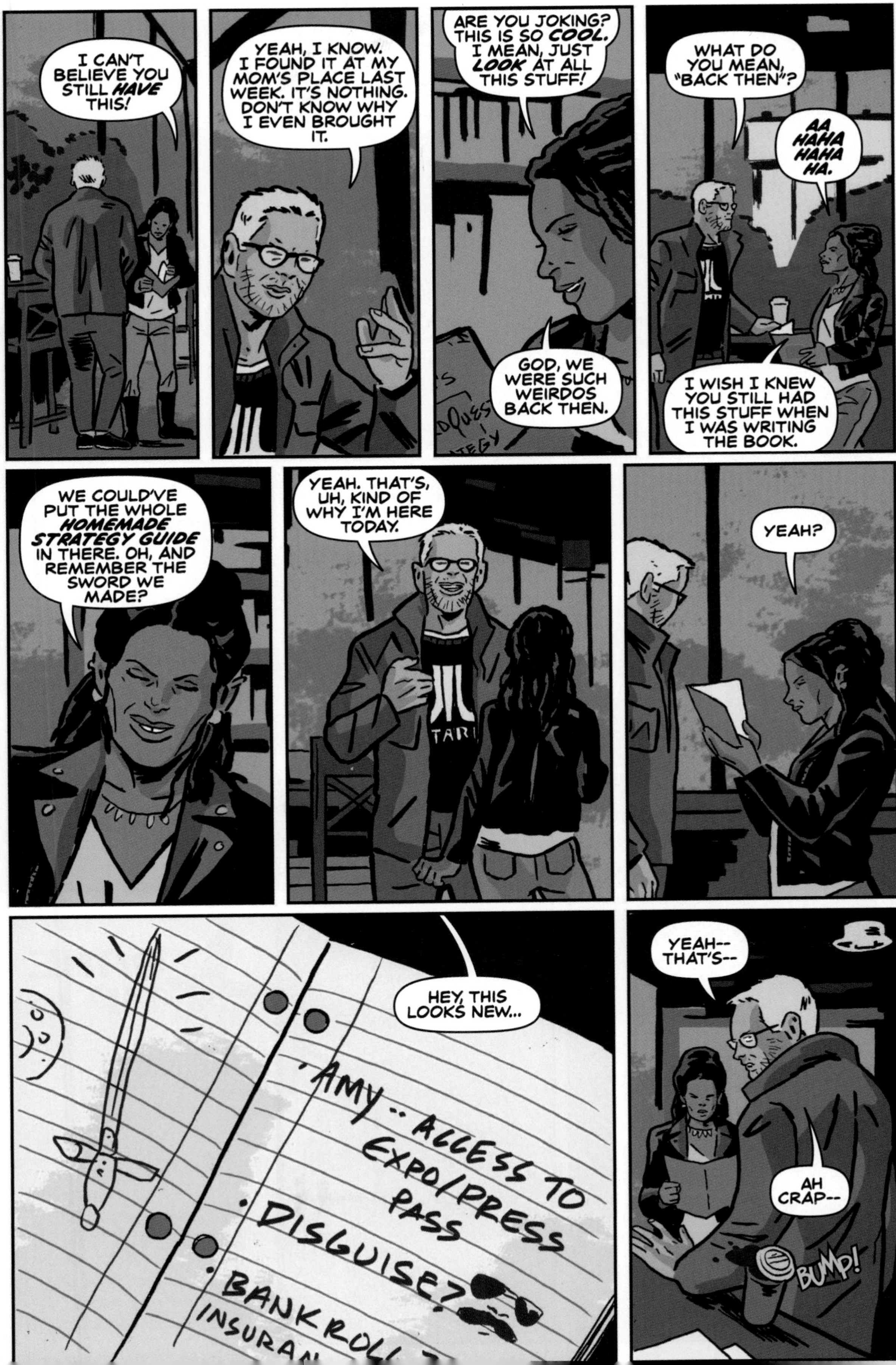
I CAN'T BELIEVE YOU STILL *HAVE* THIS!
YEAH, I KNOW. I FOUND IT AT MY MOM'S PLACE LAST WEEK. IT'S NOTHING. DON'T KNOW WHY I EVEN BROUGHT IT.
ARE YOU JOKING? THIS IS SO *COOL.* I MEAN, JUST *LOOK* AT ALL THIS STUFF!
GOD, WE WERE SUCH WEIRDOS BACK THEN.
WHAT DO YOU MEAN, "BACK THEN"?
AA HAHA HAHA HA.
I WISH I KNEW YOU STILL HAD THIS STUFF WHEN I WAS WRITING THE BOOK.
WE COULD'VE PUT THE WHOLE *HOMEMADE STRATEGY GUIDE* IN THERE. OH, AND REMEMBER THE SWORD WE MADE?
YEAH. THAT'S, UH, KIND OF WHY I'M HERE TODAY.
YEAH?
HEY, THIS LOOKS NEW...
AMY -- ACCESS TO EXPO/PRESS PASS
DISGUISE?
YEAH-- THAT'S--
AH CRAP--
BUMP!

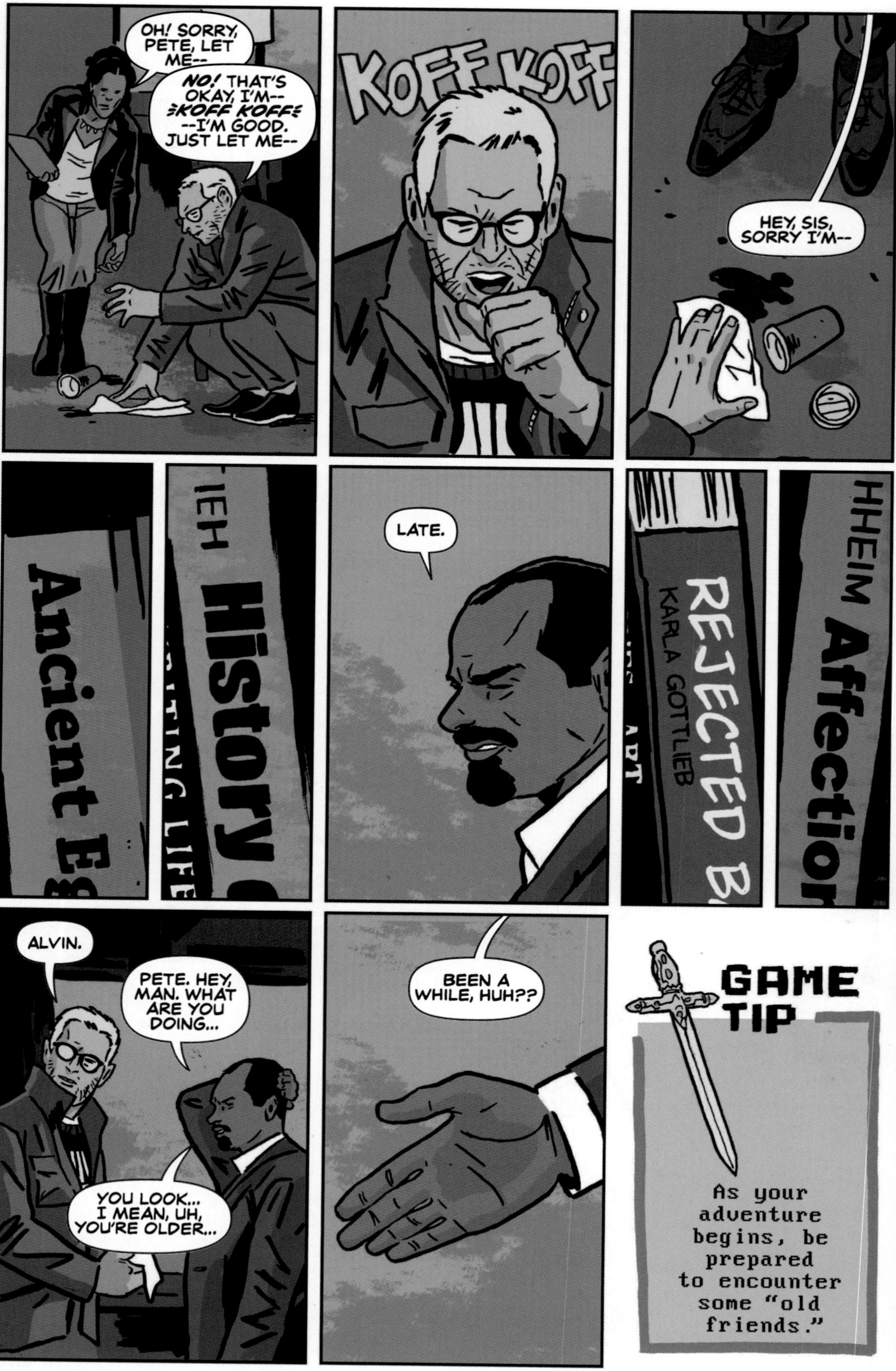
OH! SORRY, PETE, LET ME--
NO! THAT'S OKAY, I'M-- KOFF KOFF --I'M GOOD. JUST LET ME--
KOFF KOFF
HEY, SIS, SORRY I'M--
Ancient
History
LATE.
REJECTED
KARLA GOTTLIEB
ALVIN.
PETE. HEY, MAN. WHAT ARE YOU DOING...
YOU LOOK... I MEAN, UH, YOU'RE OLDER...
BEEN A WHILE, HUH??
GAME TIP
As your adventure begins, be prepared to encounter some "old friends."

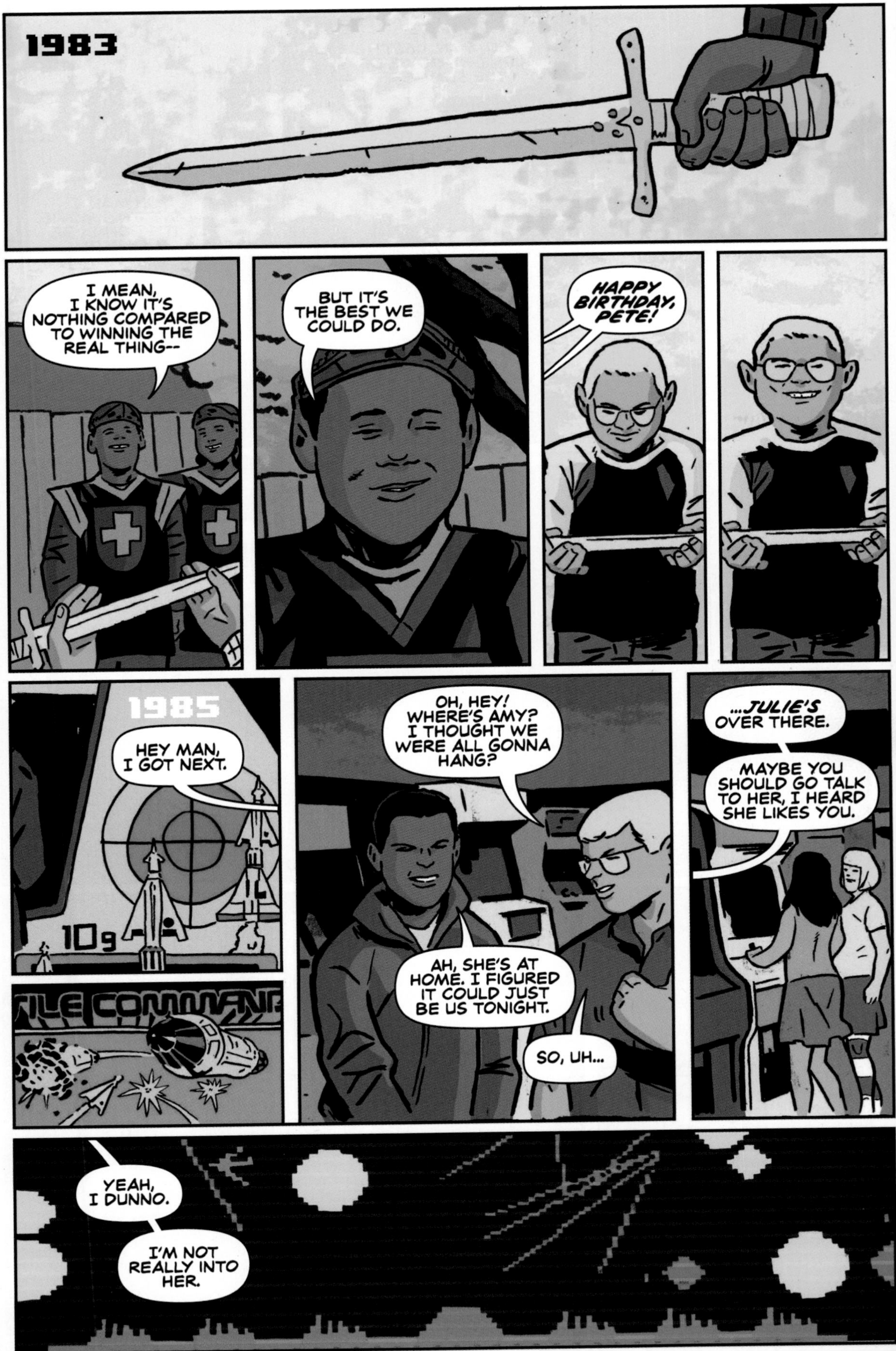
1983
I MEAN, I KNOW IT'S NOTHING COMPARED TO WINNING THE REAL THING--
BUT IT'S THE BEST WE COULD DO.
HAPPY BIRTHDAY, PETE!
1985
HEY MAN, I GOT NEXT.
10g
TILE COMMAND
OH, HEY! WHERE'S AMY? I THOUGHT WE WERE ALL GONNA HANG?
AH, SHE'S AT HOME. I FIGURED IT COULD JUST BE US TONIGHT.
SO, UH...
...JULIE'S OVER THERE.
MAYBE YOU SHOULD GO TALK TO HER, I HEARD SHE LIKES YOU.
YEAH, I DUNNO.
I'M NOT REALLY INTO HER.

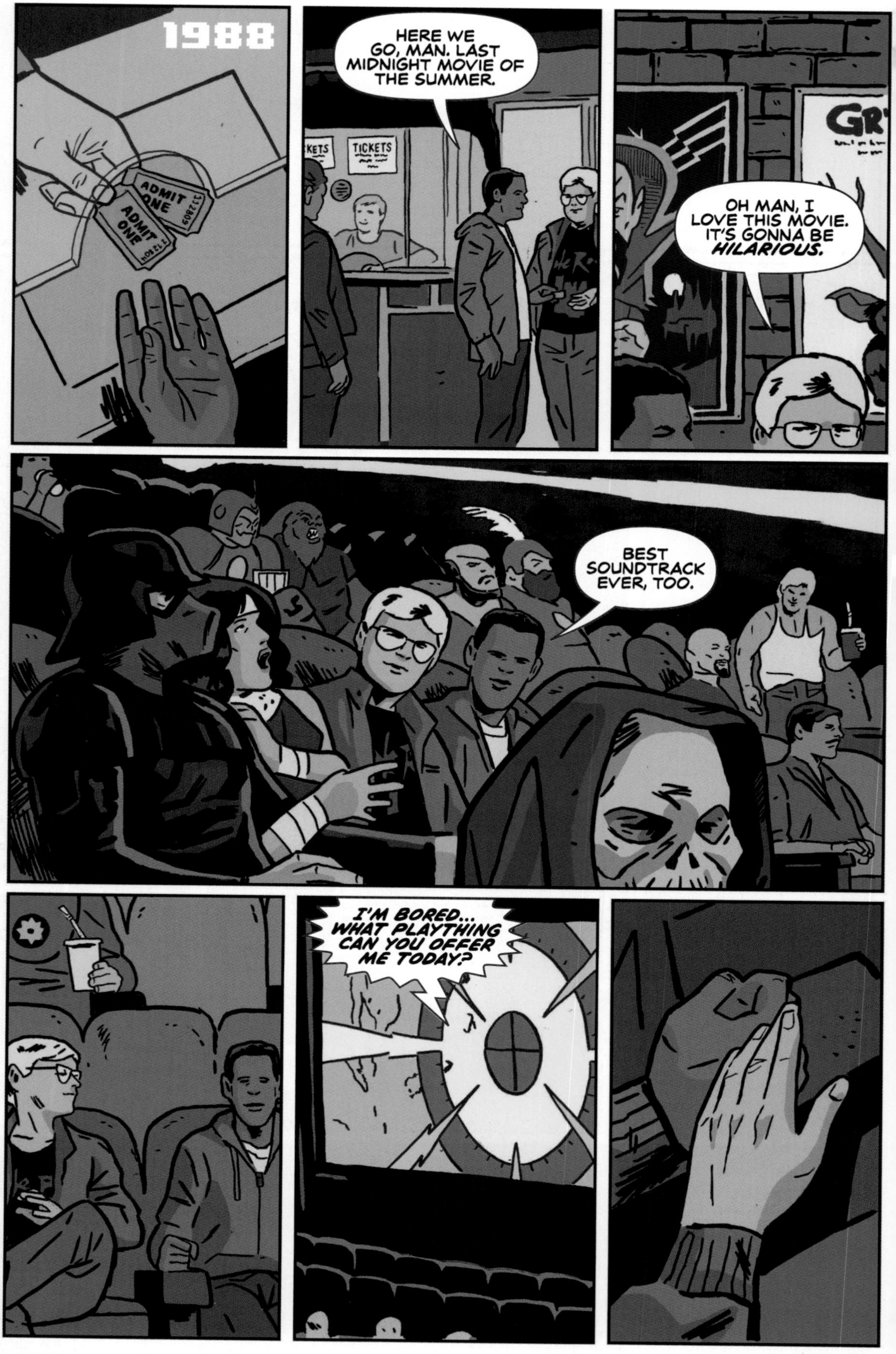

1988
ADMIT ONE
ADMIT ONE
HERE WE GO, MAN. LAST MIDNIGHT MOVIE OF THE SUMMER.
TICKETS
OH MAN, I LOVE THIS MOVIE. IT'S GONNA BE *HILARIOUS.*
BEST SOUNDTRACK EVER, TOO.
I'M BORED... WHAT PLAYTHING CAN YOU OFFER ME TODAY?

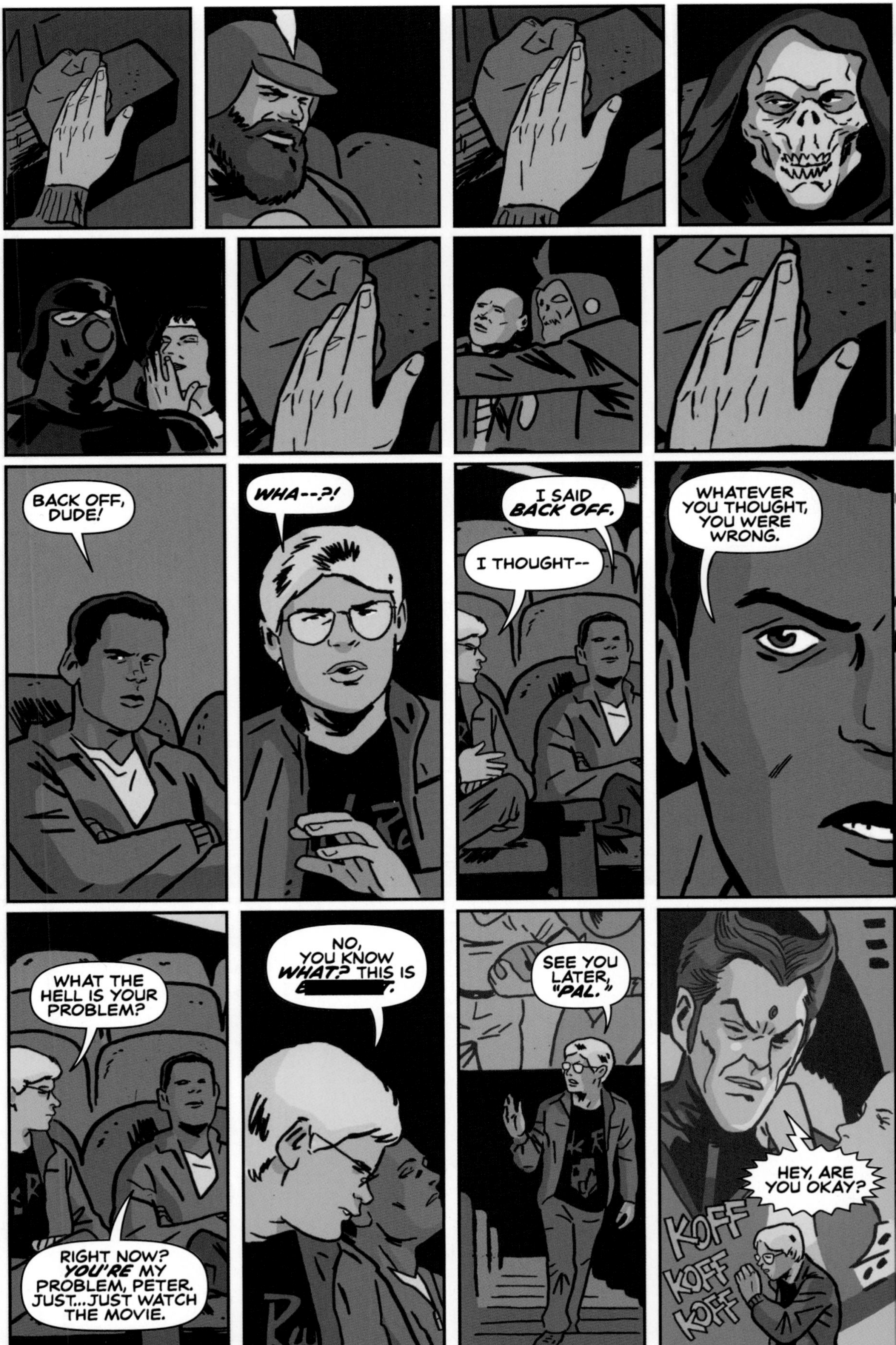
BACK OFF, DUDE!
WHA--?!
I SAID BACK OFF.
I THOUGHT--
WHATEVER YOU THOUGHT, YOU WERE WRONG.
WHAT THE HELL IS YOUR PROBLEM?
RIGHT NOW? YOU'RE MY PROBLEM, PETER. JUST...JUST WATCH THE MOVIE.
NO, YOU KNOW WHAT? THIS IS [redacted].
SEE YOU LATER, "PAL."
HEY, ARE YOU OKAY?
KOFF
KOFF
KOFF

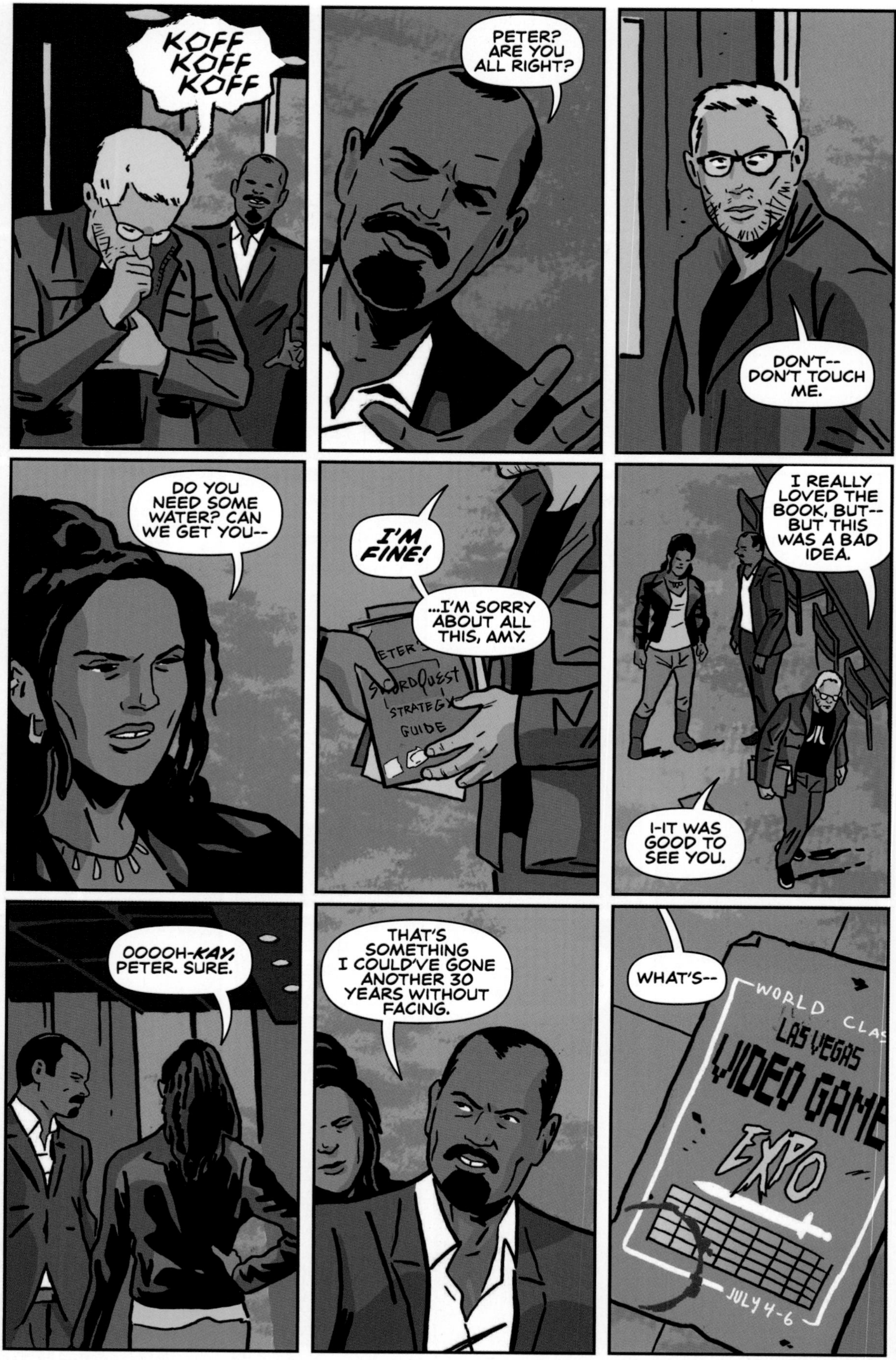
KOFF KOFF KOFF
PETER? ARE YOU ALL RIGHT?
DON'T-- DON'T TOUCH ME.
DO YOU NEED SOME WATER? CAN WE GET YOU--
I'M FINE!
...I'M SORRY ABOUT ALL THIS, AMY.
SWORDQUEST STRATEGY GUIDE
I REALLY LOVED THE BOOK, BUT-- BUT THIS WAS A BAD IDEA.
I-IT WAS GOOD TO SEE YOU.
OOOOH-KAY, PETER. SURE.
THAT'S SOMETHING I COULD'VE GONE ANOTHER 30 YEARS WITHOUT FACING.
WHAT'S--
WORLD CLAS
LAS VEGAS
VIDEO GAME
EXPO
JULY 4-6

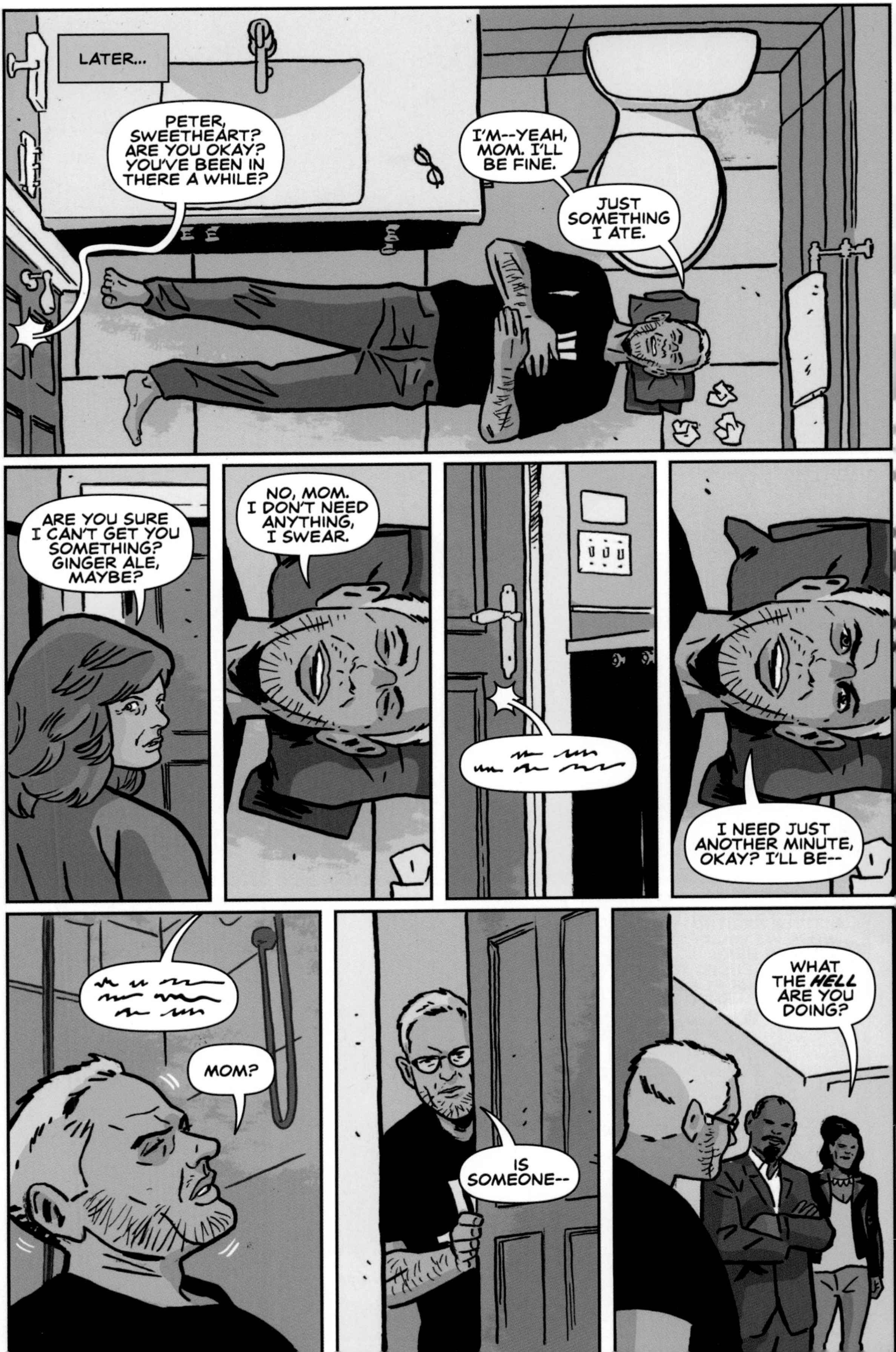
LATER...
PETER, SWEETHEART? ARE YOU OKAY? YOU'VE BEEN IN THERE A WHILE?
I'M--YEAH, MOM. I'LL BE FINE.
JUST SOMETHING I ATE.
ARE YOU SURE I CAN'T GET YOU SOMETHING? GINGER ALE, MAYBE?
NO, MOM. I DON'T NEED ANYTHING, I SWEAR.
I NEED JUST ANOTHER MINUTE, OKAY? I'LL BE--
MOM?
IS SOMEONE--
WHAT THE *HELL* ARE YOU DOING?

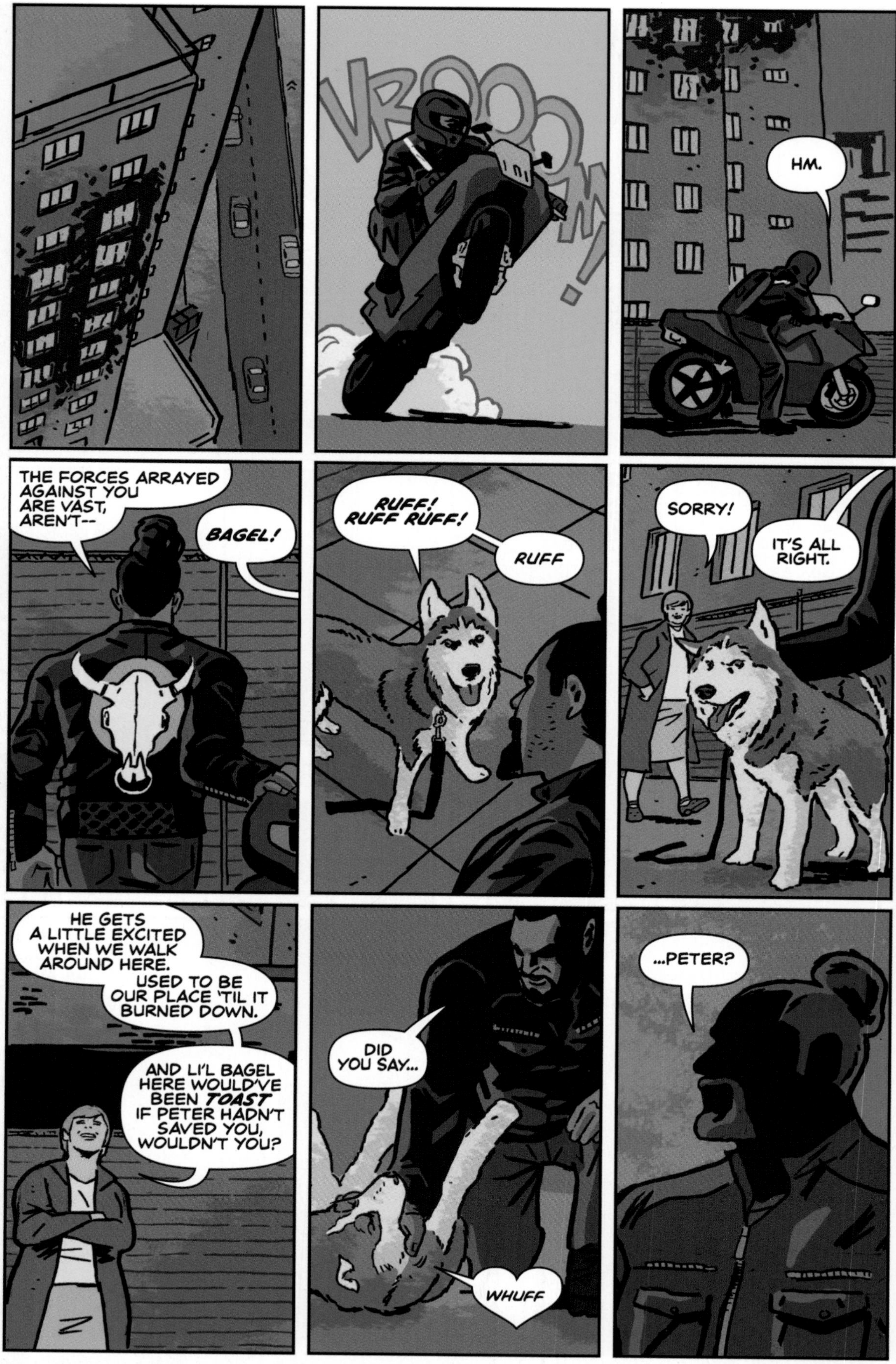
VROOOOM!
HM.
THE FORCES ARRAYED AGAINST YOU ARE VAST, AREN'T--
BAGEL!
RUFF! RUFF RUFF!
RUFF
SORRY!
IT'S ALL RIGHT.
HE GETS A LITTLE EXCITED WHEN WE WALK AROUND HERE.
USED TO BE OUR PLACE 'TIL IT BURNED DOWN.
AND LI'L BAGEL HERE WOULD'VE BEEN TOAST IF PETER HADN'T SAVED YOU, WOULDN'T YOU?
DID YOU SAY...
WHUFF
...PETER?

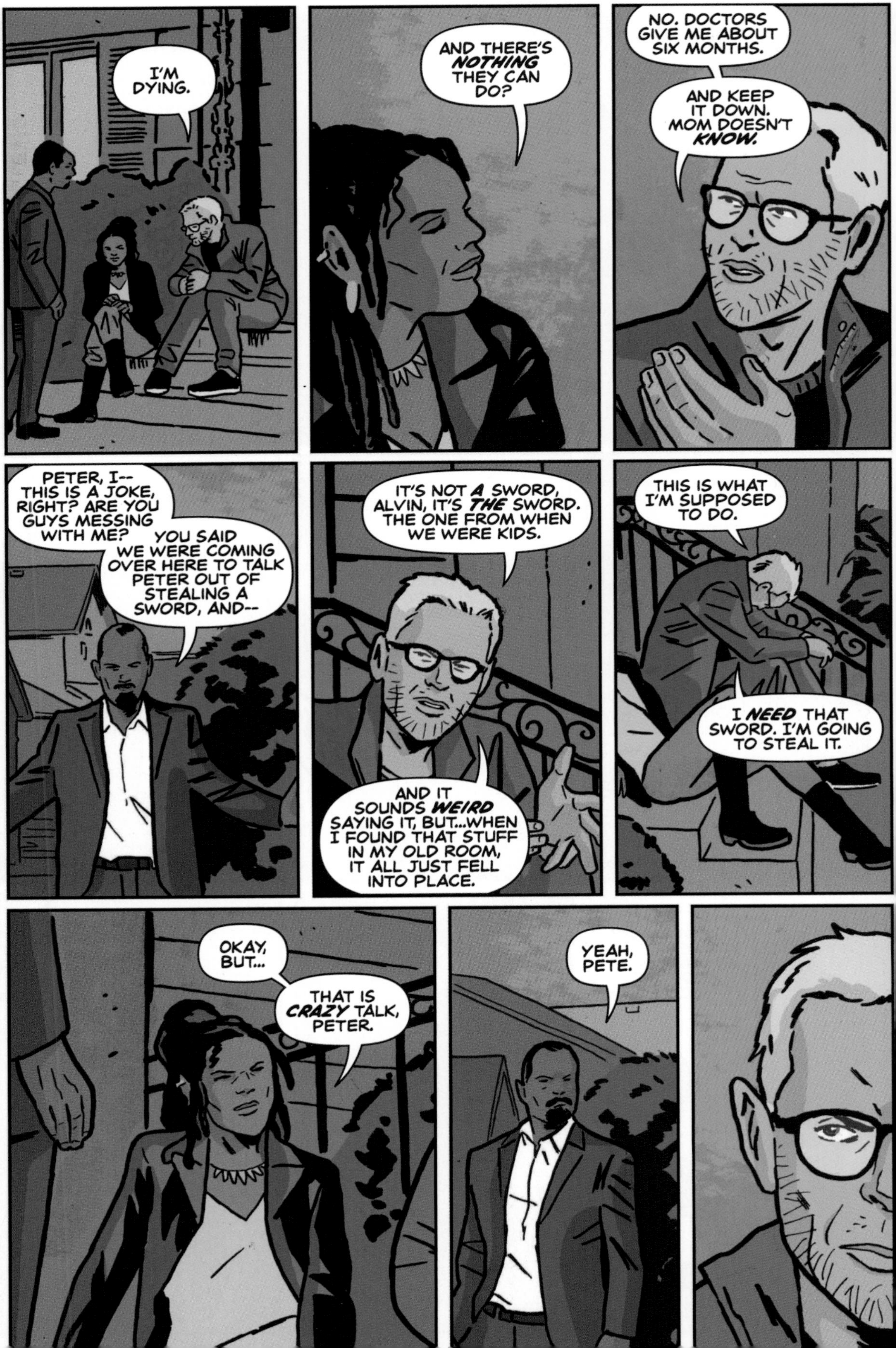
I'M DYING.
AND THERE'S NOTHING THEY CAN DO?
NO. DOCTORS GIVE ME ABOUT SIX MONTHS.
AND KEEP IT DOWN. MOM DOESN'T KNOW.
PETER, I-- THIS IS A JOKE, RIGHT? ARE YOU GUYS MESSING WITH ME?
YOU SAID WE WERE COMING OVER HERE TO TALK PETER OUT OF STEALING A SWORD, AND--
IT'S NOT A SWORD, ALVIN, IT'S THE SWORD. THE ONE FROM WHEN WE WERE KIDS.
AND IT SOUNDS WEIRD SAYING IT, BUT...WHEN I FOUND THAT STUFF IN MY OLD ROOM, IT ALL JUST FELL INTO PLACE.
THIS IS WHAT I'M SUPPOSED TO DO.
I NEED THAT SWORD. I'M GOING TO STEAL IT.
OKAY, BUT...
THAT IS CRAZY TALK, PETER.
YEAH, PETE.

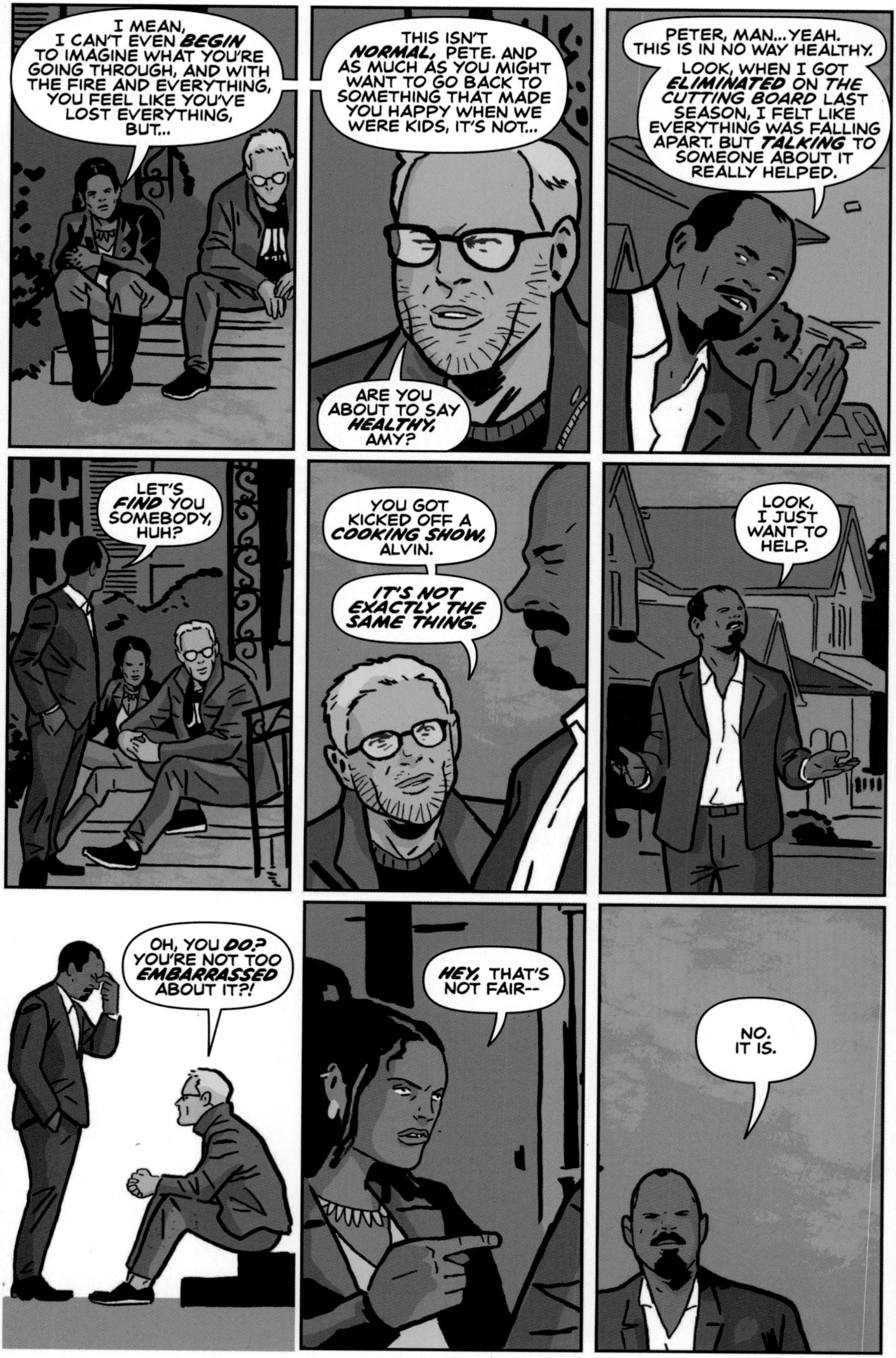
I MEAN, I CAN'T EVEN BEGIN TO IMAGINE WHAT YOU'RE GOING THROUGH, AND WITH THE FIRE AND EVERYTHING, YOU FEEL LIKE YOU'VE LOST EVERYTHING, BUT...
THIS ISN'T NORMAL, PETE. AND AS MUCH AS YOU MIGHT WANT TO GO BACK TO SOMETHING THAT MADE YOU HAPPY WHEN WE WERE KIDS, IT'S NOT...
ARE YOU ABOUT TO SAY HEALTHY, AMY?
PETER, MAN...YEAH. THIS IS IN NO WAY HEALTHY.
LOOK, WHEN I GOT ELIMINATED ON THE CUTTING BOARD LAST SEASON, I FELT LIKE EVERYTHING WAS FALLING APART. BUT TALKING TO SOMEONE ABOUT IT REALLY HELPED.
LET'S FIND YOU SOMEBODY, HUH?
YOU GOT KICKED OFF A COOKING SHOW, ALVIN.
IT'S NOT EXACTLY THE SAME THING.
LOOK, I JUST WANT TO HELP.
OH, YOU DO? YOU'RE NOT TOO EMBARRASSED ABOUT IT?!
HEY, THAT'S NOT FAIR--
NO. IT IS.

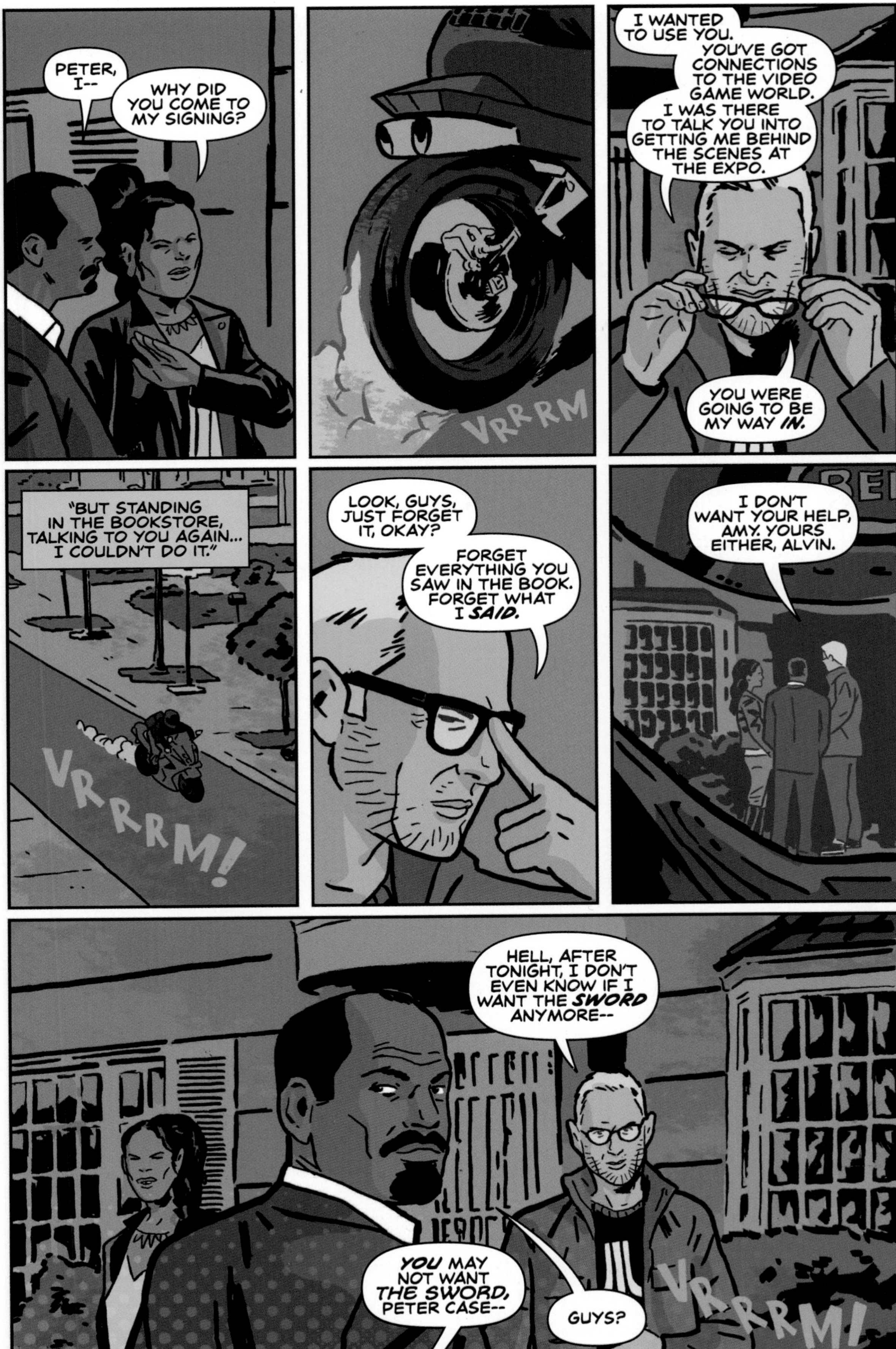
PETER, I--
WHY DID YOU COME TO MY SIGNING?
VRRRM
I WANTED TO USE YOU.
YOU'VE GOT CONNECTIONS TO THE VIDEO GAME WORLD.
I WAS THERE TO TALK YOU INTO GETTING ME BEHIND THE SCENES AT THE EXPO.
YOU WERE GOING TO BE MY WAY *IN.*
"BUT STANDING IN THE BOOKSTORE, TALKING TO YOU AGAIN... I COULDN'T DO IT."
VRRRM!
LOOK, GUYS, JUST FORGET IT, OKAY?
FORGET EVERYTHING YOU SAW IN THE BOOK. FORGET WHAT I *SAID.*
I DON'T WANT YOUR HELP, AMY. YOURS EITHER, ALVIN.
HELL, AFTER TONIGHT, I DON'T EVEN KNOW IF I WANT THE *SWORD* ANYMORE--
YOU MAY NOT WANT *THE SWORD,* PETER CASE--
GUYS?
VRRRM!

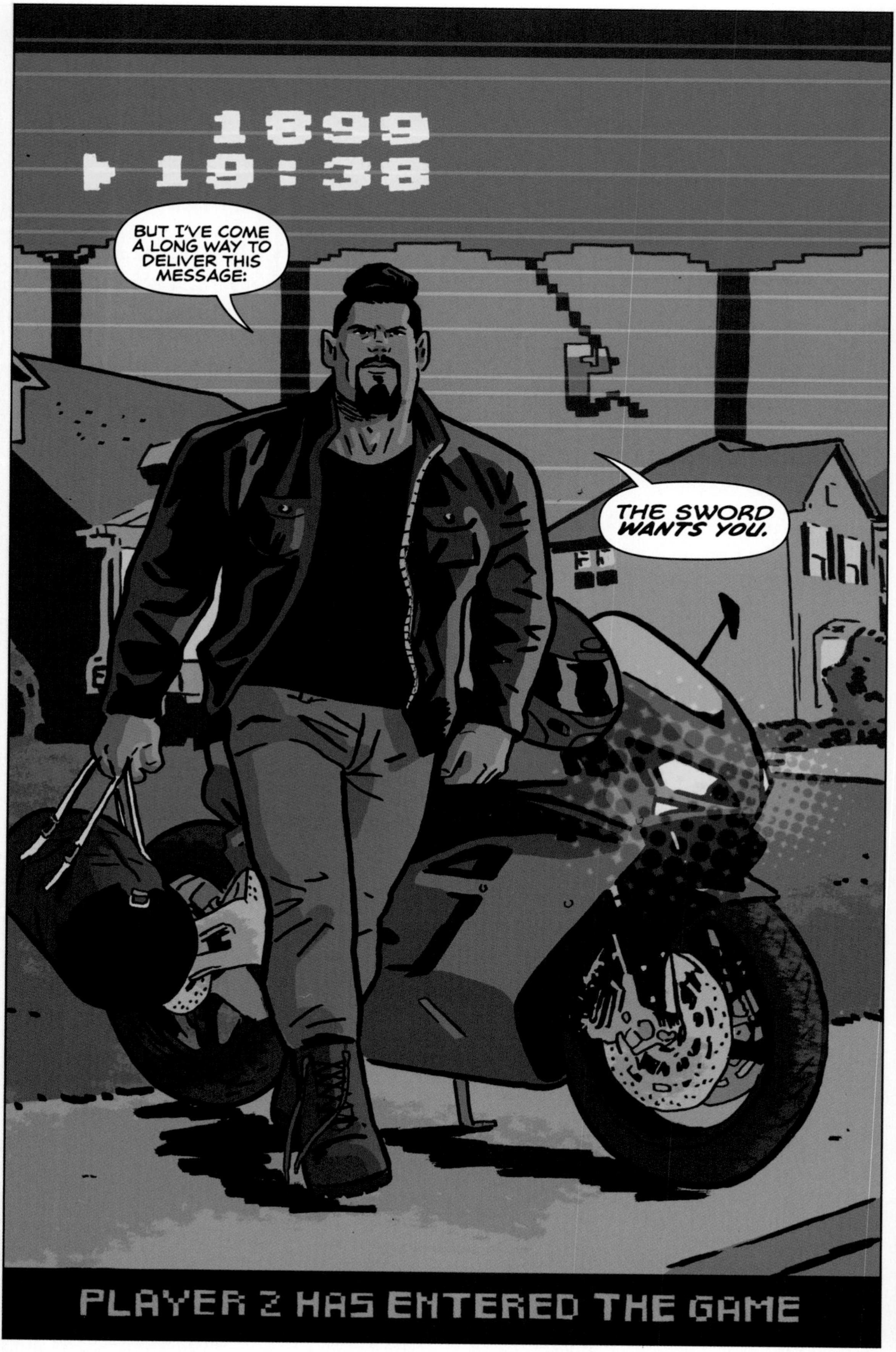
1899
19:38
BUT I'VE COME A LONG WAY TO DELIVER THIS MESSAGE:
THE SWORD WANTS YOU.
PLAYER 2 HAS ENTERED THE GAME

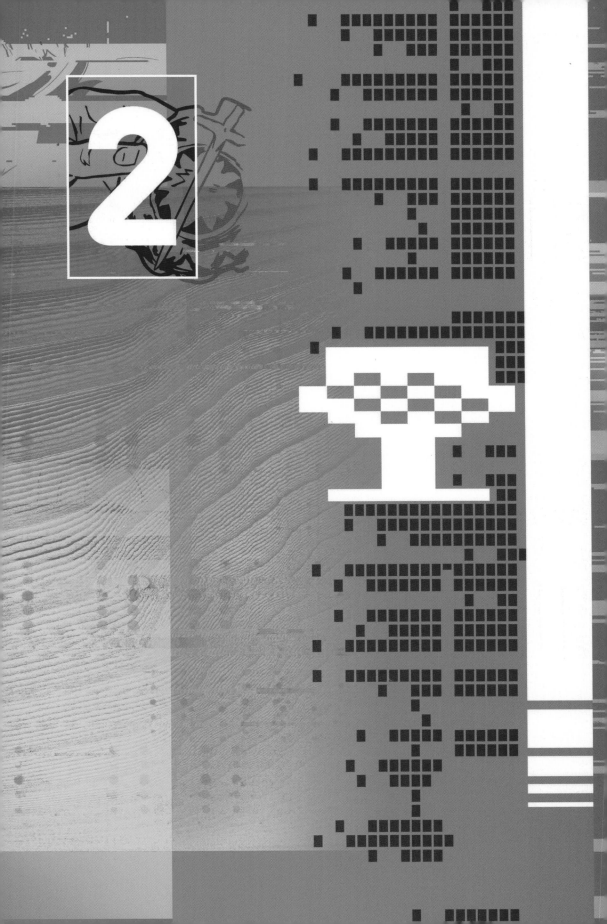

2

2

Art by GOÑI MONTES

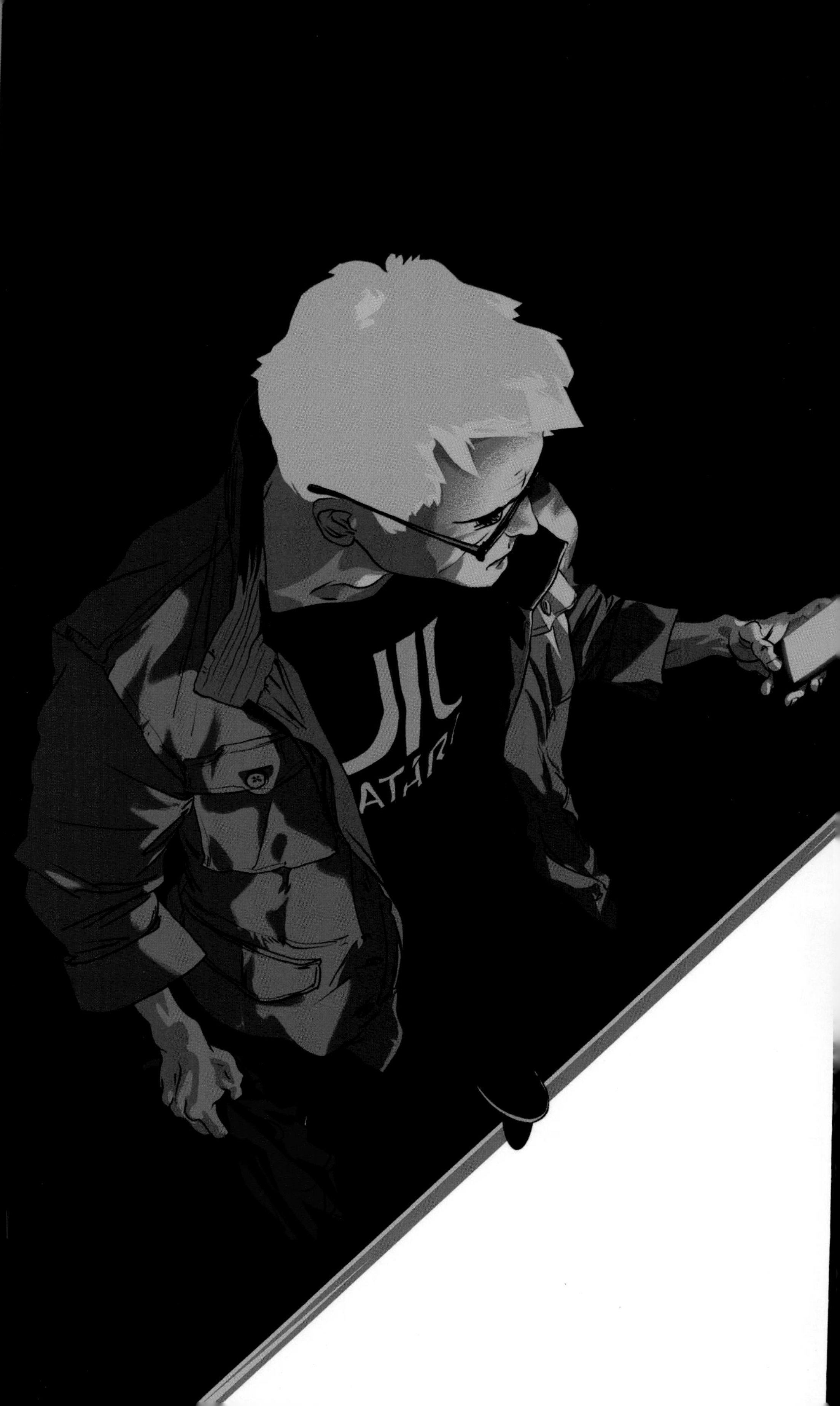

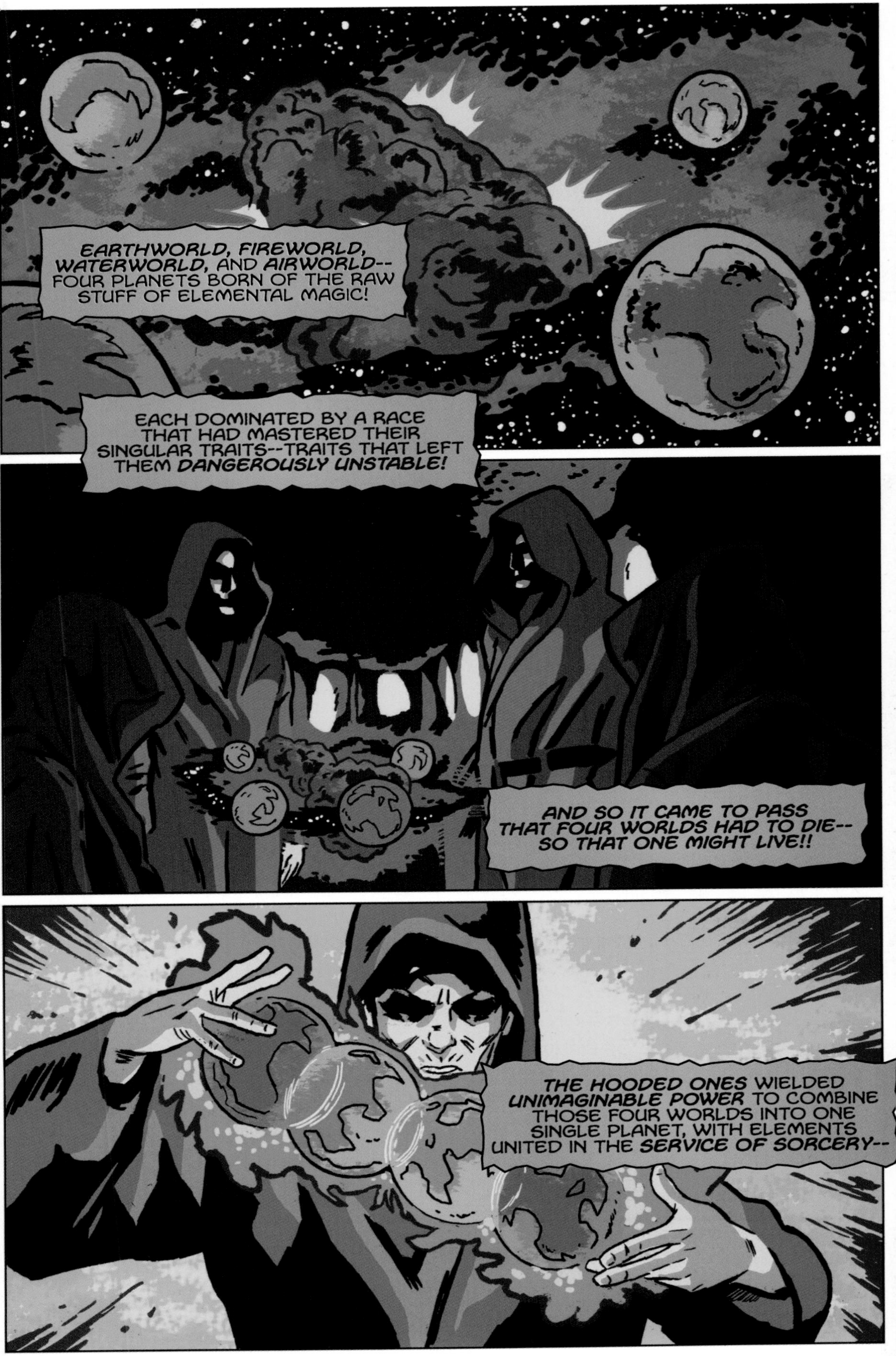
EARTHWORLD, FIREWORLD, WATERWORLD, AND AIRWORLD-- FOUR PLANETS BORN OF THE RAW STUFF OF ELEMENTAL MAGIC!
EACH DOMINATED BY A RACE THAT HAD MASTERED THEIR SINGULAR TRAITS--TRAITS THAT LEFT THEM DANGEROUSLY UNSTABLE!
AND SO IT CAME TO PASS THAT FOUR WORLDS HAD TO DIE-- SO THAT ONE MIGHT LIVE!!
THE HOODED ONES WIELDED UNIMAGINABLE POWER TO COMBINE THOSE FOUR WORLDS INTO ONE SINGLE PLANET, WITH ELEMENTS UNITED IN THE SERVICE OF SORCERY--

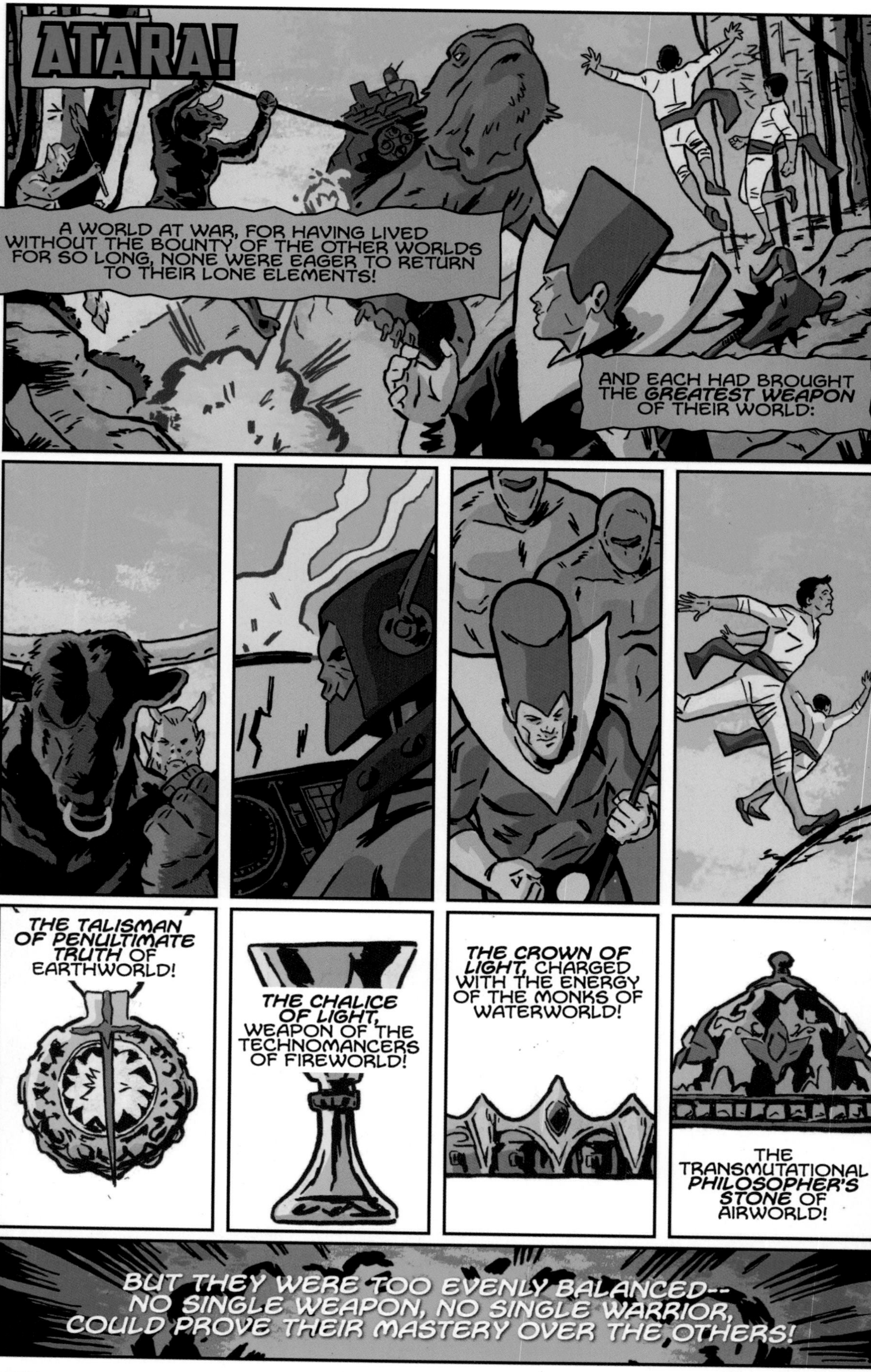
ATARA!
A WORLD AT WAR, FOR HAVING LIVED WITHOUT THE BOUNTY OF THE OTHER WORLDS FOR SO LONG, NONE WERE EAGER TO RETURN TO THEIR LONE ELEMENTS!
AND EACH HAD BROUGHT THE GREATEST WEAPON OF THEIR WORLD:
THE TALISMAN OF PENULTIMATE TRUTH OF EARTHWORLD!
THE CHALICE OF LIGHT, WEAPON OF THE TECHNOMANCERS OF FIREWORLD!
THE CROWN OF LIGHT, CHARGED WITH THE ENERGY OF THE MONKS OF WATERWORLD!
THE TRANSMUTATIONAL PHILOSOPHER'S STONE OF AIRWORLD!
BUT THEY WERE TOO EVENLY BALANCED-- NO SINGLE WEAPON, NO SINGLE WARRIOR, COULD PROVE THEIR MASTERY OVER THE OTHERS!

BUT WHERE A *WARRIOR* FEARS TO TREAD, PERHAPS A *THIEF* MAY DARE!

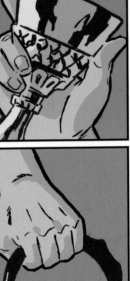

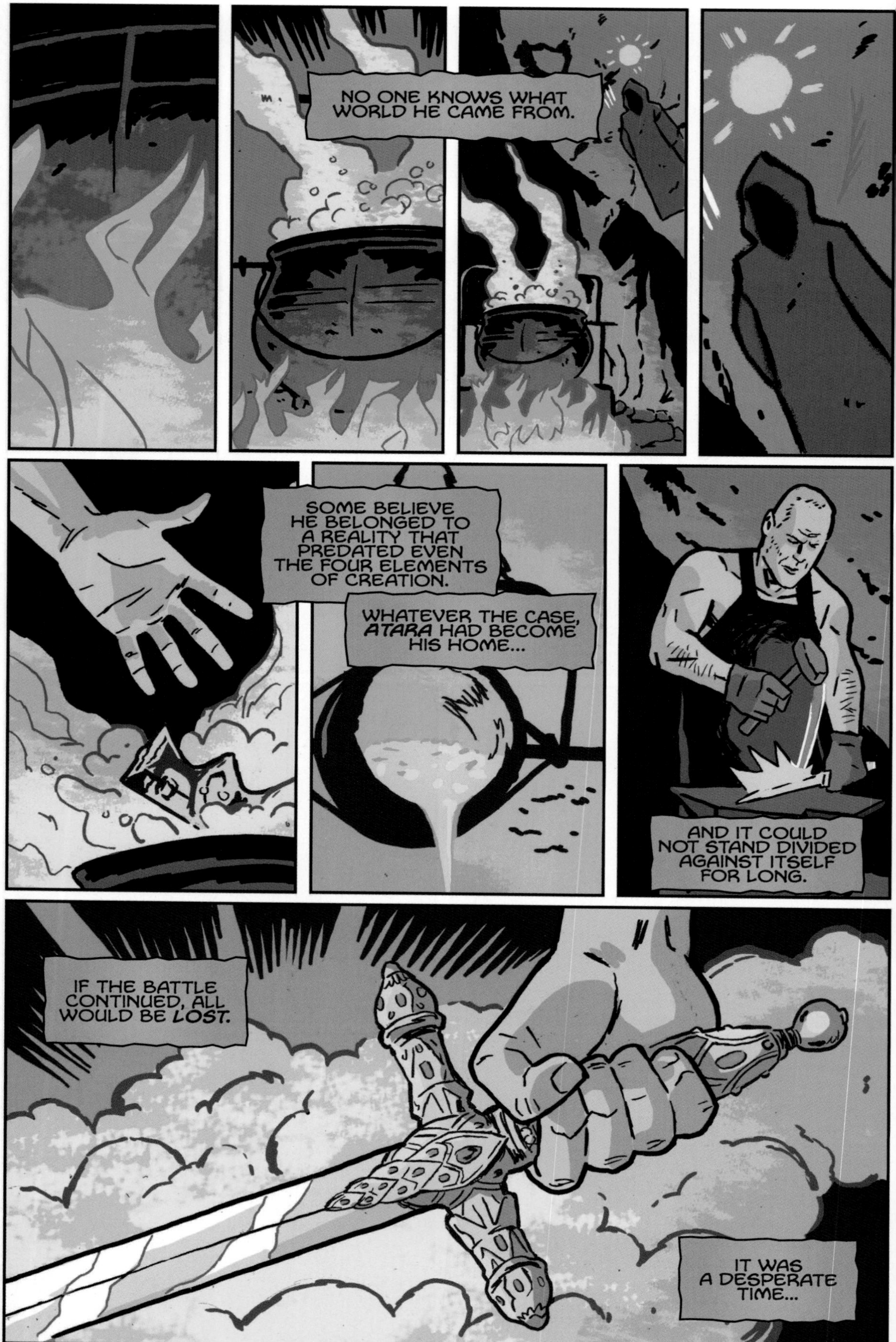
NO ONE KNOWS WHAT WORLD HE CAME FROM.
SOME BELIEVE HE BELONGED TO A REALITY THAT PREDATED EVEN THE FOUR ELEMENTS OF CREATION.
WHATEVER THE CASE, *ATARA* HAD BECOME HIS HOME...
AND IT COULD NOT STAND DIVIDED AGAINST ITSELF FOR LONG.
IF THE BATTLE CONTINUED, ALL WOULD BE *LOST*.
IT WAS A DESPERATE TIME...

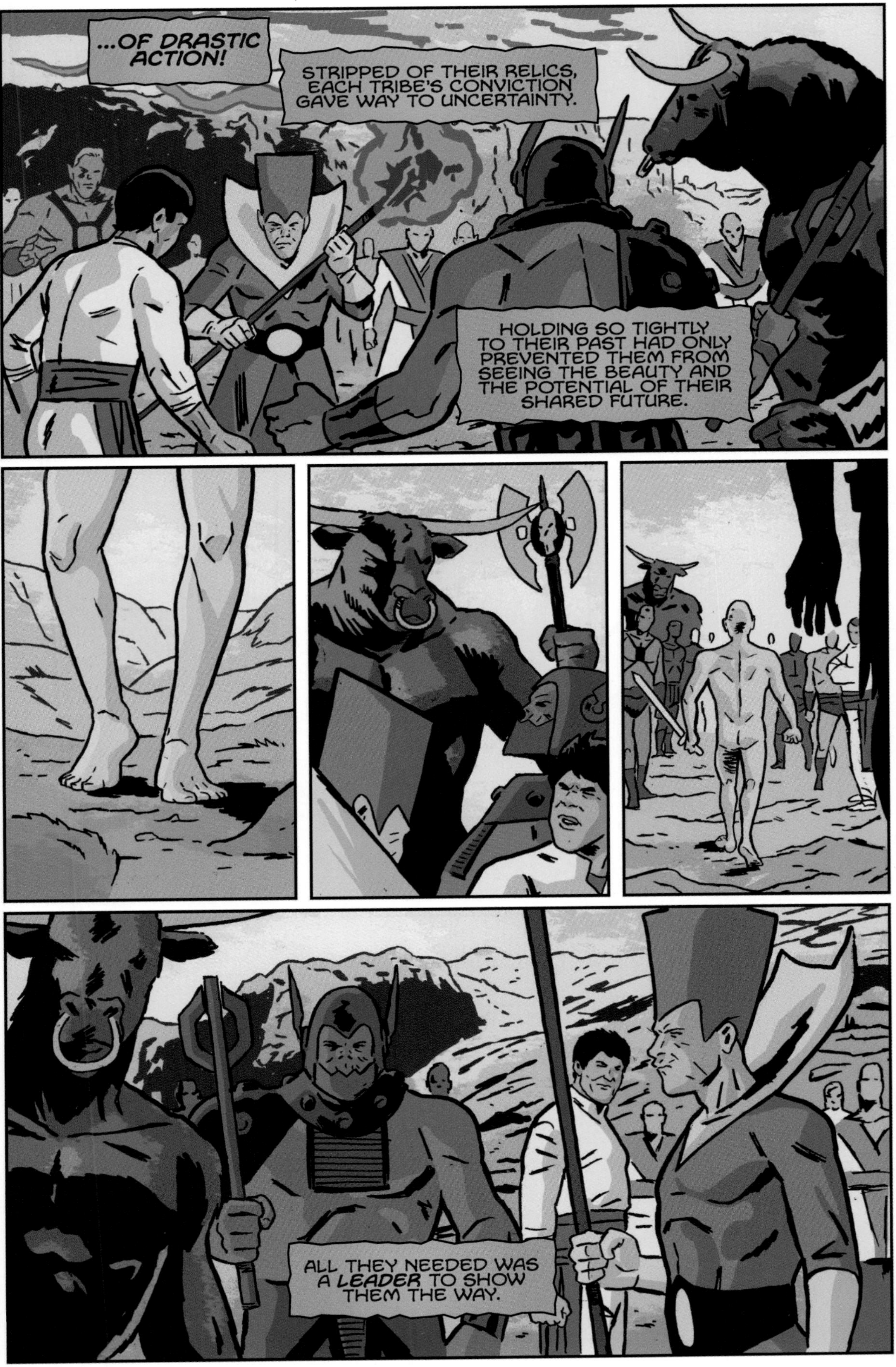
...OF DRASTIC ACTION!
STRIPPED OF THEIR RELICS, EACH TRIBE'S CONVICTION GAVE WAY TO UNCERTAINTY.
HOLDING SO TIGHTLY TO THEIR PAST HAD ONLY PREVENTED THEM FROM SEEING THE BEAUTY AND THE POTENTIAL OF THEIR SHARED FUTURE.
ALL THEY NEEDED WAS A LEADER TO SHOW THEM THE WAY.

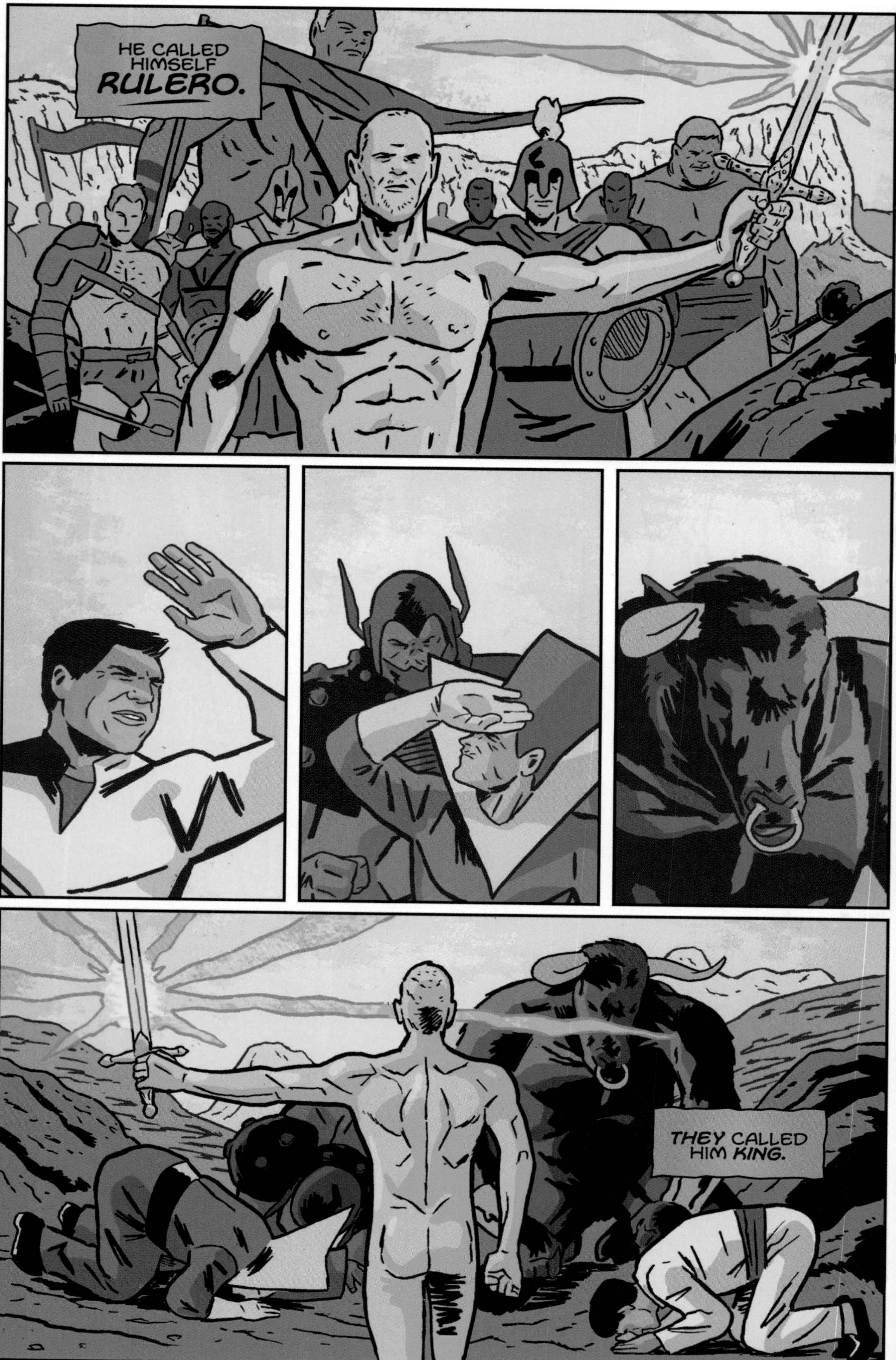
HE CALLED HIMSELF RULERO.
THEY CALLED HIM KING.

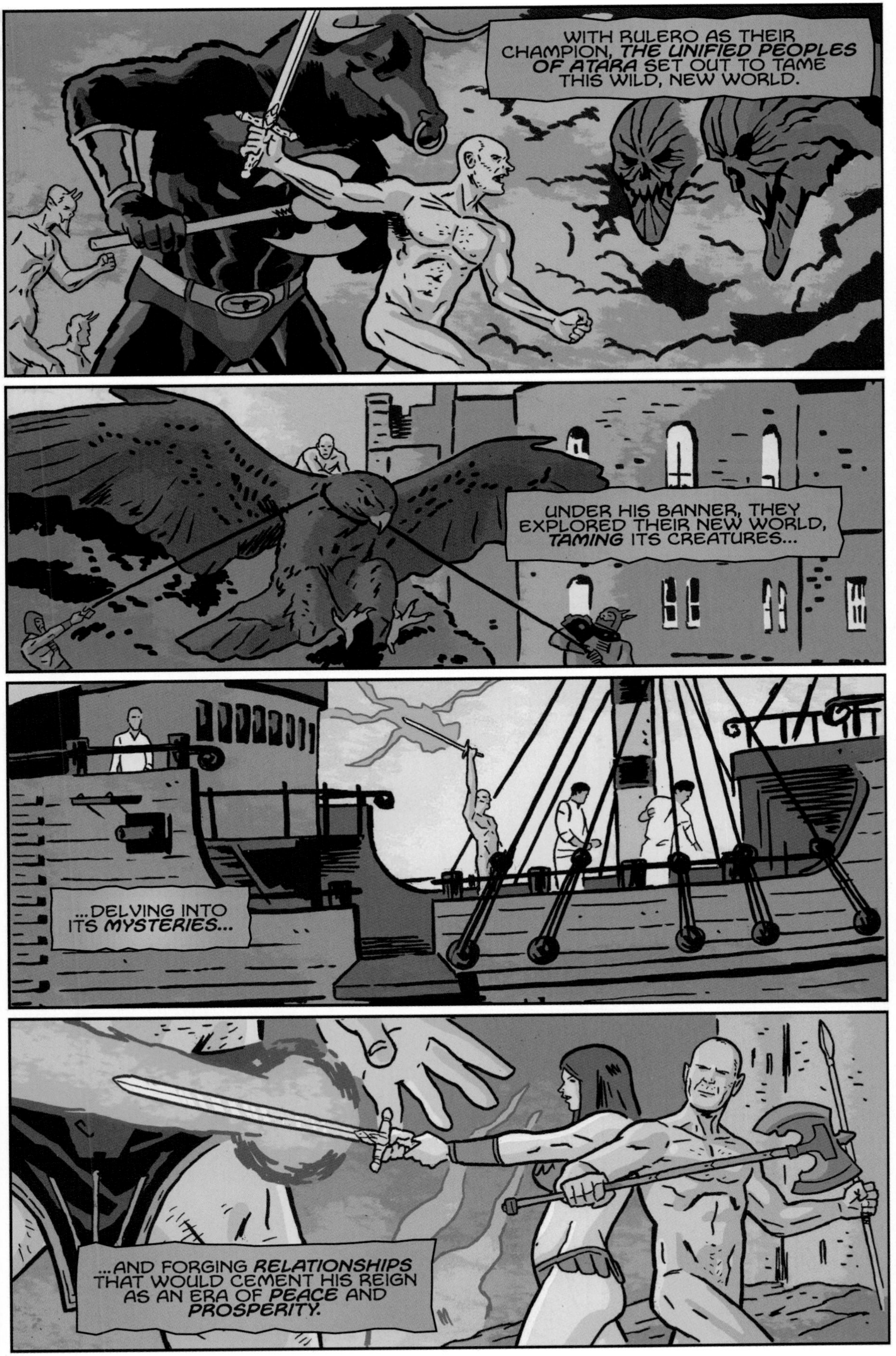
WITH RULERO AS THEIR CHAMPION, THE UNIFIED PEOPLES OF ATARA SET OUT TO TAME THIS WILD, NEW WORLD.
UNDER HIS BANNER, THEY EXPLORED THEIR NEW WORLD, TAMING ITS CREATURES...
...DELVING INTO ITS MYSTERIES...
...AND FORGING RELATIONSHIPS THAT WOULD CEMENT HIS REIGN AS AN ERA OF PEACE AND PROSPERITY.

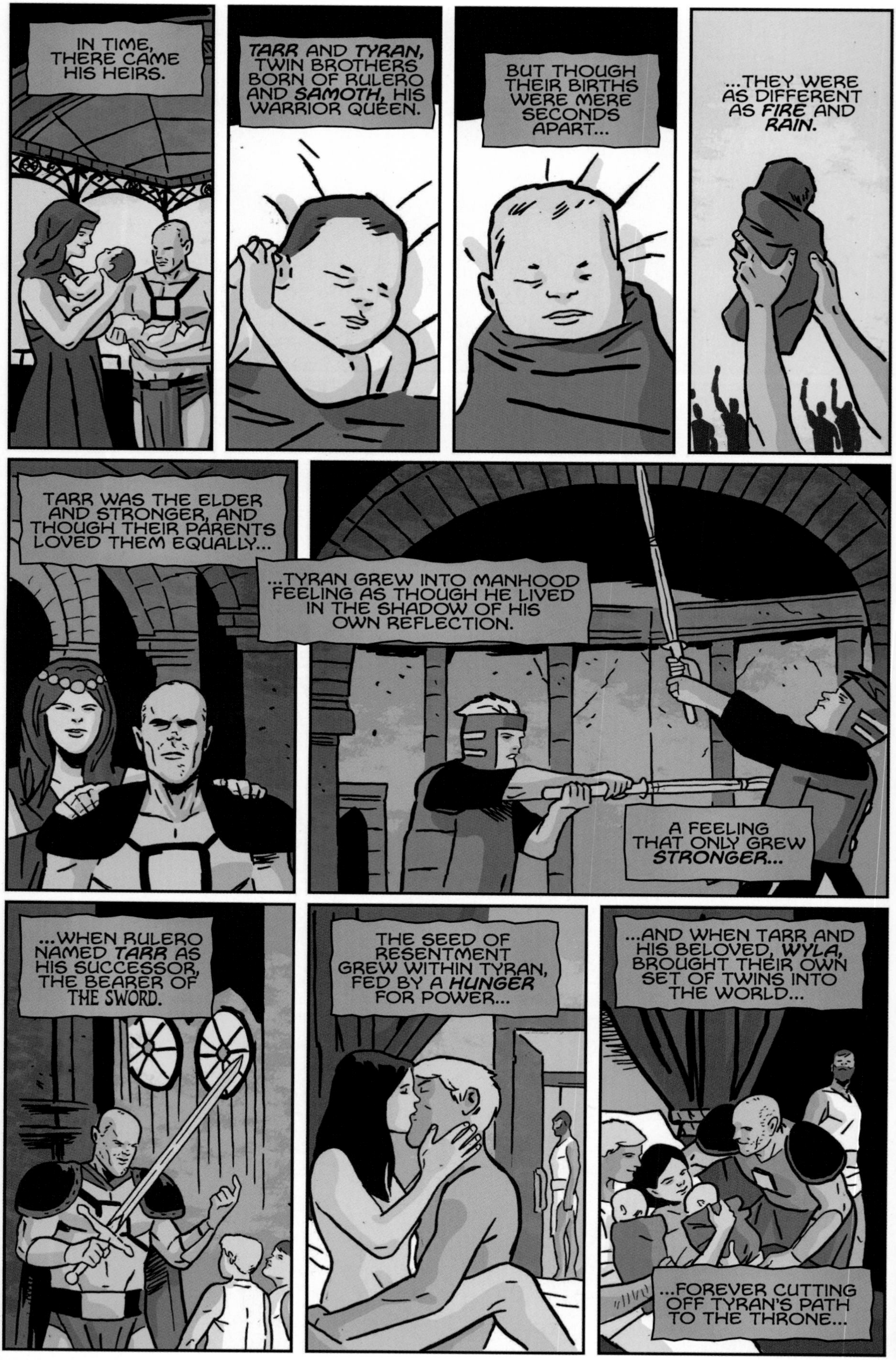
IN TIME, THERE CAME HIS HEIRS.
TARR AND TYRAN, TWIN BROTHERS BORN OF RULERO AND SAMOTH, HIS WARRIOR QUEEN.
BUT THOUGH THEIR BIRTHS WERE MERE SECONDS APART...
...THEY WERE AS DIFFERENT AS FIRE AND RAIN.
TARR WAS THE ELDER AND STRONGER, AND THOUGH THEIR PARENTS LOVED THEM EQUALLY...
...TYRAN GREW INTO MANHOOD FEELING AS THOUGH HE LIVED IN THE SHADOW OF HIS OWN REFLECTION.
A FEELING THAT ONLY GREW STRONGER...
...WHEN RULERO NAMED TARR AS HIS SUCCESSOR, THE BEARER OF THE SWORD.
THE SEED OF RESENTMENT GREW WITHIN TYRAN, FED BY A HUNGER FOR POWER...
...AND WHEN TARR AND HIS BELOVED, WYLA, BROUGHT THEIR OWN SET OF TWINS INTO THE WORLD...
...FOREVER CUTTING OFF TYRAN'S PATH TO THE THRONE...

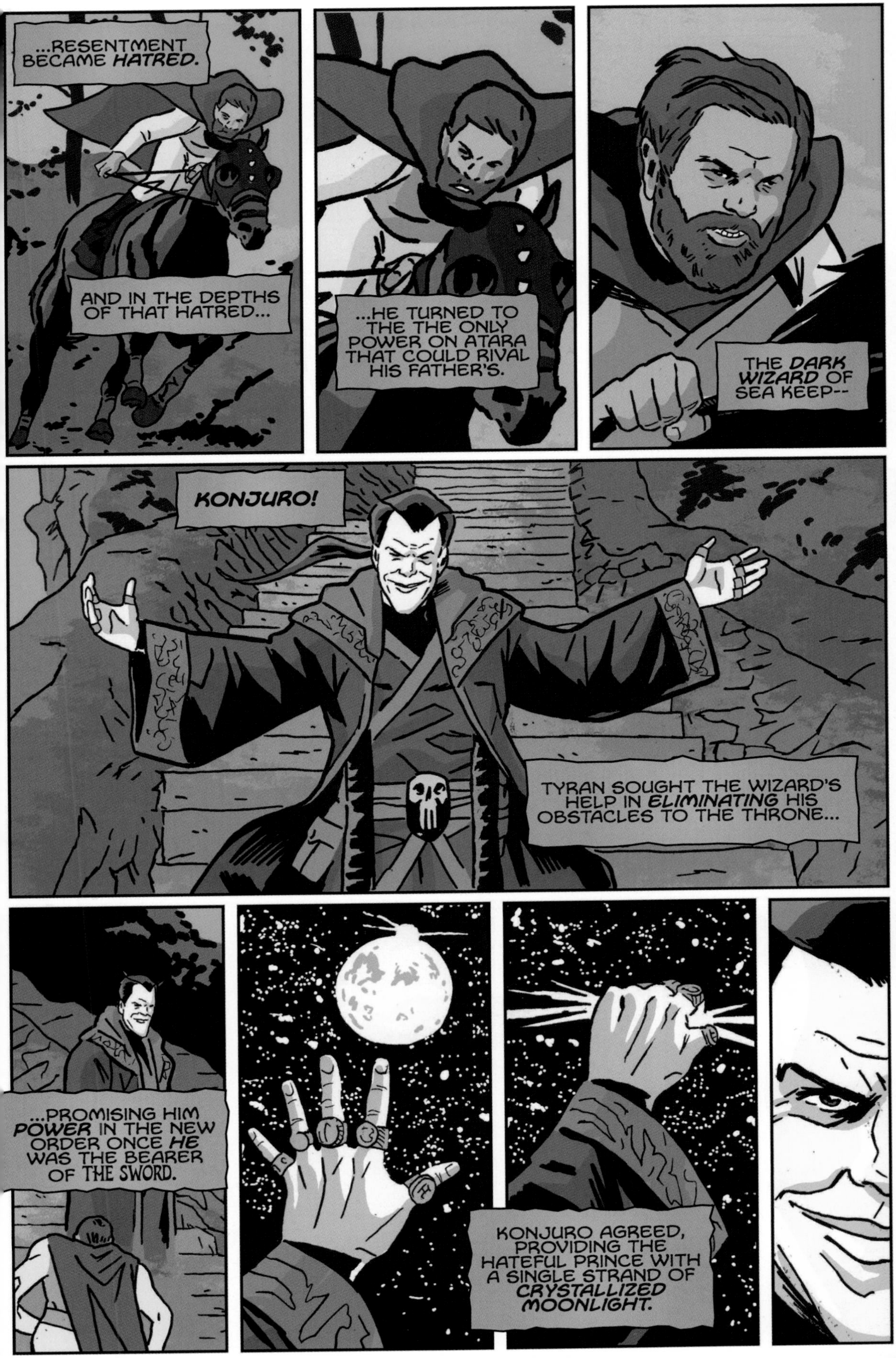
...RESENTMENT BECAME HATRED.
AND IN THE DEPTHS OF THAT HATRED...
...HE TURNED TO THE THE ONLY POWER ON ATARA THAT COULD RIVAL HIS FATHER'S.
THE DARK WIZARD OF SEA KEEP--
KONJURO!
TYRAN SOUGHT THE WIZARD'S HELP IN ELIMINATING HIS OBSTACLES TO THE THRONE...
...PROMISING HIM POWER IN THE NEW ORDER ONCE HE WAS THE BEARER OF THE SWORD.
KONJURO AGREED, PROVIDING THE HATEFUL PRINCE WITH A SINGLE STRAND OF CRYSTALLIZED MOONLIGHT.

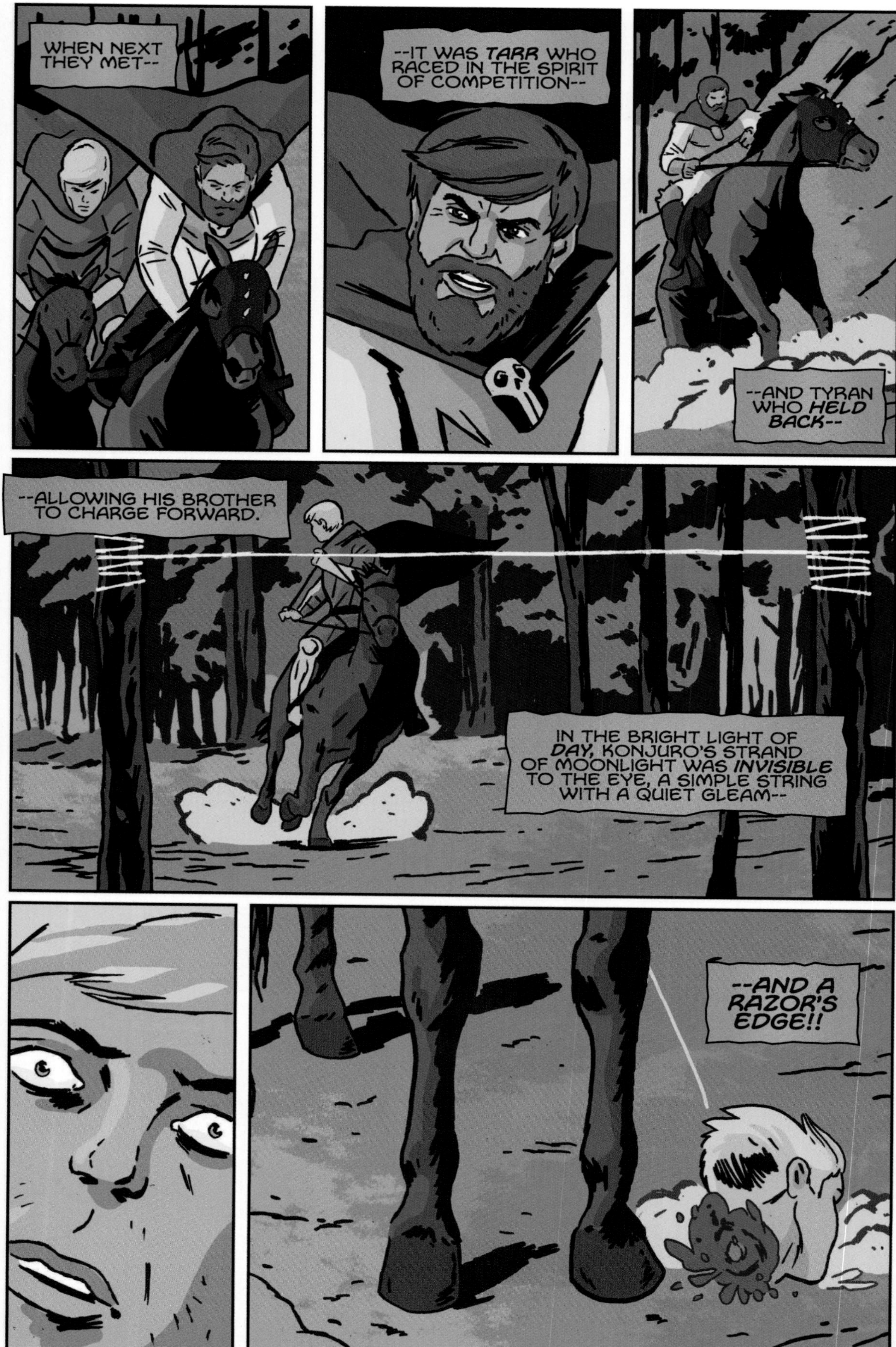
WHEN NEXT THEY MET--
--IT WAS TARR WHO RACED IN THE SPIRIT OF COMPETITION--
--AND TYRAN WHO HELD BACK--
--ALLOWING HIS BROTHER TO CHARGE FORWARD.
IN THE BRIGHT LIGHT OF DAY, KONJURO'S STRAND OF MOONLIGHT WAS INVISIBLE TO THE EYE, A SIMPLE STRING WITH A QUIET GLEAM--
--AND A RAZOR'S EDGE!!

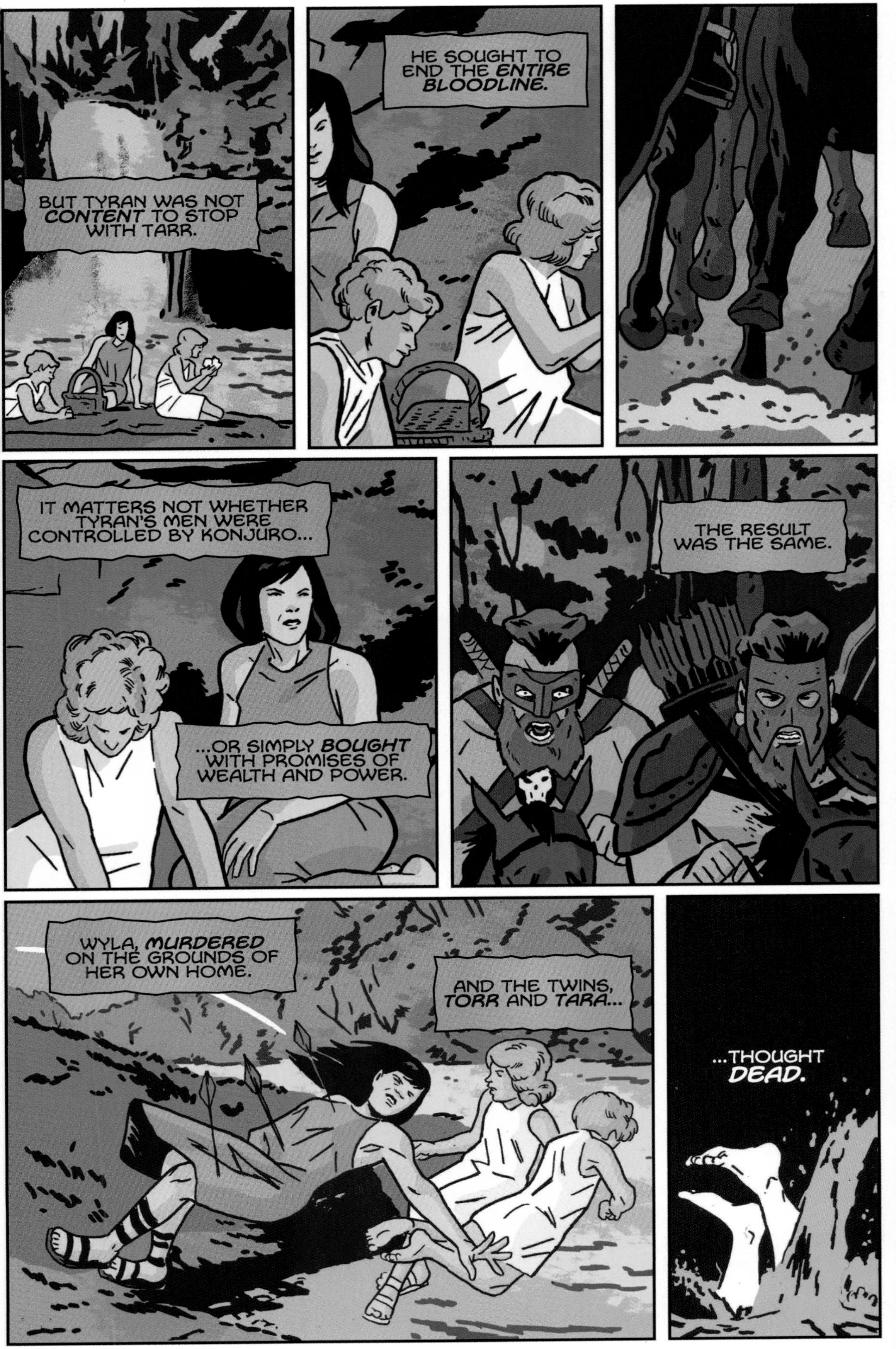
BUT TYRAN WAS NOT *CONTENT* TO STOP WITH TARR.
HE SOUGHT TO END THE *ENTIRE BLOODLINE.*
IT MATTERS NOT WHETHER TYRAN'S MEN WERE CONTROLLED BY KONJURO...
...OR SIMPLY *BOUGHT* WITH PROMISES OF WEALTH AND POWER.
THE RESULT WAS THE SAME.
WYLA, *MURDERED* ON THE GROUNDS OF HER OWN HOME.
AND THE TWINS, *TORR* AND *TARA*...
...THOUGHT *DEAD.*

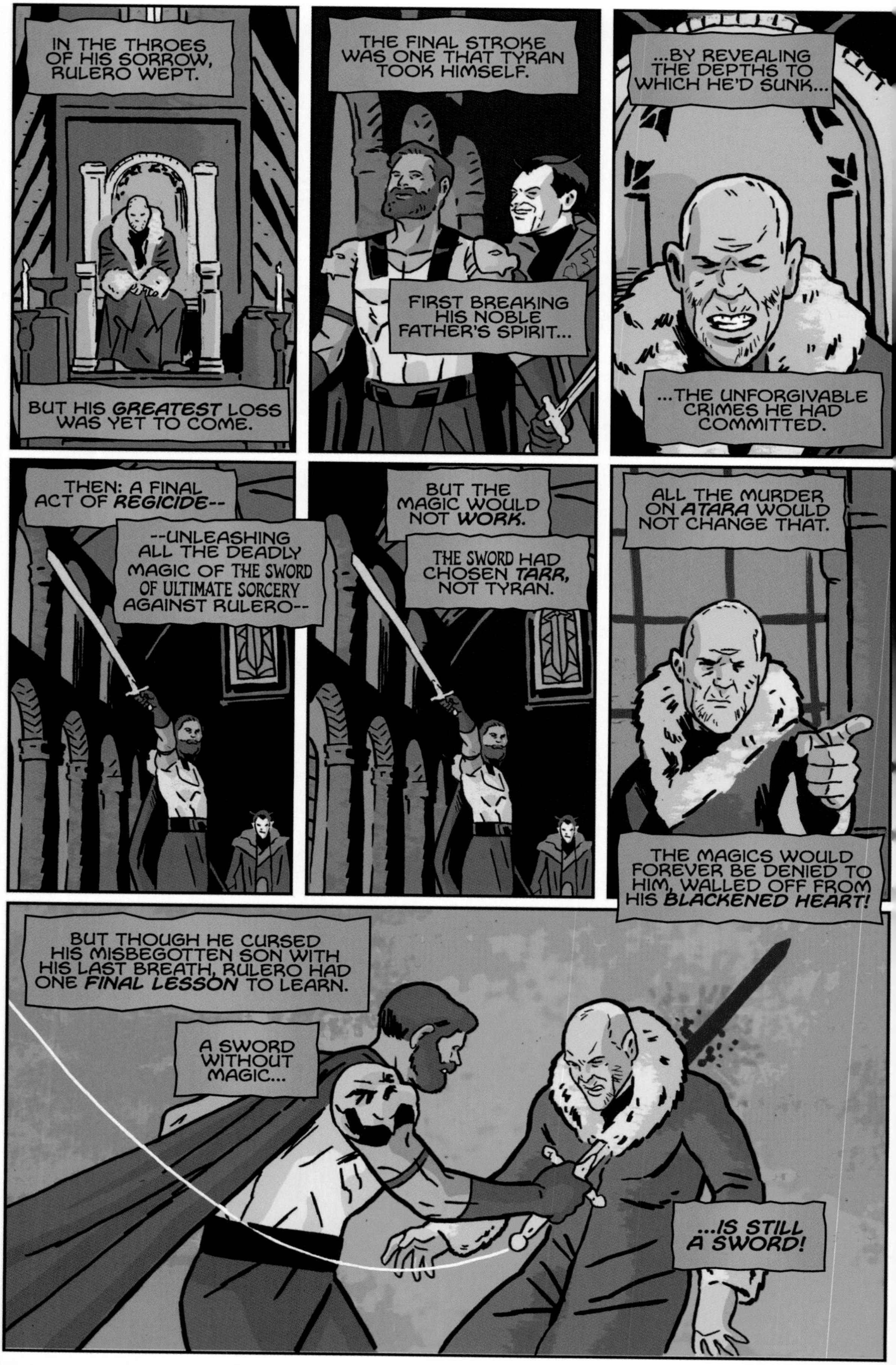

IN THE THROES OF HIS SORROW, RULERO WEPT.
BUT HIS GREATEST LOSS WAS YET TO COME.
THE FINAL STROKE WAS ONE THAT TYRAN TOOK HIMSELF.
FIRST BREAKING HIS NOBLE FATHER'S SPIRIT...
...BY REVEALING THE DEPTHS TO WHICH HE'D SUNK...
...THE UNFORGIVABLE CRIMES HE HAD COMMITTED.
THEN: A FINAL ACT OF REGICIDE--
--UNLEASHING ALL THE DEADLY MAGIC OF THE SWORD OF ULTIMATE SORCERY AGAINST RULERO--
BUT THE MAGIC WOULD NOT WORK.
THE SWORD HAD CHOSEN TARR, NOT TYRAN.
ALL THE MURDER ON ATARA WOULD NOT CHANGE THAT.
THE MAGICS WOULD FOREVER BE DENIED TO HIM, WALLED OFF FROM HIS BLACKENED HEART!
BUT THOUGH HE CURSED HIS MISBEGOTTEN SON WITH HIS LAST BREATH, RULERO HAD ONE FINAL LESSON TO LEARN.
A SWORD WITHOUT MAGIC...
...IS STILL A SWORD!

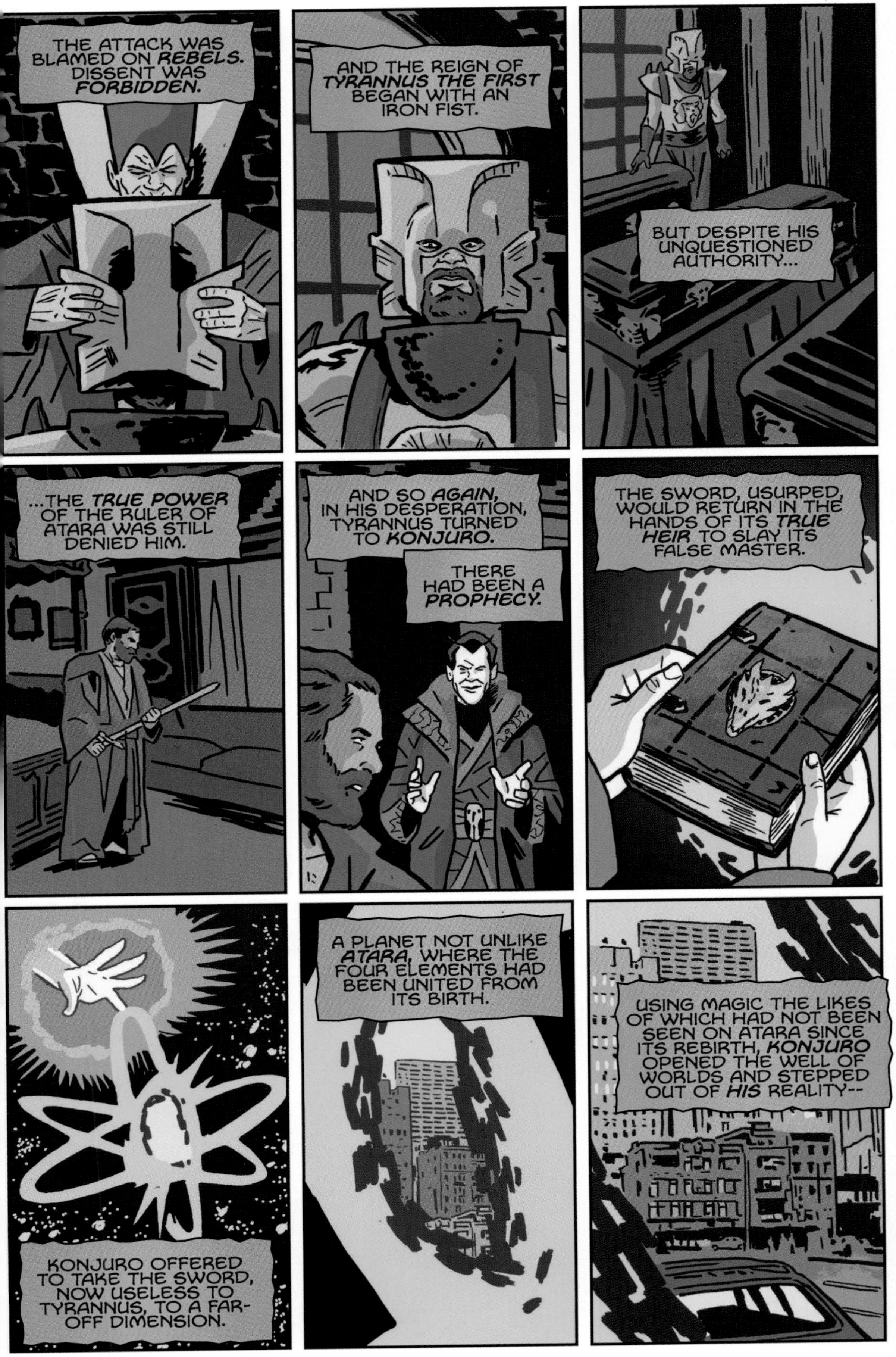
THE ATTACK WAS BLAMED ON REBELS. DISSENT WAS FORBIDDEN.
AND THE REIGN OF TYRANNUS THE FIRST BEGAN WITH AN IRON FIST.
BUT DESPITE HIS UNQUESTIONED AUTHORITY...
...THE TRUE POWER OF THE RULER OF ATARA WAS STILL DENIED HIM.
AND SO AGAIN, IN HIS DESPERATION, TYRANNUS TURNED TO KONJURO.
THERE HAD BEEN A PROPHECY.
THE SWORD, USURPED, WOULD RETURN IN THE HANDS OF ITS TRUE HEIR TO SLAY ITS FALSE MASTER.
KONJURO OFFERED TO TAKE THE SWORD, NOW USELESS TO TYRANNUS, TO A FAR-OFF DIMENSION.
A PLANET NOT UNLIKE ATARA, WHERE THE FOUR ELEMENTS HAD BEEN UNITED FROM ITS BIRTH.
USING MAGIC THE LIKES OF WHICH HAD NOT BEEN SEEN ON ATARA SINCE ITS REBIRTH, KONJURO OPENED THE WELL OF WORLDS AND STEPPED OUT OF HIS REALITY--

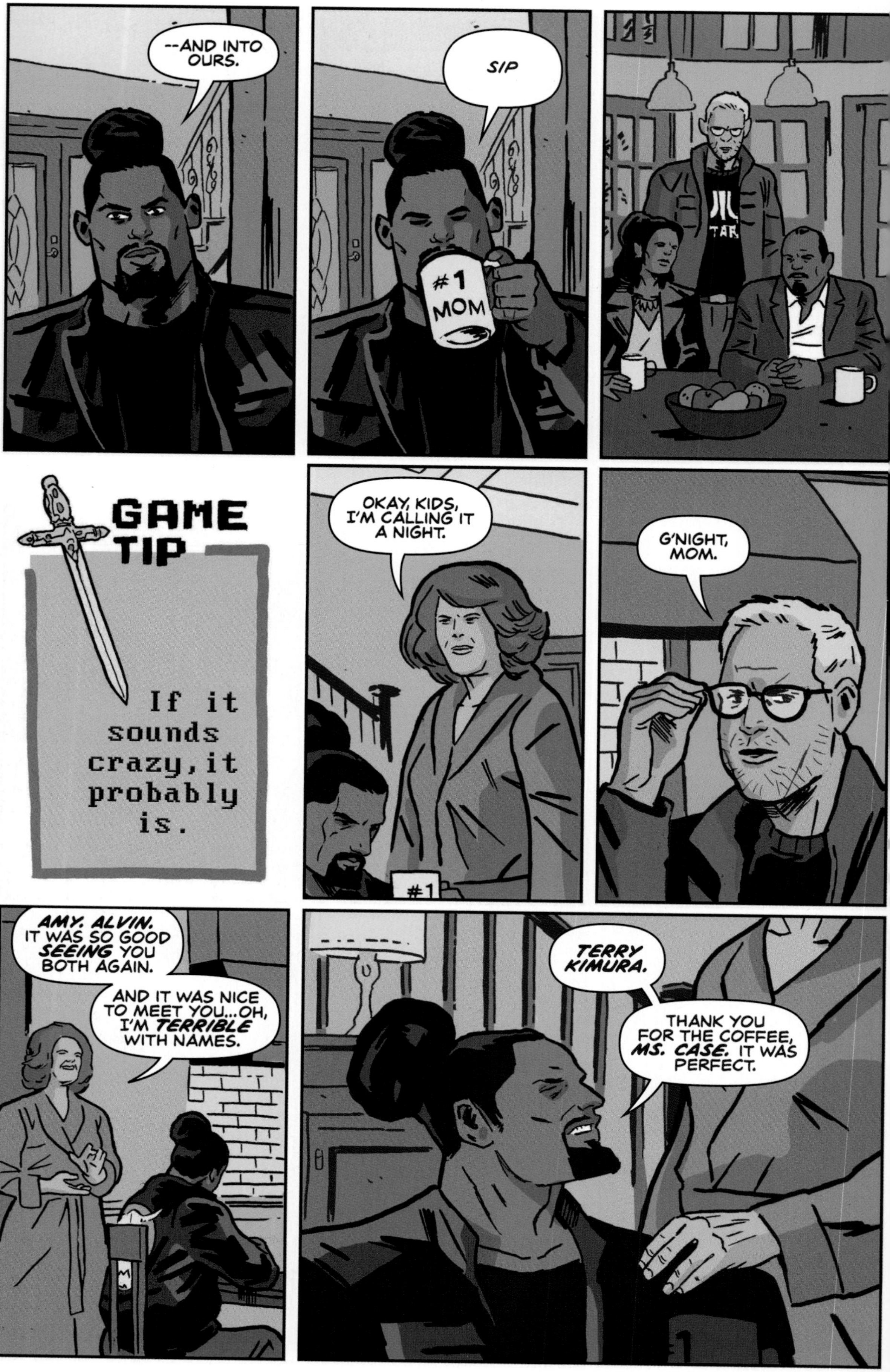
--AND INTO OURS.
SIP
#1 MOM
GAME TIP
If it sounds crazy,it probably is.
OKAY, KIDS, I'M CALLING IT A NIGHT.
#1
G'NIGHT, MOM.
AMY. ALVIN. IT WAS SO GOOD SEEING YOU BOTH AGAIN.
AND IT WAS NICE TO MEET YOU...OH, I'M TERRIBLE WITH NAMES.
TERRY KIMURA.
THANK YOU FOR THE COFFEE, MS. CASE. IT WAS PERFECT.

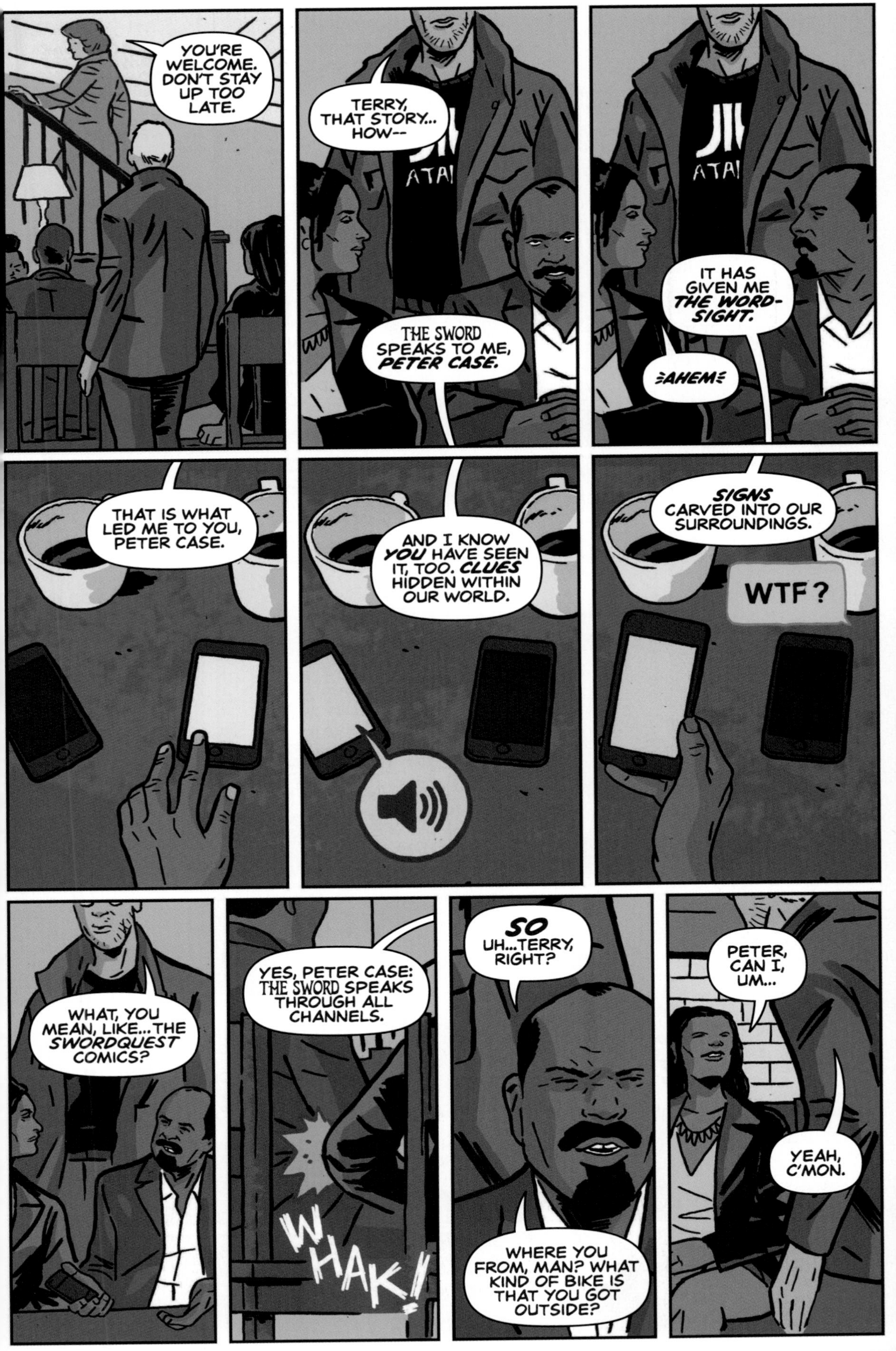
YOU'RE WELCOME. DON'T STAY UP TOO LATE.
TERRY, THAT STORY... HOW--
THE SWORD SPEAKS TO ME, PETER CASE.
IT HAS GIVEN ME THE WORD-SIGHT.
AHEM
THAT IS WHAT LED ME TO YOU, PETER CASE.
AND I KNOW YOU HAVE SEEN IT, TOO. CLUES HIDDEN WITHIN OUR WORLD.
SIGNS CARVED INTO OUR SURROUNDINGS.
WTF?
WHAT, YOU MEAN, LIKE...THE SWORDQUEST COMICS?
YES, PETER CASE: THE SWORD SPEAKS THROUGH ALL CHANNELS.
WHAK!
SO UH...TERRY, RIGHT?
WHERE YOU FROM, MAN? WHAT KIND OF BIKE IS THAT YOU GOT OUTSIDE?
PETER, CAN I, UM...
YEAH, C'MON.

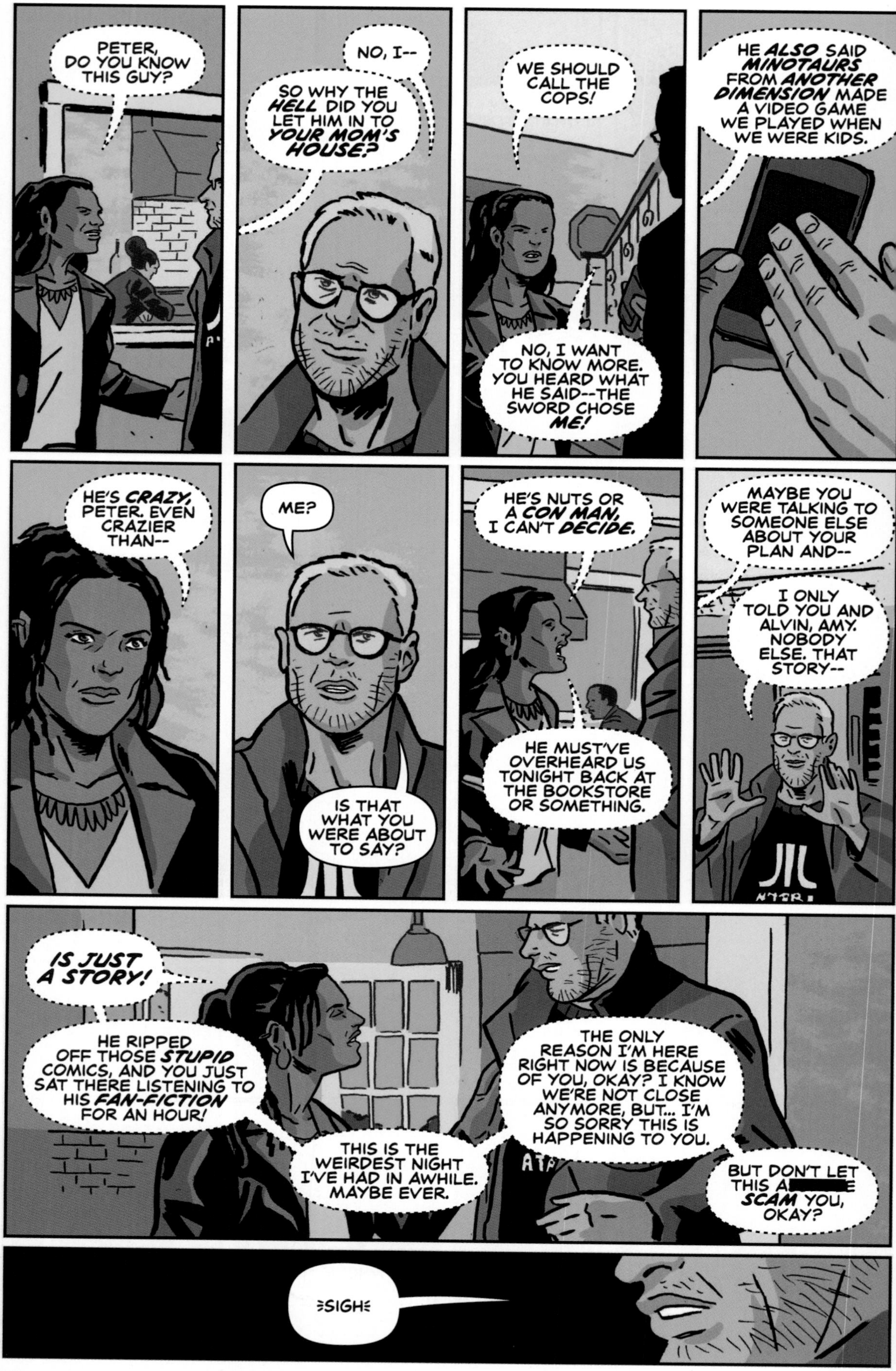
PETER, DO YOU KNOW THIS GUY?
NO, I--
SO WHY THE HELL DID YOU LET HIM IN TO YOUR MOM'S HOUSE?
WE SHOULD CALL THE COPS!
NO, I WANT TO KNOW MORE. YOU HEARD WHAT HE SAID--THE SWORD CHOSE ME!
HE ALSO SAID MINOTAURS FROM ANOTHER DIMENSION MADE A VIDEO GAME WE PLAYED WHEN WE WERE KIDS.
HE'S CRAZY, PETER. EVEN CRAZIER THAN--
ME?
IS THAT WHAT YOU WERE ABOUT TO SAY?
HE'S NUTS OR A CON MAN, I CAN'T DECIDE.
HE MUST'VE OVERHEARD US TONIGHT BACK AT THE BOOKSTORE OR SOMETHING.
MAYBE YOU WERE TALKING TO SOMEONE ELSE ABOUT YOUR PLAN AND--
I ONLY TOLD YOU AND ALVIN, AMY. NOBODY ELSE. THAT STORY--
IS JUST A STORY!
HE RIPPED OFF THOSE STUPID COMICS, AND YOU JUST SAT THERE LISTENING TO HIS FAN-FICTION FOR AN HOUR!
THIS IS THE WEIRDEST NIGHT I'VE HAD IN AWHILE. MAYBE EVER.
THE ONLY REASON I'M HERE RIGHT NOW IS BECAUSE OF YOU, OKAY? I KNOW WE'RE NOT CLOSE ANYMORE, BUT... I'M SO SORRY THIS IS HAPPENING TO YOU.
BUT DON'T LET THIS A[redacted]E SCAM YOU, OKAY?
SIGH

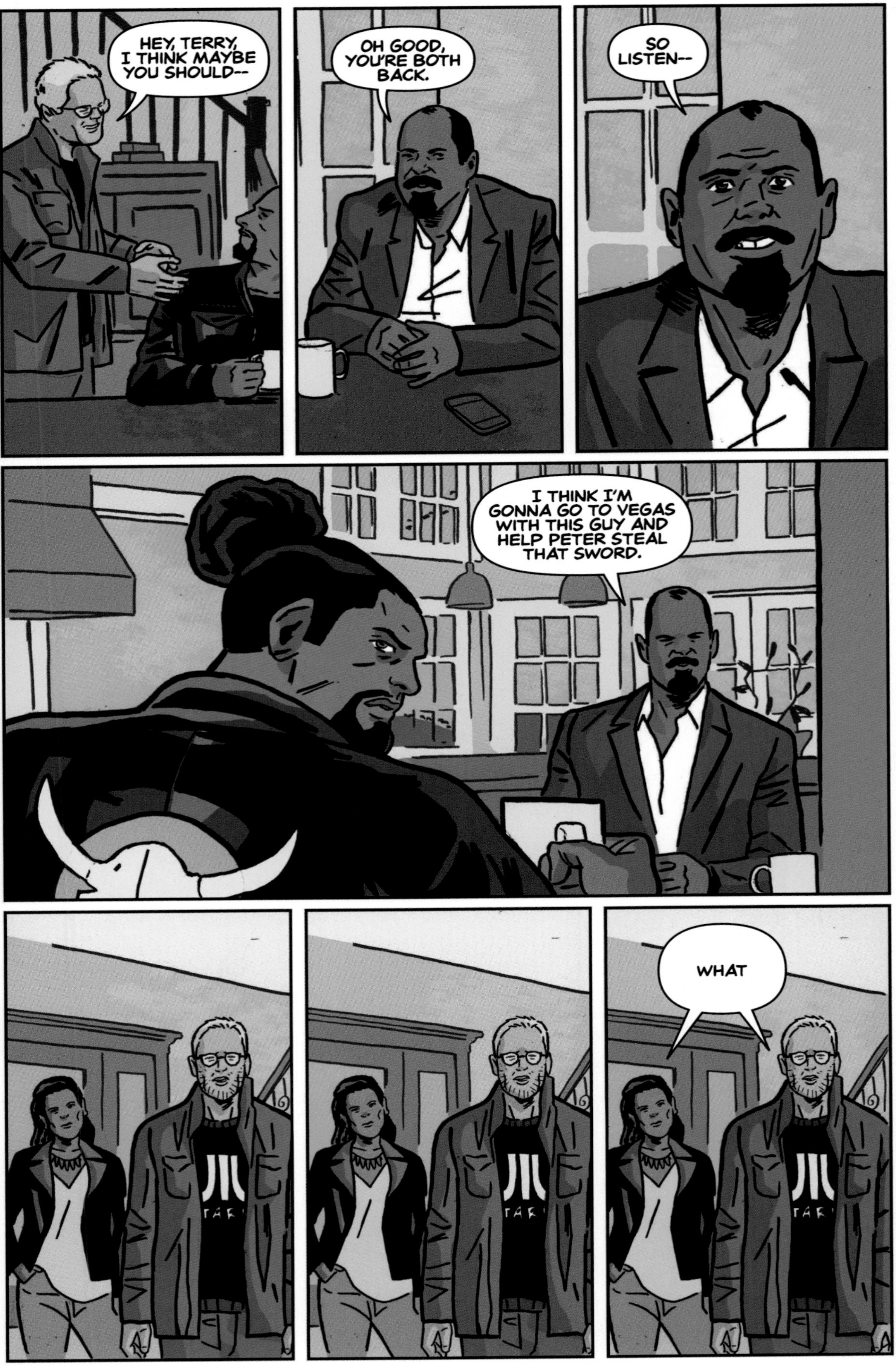
HEY, TERRY, I THINK MAYBE YOU SHOULD--
OH GOOD, YOU'RE BOTH BACK.
SO LISTEN--
I THINK I'M GONNA GO TO VEGAS WITH THIS GUY AND HELP PETER STEAL THAT SWORD.
WHAT

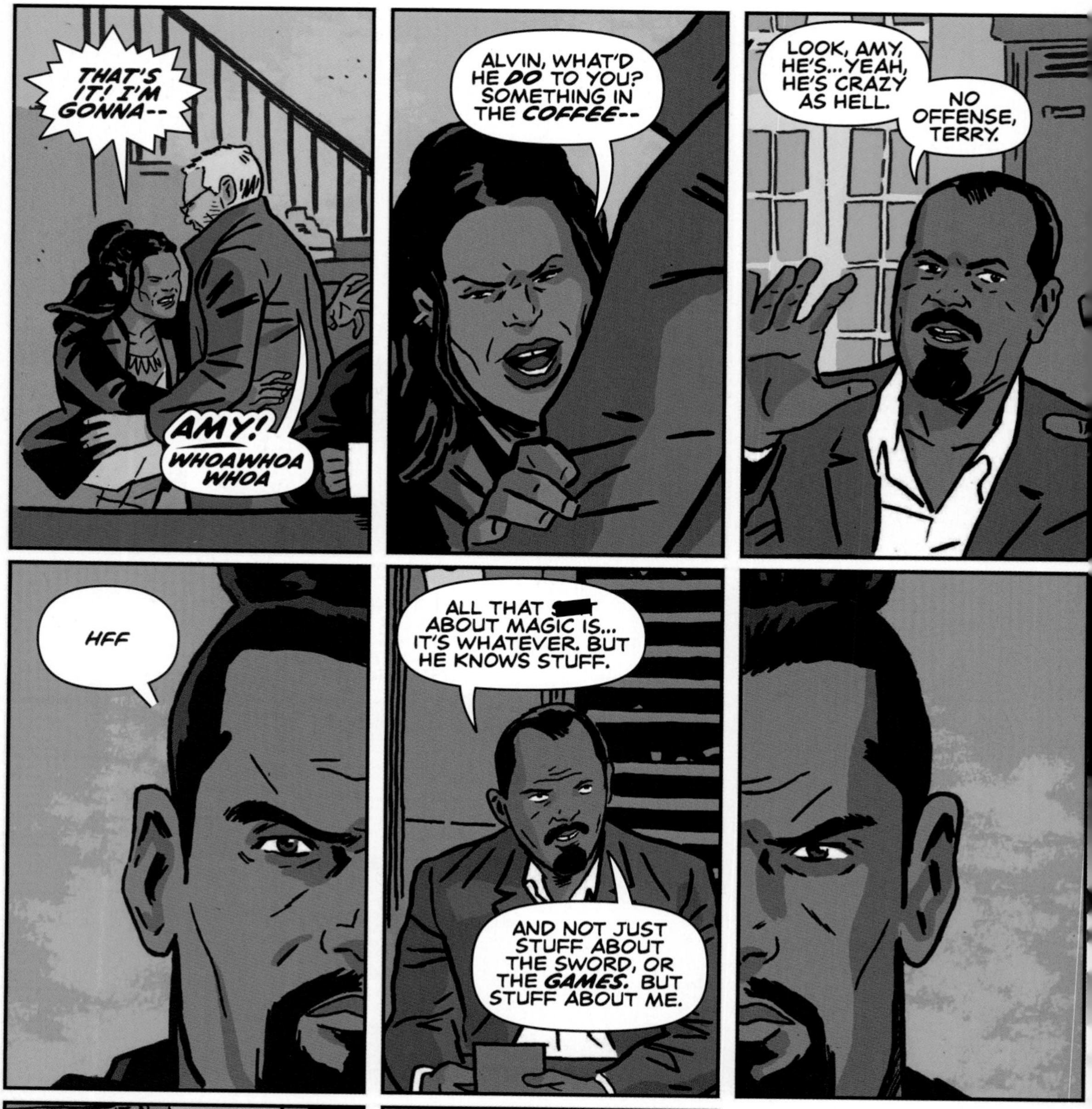
THAT'S IT! I'M GONNA--
AMY! WHOAWHOA WHOA
ALVIN, WHAT'D HE *DO* TO YOU? SOMETHING IN THE *COFFEE*--
LOOK, AMY, HE'S...YEAH, HE'S CRAZY AS HELL.
NO OFFENSE, TERRY.
HFF
ALL THAT [redacted] ABOUT MAGIC IS... IT'S WHATEVER. BUT HE KNOWS STUFF.
AND NOT JUST STUFF ABOUT THE SWORD, OR THE *GAMES.* BUT STUFF ABOUT ME.

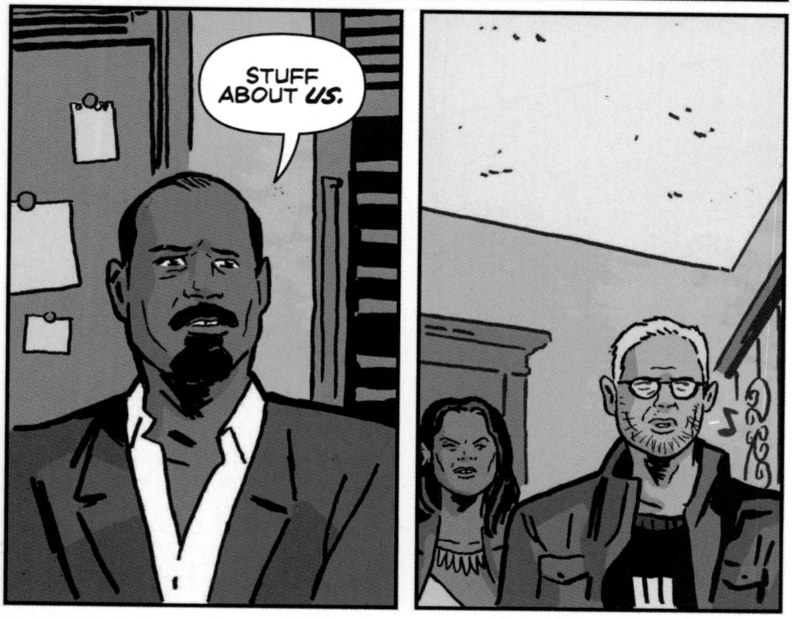
STUFF ABOUT *US.*

GAME TIP

Always make sure you know what you're getting into.

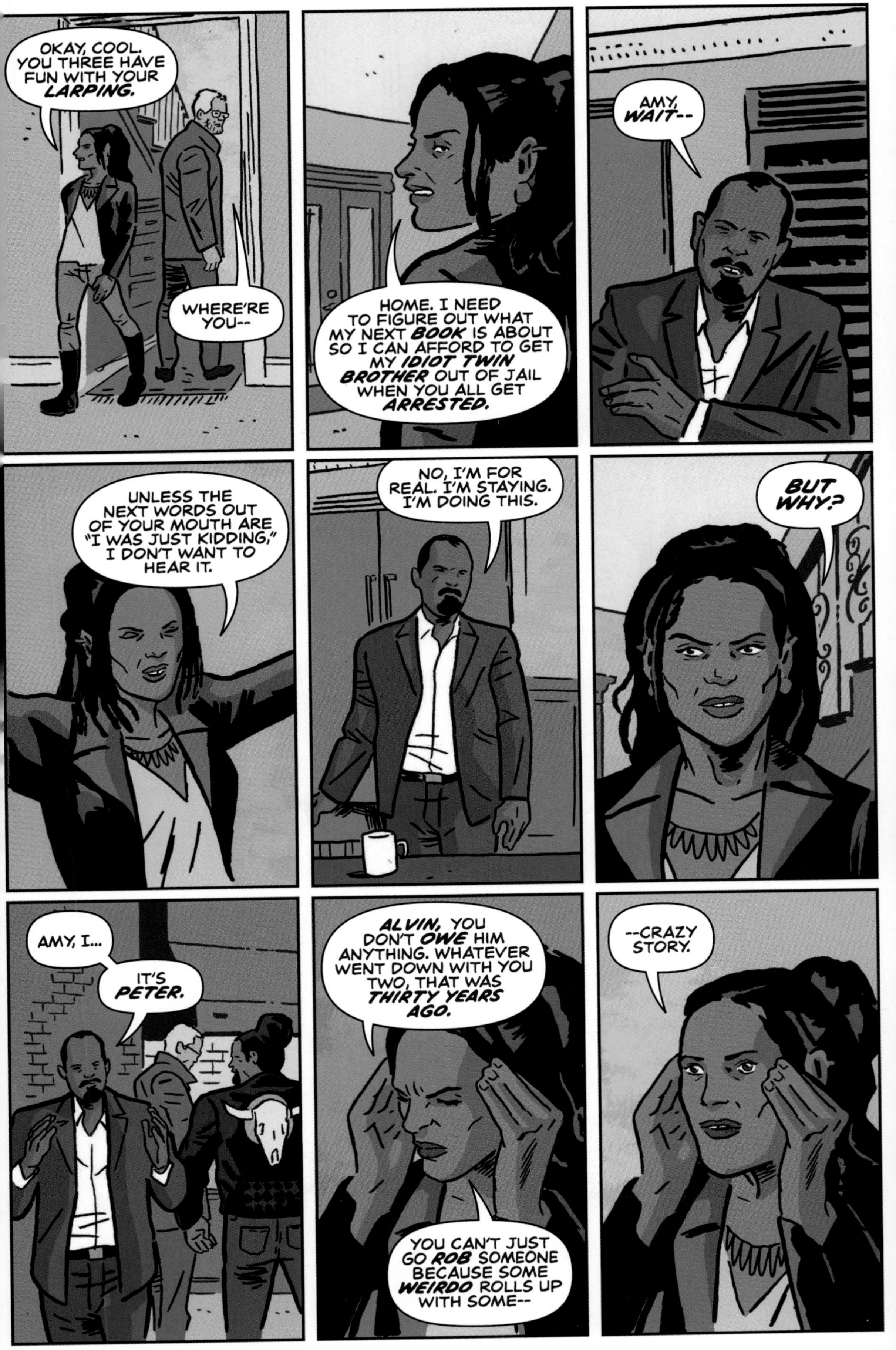
OKAY, COOL. YOU THREE HAVE FUN WITH YOUR LARPING.
WHERE'RE YOU--
HOME. I NEED TO FIGURE OUT WHAT MY NEXT BOOK IS ABOUT SO I CAN AFFORD TO GET MY IDIOT TWIN BROTHER OUT OF JAIL WHEN YOU ALL GET ARRESTED.
AMY, WAIT--
UNLESS THE NEXT WORDS OUT OF YOUR MOUTH ARE "I WAS JUST KIDDING," I DON'T WANT TO HEAR IT.
NO, I'M FOR REAL. I'M STAYING. I'M DOING THIS.
BUT WHY?
AMY, I...
IT'S PETER.
ALVIN, YOU DON'T OWE HIM ANYTHING. WHATEVER WENT DOWN WITH YOU TWO, THAT WAS THIRTY YEARS AGO.
YOU CAN'T JUST GO ROB SOMEONE BECAUSE SOME WEIRDO ROLLS UP WITH SOME--
--CRAZY STORY.

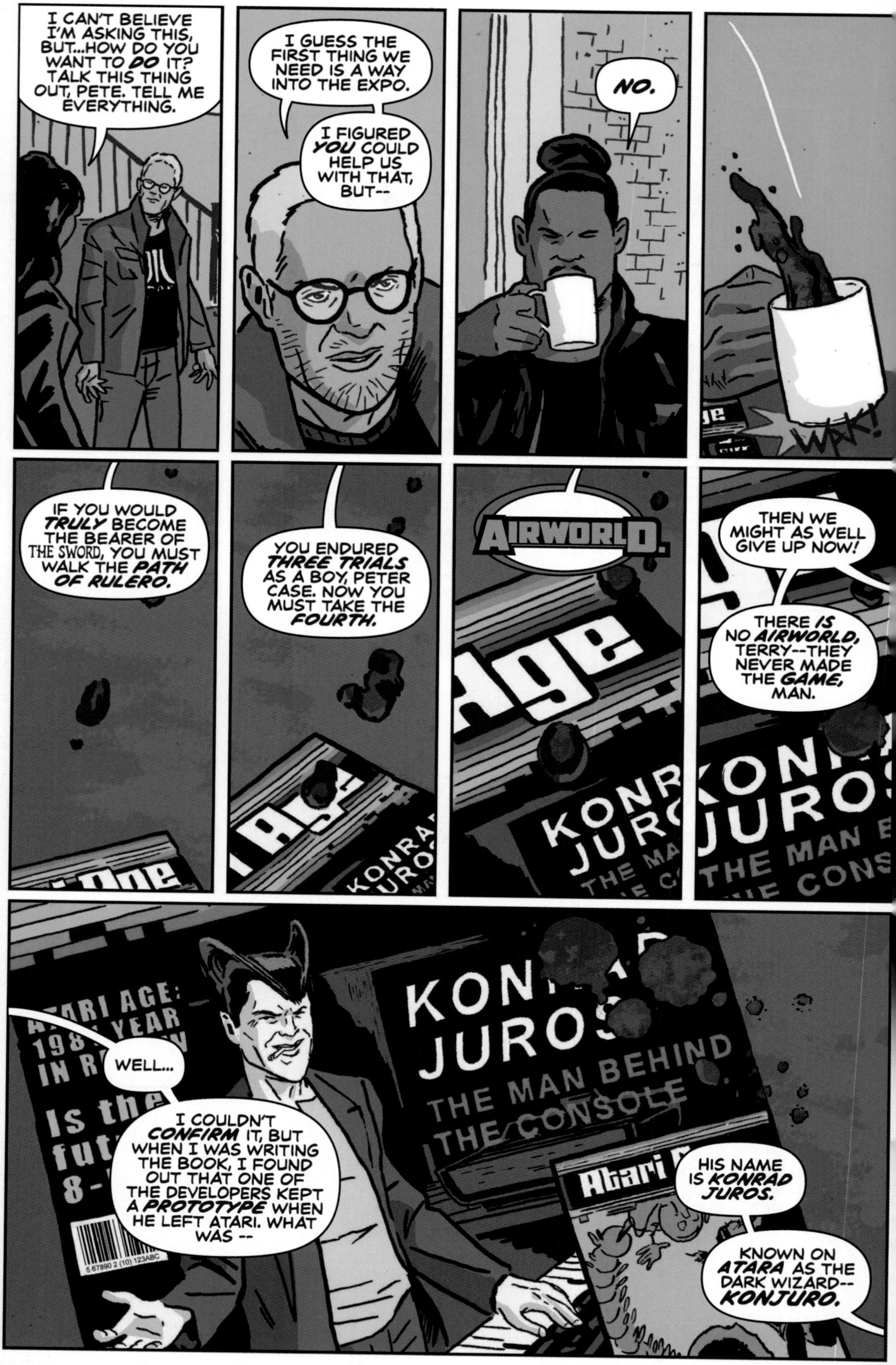

I CAN'T BELIEVE I'M ASKING THIS, BUT...HOW DO YOU WANT TO DO IT? TALK THIS THING OUT, PETE. TELL ME EVERYTHING.
I GUESS THE FIRST THING WE NEED IS A WAY INTO THE EXPO.
I FIGURED YOU COULD HELP US WITH THAT, BUT--
NO.
WAK!
IF YOU WOULD TRULY BECOME THE BEARER OF THE SWORD, YOU MUST WALK THE PATH OF RULERO.
YOU ENDURED THREE TRIALS AS A BOY, PETER CASE. NOW YOU MUST TAKE THE FOURTH.
AIRWORLD.
THEN WE MIGHT AS WELL GIVE UP NOW!
THERE IS NO AIRWORLD, TERRY--THEY NEVER MADE THE GAME, MAN.
ATARI AGE:
KONRAD JUROS THE MAN BEHIND THE CONSOLE
WELL...
I COULDN'T CONFIRM IT, BUT WHEN I WAS WRITING THE BOOK, I FOUND OUT THAT ONE OF THE DEVELOPERS KEPT A PROTOTYPE WHEN HE LEFT ATARI. WHAT WAS --
HIS NAME IS KONRAD JUROS.
KNOWN ON ATARA AS THE DARK WIZARD--KONJURO.

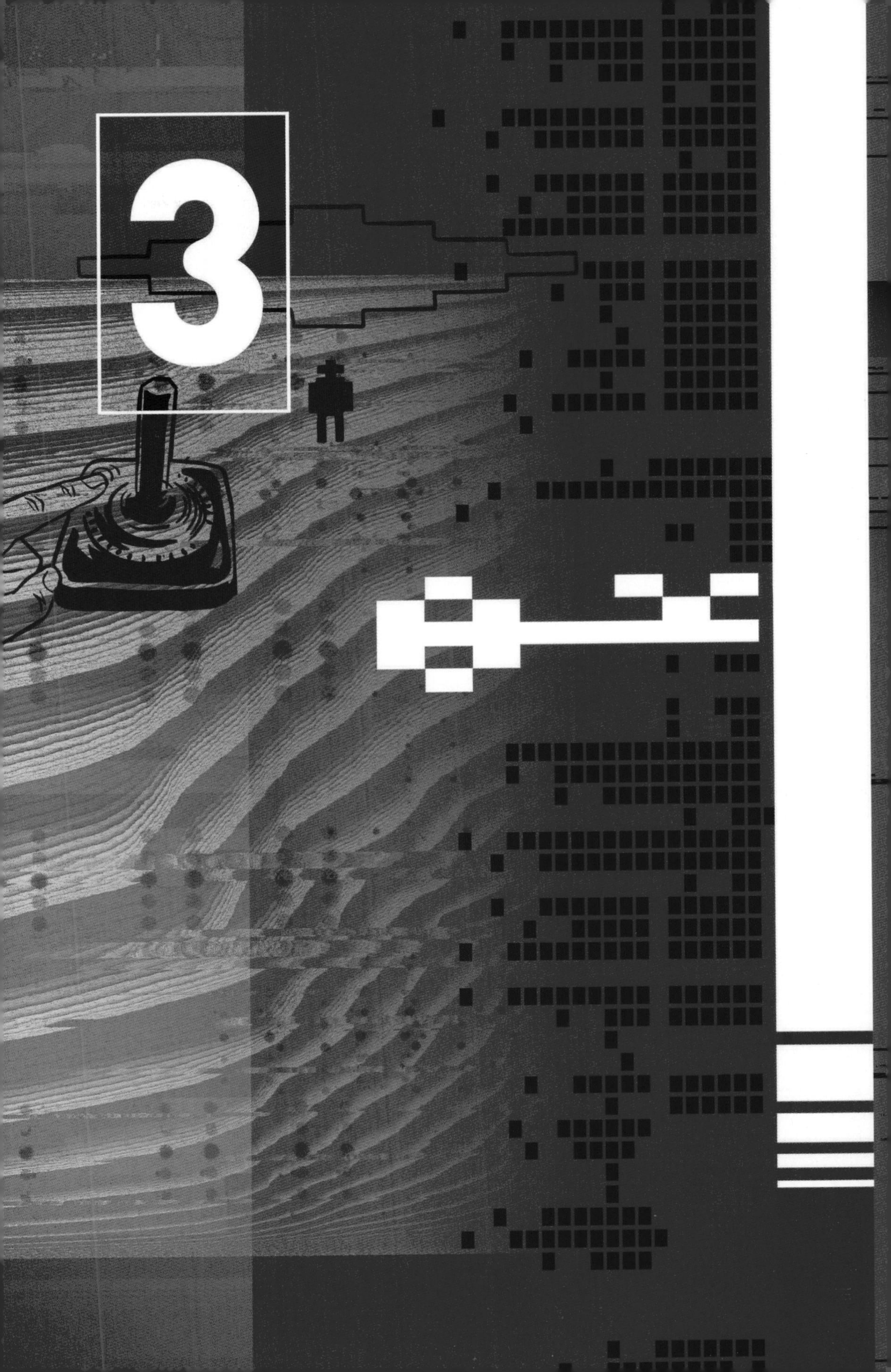
3

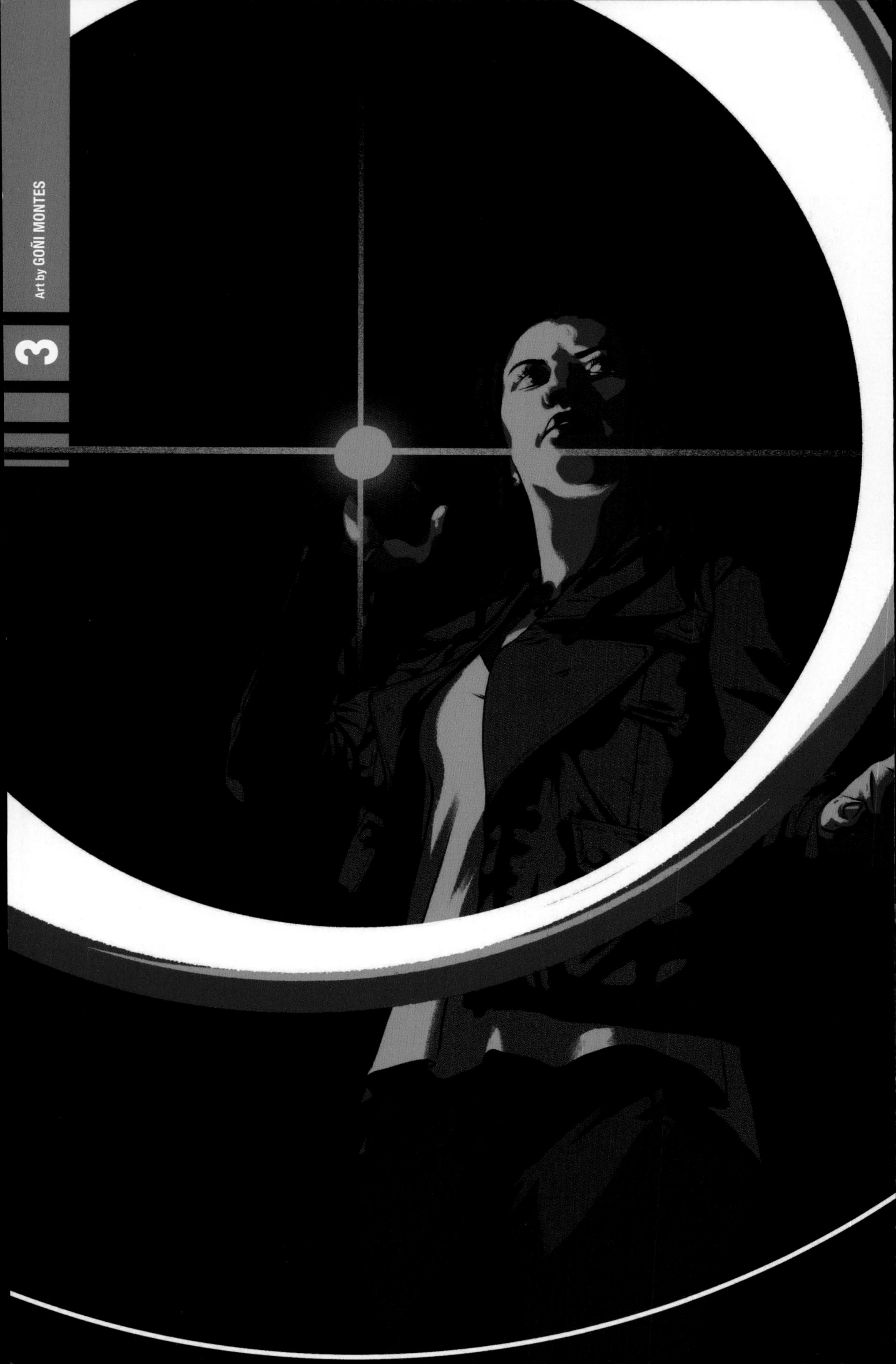
Art by GOÑI MONTES
3

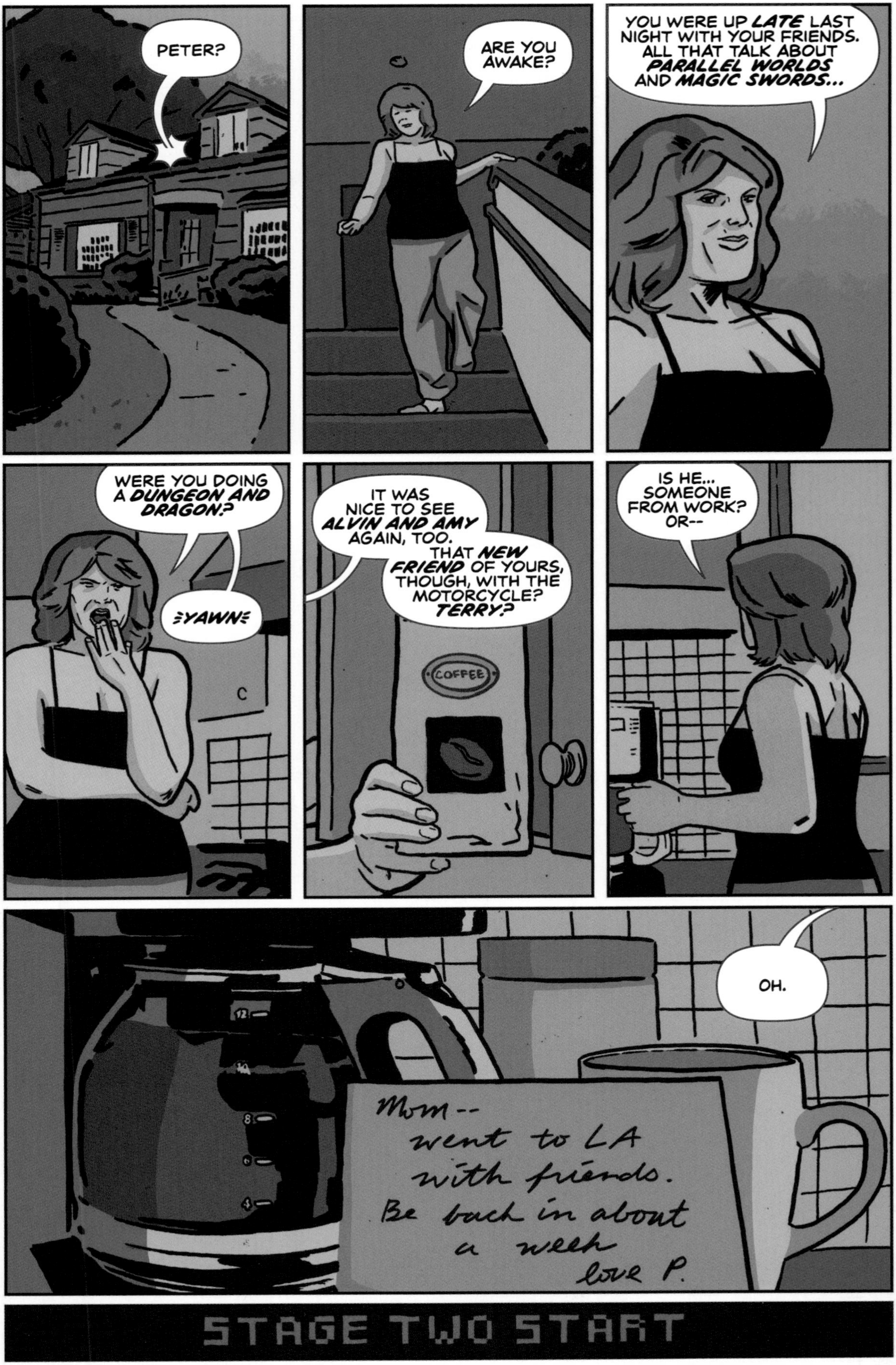
PETER?
ARE YOU AWAKE?
YOU WERE UP LATE LAST NIGHT WITH YOUR FRIENDS. ALL THAT TALK ABOUT PARALLEL WORLDS AND MAGIC SWORDS...
WERE YOU DOING A DUNGEON AND DRAGON?
YAWN
IT WAS NICE TO SEE ALVIN AND AMY AGAIN, TOO.
THAT NEW FRIEND OF YOURS, THOUGH, WITH THE MOTORCYCLE? TERRY?
COFFEE
IS HE... SOMEONE FROM WORK? OR--
OH.
Mom -- went to LA with friends. Be back in about a week love P.
STAGE TWO START

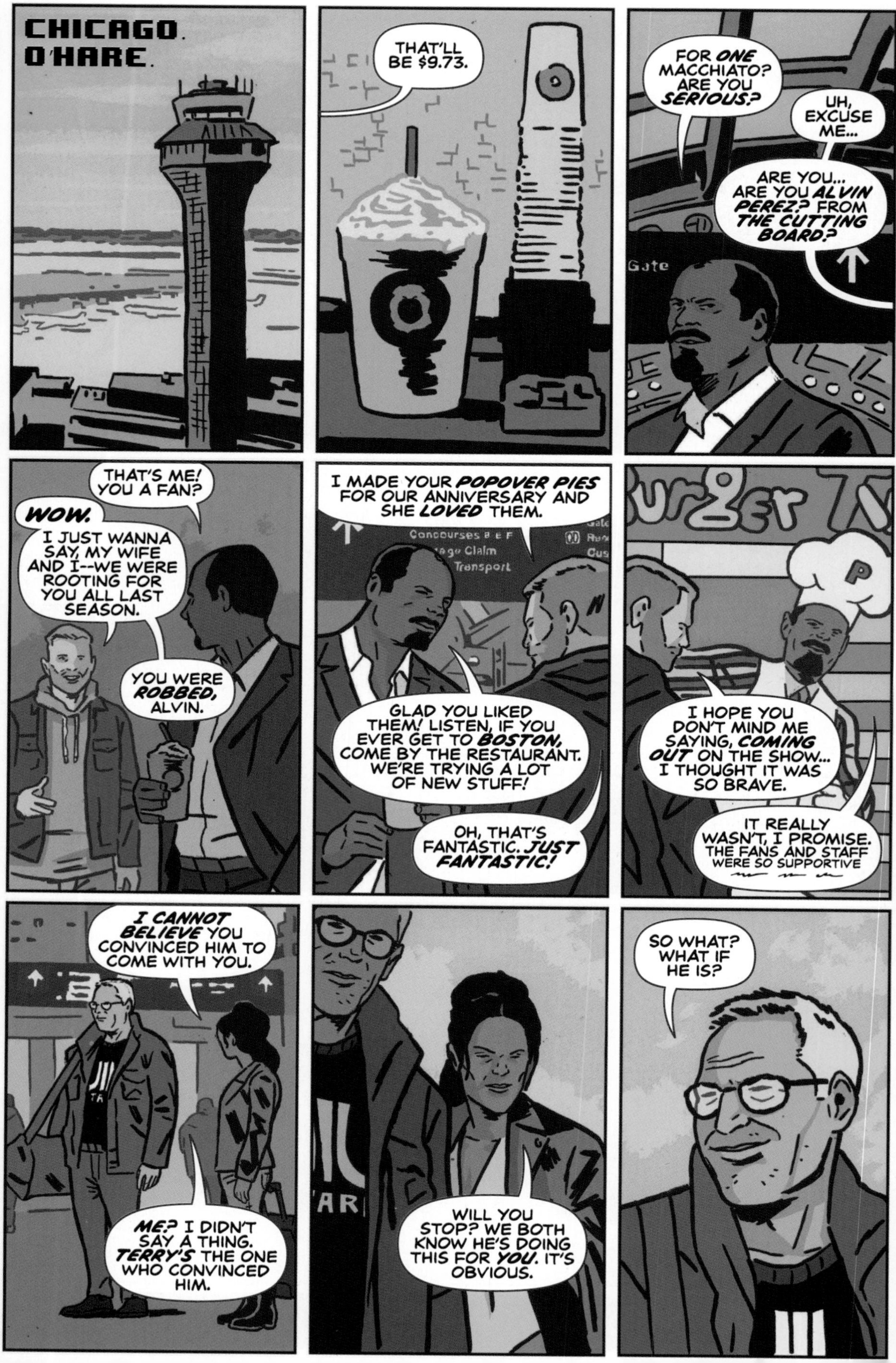
CHICAGO.
O'HARE.
THAT'LL BE $9.73.
FOR ONE MACCHIATO? ARE YOU SERIOUS?
UH, EXCUSE ME...
ARE YOU... ARE YOU ALVIN PEREZ? FROM THE CUTTING BOARD?
Gate
THAT'S ME! YOU A FAN?
WOW. I JUST WANNA SAY, MY WIFE AND I--WE WERE ROOTING FOR YOU ALL LAST SEASON.
YOU WERE ROBBED, ALVIN.
I MADE YOUR POPOVER PIES FOR OUR ANNIVERSARY AND SHE LOVED THEM.
Concourses E F
Transport
GLAD YOU LIKED THEM! LISTEN, IF YOU EVER GET TO BOSTON, COME BY THE RESTAURANT. WE'RE TRYING A LOT OF NEW STUFF!
OH, THAT'S FANTASTIC. JUST FANTASTIC!
I HOPE YOU DON'T MIND ME SAYING, COMING OUT ON THE SHOW... I THOUGHT IT WAS SO BRAVE.
IT REALLY WASN'T, I PROMISE. THE FANS AND STAFF WERE SO SUPPORTIVE
I CANNOT BELIEVE YOU CONVINCED HIM TO COME WITH YOU.
ME? I DIDN'T SAY A THING. TERRY'S THE ONE WHO CONVINCED HIM.
WILL YOU STOP? WE BOTH KNOW HE'S DOING THIS FOR YOU. IT'S OBVIOUS.
SO WHAT? WHAT IF HE IS?

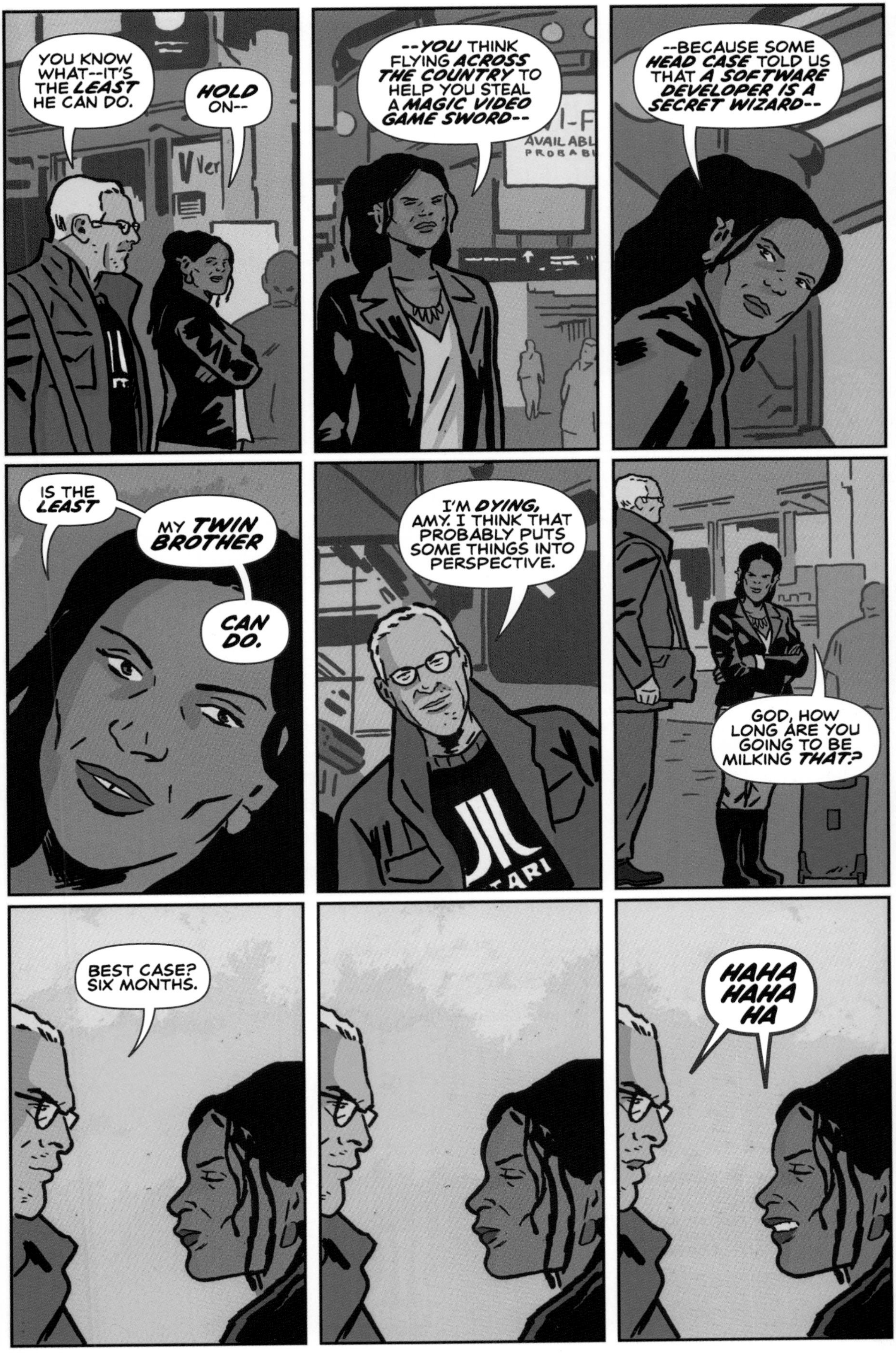
YOU KNOW WHAT--IT'S THE LEAST HE CAN DO.
HOLD ON--
--YOU THINK FLYING ACROSS THE COUNTRY TO HELP YOU STEAL A MAGIC VIDEO GAME SWORD--
--BECAUSE SOME HEAD CASE TOLD US THAT A SOFTWARE DEVELOPER IS A SECRET WIZARD--
IS THE LEAST
MY TWIN BROTHER
CAN DO.
I'M DYING, AMY. I THINK THAT PROBABLY PUTS SOME THINGS INTO PERSPECTIVE.
GOD, HOW LONG ARE YOU GOING TO BE MILKING THAT?
BEST CASE? SIX MONTHS.
HAHA HAHA HA

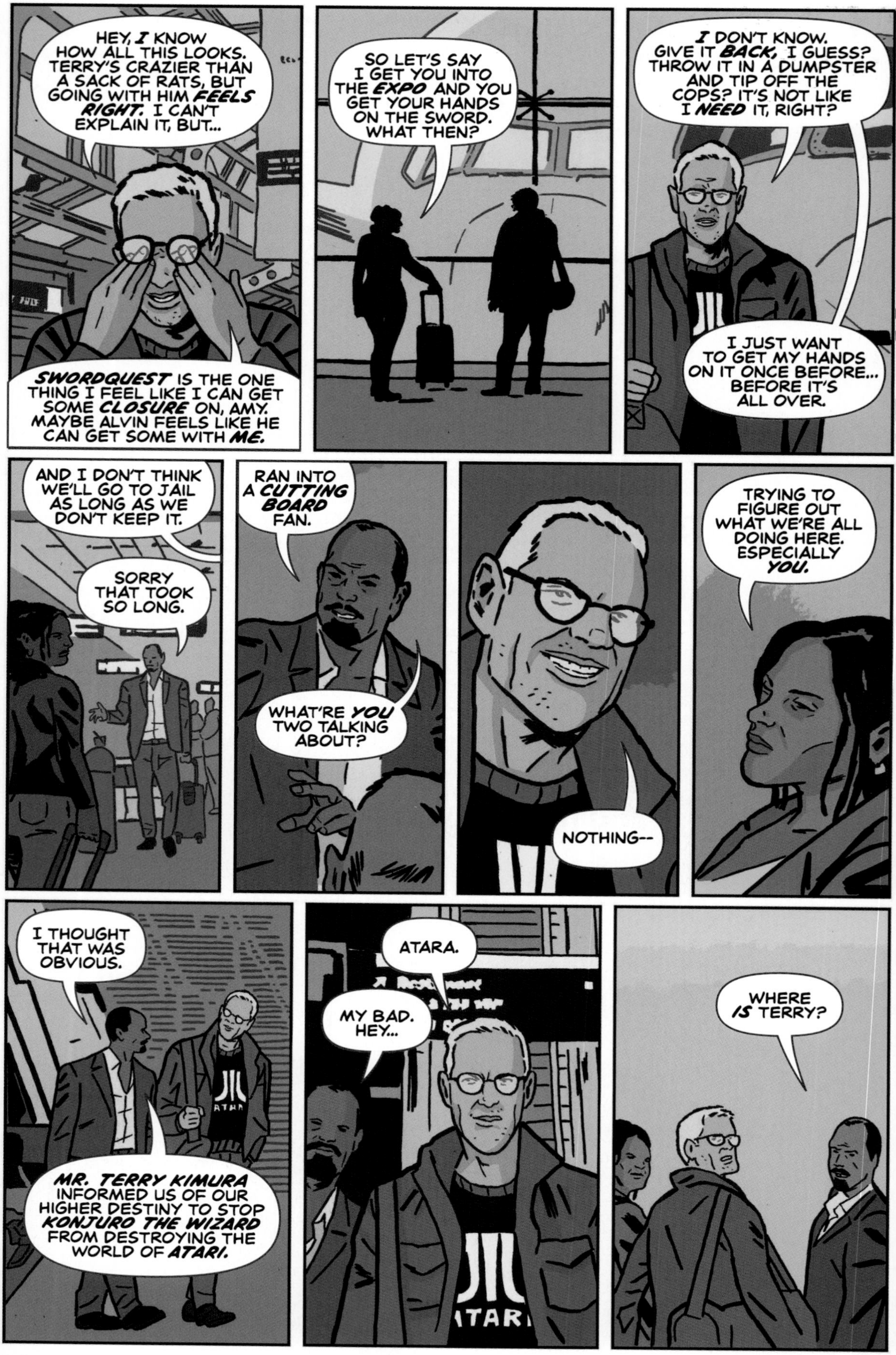
HEY, I KNOW HOW ALL THIS LOOKS. TERRY'S CRAZIER THAN A SACK OF RATS, BUT GOING WITH HIM FEELS RIGHT. I CAN'T EXPLAIN IT, BUT...
SWORDQUEST IS THE ONE THING I FEEL LIKE I CAN GET SOME CLOSURE ON, AMY. MAYBE ALVIN FEELS LIKE HE CAN GET SOME WITH ME.
SO LET'S SAY I GET YOU INTO THE EXPO AND YOU GET YOUR HANDS ON THE SWORD. WHAT THEN?
I DON'T KNOW. GIVE IT BACK, I GUESS? THROW IT IN A DUMPSTER AND TIP OFF THE COPS? IT'S NOT LIKE I NEED IT, RIGHT?
I JUST WANT TO GET MY HANDS ON IT ONCE BEFORE... BEFORE IT'S ALL OVER.
AND I DON'T THINK WE'LL GO TO JAIL AS LONG AS WE DON'T KEEP IT.
SORRY THAT TOOK SO LONG.
RAN INTO A CUTTING BOARD FAN.
WHAT'RE YOU TWO TALKING ABOUT?
NOTHING--
TRYING TO FIGURE OUT WHAT WE'RE ALL DOING HERE. ESPECIALLY YOU.
I THOUGHT THAT WAS OBVIOUS.
MR. TERRY KIMURA INFORMED US OF OUR HIGHER DESTINY TO STOP KONJURO THE WIZARD FROM DESTROYING THE WORLD OF ATARI.
ATARA.
MY BAD. HEY...
WHERE IS TERRY?

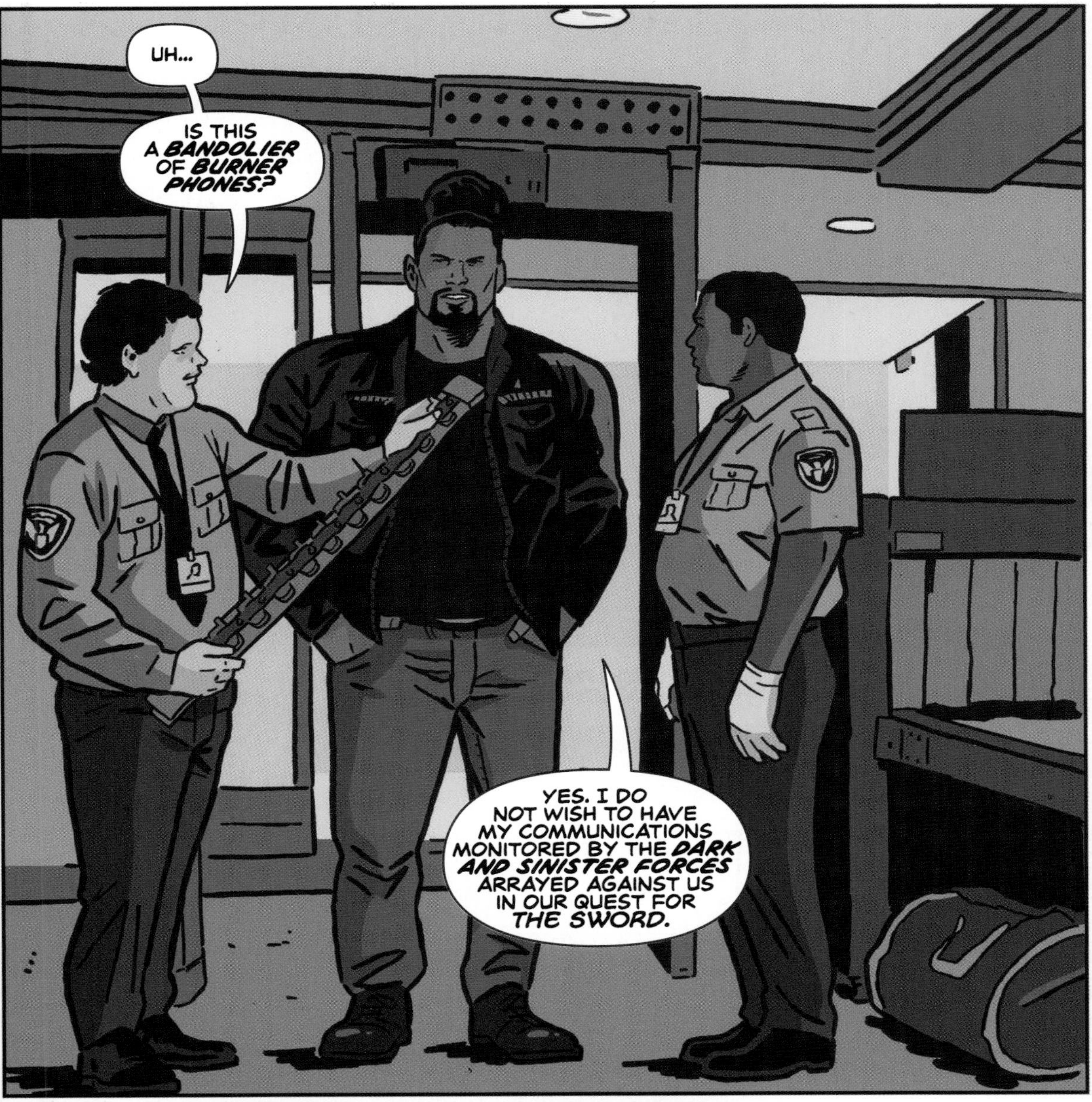
UH...
IS THIS A *BANDOLIER* OF *BURNER PHONES?*
YES. I DO NOT WISH TO HAVE MY COMMUNICATIONS MONITORED BY THE *DARK AND SINISTER FORCES* ARRAYED AGAINST US IN OUR QUEST FOR *THE SWORD.*

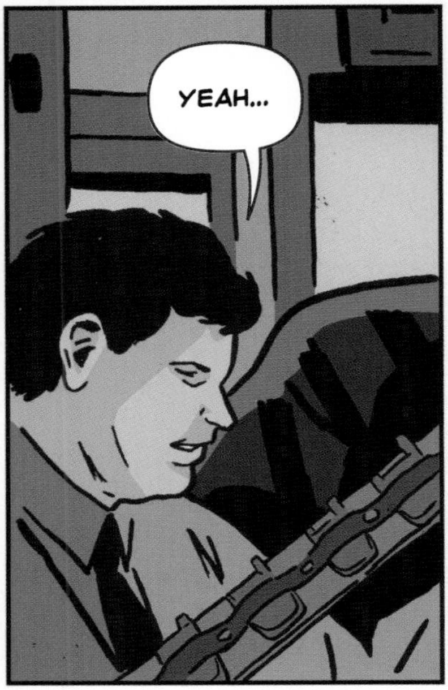
YEAH...

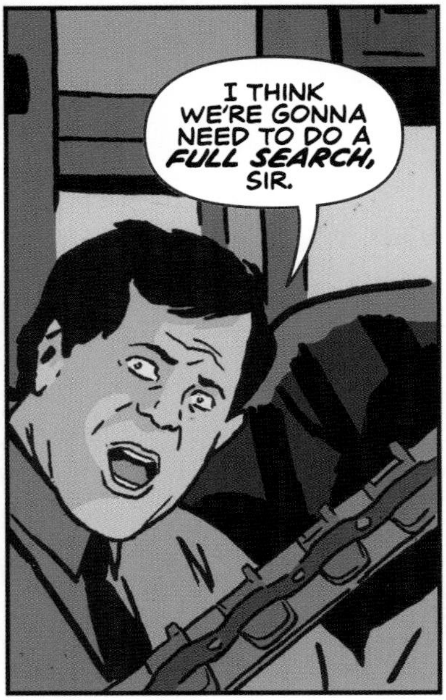
I THINK WE'RE GONNA NEED TO DO A *FULL SEARCH,* SIR.

GAME TIP

Inventory management is key-- make sure you bring the right tools for each adventure!

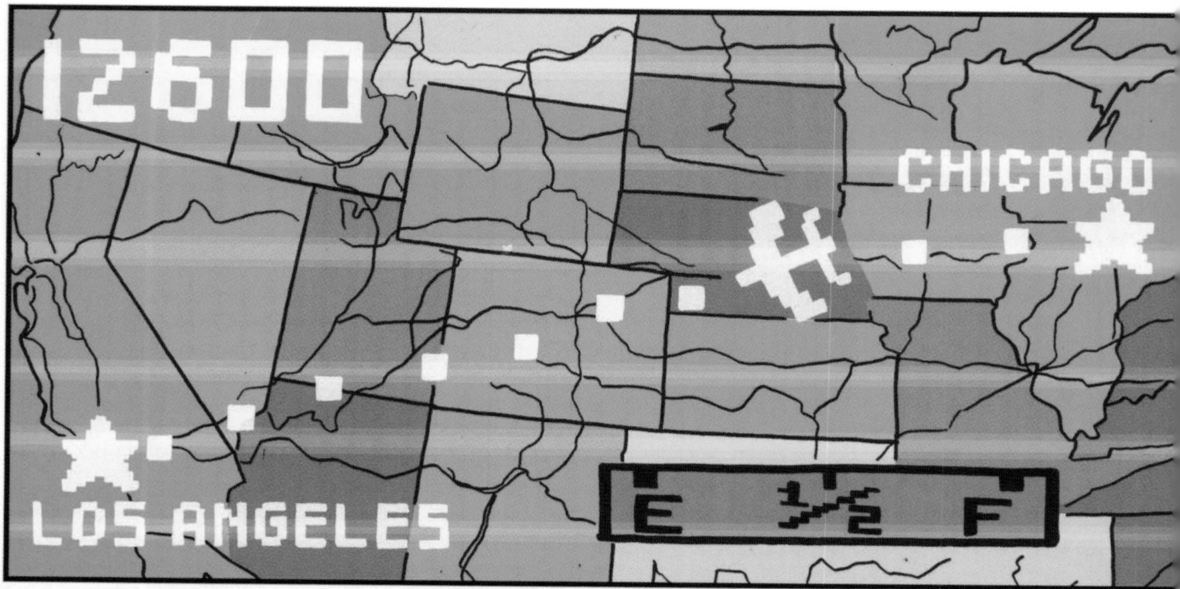
12600
CHICAGO
LOS ANGELES
E 1/2 F

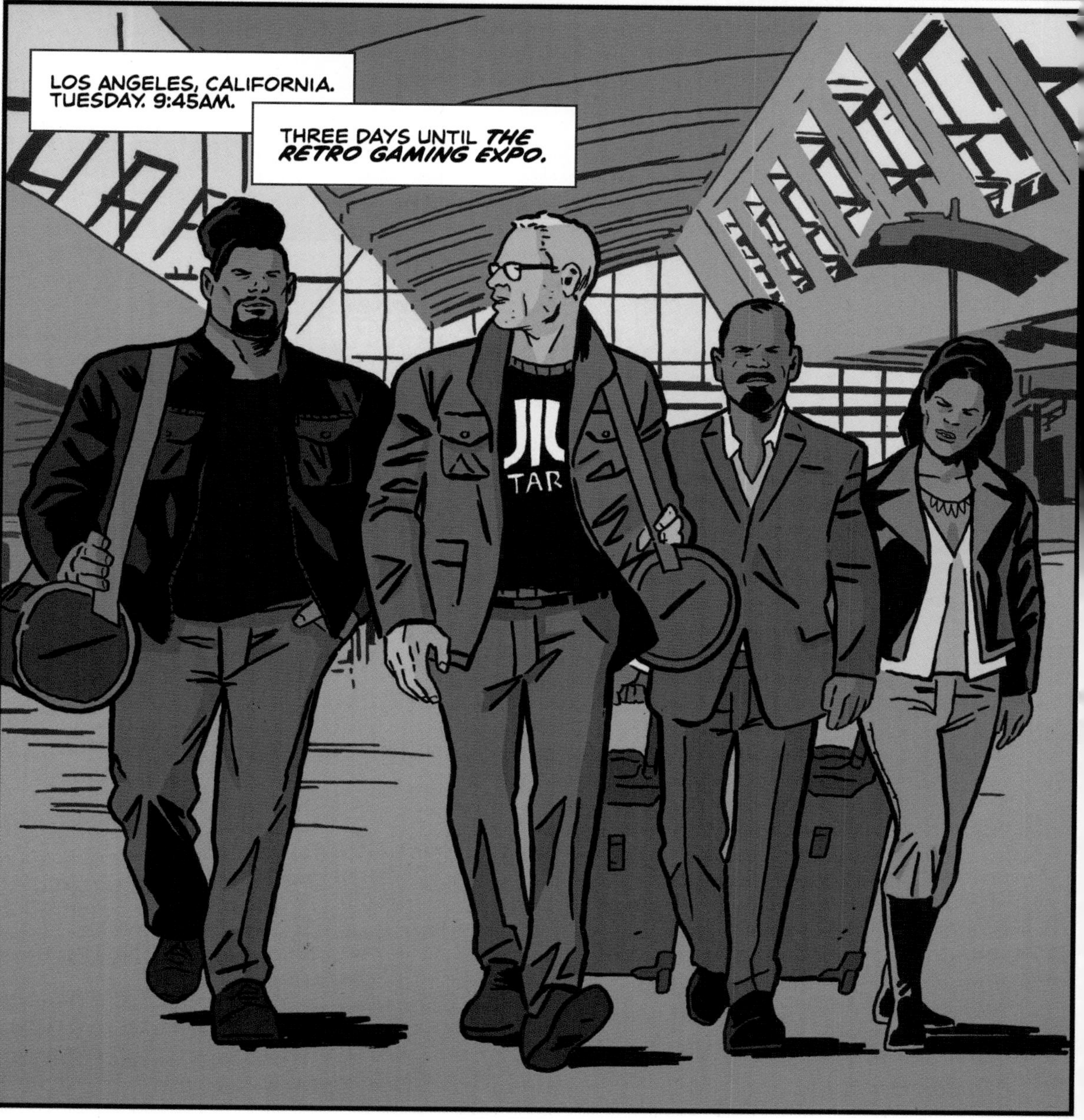
LOS ANGELES, CALIFORNIA.
TUESDAY. 9:45AM.
THREE DAYS UNTIL *THE RETRO GAMING EXPO.*

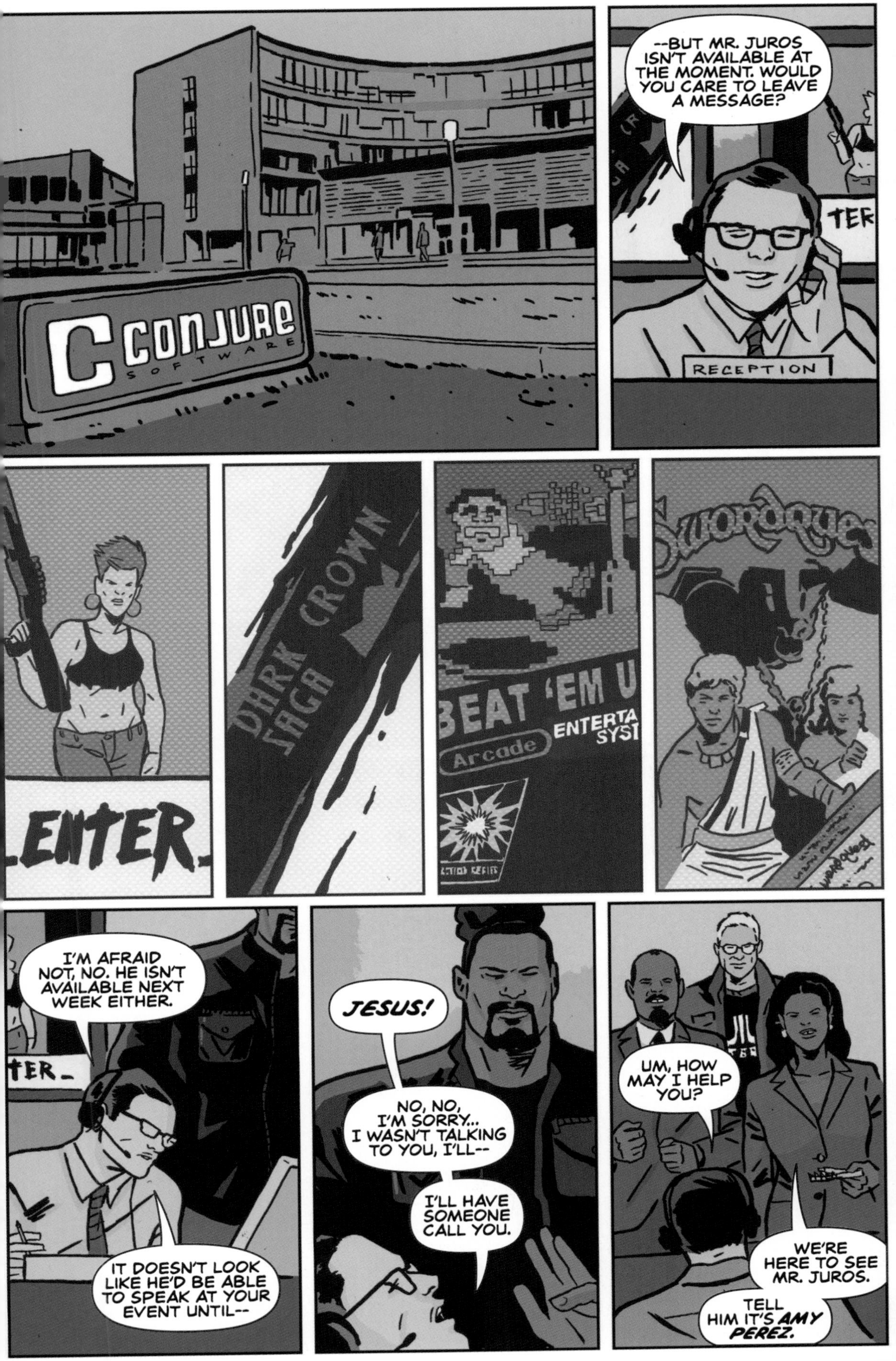
CONJURE SOFTWARE
--BUT MR. JUROS ISN'T AVAILABLE AT THE MOMENT. WOULD YOU CARE TO LEAVE A MESSAGE?
RECEPTION
ENTER
DARK CROWN SAGA
BEAT 'EM U
Arcade
ENTERTA SYST
I'M AFRAID NOT, NO. HE ISN'T AVAILABLE NEXT WEEK EITHER.
IT DOESN'T LOOK LIKE HE'D BE ABLE TO SPEAK AT YOUR EVENT UNTIL--
JESUS!
NO, NO, I'M SORRY... I WASN'T TALKING TO YOU, I'LL--
I'LL HAVE SOMEONE CALL YOU.
UM, HOW MAY I HELP YOU?
WE'RE HERE TO SEE MR. JUROS.
TELL HIM IT'S AMY PEREZ.

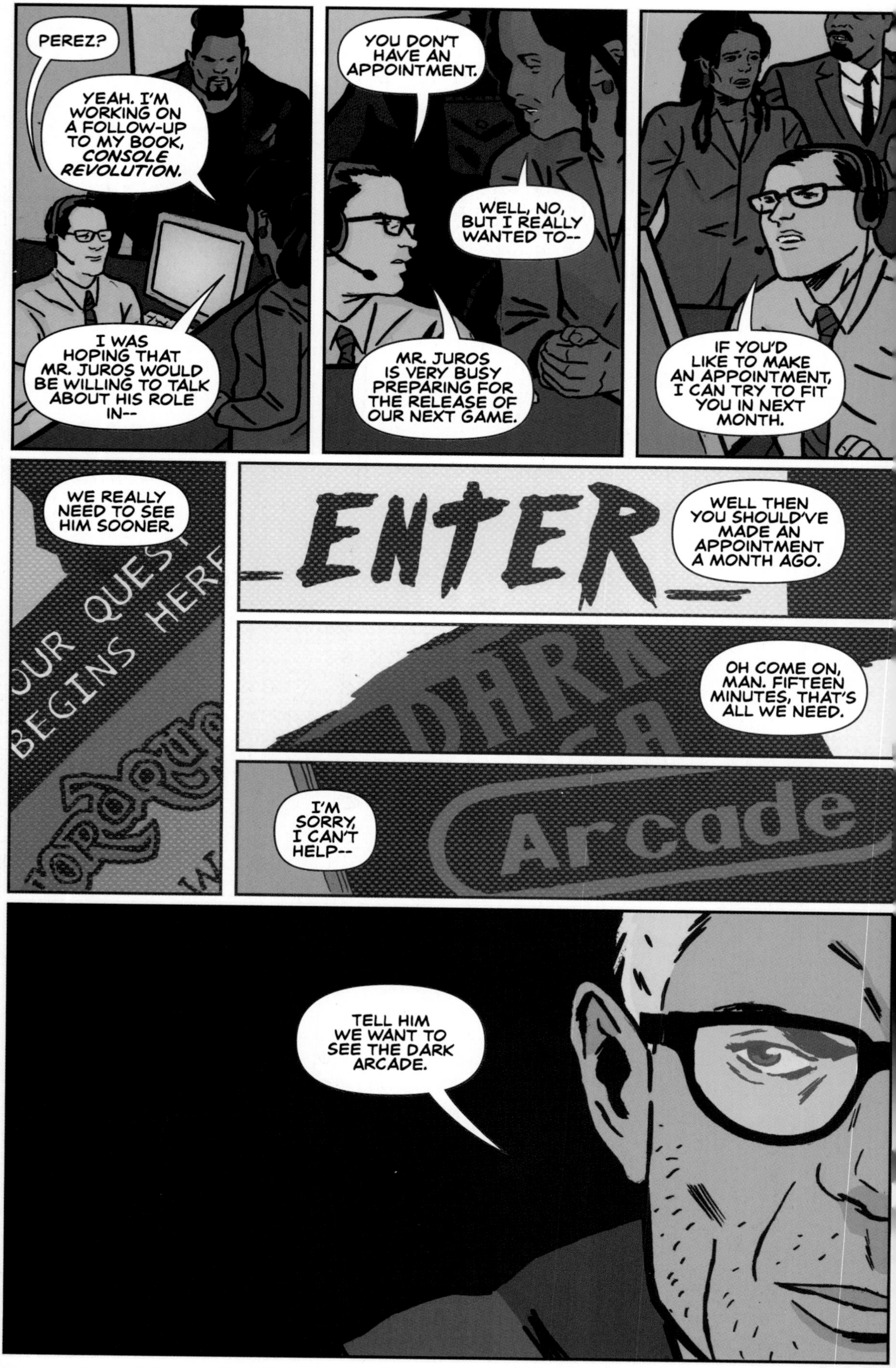
PEREZ?
YEAH. I'M WORKING ON A FOLLOW-UP TO MY BOOK, *CONSOLE REVOLUTION.*
I WAS HOPING THAT MR. JUROS WOULD BE WILLING TO TALK ABOUT HIS ROLE IN--
YOU DON'T HAVE AN APPOINTMENT.
WELL, NO, BUT I REALLY WANTED TO--
MR. JUROS IS VERY BUSY PREPARING FOR THE RELEASE OF OUR NEXT GAME.
IF YOU'D LIKE TO MAKE AN APPOINTMENT, I CAN TRY TO FIT YOU IN NEXT MONTH.
WE REALLY NEED TO SEE HIM SOONER.
OUR QUEST BEGINS HERE
ENTER
WELL THEN YOU SHOULD'VE MADE AN APPOINTMENT A MONTH AGO.
OH COME ON, MAN. FIFTEEN MINUTES, THAT'S ALL WE NEED.
I'M SORRY, I CAN'T HELP--
Arcade
TELL HIM WE WANT TO SEE THE DARK ARCADE.

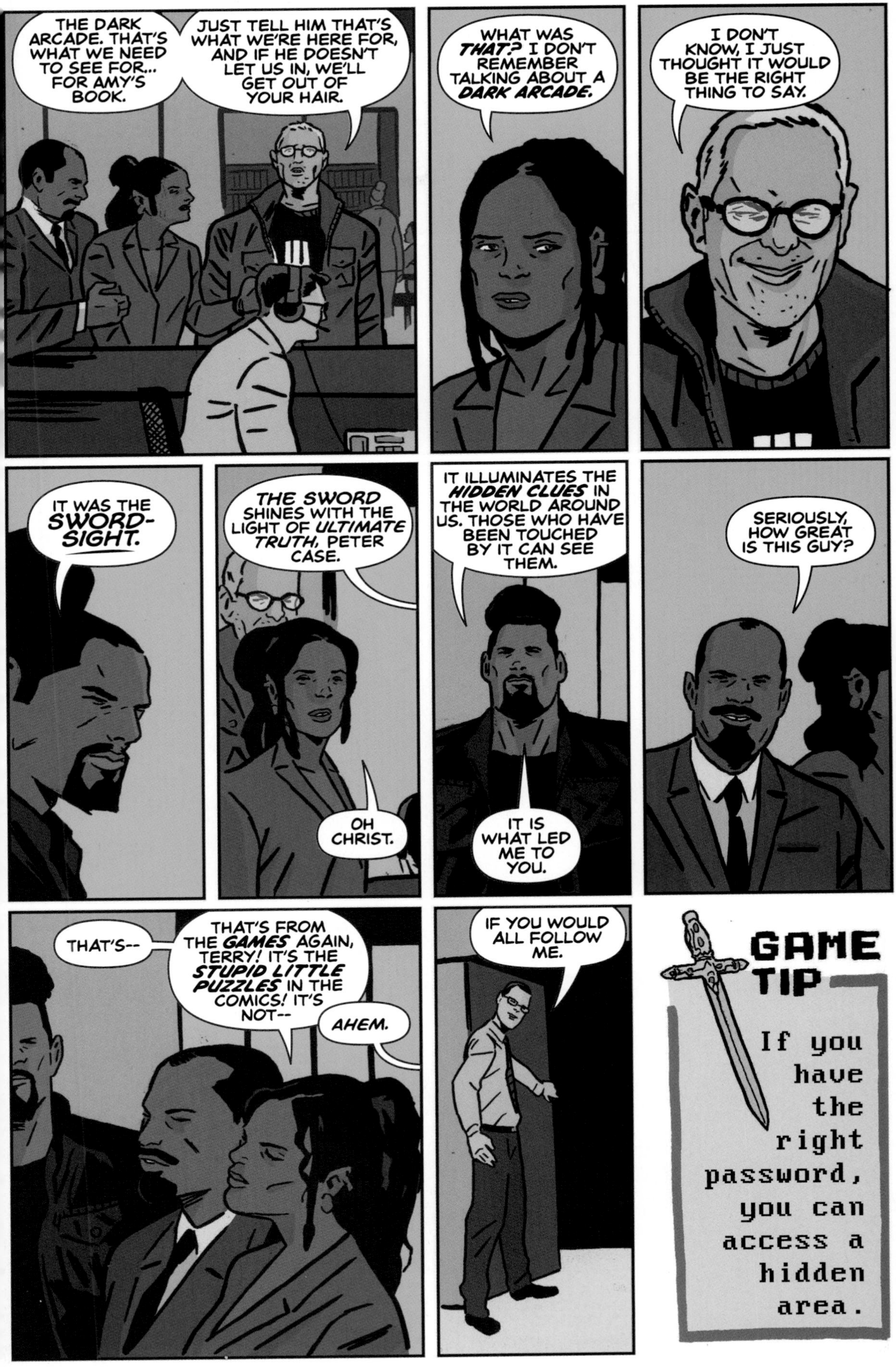
THE DARK ARCADE. THAT'S WHAT WE NEED TO SEE FOR... FOR AMY'S BOOK.
JUST TELL HIM THAT'S WHAT WE'RE HERE FOR, AND IF HE DOESN'T LET US IN, WE'LL GET OUT OF YOUR HAIR.
WHAT WAS *THAT?* I DON'T REMEMBER TALKING ABOUT A *DARK ARCADE.*
I DON'T KNOW, I JUST THOUGHT IT WOULD BE THE RIGHT THING TO SAY.
IT WAS THE *SWORD-SIGHT.*
THE SWORD SHINES WITH THE LIGHT OF *ULTIMATE TRUTH,* PETER CASE.
OH CHRIST.
IT ILLUMINATES THE *HIDDEN CLUES* IN THE WORLD AROUND US. THOSE WHO HAVE BEEN TOUCHED BY IT CAN SEE THEM.
IT IS WHAT LED ME TO YOU.
SERIOUSLY, HOW GREAT IS THIS GUY?
THAT'S--
THAT'S FROM THE *GAMES* AGAIN, TERRY! IT'S THE *STUPID LITTLE PUZZLES* IN THE COMICS! IT'S NOT--
AHEM.
IF YOU WOULD ALL FOLLOW ME.
GAME TIP
If you have the right password, you can access a hidden area.

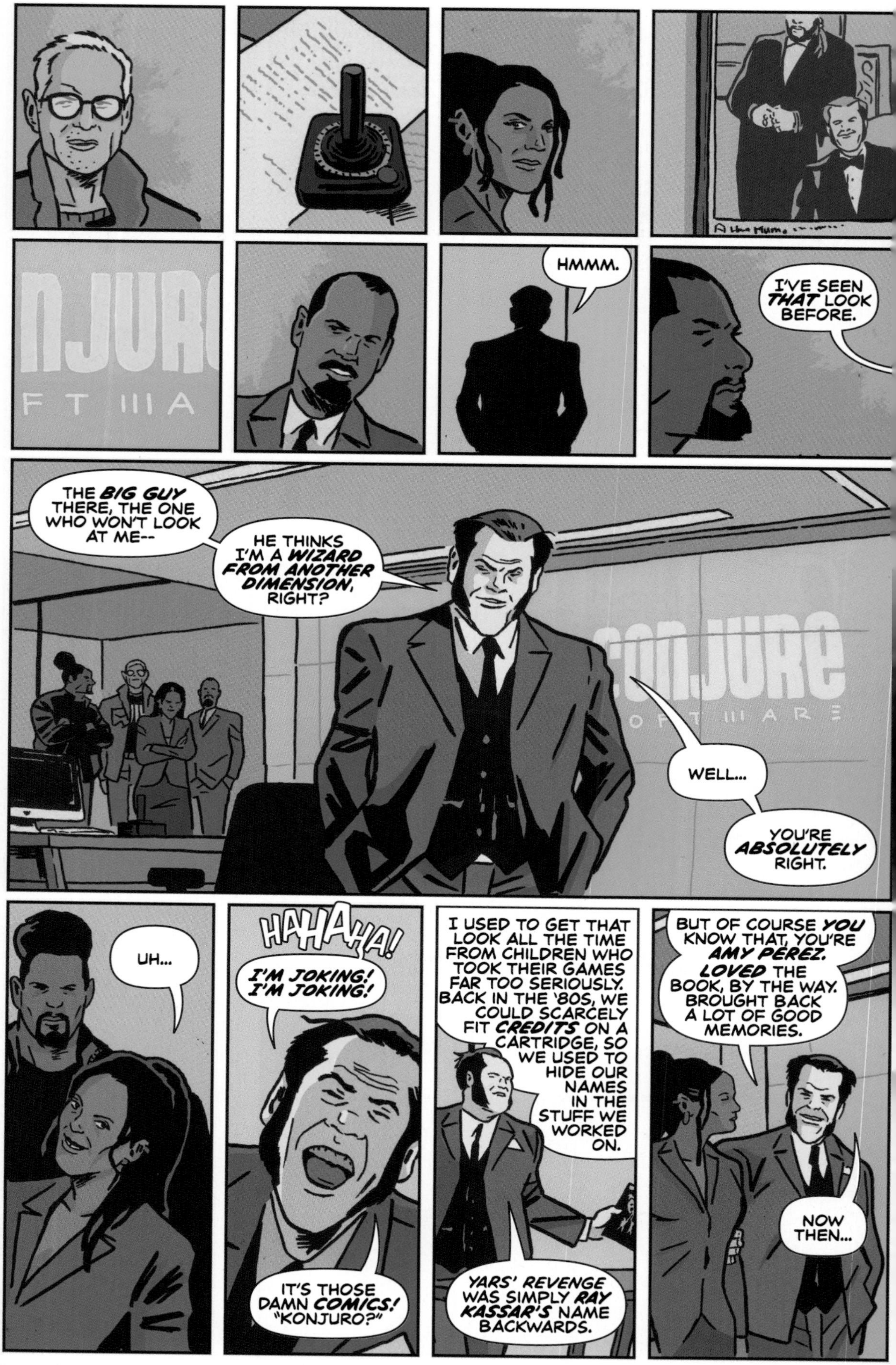
HMMM.
I'VE SEEN THAT LOOK BEFORE.
THE BIG GUY THERE, THE ONE WHO WON'T LOOK AT ME--
HE THINKS I'M A WIZARD FROM ANOTHER DIMENSION, RIGHT?
CONJURE
WELL...
YOU'RE ABSOLUTELY RIGHT.
UH...
HAHAHAHA!
I'M JOKING! I'M JOKING!
IT'S THOSE DAMN COMICS! "KONJURO?"
I USED TO GET THAT LOOK ALL THE TIME FROM CHILDREN WHO TOOK THEIR GAMES FAR TOO SERIOUSLY. BACK IN THE '80S, WE COULD SCARCELY FIT CREDITS ON A CARTRIDGE, SO WE USED TO HIDE OUR NAMES IN THE STUFF WE WORKED ON.
YARS' REVENGE WAS SIMPLY RAY KASSAR'S NAME BACKWARDS.
BUT OF COURSE YOU KNOW THAT, YOU'RE AMY PEREZ. LOVED THE BOOK, BY THE WAY. BROUGHT BACK A LOT OF GOOD MEMORIES.
NOW THEN...

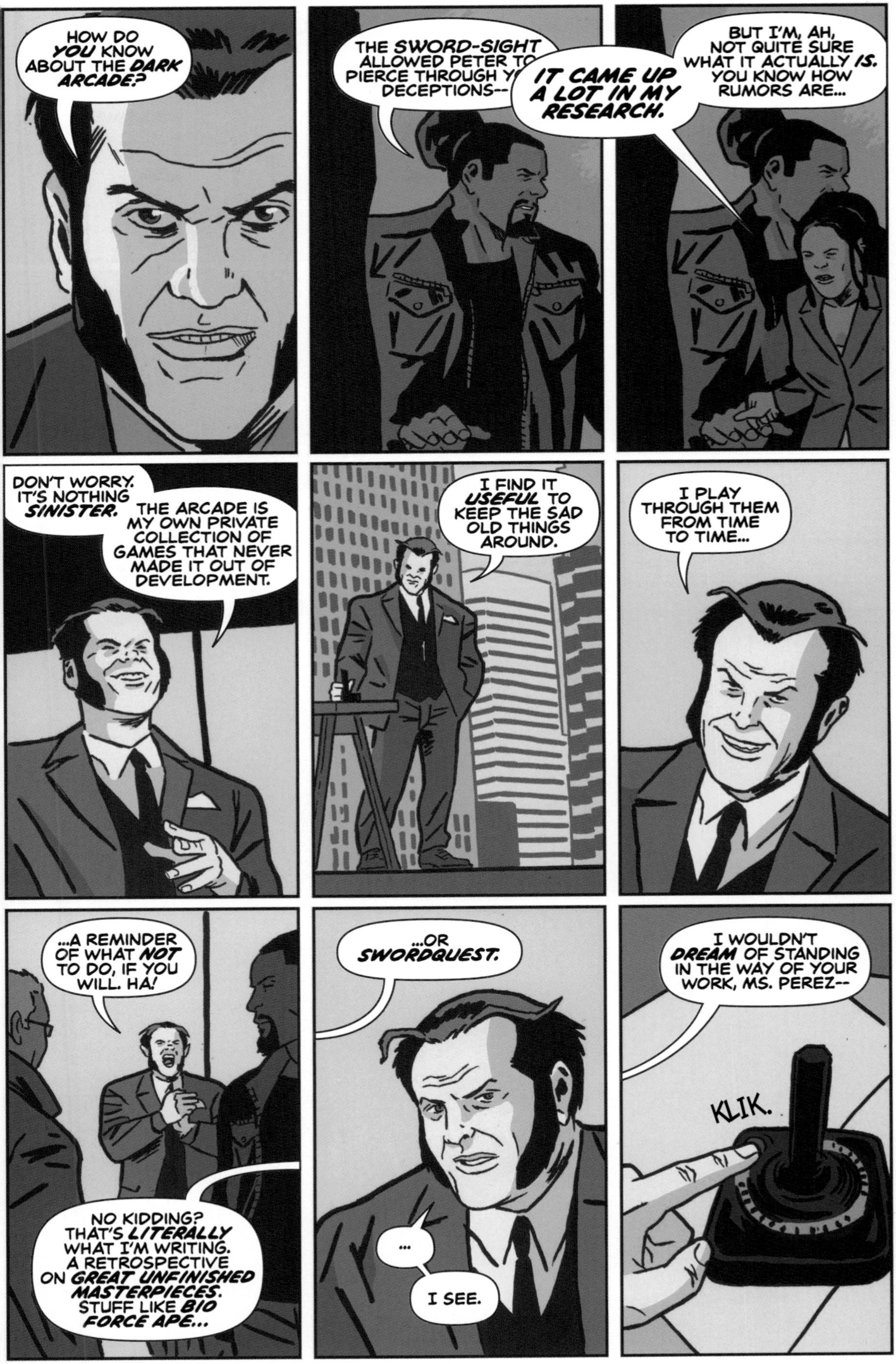
HOW DO YOU KNOW ABOUT THE DARK ARCADE?
THE SWORD-SIGHT ALLOWED PETER TO PIERCE THROUGH Y DECEPTIONS--
IT CAME UP A LOT IN MY RESEARCH.
BUT I'M, AH, NOT QUITE SURE WHAT IT ACTUALLY IS. YOU KNOW HOW RUMORS ARE...
DON'T WORRY. IT'S NOTHING SINISTER.
THE ARCADE IS MY OWN PRIVATE COLLECTION OF GAMES THAT NEVER MADE IT OUT OF DEVELOPMENT.
I FIND IT USEFUL TO KEEP THE SAD OLD THINGS AROUND.
I PLAY THROUGH THEM FROM TIME TO TIME...
...A REMINDER OF WHAT NOT TO DO, IF YOU WILL. HA!
NO KIDDING? THAT'S LITERALLY WHAT I'M WRITING. A RETROSPECTIVE ON GREAT UNFINISHED MASTERPIECES. STUFF LIKE BIO FORCE APE...
...OR SWORDQUEST.
...
I SEE.
I WOULDN'T DREAM OF STANDING IN THE WAY OF YOUR WORK, MS. PEREZ--
KLIK.

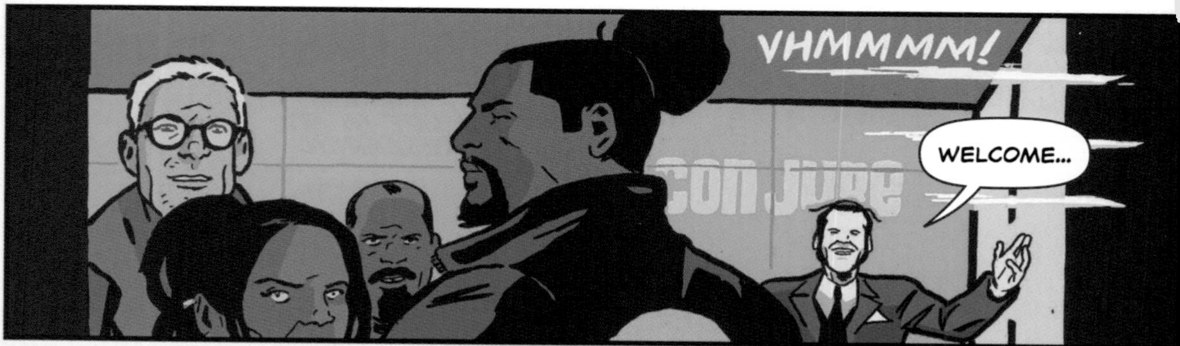
VHMMMM!
WELCOME...

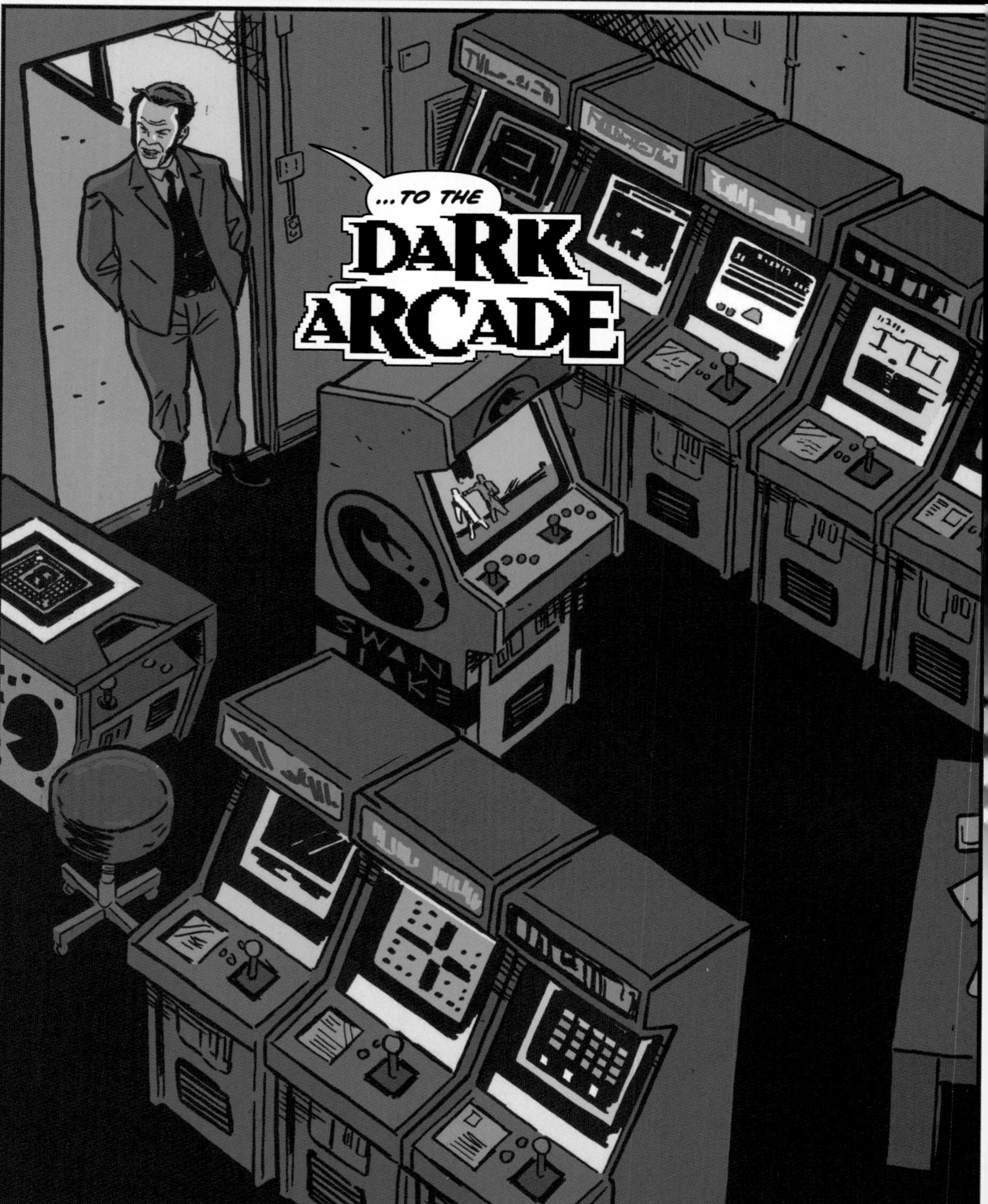
...TO THE
DARK ARCADE

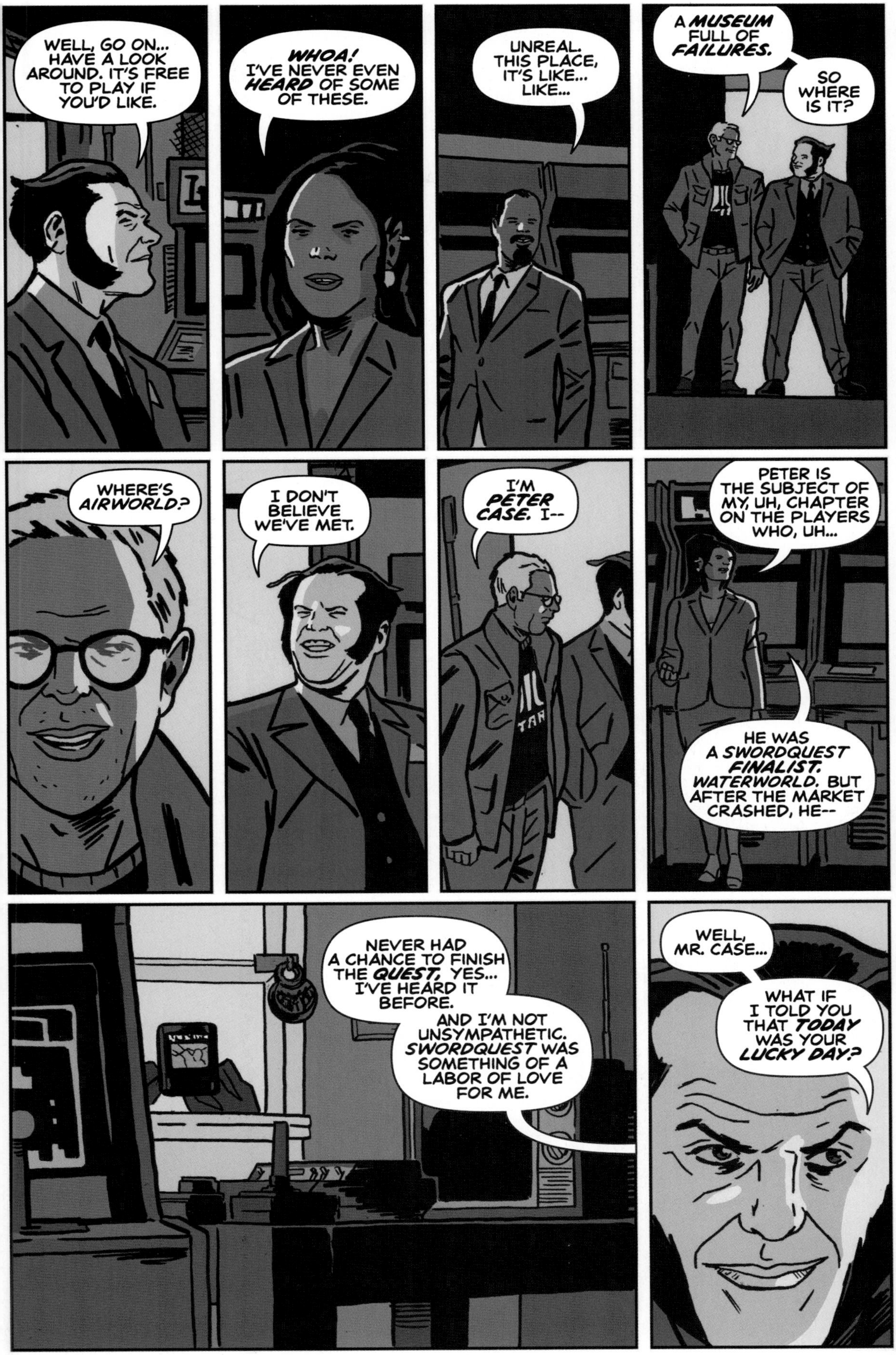
WELL, GO ON... HAVE A LOOK AROUND. IT'S FREE TO PLAY IF YOU'D LIKE.
WHOA! I'VE NEVER EVEN HEARD OF SOME OF THESE.
UNREAL. THIS PLACE, IT'S LIKE... LIKE...
A MUSEUM FULL OF FAILURES.
SO WHERE IS IT?
WHERE'S AIRWORLD?
I DON'T BELIEVE WE'VE MET.
I'M PETER CASE. I--
PETER IS THE SUBJECT OF MY, UH, CHAPTER ON THE PLAYERS WHO, UH...
HE WAS A SWORDQUEST FINALIST. WATERWORLD. BUT AFTER THE MARKET CRASHED, HE--
NEVER HAD A CHANCE TO FINISH THE QUEST, YES... I'VE HEARD IT BEFORE.
AND I'M NOT UNSYMPATHETIC. SWORDQUEST WAS SOMETHING OF A LABOR OF LOVE FOR ME.
WELL, MR. CASE...
WHAT IF I TOLD YOU THAT TODAY WAS YOUR LUCKY DAY?

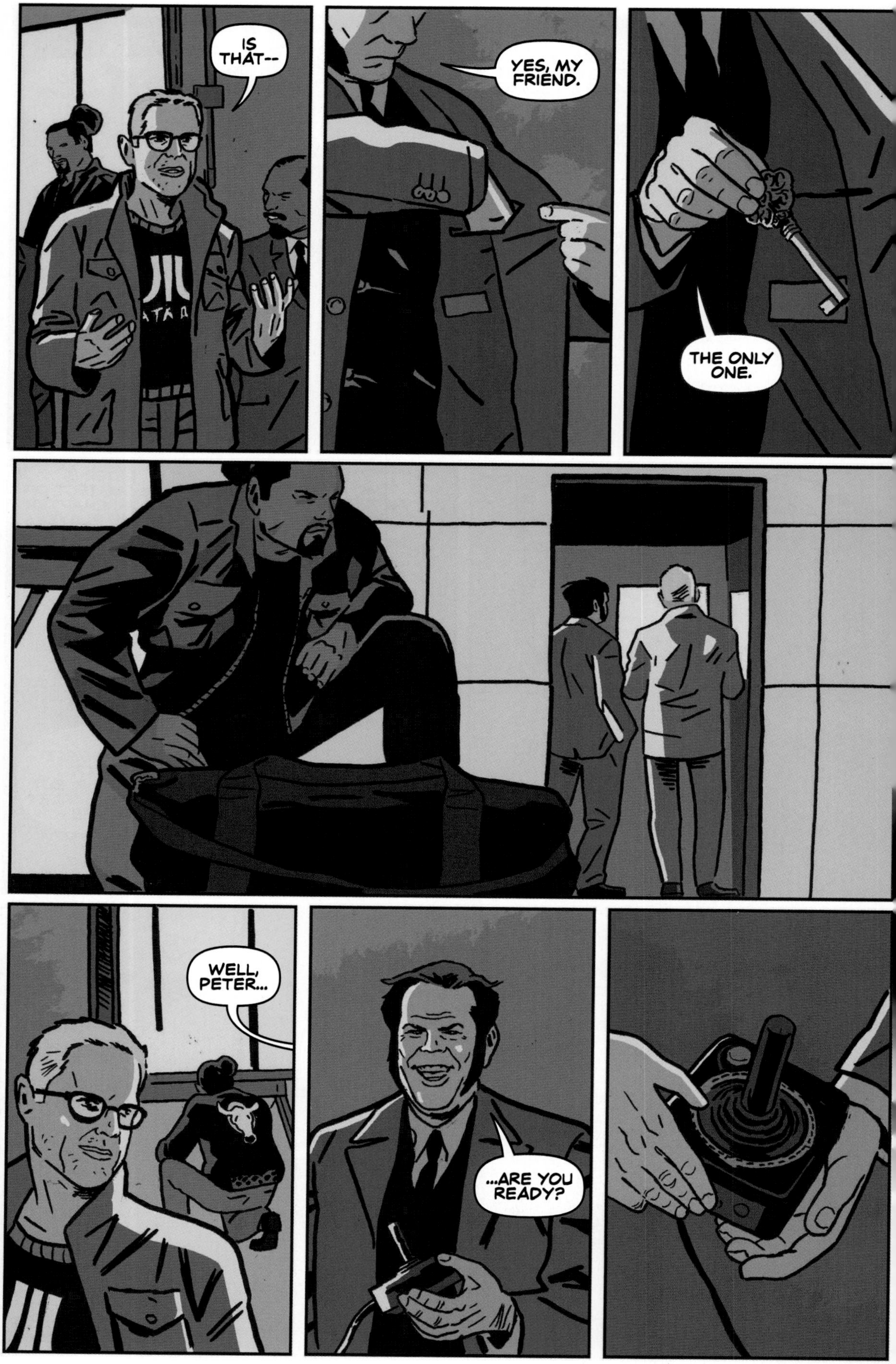
IS THAT--
YES, MY FRIEND.
THE ONLY ONE.
WELL, PETER...
...ARE YOU READY?

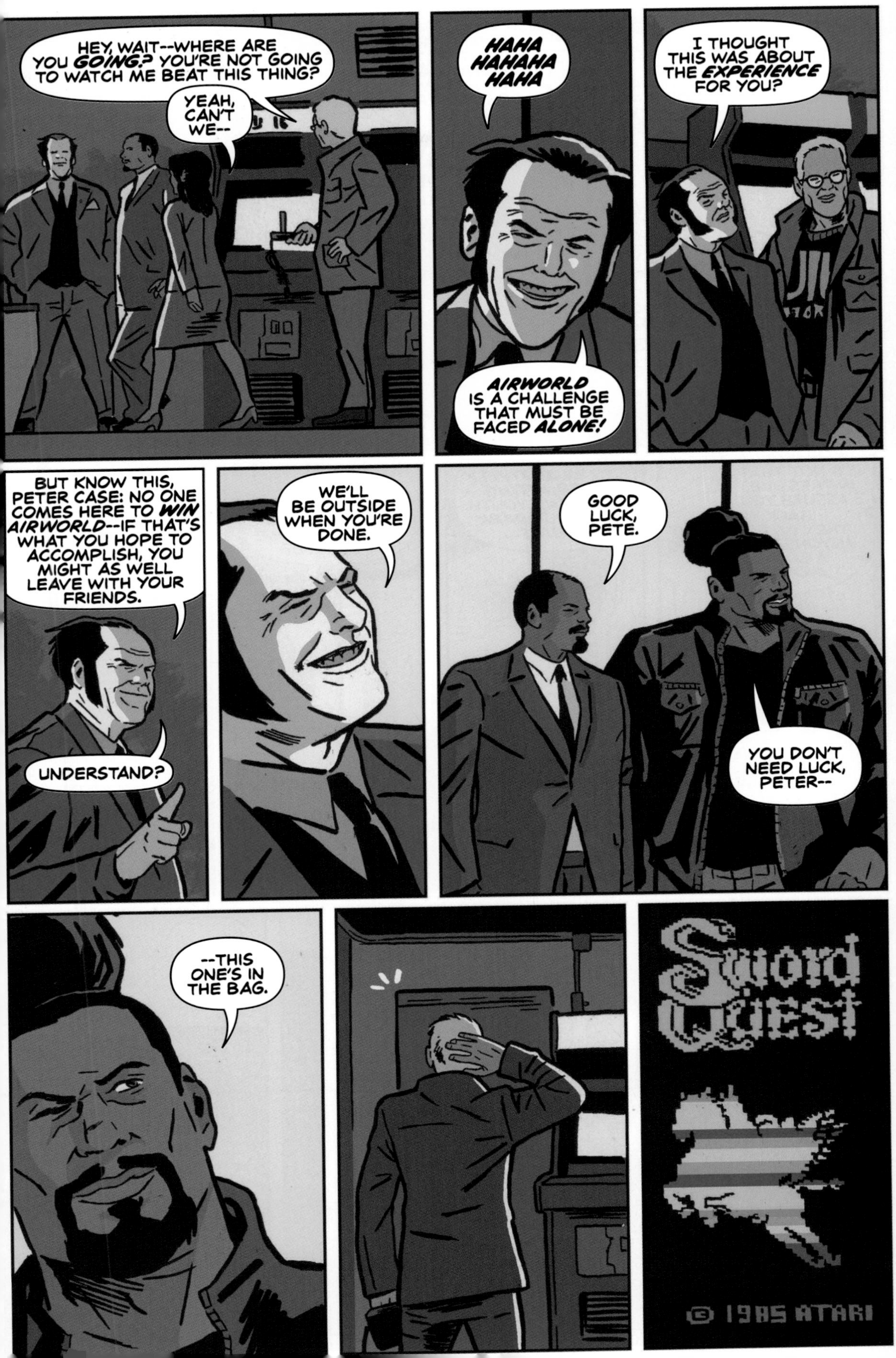
HEY, WAIT--WHERE ARE YOU GOING? YOU'RE NOT GOING TO WATCH ME BEAT THIS THING?
YEAH, CAN'T WE--
HAHA HAHAHA HAHA
AIRWORLD IS A CHALLENGE THAT MUST BE FACED ALONE!
I THOUGHT THIS WAS ABOUT THE EXPERIENCE FOR YOU?
BUT KNOW THIS, PETER CASE: NO ONE COMES HERE TO WIN AIRWORLD--IF THAT'S WHAT YOU HOPE TO ACCOMPLISH, YOU MIGHT AS WELL LEAVE WITH YOUR FRIENDS.
UNDERSTAND?
WE'LL BE OUTSIDE WHEN YOU'RE DONE.
GOOD LUCK, PETE.
YOU DON'T NEED LUCK, PETER--
--THIS ONE'S IN THE BAG.
Sword Quest
© 1985 ATARI

SO...YOU GET THAT WIZARD STUFF A LOT?

NOT SO MUCH ANYMORE, OUTSIDE OF A FEW *CONSPIRACY THEORY* SITES.

IN THE '80S, HOWEVER...OOOH *THE '80S.*

COOKIE?

DURING THE HEIGHT OF THE *SATANIC PANIC,* THE *FBI* EVEN OPENED A FILE ON ME.

FOR REAL?

SEE FOR YOURSELF.

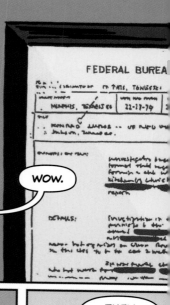

FEDERAL BUREA

WOW.

IT'S NOT THAT IMPRESSIVE, I ASSURE YOU. BACK THEN, THEY INVESTIGATED ANYONE WHO OWNED A BOOK WITH A *DRAGON* IN IT.

BUT THOSE OF US WHO WERE LUCKY ENOUGH...

...TO BE *ACTIVELY CORRUPTING* AMERICA'S YOUTH WITH OUR *DARK MAGICS...*

...WERE EVEN *MORE* SUSPECT.

TERRY, YOU SURE YOU DON'T WANT ONE OF THESE?

THEY ARE LIKELY POISONED.

C'MON, MAN. THEY'RE *DOUBLE STUF.*

...

PERHAPS--

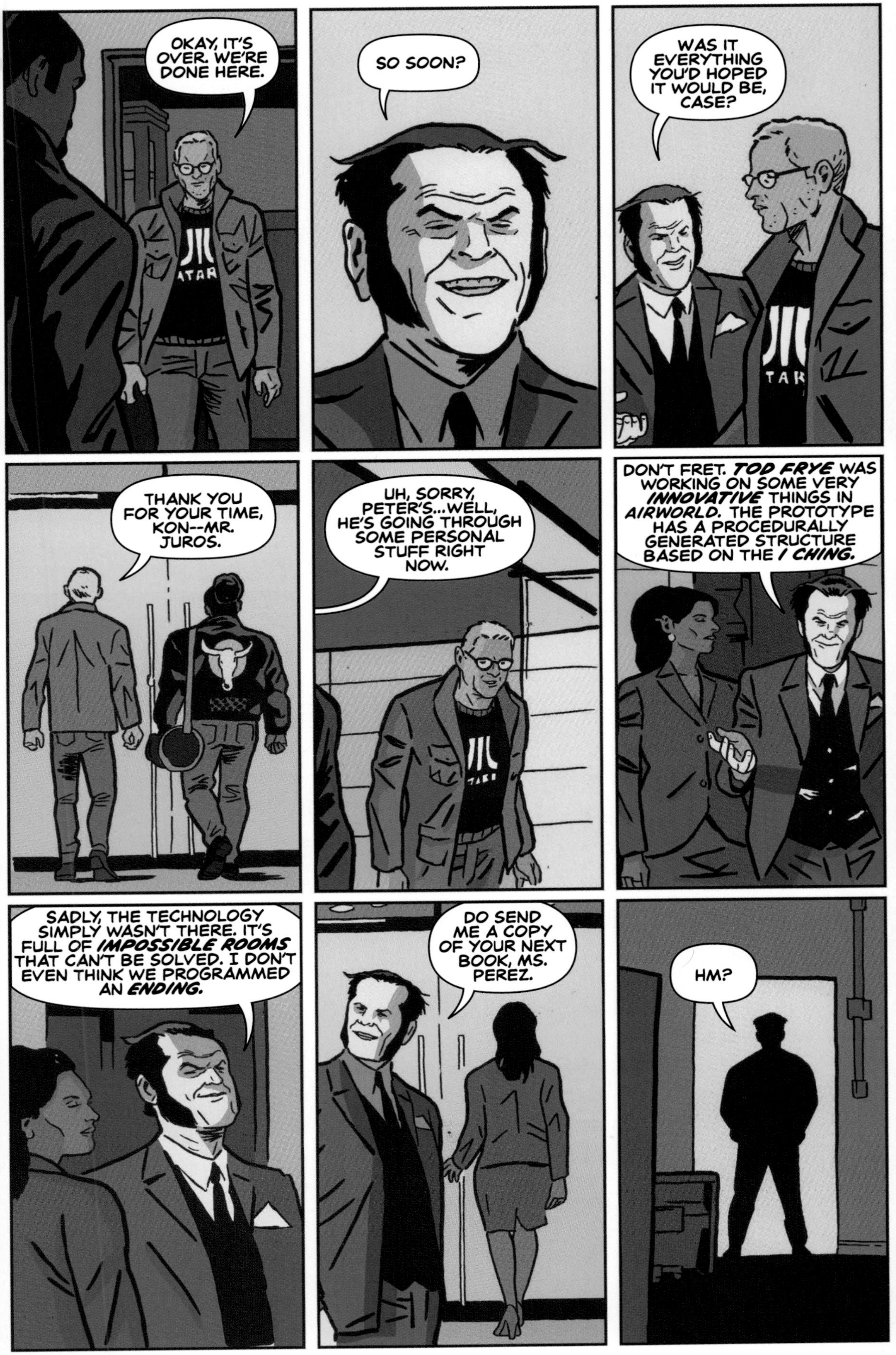
OKAY, IT'S OVER. WE'RE DONE HERE.
SO SOON?
WAS IT EVERYTHING YOU'D HOPED IT WOULD BE, CASE?
THANK YOU FOR YOUR TIME, KON--MR. JUROS.
UH, SORRY, PETER'S...WELL, HE'S GOING THROUGH SOME PERSONAL STUFF RIGHT NOW.
DON'T FRET. TOD FRYE WAS WORKING ON SOME VERY INNOVATIVE THINGS IN AIRWORLD. THE PROTOTYPE HAS A PROCEDURALLY GENERATED STRUCTURE BASED ON THE I CHING.
SADLY, THE TECHNOLOGY SIMPLY WASN'T THERE. IT'S FULL OF IMPOSSIBLE ROOMS THAT CAN'T BE SOLVED. I DON'T EVEN THINK WE PROGRAMMED AN ENDING.
DO SEND ME A COPY OF YOUR NEXT BOOK, MS. PEREZ.
HM?

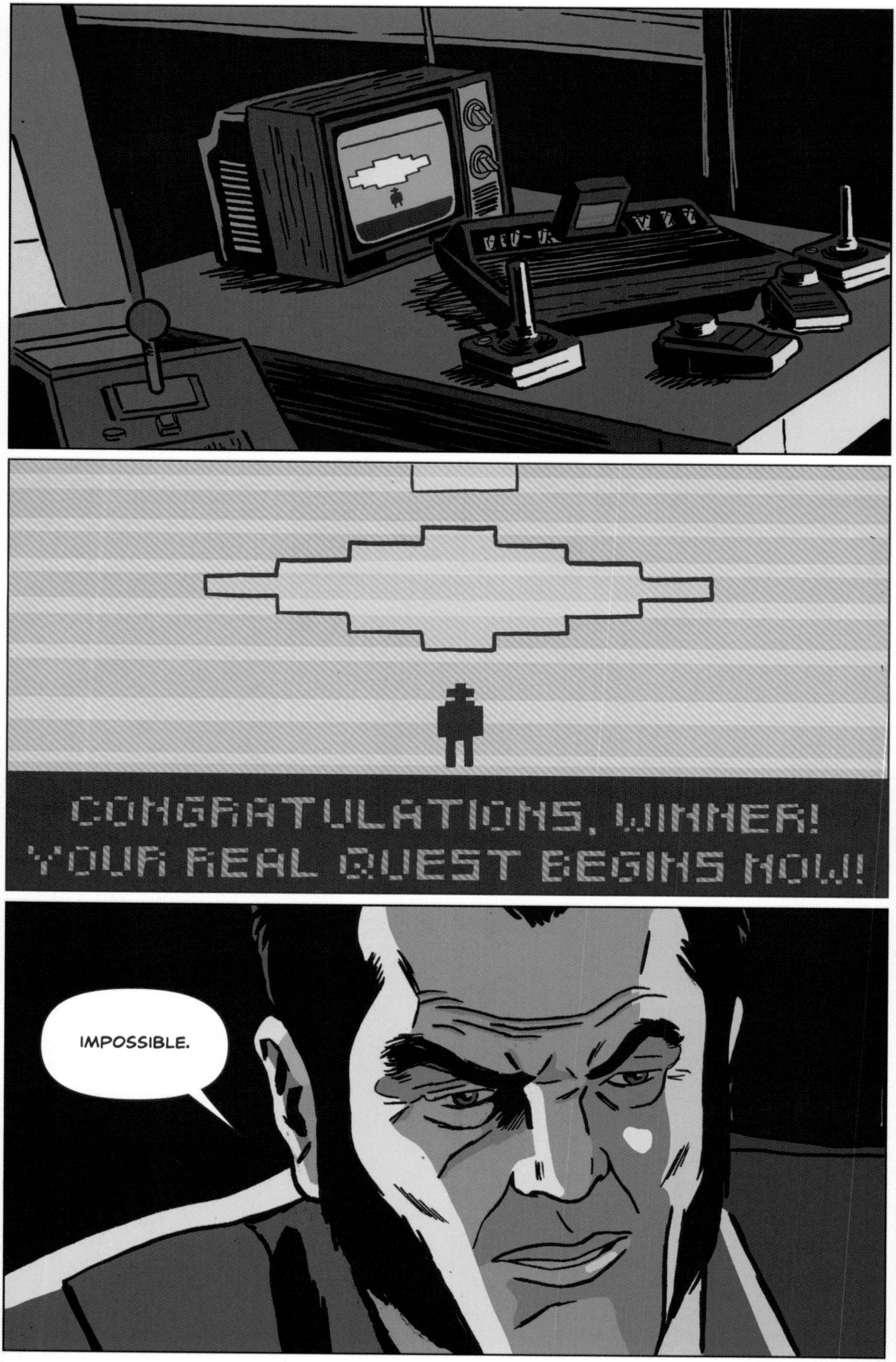
CONGRATULATIONS, WINNER!
YOUR REAL QUEST BEGINS NOW!
IMPOSSIBLE.

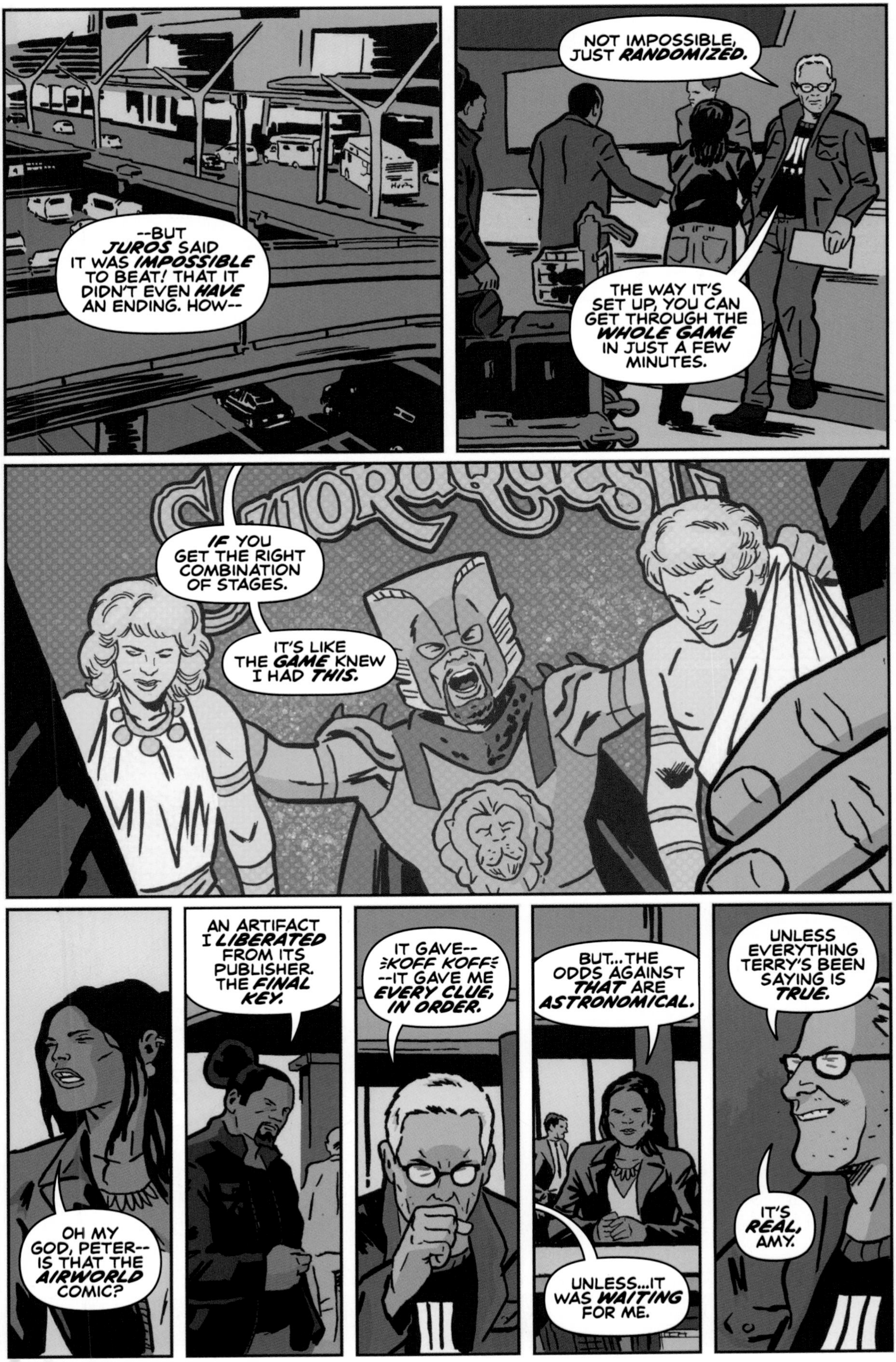
--BUT JUROS SAID IT WAS IMPOSSIBLE TO BEAT! THAT IT DIDN'T EVEN HAVE AN ENDING. HOW--
NOT IMPOSSIBLE, JUST RANDOMIZED.
THE WAY IT'S SET UP, YOU CAN GET THROUGH THE WHOLE GAME IN JUST A FEW MINUTES.
IF YOU GET THE RIGHT COMBINATION OF STAGES.
IT'S LIKE THE GAME KNEW I HAD THIS.
OH MY GOD, PETER-- IS THAT THE AIRWORLD COMIC?
AN ARTIFACT I LIBERATED FROM ITS PUBLISHER. THE FINAL KEY.
IT GAVE-- KOFF KOFF --IT GAVE ME EVERY CLUE, IN ORDER.
BUT...THE ODDS AGAINST THAT ARE ASTRONOMICAL.
UNLESS...IT WAS WAITING FOR ME.
UNLESS EVERYTHING TERRY'S BEEN SAYING IS TRUE.
IT'S REAL, AMY.

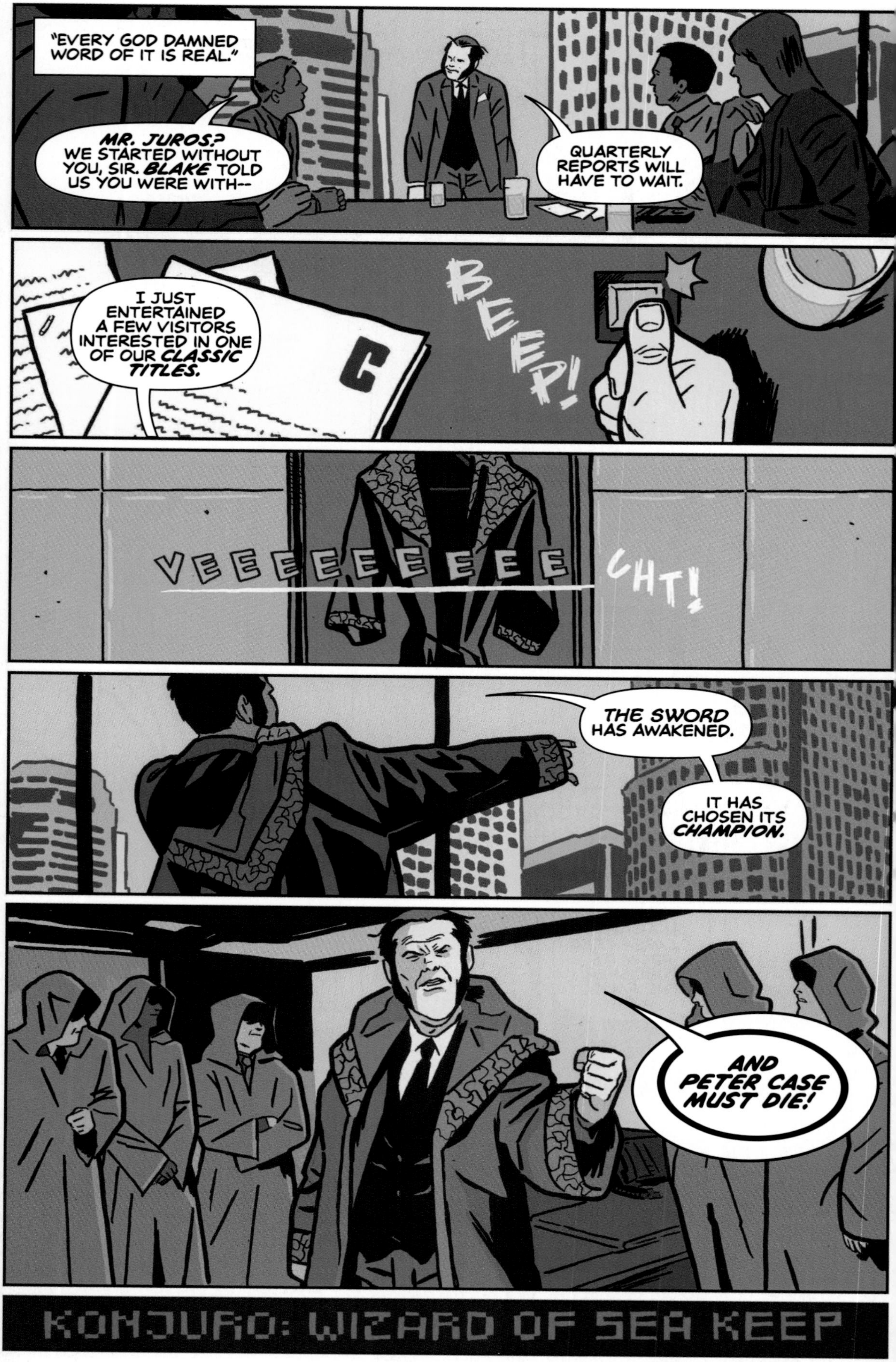
"EVERY GOD DAMNED WORD OF IT IS REAL."
MR. JUROS? WE STARTED WITHOUT YOU, SIR. BLAKE TOLD US YOU WERE WITH--
QUARTERLY REPORTS WILL HAVE TO WAIT.
I JUST ENTERTAINED A FEW VISITORS INTERESTED IN ONE OF OUR CLASSIC TITLES.
BEEP!
VEEEEEEEEEE CHT!
THE SWORD HAS AWAKENED.
IT HAS CHOSEN ITS CHAMPION.
AND PETER CASE MUST DIE!
KONJURO: WIZARD OF SEA KEEP

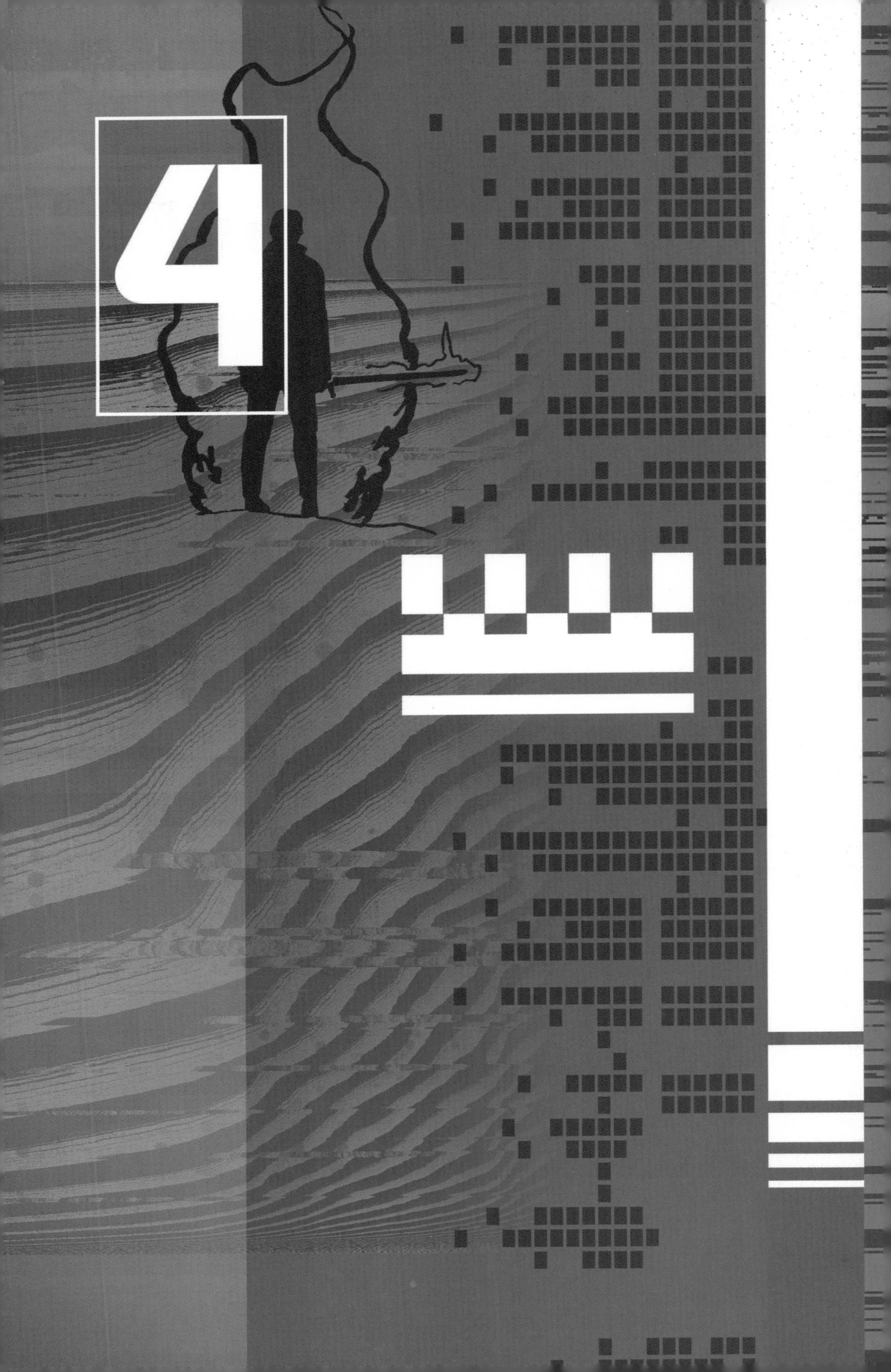
4

Art by GOÑI MONTES

4

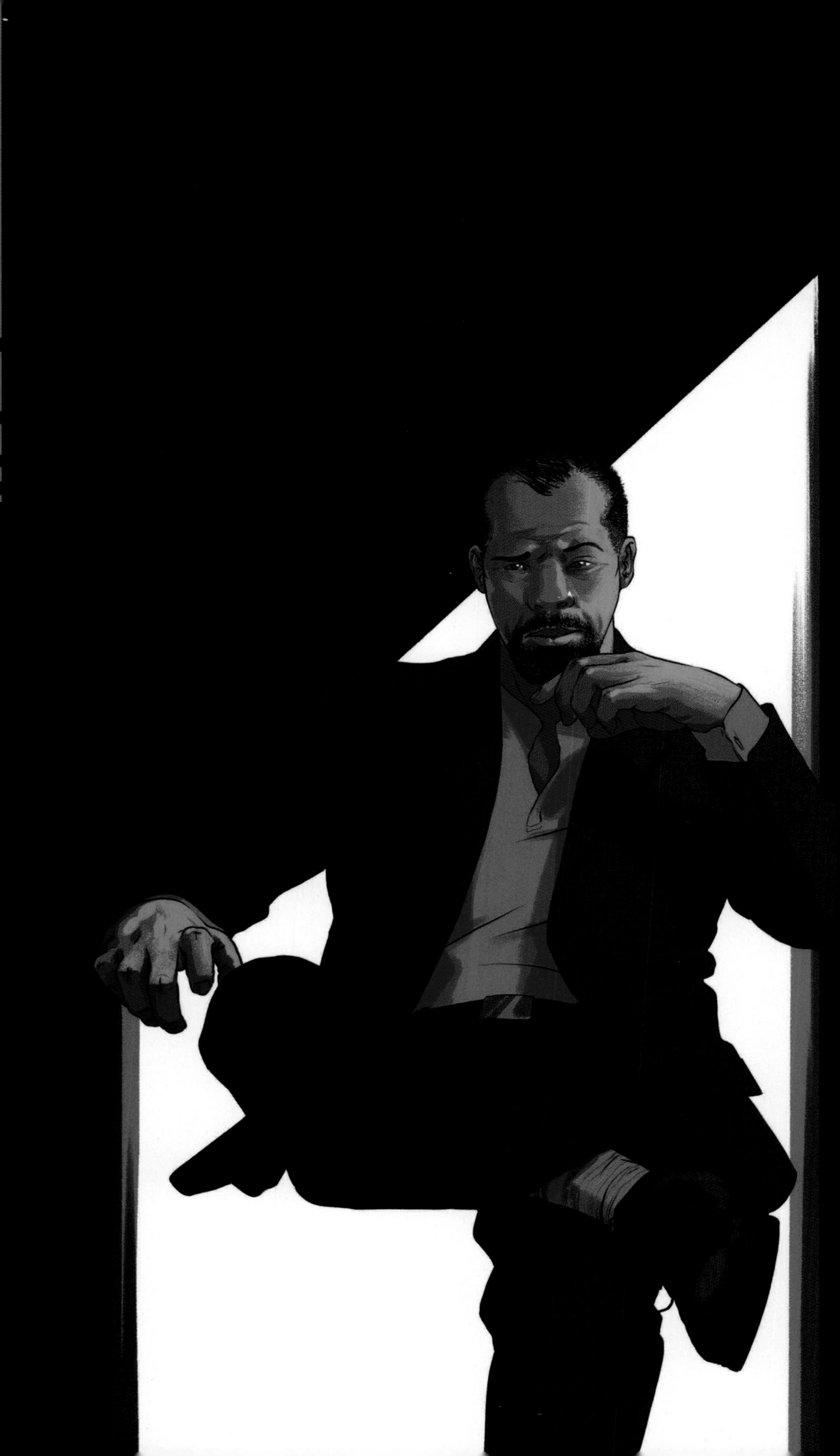

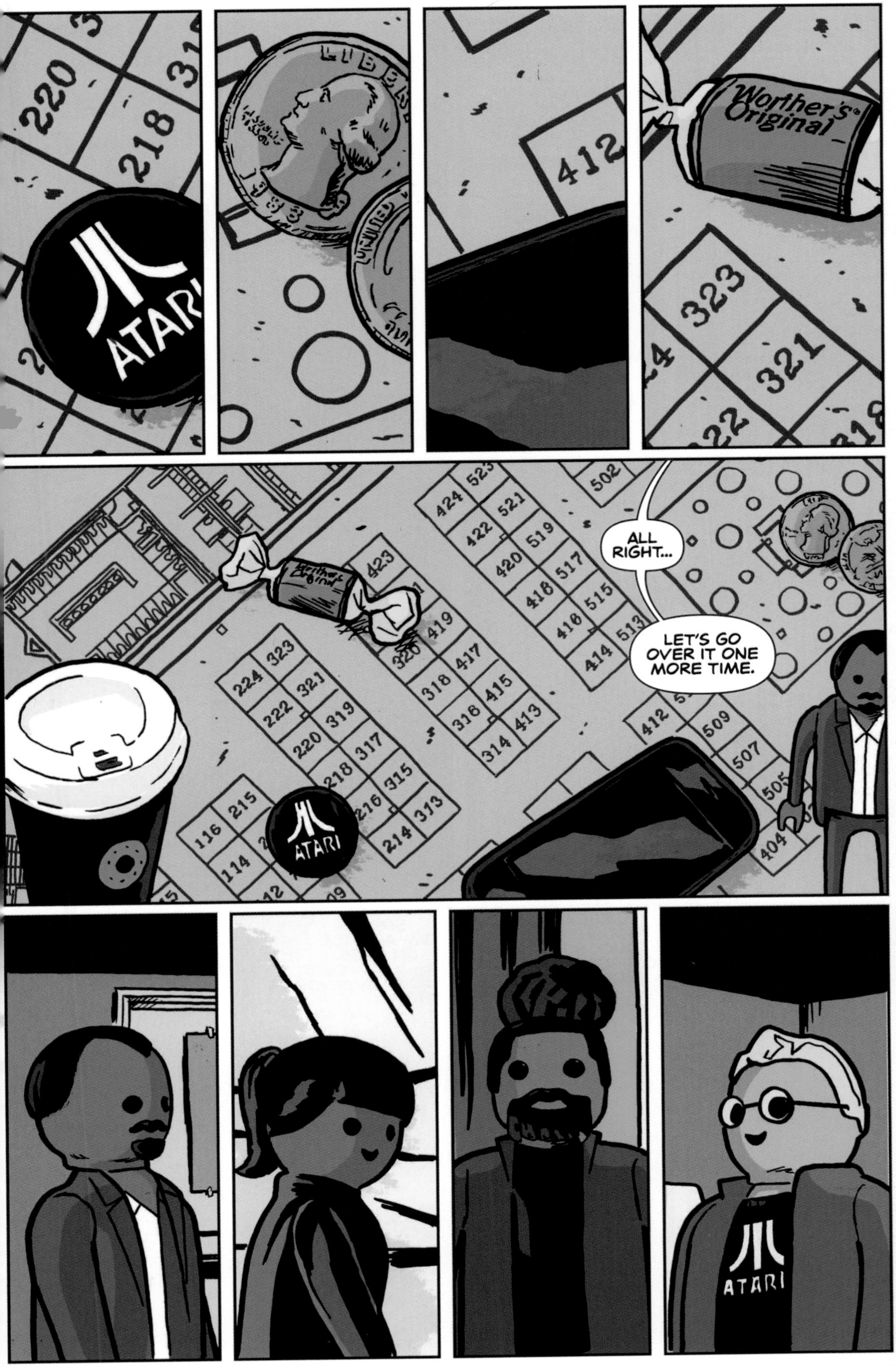
ATARI
Worther's Original
ALL RIGHT...
LET'S GO OVER IT ONE MORE TIME.
ATARI

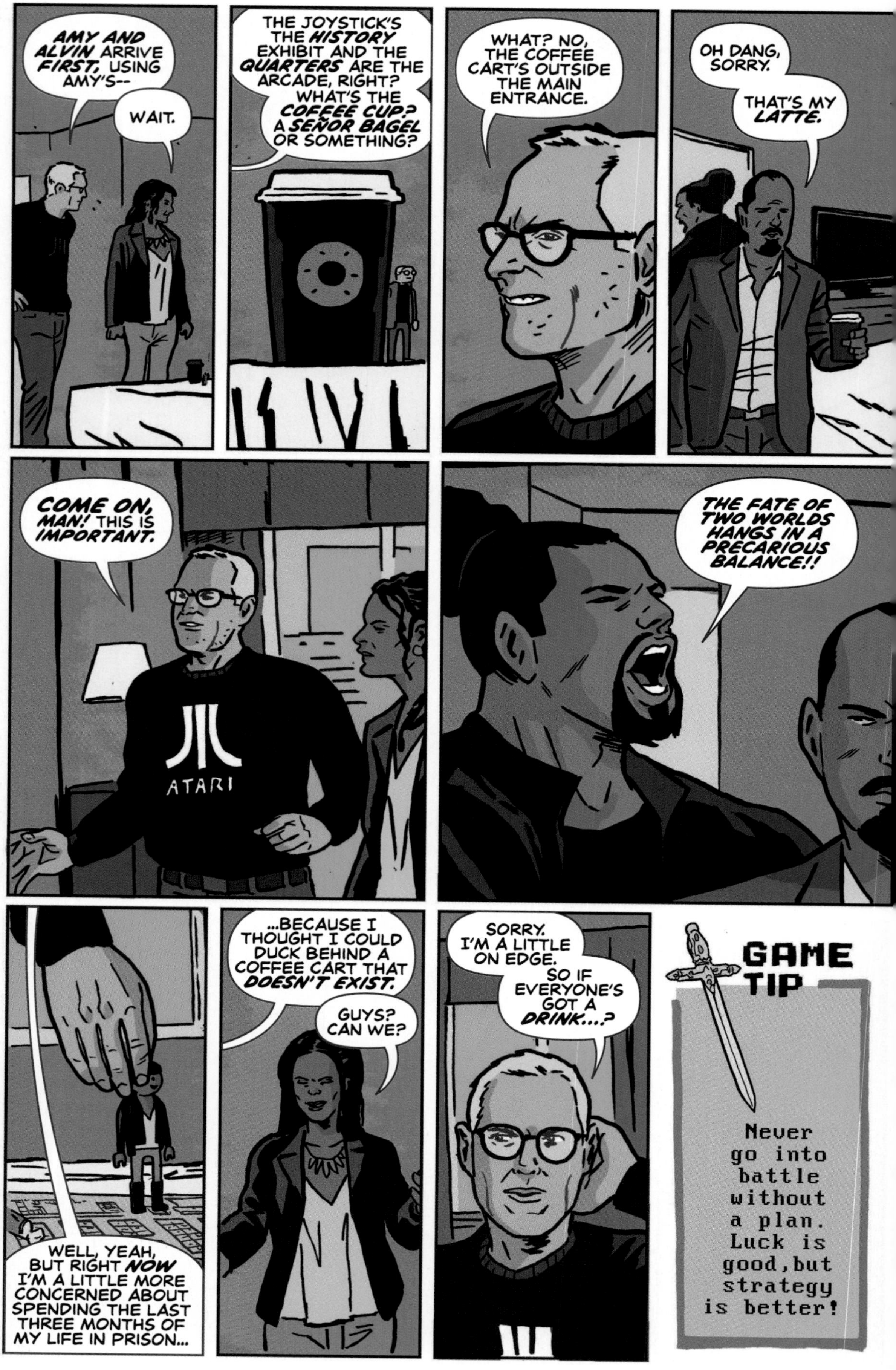
AMY AND ALVIN ARRIVE FIRST, USING AMY'S--
WAIT.
THE JOYSTICK'S THE HISTORY EXHIBIT AND THE QUARTERS ARE THE ARCADE, RIGHT?
WHAT'S THE COFFEE CUP? A SEÑOR BAGEL OR SOMETHING?
WHAT? NO, THE COFFEE CART'S OUTSIDE THE MAIN ENTRANCE.
OH DANG, SORRY.
THAT'S MY LATTE.
COME ON, MAN! THIS IS IMPORTANT.
ATARI
THE FATE OF TWO WORLDS HANGS IN A PRECARIOUS BALANCE!!
WELL, YEAH, BUT RIGHT NOW I'M A LITTLE MORE CONCERNED ABOUT SPENDING THE LAST THREE MONTHS OF MY LIFE IN PRISON...
...BECAUSE I THOUGHT I COULD DUCK BEHIND A COFFEE CART THAT DOESN'T EXIST.
GUYS? CAN WE?
SORRY. I'M A LITTLE ON EDGE.
SO IF EVERYONE'S GOT A DRINK...?
GAME TIP
Never go into battle without a plan. Luck is good, but strategy is better!

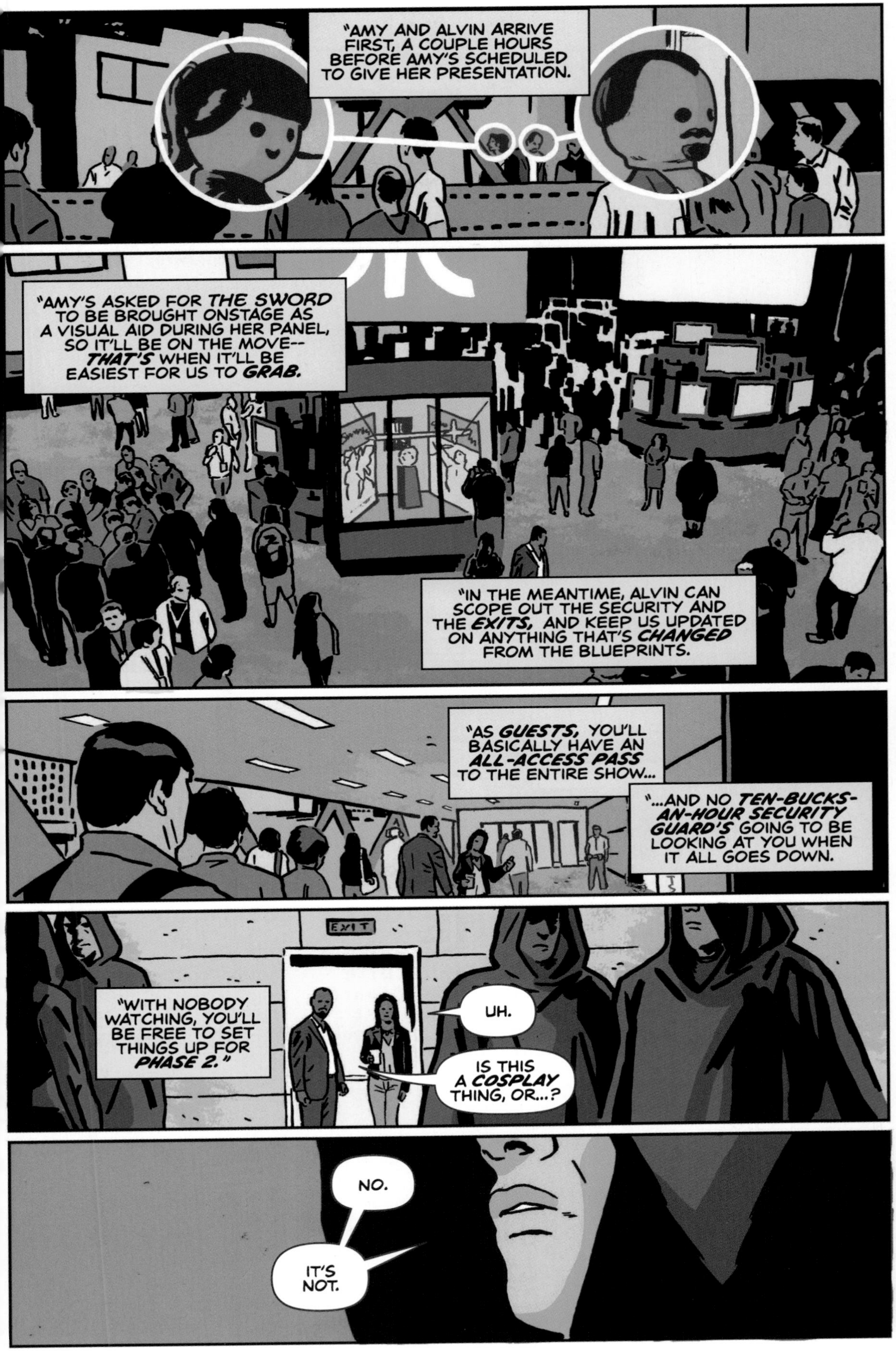
"AMY AND ALVIN ARRIVE FIRST, A COUPLE HOURS BEFORE AMY'S SCHEDULED TO GIVE HER PRESENTATION.
"AMY'S ASKED FOR *THE SWORD* TO BE BROUGHT ONSTAGE AS A VISUAL AID DURING HER PANEL, SO IT'LL BE ON THE MOVE-- *THAT'S* WHEN IT'LL BE EASIEST FOR US TO *GRAB.*
"IN THE MEANTIME, ALVIN CAN SCOPE OUT THE SECURITY AND THE *EXITS,* AND KEEP US UPDATED ON ANYTHING THAT'S *CHANGED* FROM THE BLUEPRINTS.
"AS *GUESTS,* YOU'LL BASICALLY HAVE AN *ALL-ACCESS PASS* TO THE ENTIRE SHOW...
"...AND NO *TEN-BUCKS-AN-HOUR SECURITY GUARD'S* GOING TO BE LOOKING AT YOU WHEN IT ALL GOES DOWN.
EXIT
"WITH NOBODY WATCHING, YOU'LL BE FREE TO SET THINGS UP FOR *PHASE 2.*"
UH.
IS THIS A *COSPLAY* THING, OR...?
NO.
IT'S NOT.

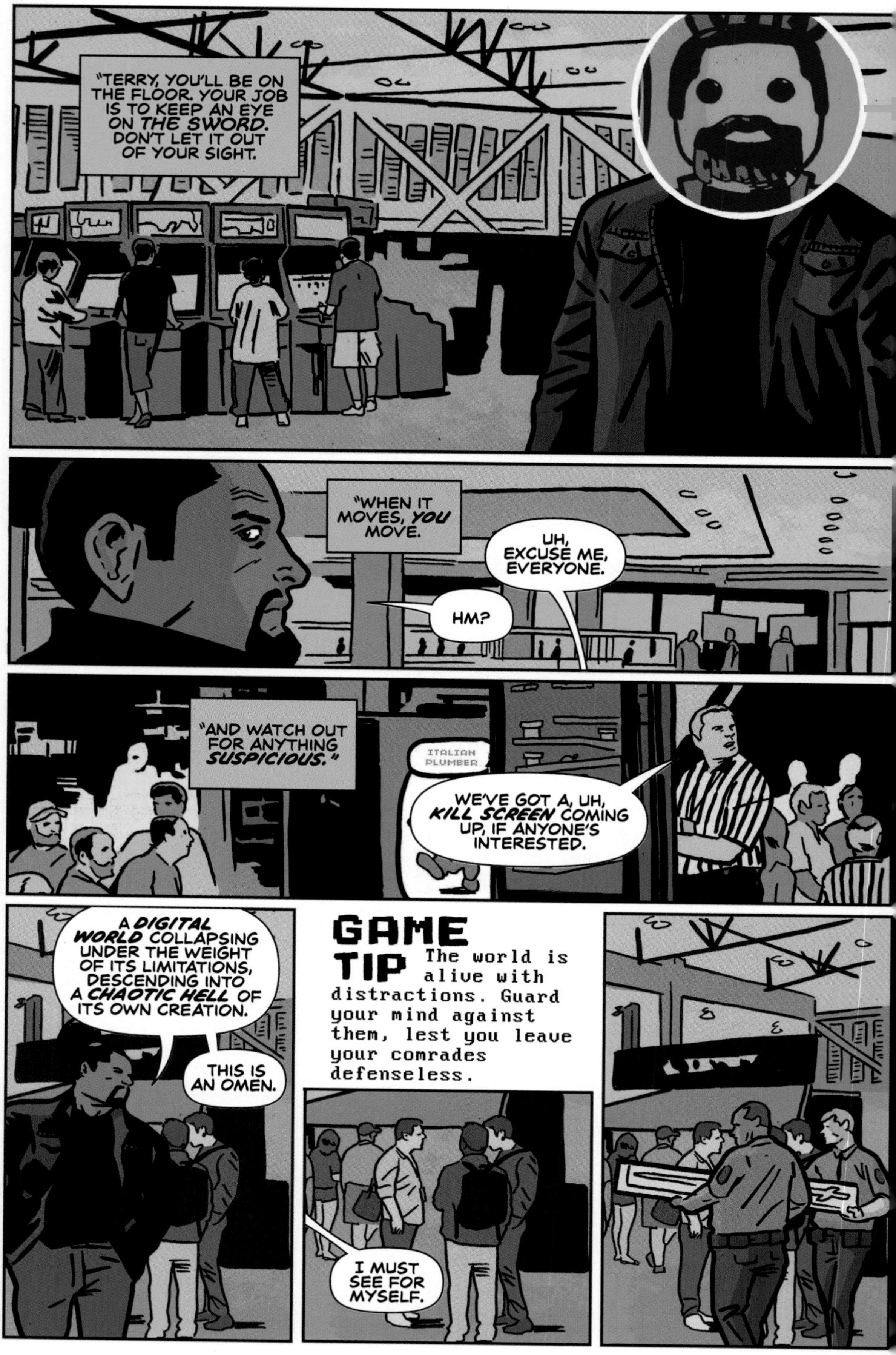
"TERRY, YOU'LL BE ON THE FLOOR. YOUR JOB IS TO KEEP AN EYE ON THE SWORD. DON'T LET IT OUT OF YOUR SIGHT.
"WHEN IT MOVES, YOU MOVE.
UH, EXCUSE ME, EVERYONE.
HM?
"AND WATCH OUT FOR ANYTHING SUSPICIOUS."
ITALIAN PLUMBER
WE'VE GOT A, UH, KILL SCREEN COMING UP, IF ANYONE'S INTERESTED.
A DIGITAL WORLD COLLAPSING UNDER THE WEIGHT OF ITS LIMITATIONS, DESCENDING INTO A CHAOTIC HELL OF ITS OWN CREATION.
THIS IS AN OMEN.
GAME TIP The world is alive with distractions. Guard your mind against them, lest you leave your comrades defenseless.
I MUST SEE FOR MYSELF.

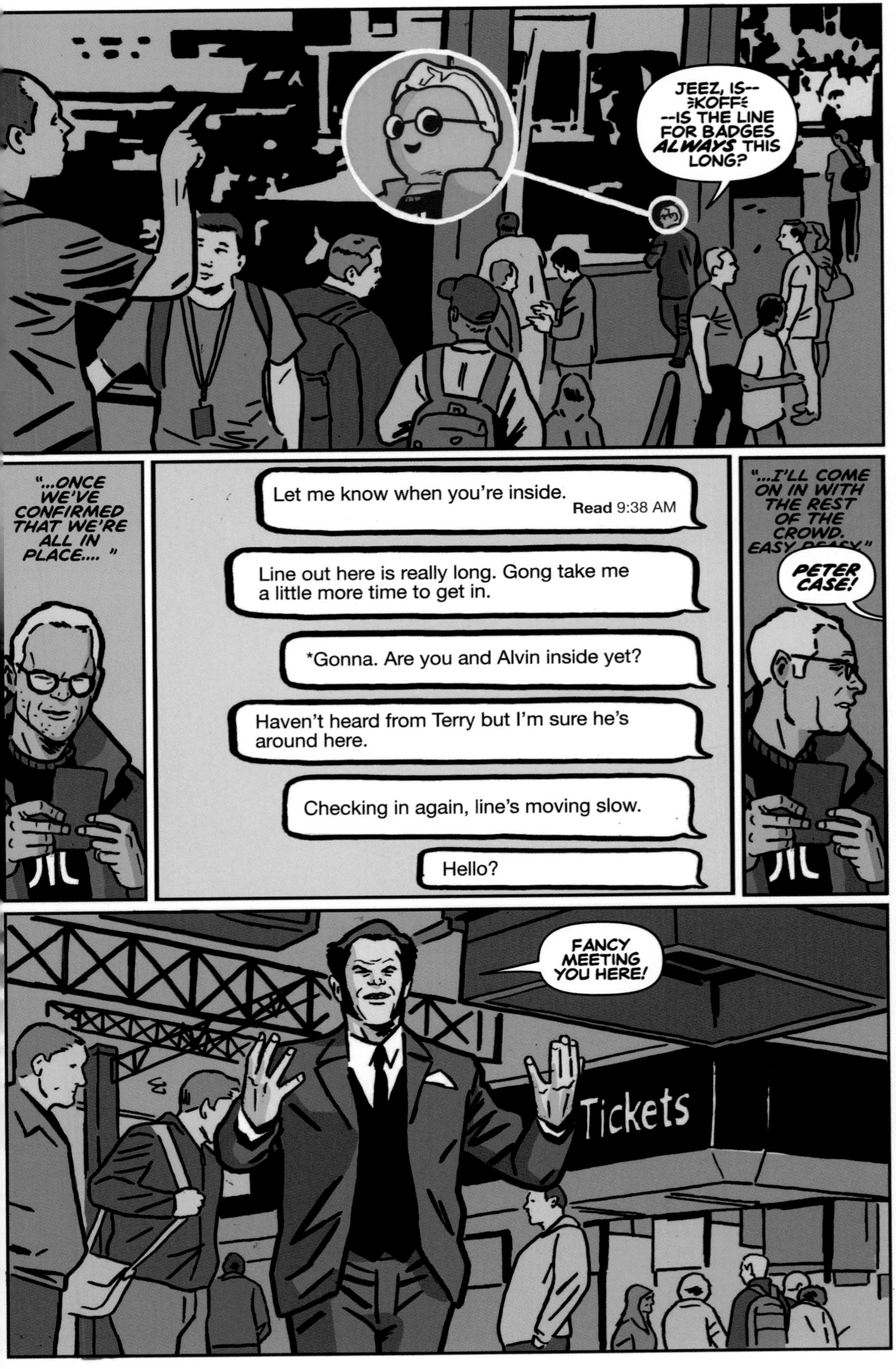
JEEZ, IS--
≈KOFF≈
--IS THE LINE FOR BADGES *ALWAYS* THIS LONG?
"...ONCE WE'VE CONFIRMED THAT WE'RE ALL IN PLACE.... "
Let me know when you're inside.
Read 9:38 AM
Line out here is really long. Gong take me a little more time to get in.
*Gonna. Are you and Alvin inside yet?
Haven't heard from Terry but I'm sure he's around here.
Checking in again, line's moving slow.
Hello?
"...I'LL COME ON IN WITH THE REST OF THE CROWD. EASY
PETER CASE!
FANCY MEETING YOU HERE!
Tickets

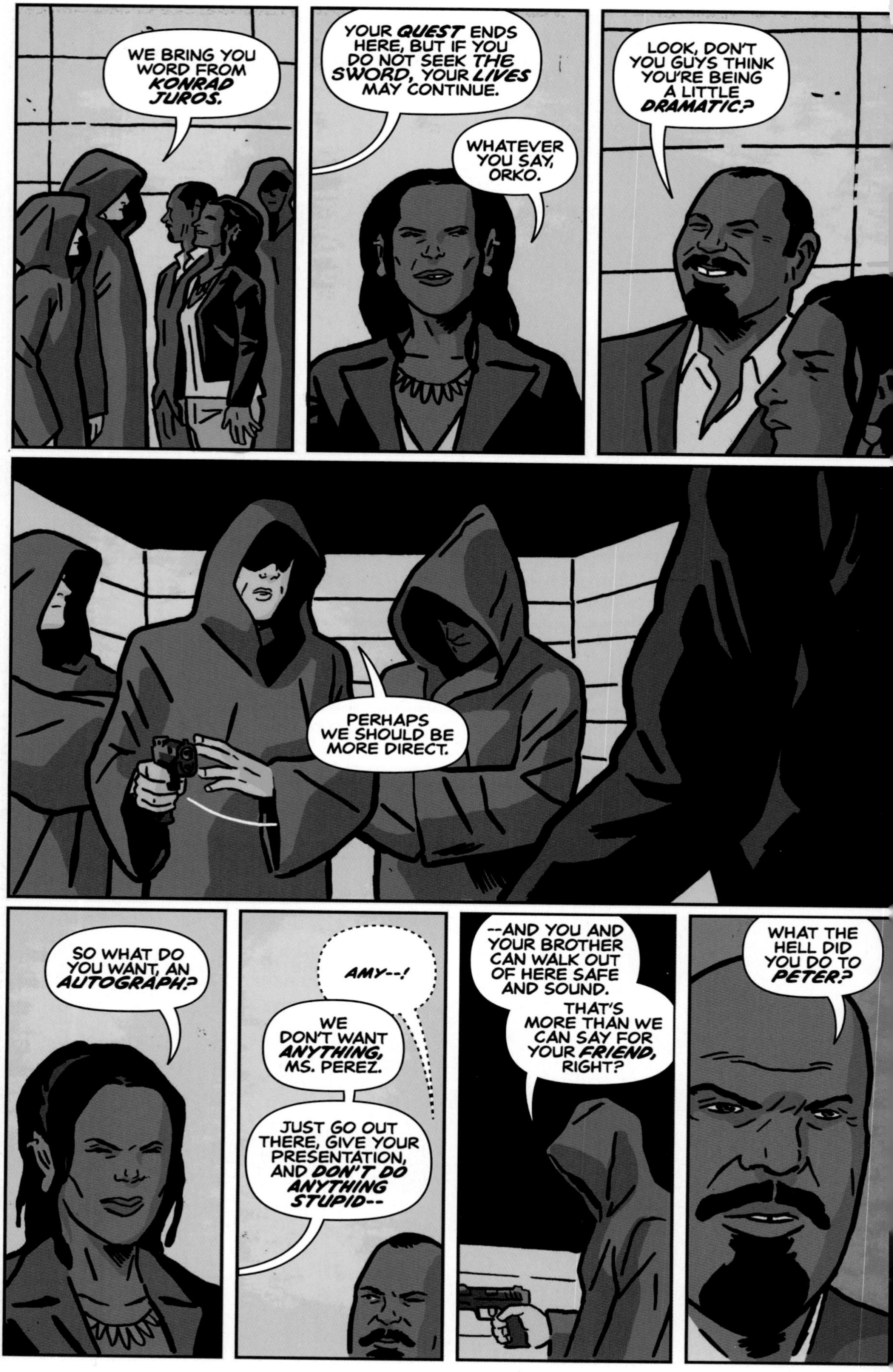
WE BRING YOU WORD FROM KONRAD JUROS.
YOUR QUEST ENDS HERE, BUT IF YOU DO NOT SEEK THE SWORD, YOUR LIVES MAY CONTINUE.
WHATEVER YOU SAY, ORKO.
LOOK, DON'T YOU GUYS THINK YOU'RE BEING A LITTLE DRAMATIC?
PERHAPS WE SHOULD BE MORE DIRECT.
SO WHAT DO YOU WANT, AN AUTOGRAPH?
AMY--!
WE DON'T WANT ANYTHING, MS. PEREZ.
JUST GO OUT THERE, GIVE YOUR PRESENTATION, AND DON'T DO ANYTHING STUPID--
--AND YOU AND YOUR BROTHER CAN WALK OUT OF HERE SAFE AND SOUND.
THAT'S MORE THAN WE CAN SAY FOR YOUR FRIEND, RIGHT?
WHAT THE HELL DID YOU DO TO PETER?

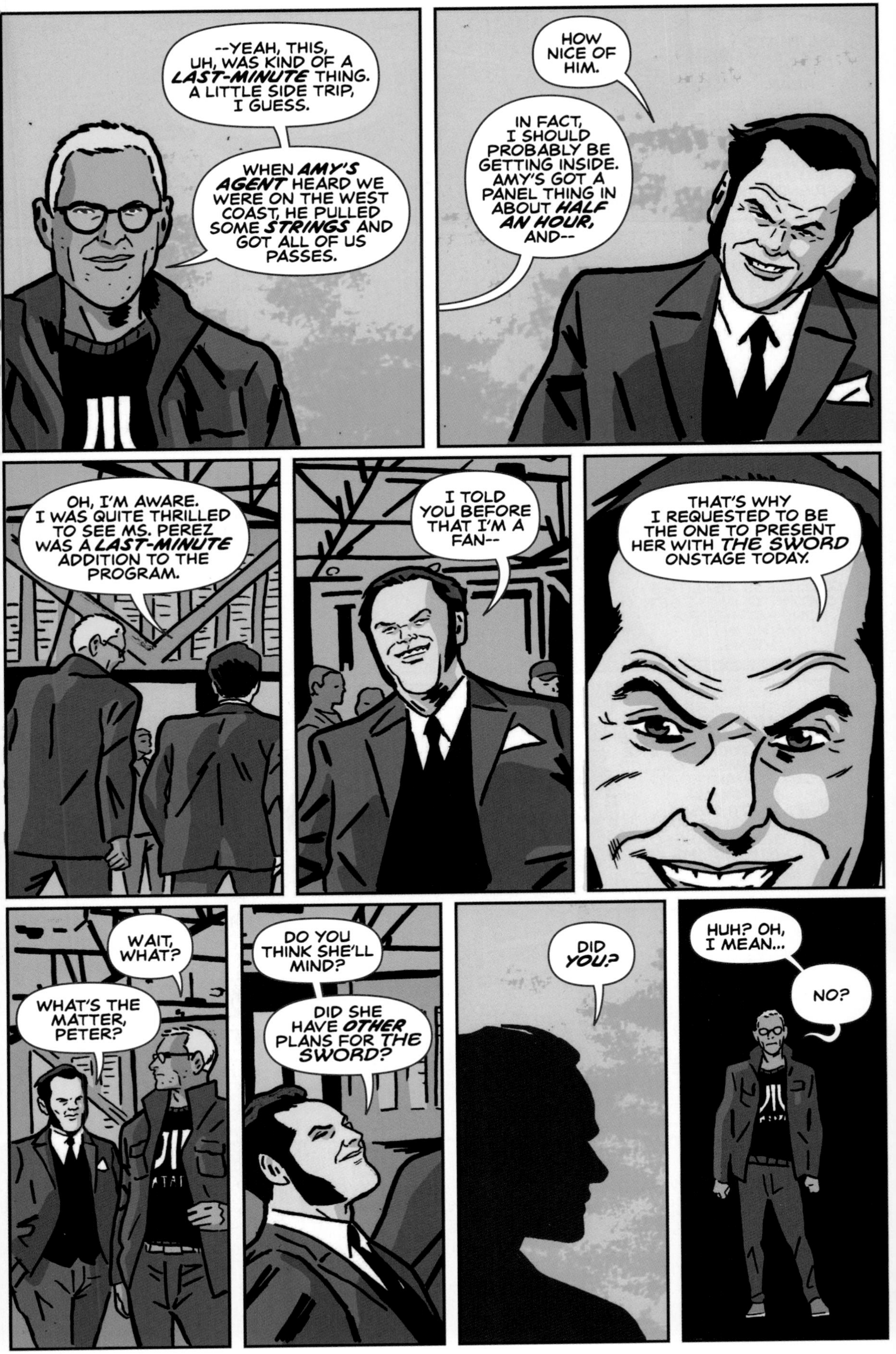
--YEAH, THIS, UH, WAS KIND OF A *LAST-MINUTE* THING. A LITTLE SIDE TRIP, I GUESS.
WHEN *AMY'S AGENT* HEARD WE WERE ON THE WEST COAST, HE PULLED SOME *STRINGS* AND GOT ALL OF US PASSES.
HOW NICE OF HIM.
IN FACT, I SHOULD PROBABLY BE GETTING INSIDE. AMY'S GOT A PANEL THING IN ABOUT *HALF AN HOUR,* AND--
OH, I'M AWARE. I WAS QUITE THRILLED TO SEE MS. PEREZ WAS A *LAST-MINUTE* ADDITION TO THE PROGRAM.
I TOLD YOU BEFORE THAT I'M A FAN--
THAT'S WHY I REQUESTED TO BE THE ONE TO PRESENT HER WITH *THE SWORD* ONSTAGE TODAY.
WAIT, WHAT?
WHAT'S THE MATTER, PETER?
DO YOU THINK SHE'LL MIND?
DID SHE HAVE *OTHER* PLANS FOR *THE SWORD?*
DID *YOU?*
HUH? OH, I MEAN...
NO?

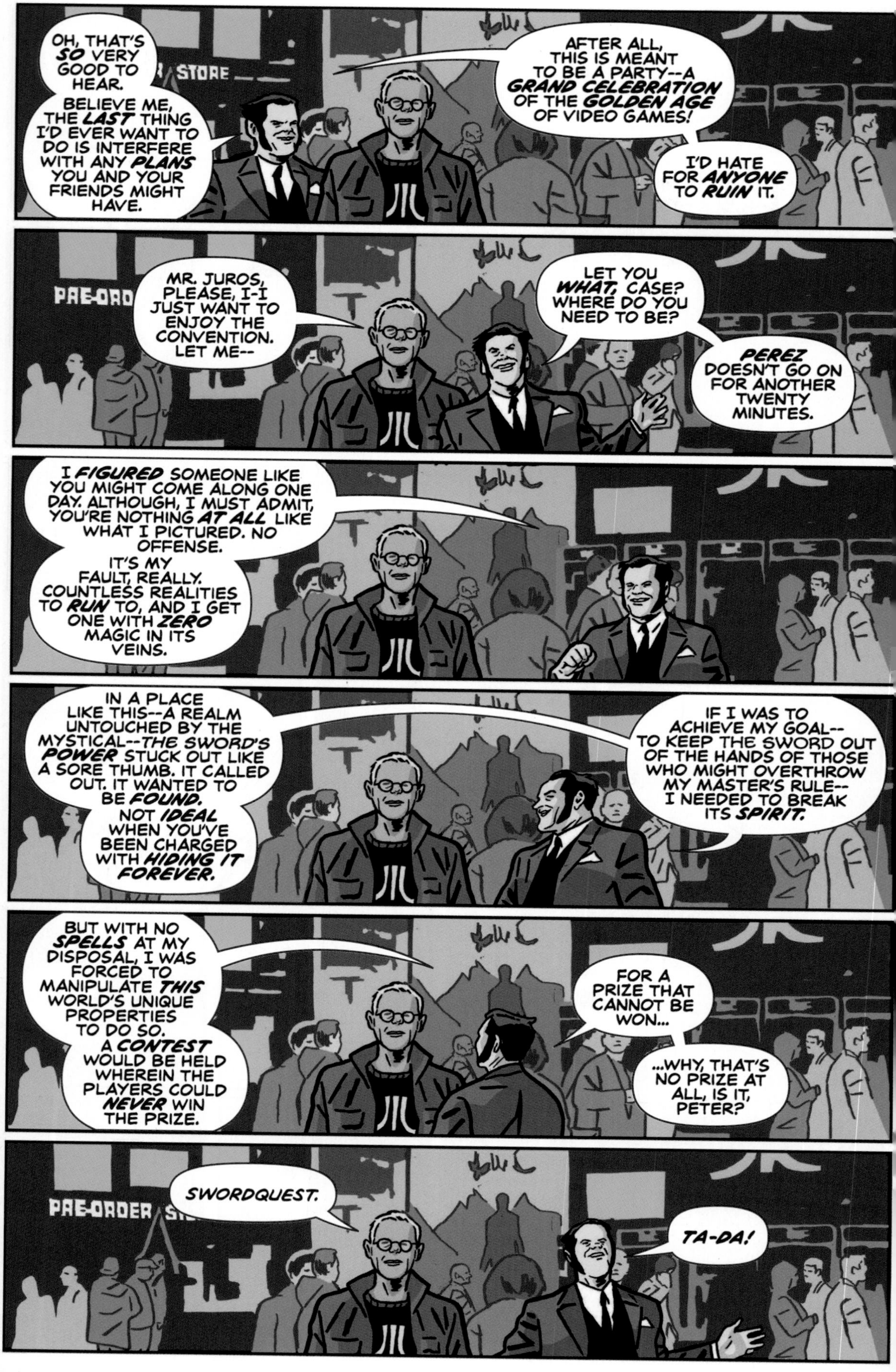
OH, THAT'S SO VERY GOOD TO HEAR.
BELIEVE ME, THE LAST THING I'D EVER WANT TO DO IS INTERFERE WITH ANY PLANS YOU AND YOUR FRIENDS MIGHT HAVE.
STORE
AFTER ALL, THIS IS MEANT TO BE A PARTY--A GRAND CELEBRATION OF THE GOLDEN AGE OF VIDEO GAMES!
I'D HATE FOR ANYONE TO RUIN IT.
MR. JUROS, PLEASE, I-I JUST WANT TO ENJOY THE CONVENTION. LET ME--
LET YOU WHAT, CASE? WHERE DO YOU NEED TO BE?
PEREZ DOESN'T GO ON FOR ANOTHER TWENTY MINUTES.
I FIGURED SOMEONE LIKE YOU MIGHT COME ALONG ONE DAY. ALTHOUGH, I MUST ADMIT, YOU'RE NOTHING AT ALL LIKE WHAT I PICTURED. NO OFFENSE.
IT'S MY FAULT, REALLY. COUNTLESS REALITIES TO RUN TO, AND I GET ONE WITH ZERO MAGIC IN ITS VEINS.
IN A PLACE LIKE THIS--A REALM UNTOUCHED BY THE MYSTICAL--THE SWORD'S POWER STUCK OUT LIKE A SORE THUMB. IT CALLED OUT. IT WANTED TO BE FOUND.
NOT IDEAL WHEN YOU'VE BEEN CHARGED WITH HIDING IT FOREVER.
IF I WAS TO ACHIEVE MY GOAL--TO KEEP THE SWORD OUT OF THE HANDS OF THOSE WHO MIGHT OVERTHROW MY MASTER'S RULE--I NEEDED TO BREAK ITS SPIRIT.
BUT WITH NO SPELLS AT MY DISPOSAL, I WAS FORCED TO MANIPULATE THIS WORLD'S UNIQUE PROPERTIES TO DO SO.
A CONTEST WOULD BE HELD WHEREIN THE PLAYERS COULD NEVER WIN THE PRIZE.
FOR A PRIZE THAT CANNOT BE WON...
...WHY, THAT'S NO PRIZE AT ALL, IS IT, PETER?
PRE-ORDER
SWORDQUEST.
TA-DA!

BUT-- WHY DOES IT WANT *ME?* WHY NOW?

I HAVE NO IDEA!

MAYBE IT FEELS SORRY FOR YOU. MAYBE YOU REMIND THE DAMN THING OF *RULERO,* BEFORE HE WAS...

TOLERABLE.

WHATEVER THE CASE IS-- NO PUN INTENDED-- WHATEVER *THE SWORD'S* LEADING YOU TO DO--

IGNORE IT!

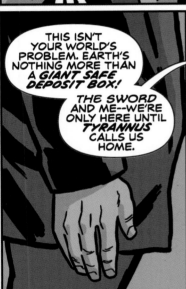

THIS ISN'T YOUR WORLD'S PROBLEM. EARTH'S NOTHING MORE THAN A *GIANT SAFE DEPOSIT BOX!*

THE SWORD AND ME--WE'RE ONLY HERE UNTIL *TYRANNUS* CALLS US HOME.

LEAVE *NOW,* AND I SWEAR I'LL FORGET I EVER SAW YOU. SAVE YOUR FRIENDS THE EMBARRASSMENT OF GOING TO JAIL, AND YOURSELF THE--WELL...

JUST SAVE YOURSELF, PETER.

I CAN'T.

IT WON'T LET ME.

SO *THE SWORD* SPEAKS TO YOU, THEN? GUIDES YOU? TELLS YOU WHAT TO *DO?*

TELL ME, PETER, I'VE GOT TO KNOW--

WHAT'S IT TELLING YOU TO DO *RIGHT NOW?*

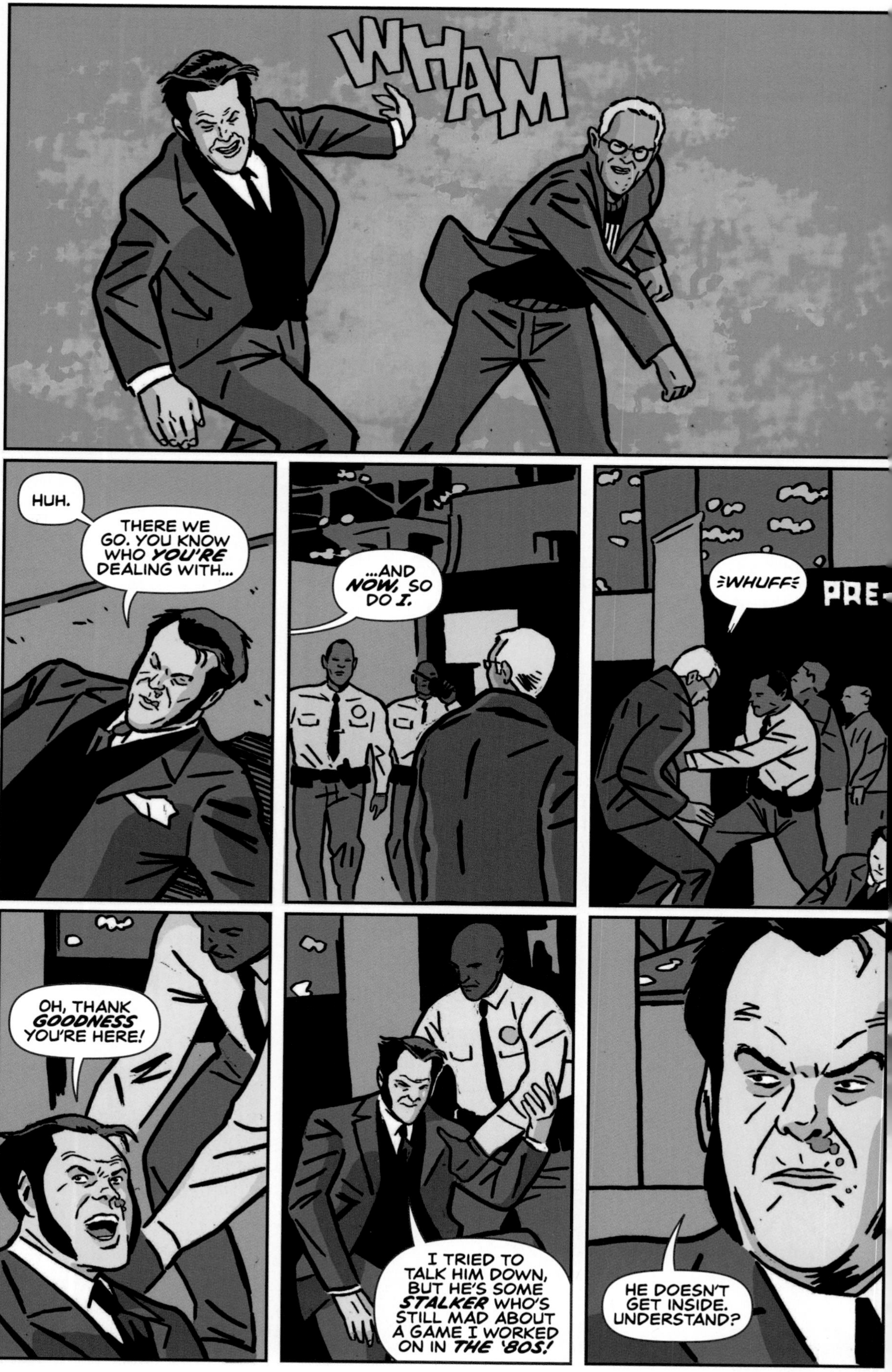
WHAM
HUH.
THERE WE GO. YOU KNOW WHO *YOU'RE* DEALING WITH...
...AND *NOW,* SO DO *I.*
WHUFF
PRE-
OH, THANK *GOODNESS* YOU'RE HERE!
I TRIED TO TALK HIM DOWN, BUT HE'S SOME *STALKER* WHO'S STILL MAD ABOUT A GAME I WORKED ON IN *THE '80S!*
HE DOESN'T GET INSIDE. UNDERSTAND?

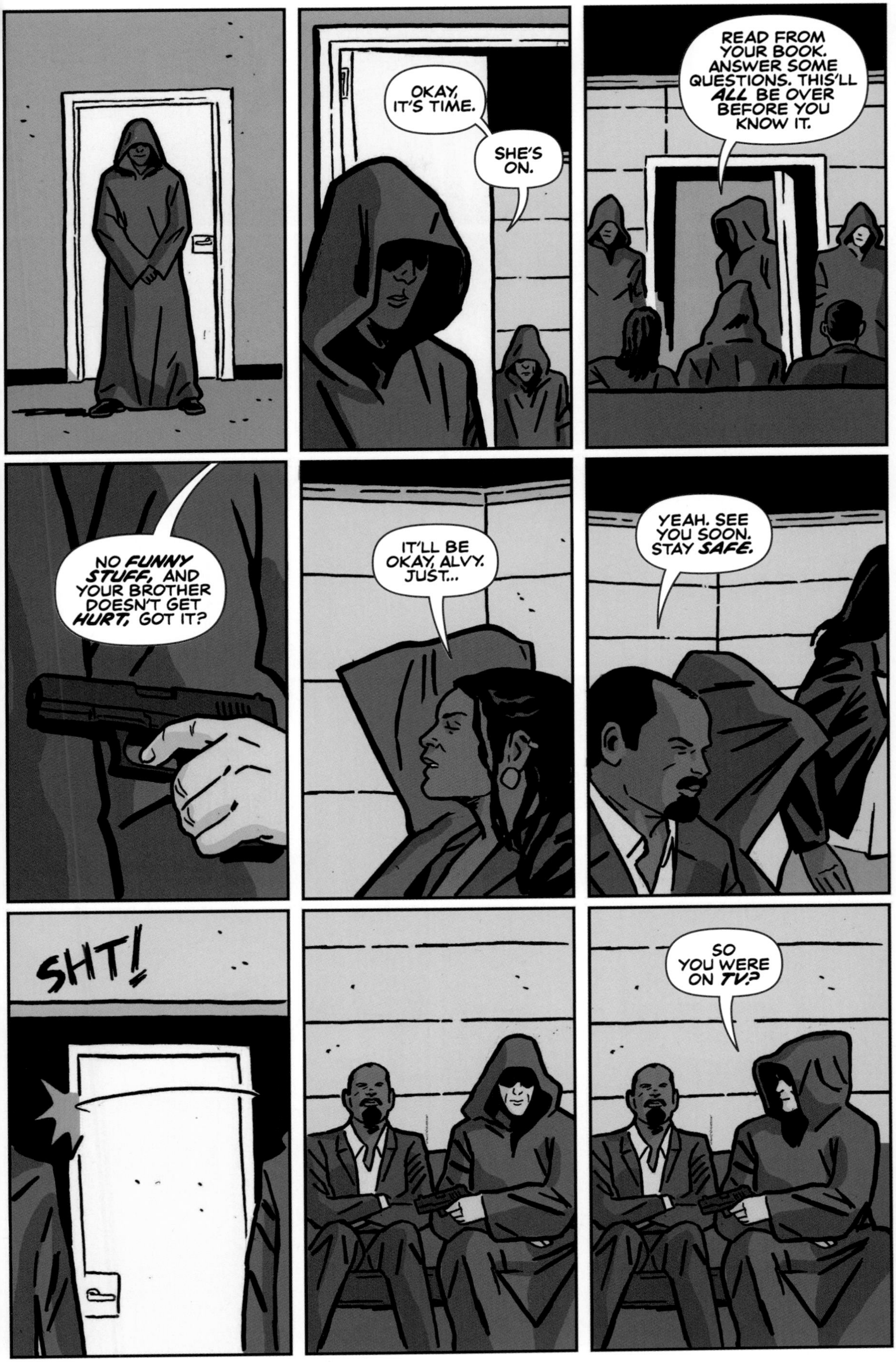
OKAY, IT'S TIME.
SHE'S ON.
READ FROM YOUR BOOK. ANSWER SOME QUESTIONS. THIS'LL ALL BE OVER BEFORE YOU KNOW IT.
NO FUNNY STUFF, AND YOUR BROTHER DOESN'T GET HURT, GOT IT?
IT'LL BE OKAY, ALVY. JUST...
YEAH. SEE YOU SOON. STAY SAFE.
SHT!
SO YOU WERE ON TV?

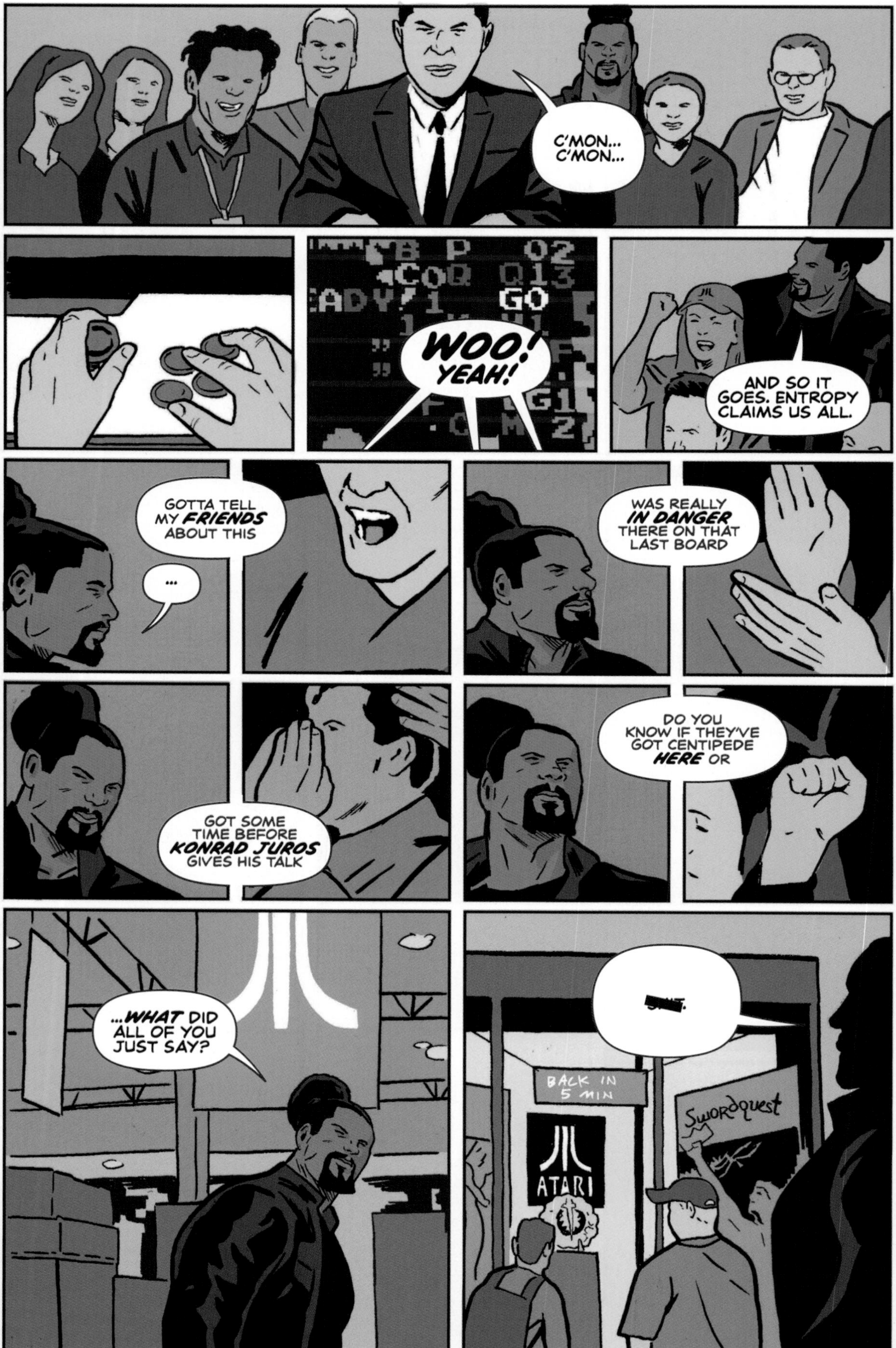
C'MON... C'MON...
WOO! YEAH!
AND SO IT GOES. ENTROPY CLAIMS US ALL.
GOTTA TELL MY FRIENDS ABOUT THIS
...
WAS REALLY IN DANGER THERE ON THAT LAST BOARD
GOT SOME TIME BEFORE KONRAD JUROS GIVES HIS TALK
DO YOU KNOW IF THEY'VE GOT CENTIPEDE HERE OR
...WHAT DID ALL OF YOU JUST SAY?
[redacted].
BACK IN 5 MIN
ATARI
Swordquest

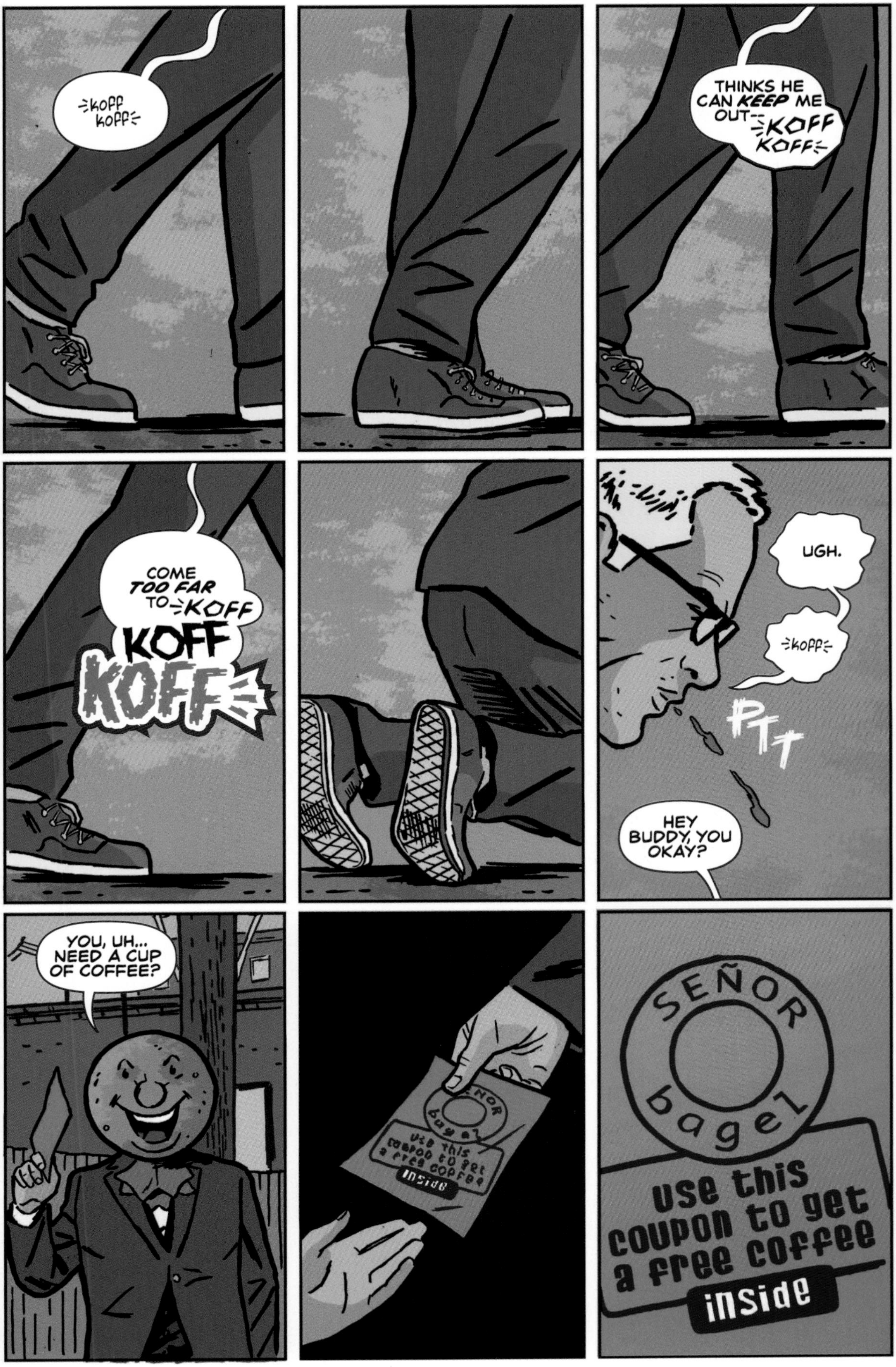

koff koff
THINKS HE CAN KEEP ME OUT- KOFF KOFF
COME TOO FAR TO- KOFF
KOFF
KOFF
UGH.
koff
PTT
HEY BUDDY, YOU OKAY?
YOU, UH... NEED A CUP OF COFFEE?
SEÑOR bagel
use this coupon to get a free coffee
inside

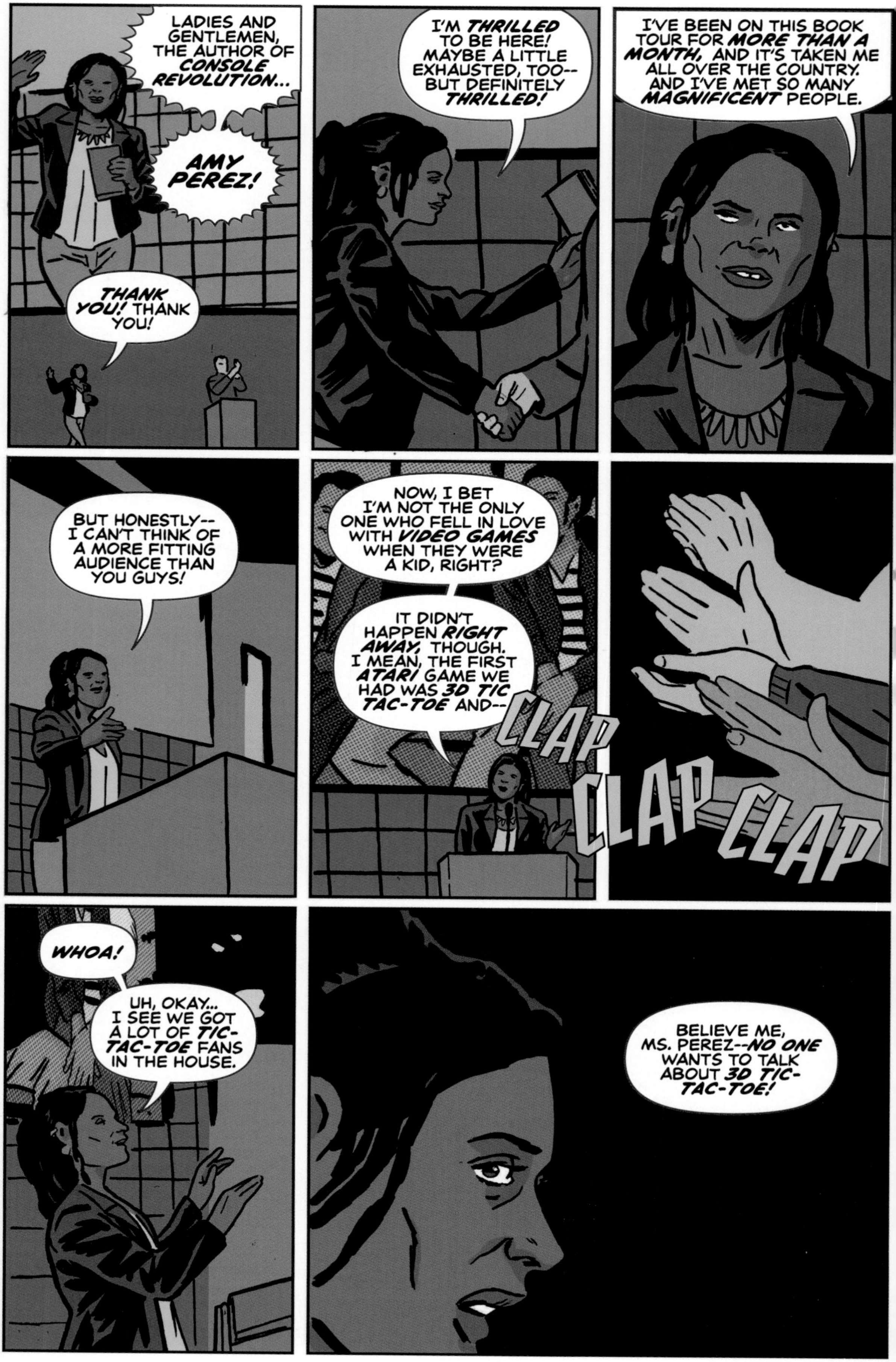
LADIES AND GENTLEMEN, THE AUTHOR OF CONSOLE REVOLUTION...
AMY PEREZ!
THANK YOU! THANK YOU!
I'M THRILLED TO BE HERE! MAYBE A LITTLE EXHAUSTED, TOO-- BUT DEFINITELY THRILLED!
I'VE BEEN ON THIS BOOK TOUR FOR MORE THAN A MONTH, AND IT'S TAKEN ME ALL OVER THE COUNTRY. AND I'VE MET SO MANY MAGNIFICENT PEOPLE.
BUT HONESTLY-- I CAN'T THINK OF A MORE FITTING AUDIENCE THAN YOU GUYS!
NOW, I BET I'M NOT THE ONLY ONE WHO FELL IN LOVE WITH VIDEO GAMES WHEN THEY WERE A KID, RIGHT?
IT DIDN'T HAPPEN RIGHT AWAY, THOUGH. I MEAN, THE FIRST ATARI GAME WE HAD WAS 3D TIC TAC-TOE AND--
CLAP
CLAP
CLAP
WHOA!
UH, OKAY... I SEE WE GOT A LOT OF TIC-TAC-TOE FANS IN THE HOUSE.
BELIEVE ME, MS. PEREZ--NO ONE WANTS TO TALK ABOUT 3D TIC-TAC-TOE!

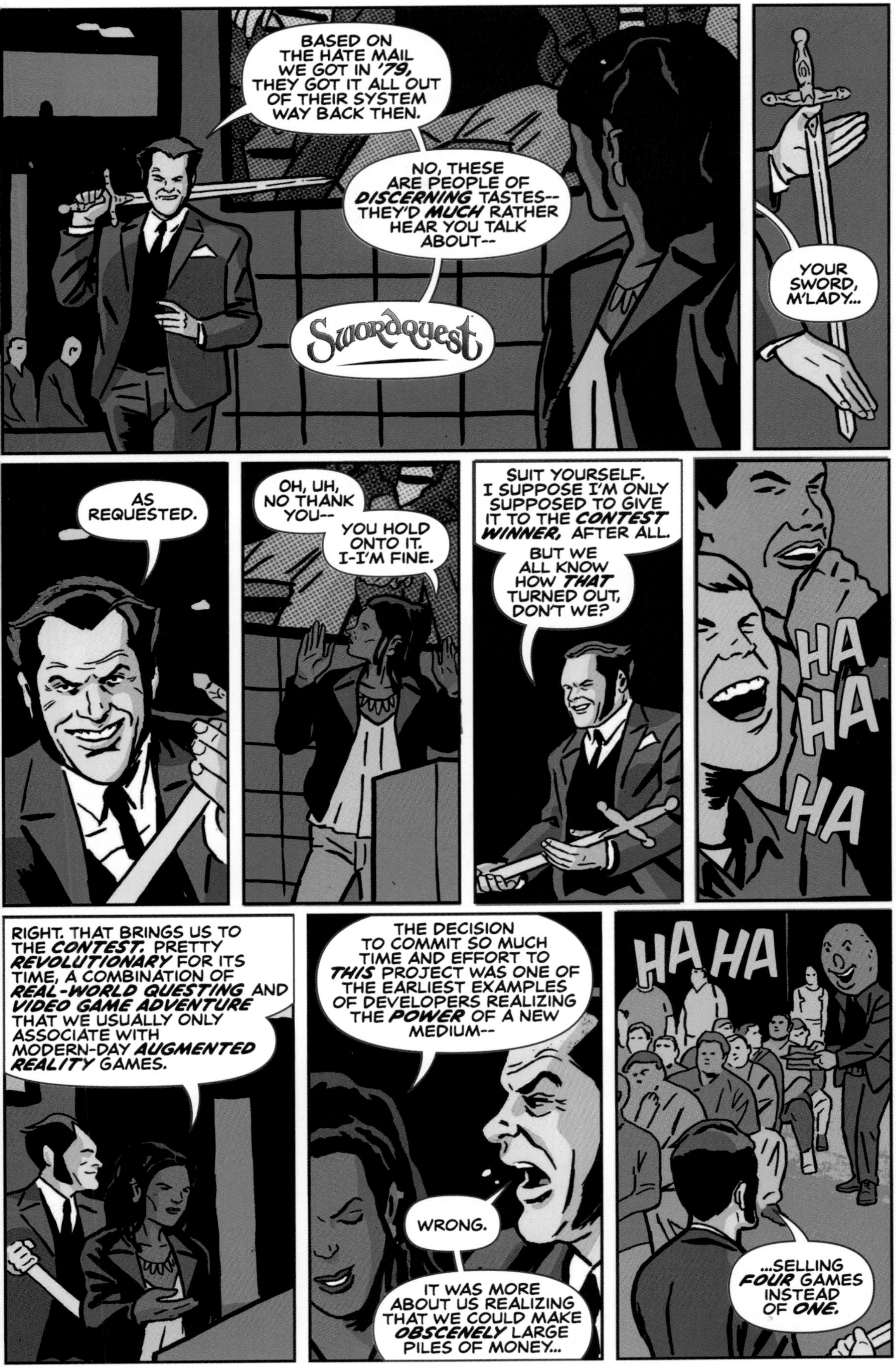
BASED ON THE HATE MAIL WE GOT IN '79, THEY GOT IT ALL OUT OF THEIR SYSTEM WAY BACK THEN.
NO, THESE ARE PEOPLE OF DISCERNING TASTES-- THEY'D MUCH RATHER HEAR YOU TALK ABOUT--
Swordquest
YOUR SWORD, M'LADY...
AS REQUESTED.
OH, UH, NO THANK YOU--
YOU HOLD ONTO IT. I-I'M FINE.
SUIT YOURSELF. I SUPPOSE I'M ONLY SUPPOSED TO GIVE IT TO THE CONTEST WINNER, AFTER ALL.
BUT WE ALL KNOW HOW THAT TURNED OUT, DON'T WE?
HA HA HA
RIGHT. THAT BRINGS US TO THE CONTEST. PRETTY REVOLUTIONARY FOR ITS TIME, A COMBINATION OF REAL-WORLD QUESTING AND VIDEO GAME ADVENTURE THAT WE USUALLY ONLY ASSOCIATE WITH MODERN-DAY AUGMENTED REALITY GAMES.
THE DECISION TO COMMIT SO MUCH TIME AND EFFORT TO THIS PROJECT WAS ONE OF THE EARLIEST EXAMPLES OF DEVELOPERS REALIZING THE POWER OF A NEW MEDIUM--
WRONG.
IT WAS MORE ABOUT US REALIZING THAT WE COULD MAKE OBSCENELY LARGE PILES OF MONEY...
HAHA
...SELLING FOUR GAMES INSTEAD OF ONE.

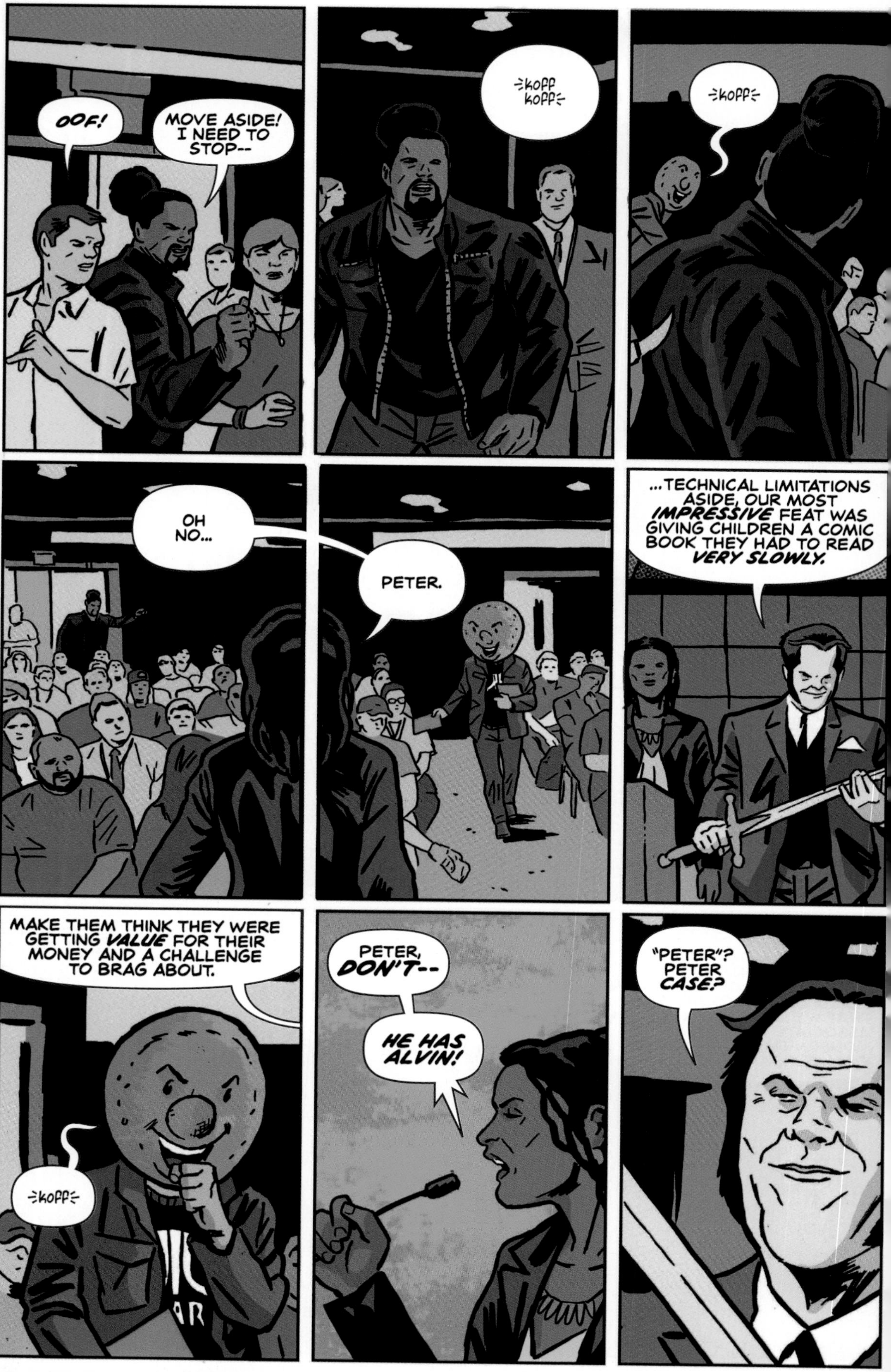
OOF!
MOVE ASIDE! I NEED TO STOP--
KOFF KOFF
KOFF
OH NO...
PETER.
...TECHNICAL LIMITATIONS ASIDE, OUR MOST IMPRESSIVE FEAT WAS GIVING CHILDREN A COMIC BOOK THEY HAD TO READ VERY SLOWLY.
MAKE THEM THINK THEY WERE GETTING VALUE FOR THEIR MONEY AND A CHALLENGE TO BRAG ABOUT.
KOFF
PETER, DON'T--
HE HAS ALVIN!
"PETER"? PETER CASE?

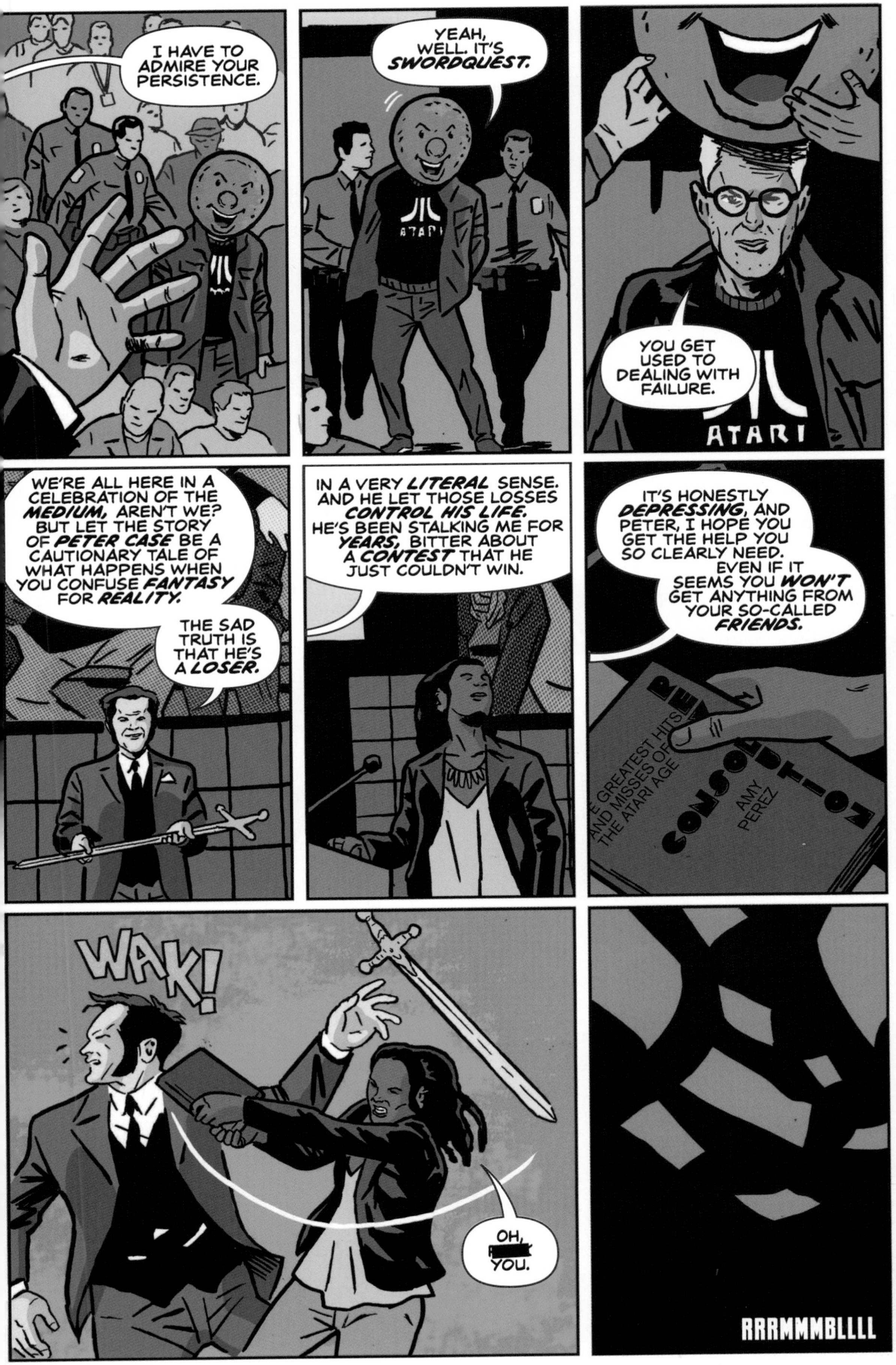
I HAVE TO ADMIRE YOUR PERSISTENCE.
YEAH, WELL. IT'S *SWORDQUEST.*
YOU GET USED TO DEALING WITH FAILURE.
ATARI
WE'RE ALL HERE IN A CELEBRATION OF THE *MEDIUM,* AREN'T WE? BUT LET THE STORY OF *PETER CASE* BE A CAUTIONARY TALE OF WHAT HAPPENS WHEN YOU CONFUSE *FANTASY* FOR *REALITY.*
THE SAD TRUTH IS THAT HE'S A *LOSER.*
IN A VERY *LITERAL* SENSE. AND HE LET THOSE LOSSES *CONTROL HIS LIFE.* HE'S BEEN STALKING ME FOR *YEARS,* BITTER ABOUT A *CONTEST* THAT HE JUST COULDN'T WIN.
IT'S HONESTLY *DEPRESSING*, AND PETER, I HOPE YOU GET THE HELP YOU SO CLEARLY NEED.
EVEN IF IT SEEMS YOU *WON'T* GET ANYTHING FROM YOUR SO-CALLED *FRIENDS.*
E GREATEST HITS AND MISSES OF THE ATARI AGE
AMY PEREZ
WAK!
OH, [redacted] YOU.
RRRMMMBLLLL

PETER, GRAB IT!

≈KOFF KOFF≈ TRYING!

WE HAVE TO GET *ALVIN!* HE'S GOT HIS *GOON SQUAD* ON THEM!

SECURITY! THEY'RE AFTER THE SWORD!

C'MON...

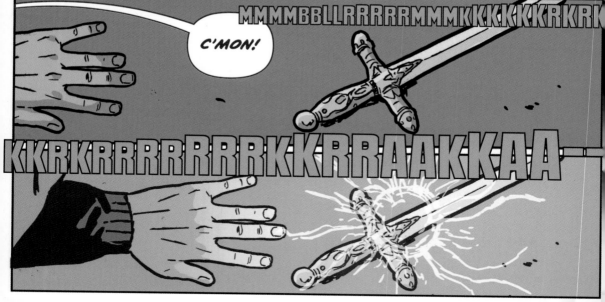

MMMMBBLLRRRRRMMMKKKKKKRKRK

C'MON!

KKRKRRRRRRRRKKRRAAKKAA

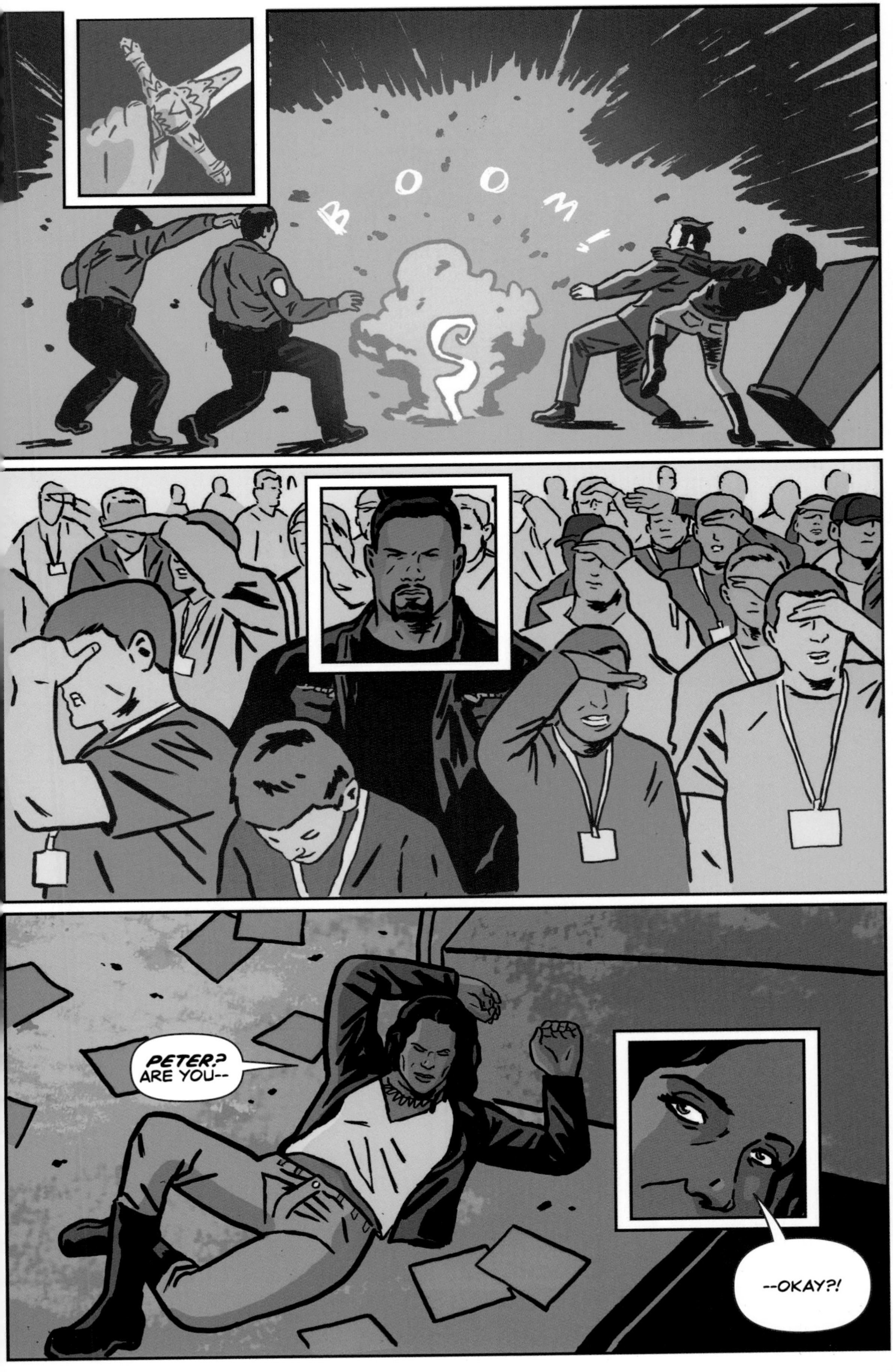
BOOOM!
PETER? ARE YOU--
--OKAY?!

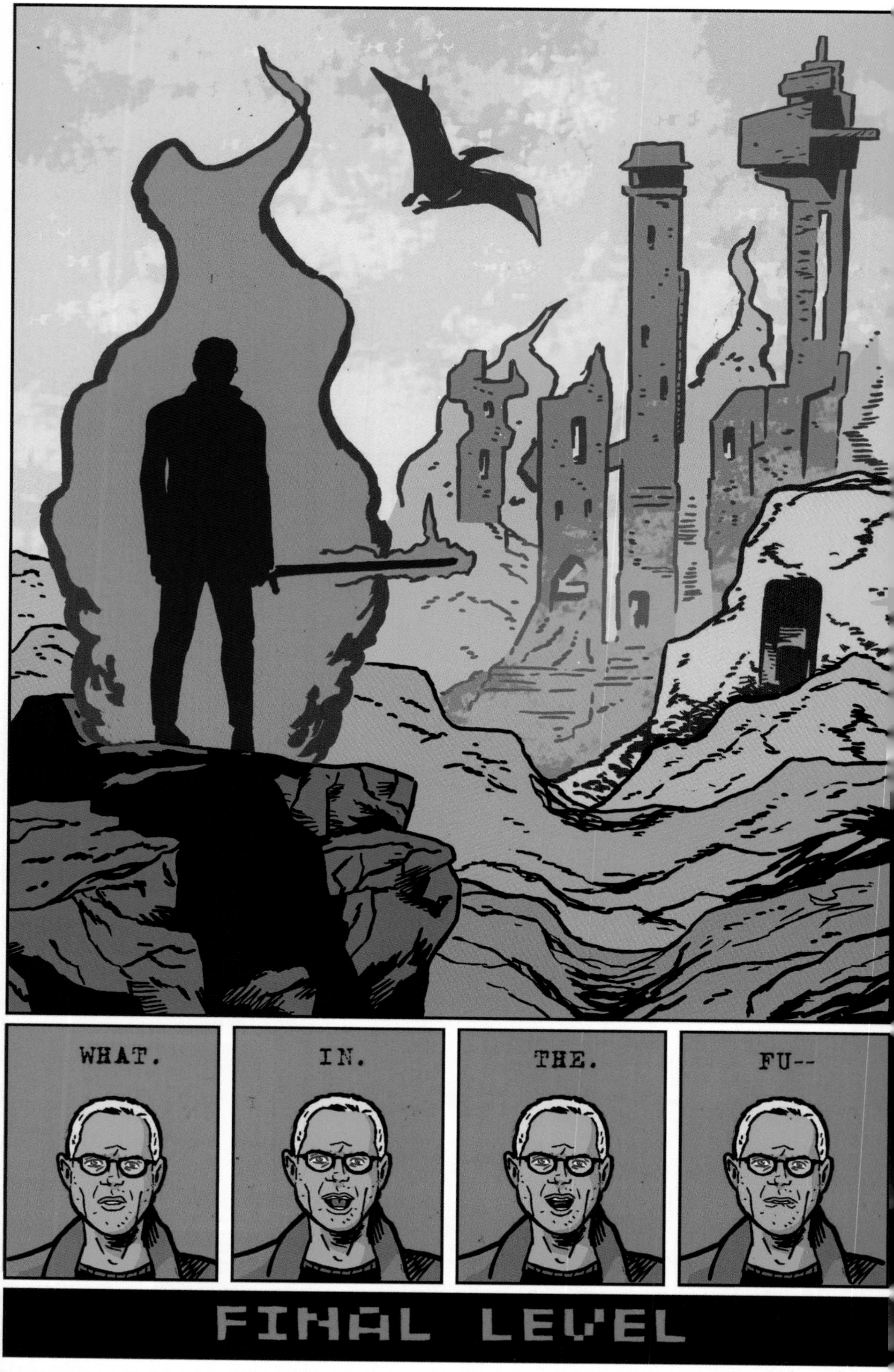
WHAT.
IN.
THE.
FU--
FINAL LEVEL

5

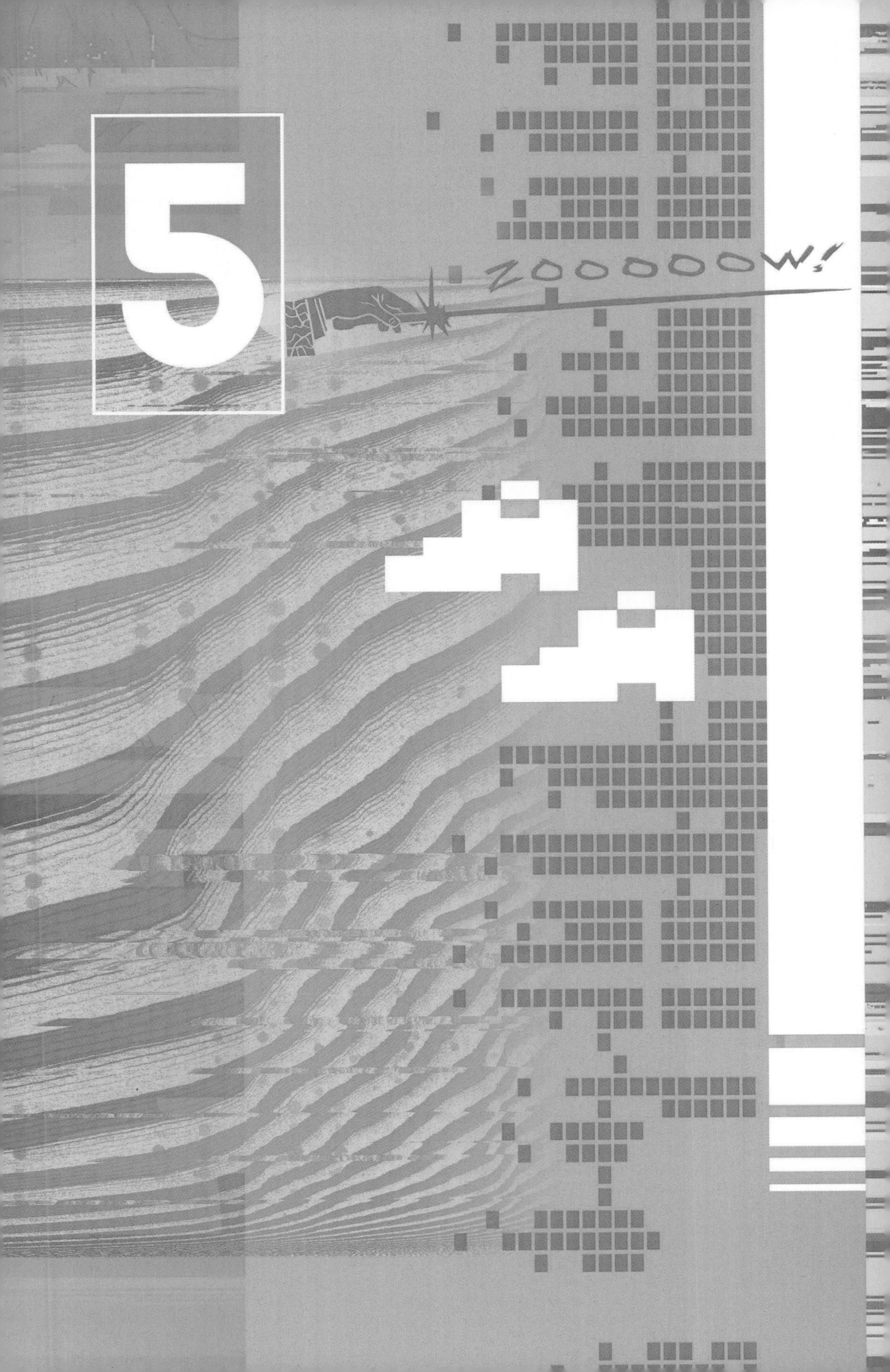
ZOOOOOW!

5

Art by GOÑI MONTES

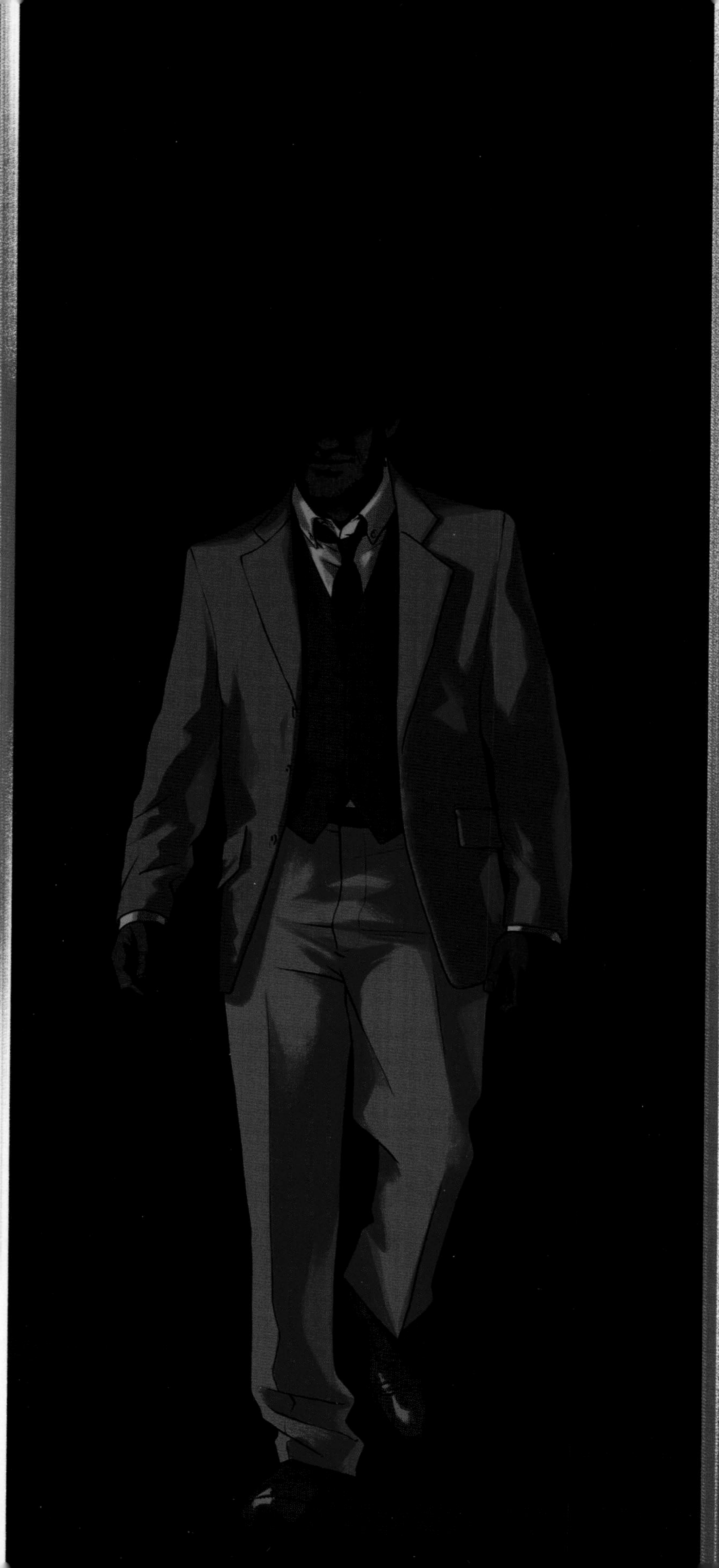

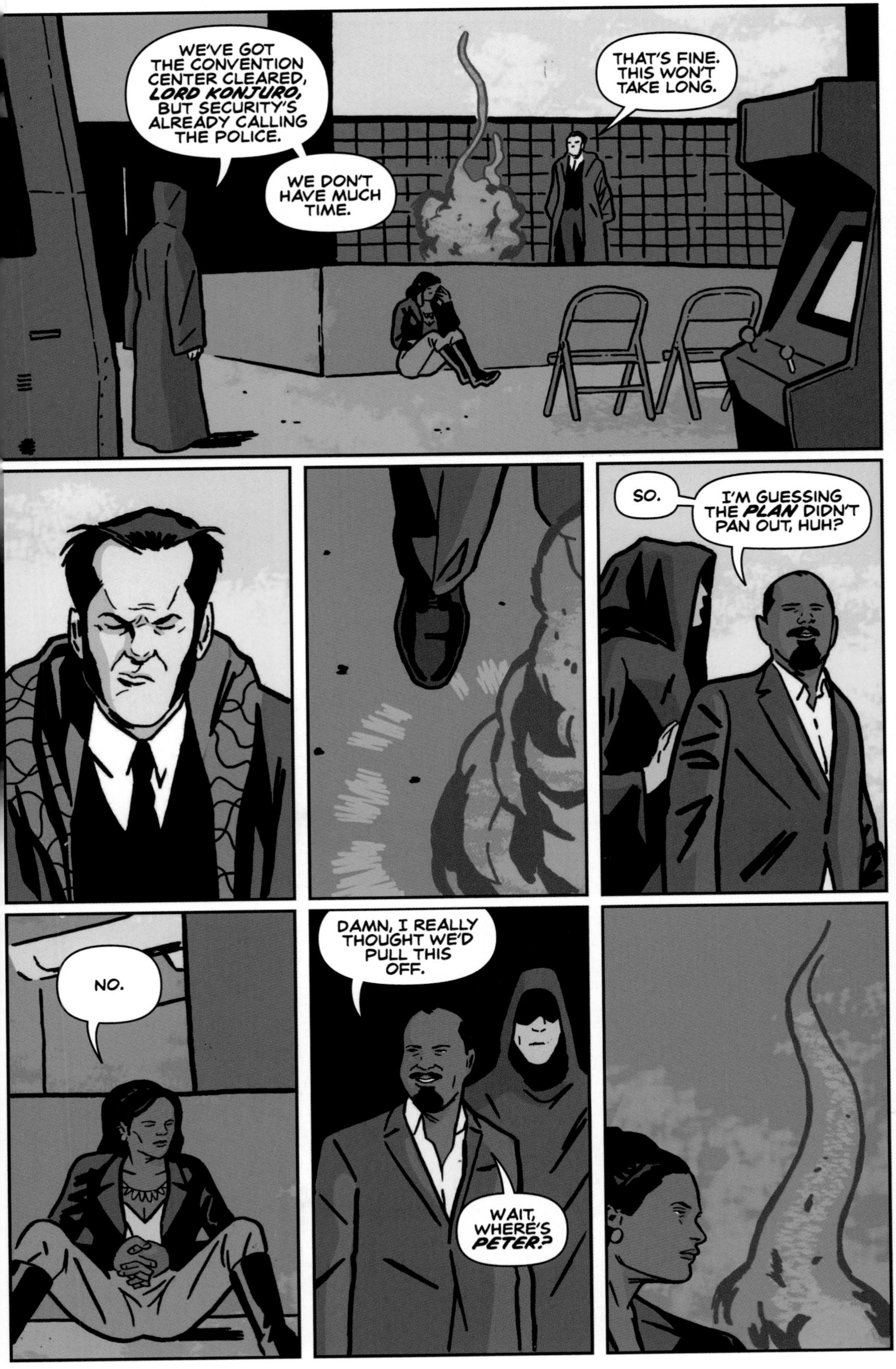
WE'VE GOT THE CONVENTION CENTER CLEARED, *LORD KONJURO,* BUT SECURITY'S ALREADY CALLING THE POLICE.
WE DON'T HAVE MUCH TIME.
THAT'S FINE. THIS WON'T TAKE LONG.
SO.
I'M GUESSING THE *PLAN* DIDN'T PAN OUT, HUH?
NO.
DAMN, I REALLY THOUGHT WE'D PULL THIS OFF.
WAIT, WHERE'S *PETER?*

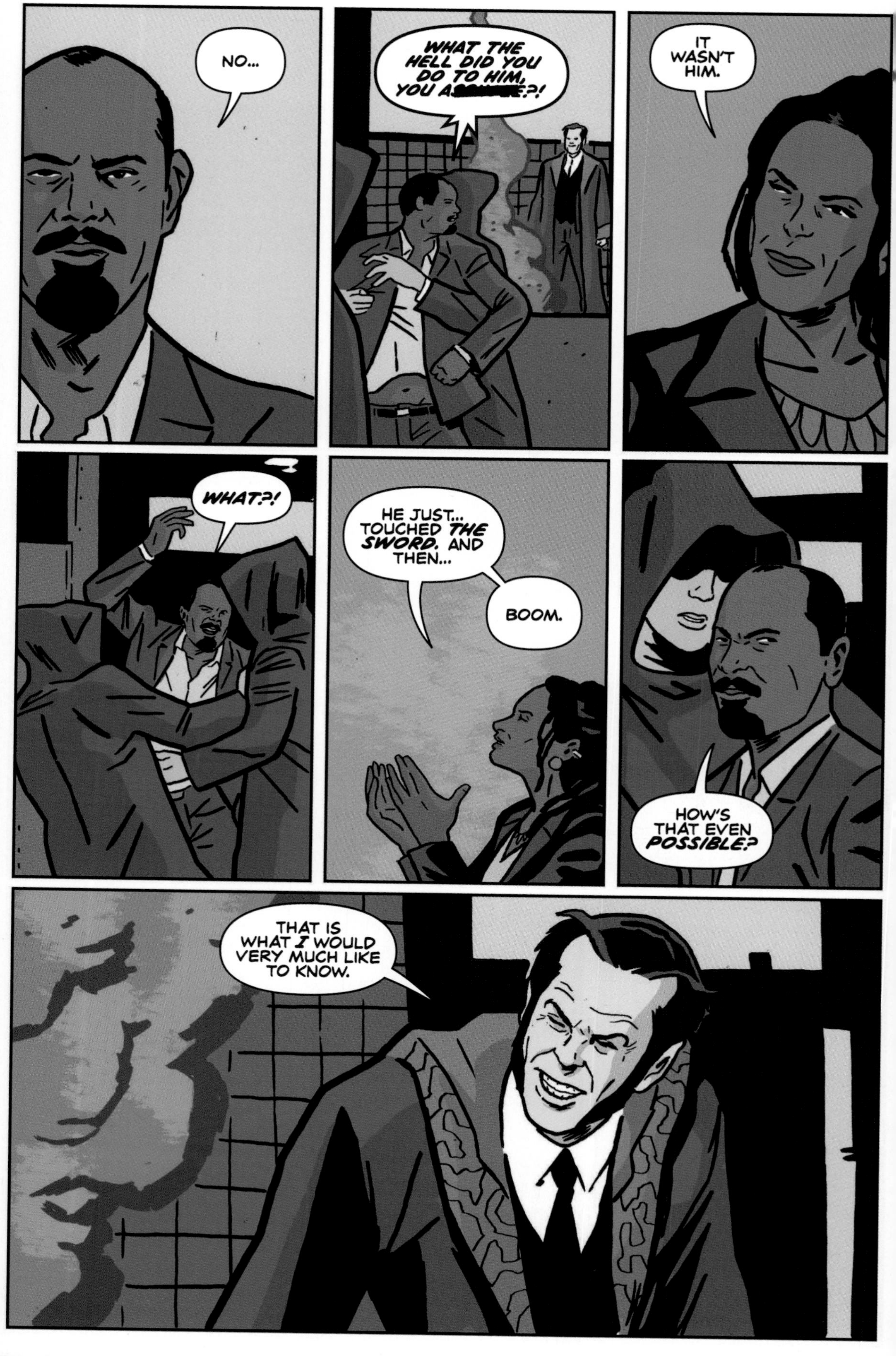
NO...
WHAT THE HELL DID YOU DO TO HIM, YOU A[redacted]E?!
IT WASN'T HIM.
WHAT?!
HE JUST... TOUCHED THE SWORD. AND THEN...
BOOM.
HOW'S THAT EVEN POSSIBLE?
THAT IS WHAT I WOULD VERY MUCH LIKE TO KNOW.

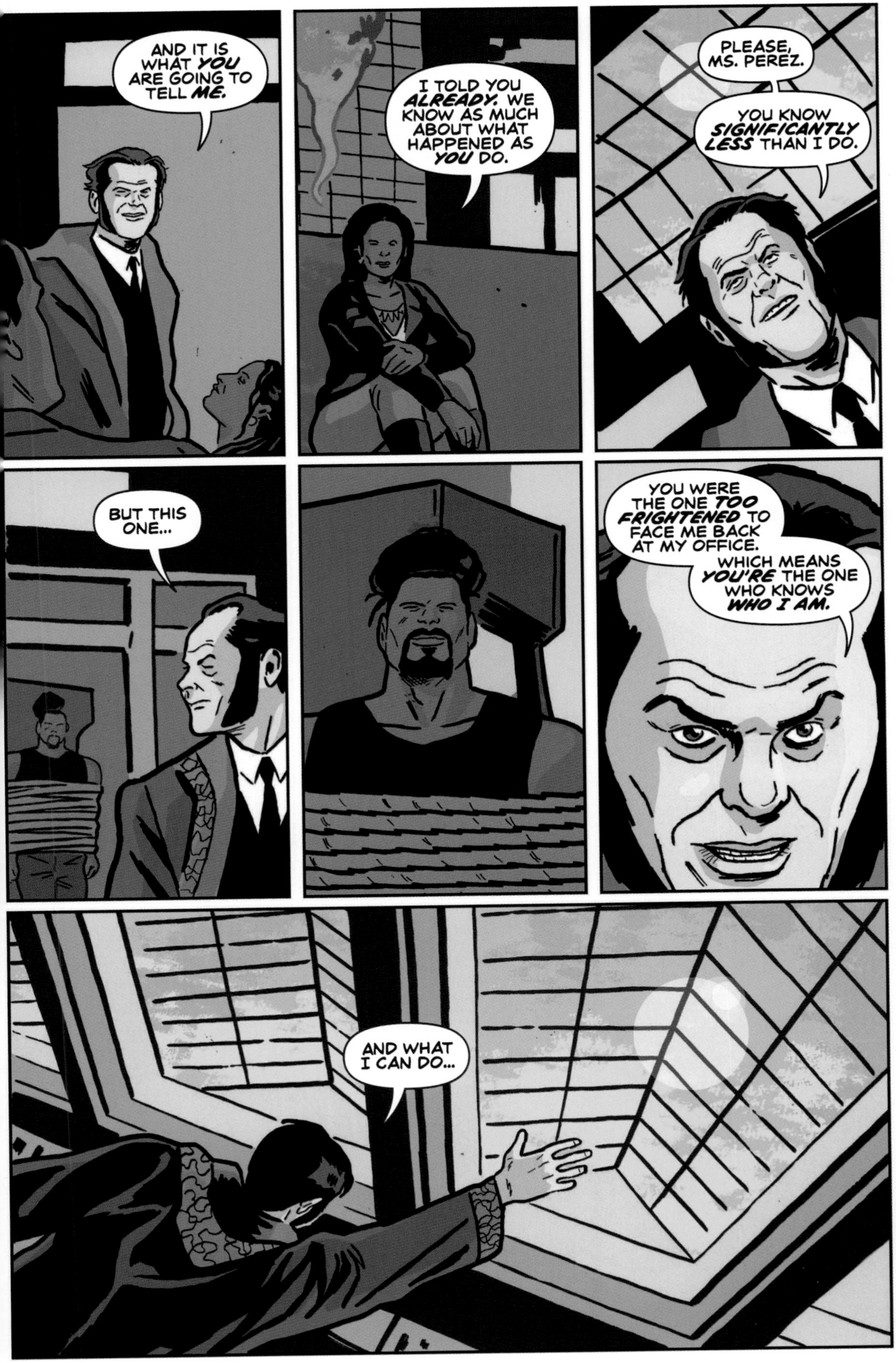
AND IT IS WHAT YOU ARE GOING TO TELL ME.
I TOLD YOU ALREADY. WE KNOW AS MUCH ABOUT WHAT HAPPENED AS YOU DO.
PLEASE, MS. PEREZ.
YOU KNOW SIGNIFICANTLY LESS THAN I DO.
BUT THIS ONE...
YOU WERE THE ONE TOO FRIGHTENED TO FACE ME BACK AT MY OFFICE.
WHICH MEANS YOU'RE THE ONE WHO KNOWS WHO I AM.
AND WHAT I CAN DO...

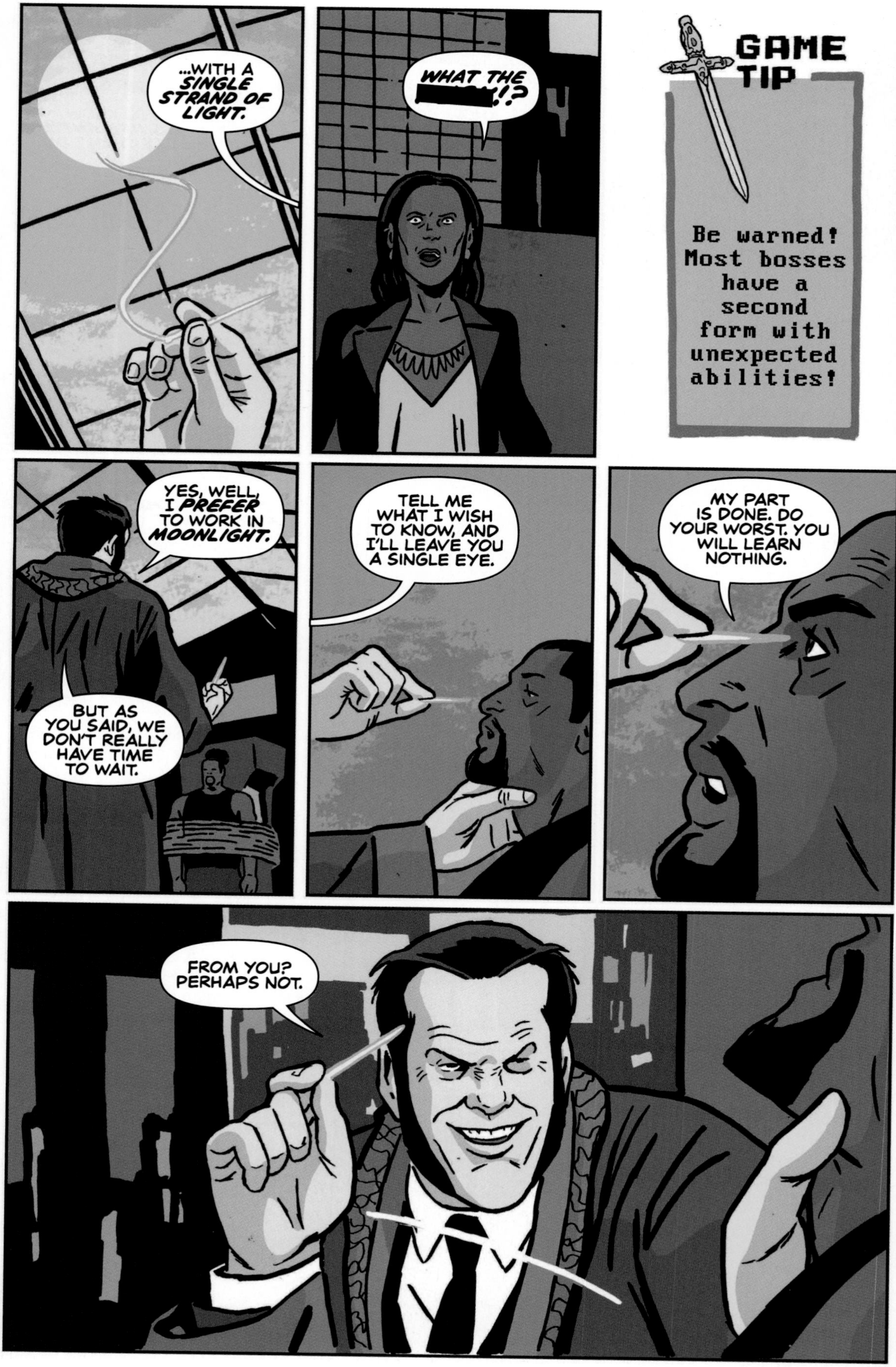
...WITH A SINGLE STRAND OF LIGHT.
WHAT THE [redacted]!?
GAME TIP
Be warned! Most bosses have a second form with unexpected abilities!
YES, WELL, I PREFER TO WORK IN MOONLIGHT.
BUT AS YOU SAID, WE DON'T REALLY HAVE TIME TO WAIT.
TELL ME WHAT I WISH TO KNOW, AND I'LL LEAVE YOU A SINGLE EYE.
MY PART IS DONE. DO YOUR WORST. YOU WILL LEARN NOTHING.
FROM YOU? PERHAPS NOT.

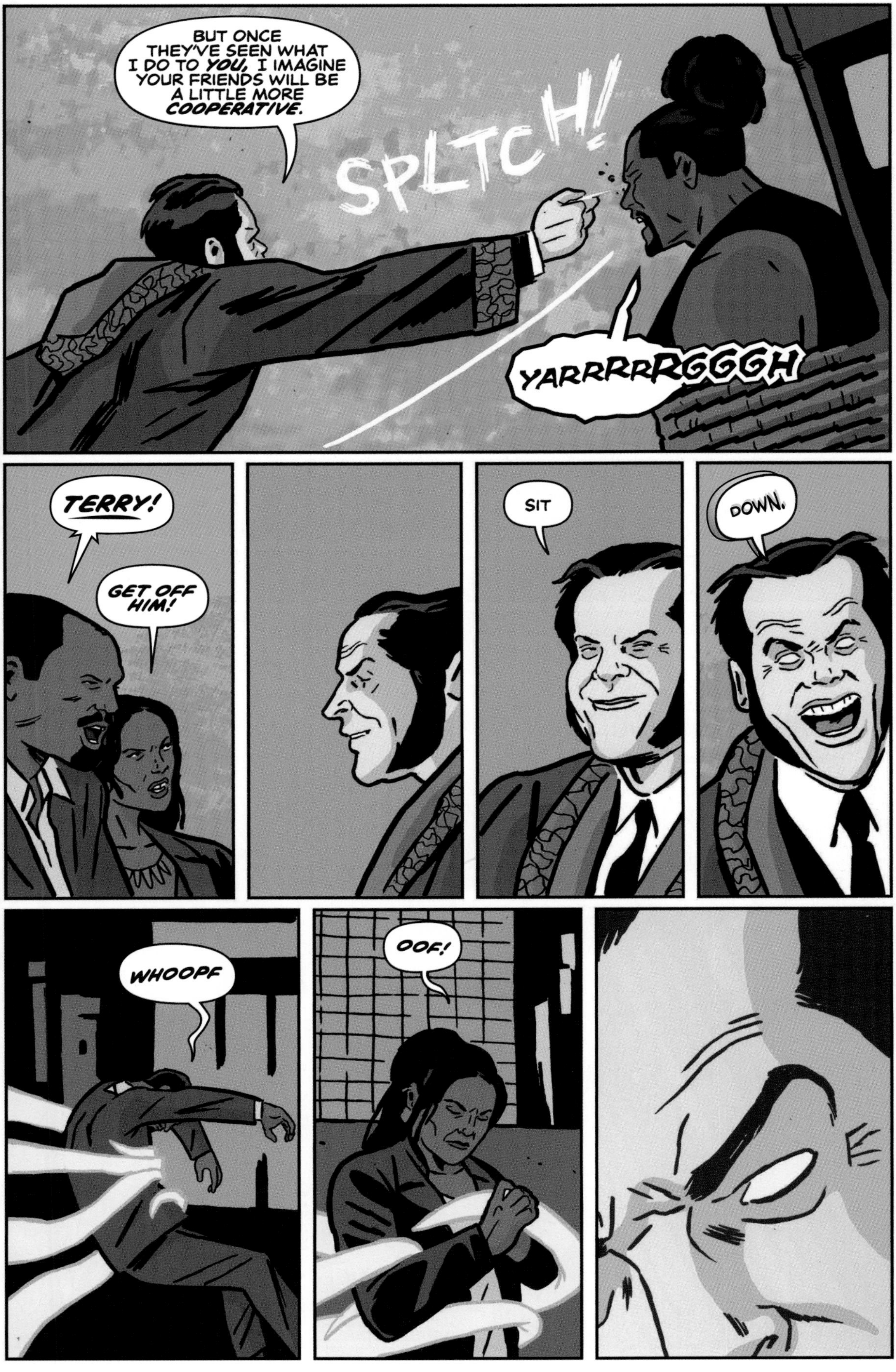
BUT ONCE THEY'VE SEEN WHAT I DO TO *YOU,* I IMAGINE YOUR FRIENDS WILL BE A LITTLE MORE *COOPERATIVE.*
SPLTCH!
YARRRRRGGGH
TERRY!
GET OFF HIM!
SIT
DOWN.
WHOOPF
OOF!

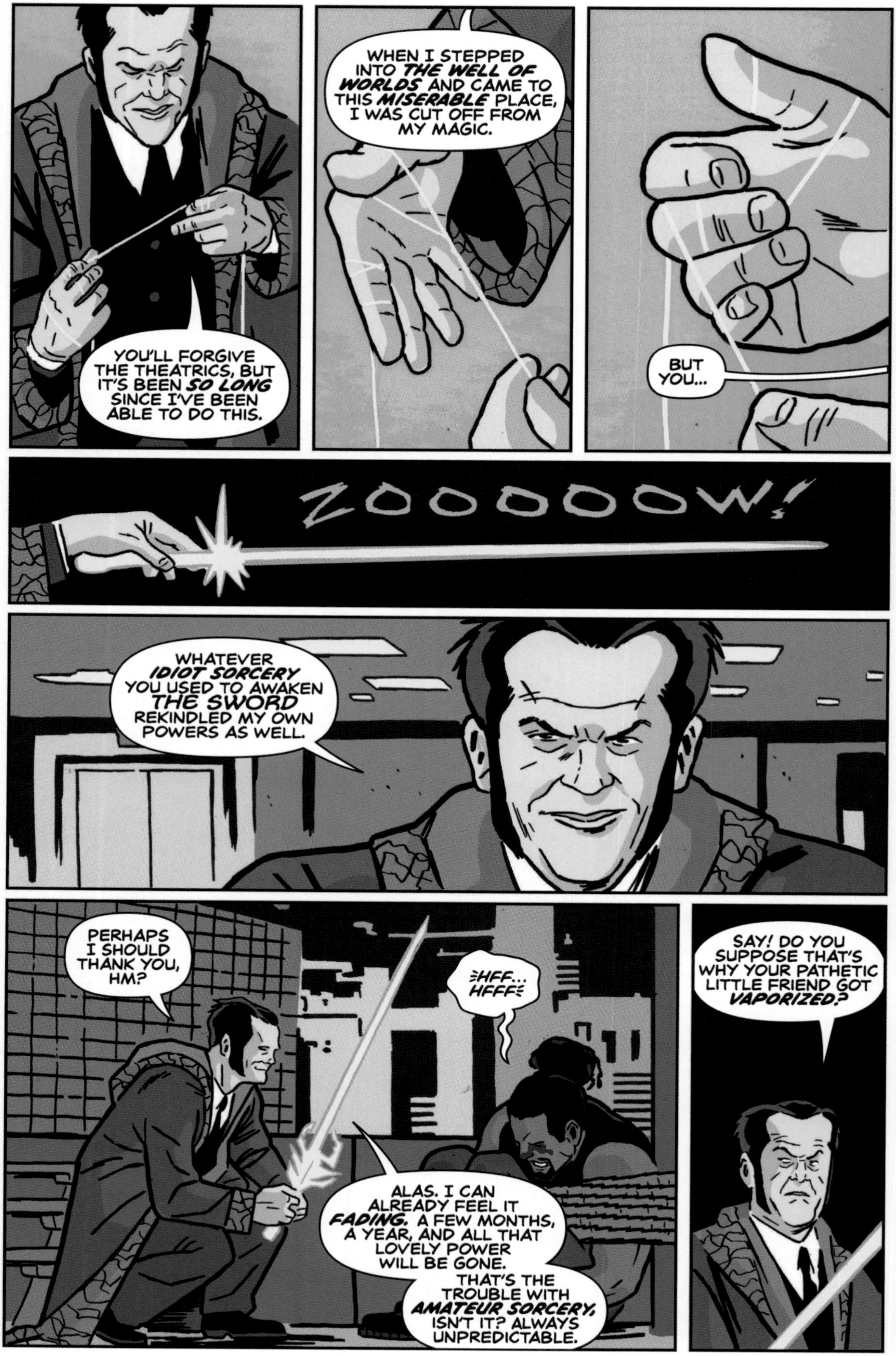
YOU'LL FORGIVE THE THEATRICS, BUT IT'S BEEN SO LONG SINCE I'VE BEEN ABLE TO DO THIS.
WHEN I STEPPED INTO THE WELL OF WORLDS AND CAME TO THIS MISERABLE PLACE, I WAS CUT OFF FROM MY MAGIC.
BUT YOU...
ZOOOOOOW!
WHATEVER IDIOT SORCERY YOU USED TO AWAKEN THE SWORD REKINDLED MY OWN POWERS AS WELL.
PERHAPS I SHOULD THANK YOU, HM?
HFF... HFFF
ALAS. I CAN ALREADY FEEL IT FADING. A FEW MONTHS, A YEAR, AND ALL THAT LOVELY POWER WILL BE GONE.
THAT'S THE TROUBLE WITH AMATEUR SORCERY, ISN'T IT? ALWAYS UNPREDICTABLE.
SAY! DO YOU SUPPOSE THAT'S WHY YOUR PATHETIC LITTLE FRIEND GOT VAPORIZED?

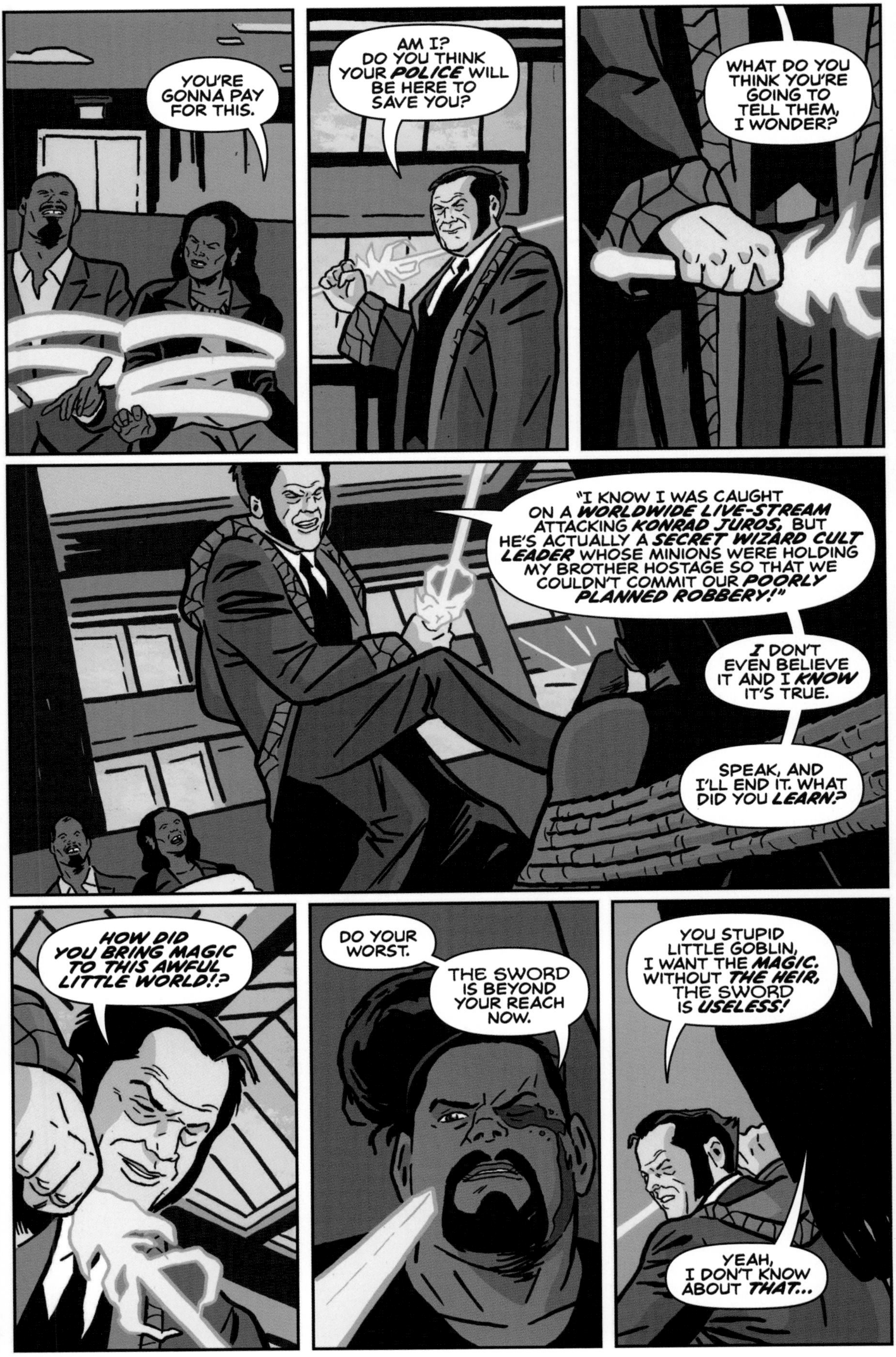
YOU'RE GONNA PAY FOR THIS.
AM I? DO YOU THINK YOUR *POLICE* WILL BE HERE TO SAVE YOU?
WHAT DO YOU THINK YOU'RE GOING TO TELL THEM, I WONDER?
"I KNOW I WAS CAUGHT ON A *WORLDWIDE LIVE-STREAM* ATTACKING *KONRAD JUROS,* BUT HE'S ACTUALLY A *SECRET WIZARD CULT LEADER* WHOSE MINIONS WERE HOLDING MY BROTHER HOSTAGE SO THAT WE COULDN'T COMMIT OUR *POORLY PLANNED ROBBERY!*"
I DON'T EVEN BELIEVE IT AND I *KNOW* IT'S TRUE.
SPEAK, AND I'LL END IT. WHAT DID YOU *LEARN?*
HOW DID YOU BRING MAGIC TO THIS AWFUL LITTLE WORLD!?
DO YOUR WORST.
THE SWORD IS BEYOND YOUR REACH NOW.
YOU STUPID LITTLE GOBLIN, I WANT THE *MAGIC.* WITHOUT *THE HEIR,* THE SWORD IS *USELESS!*
YEAH, I DON'T KNOW ABOUT *THAT...*

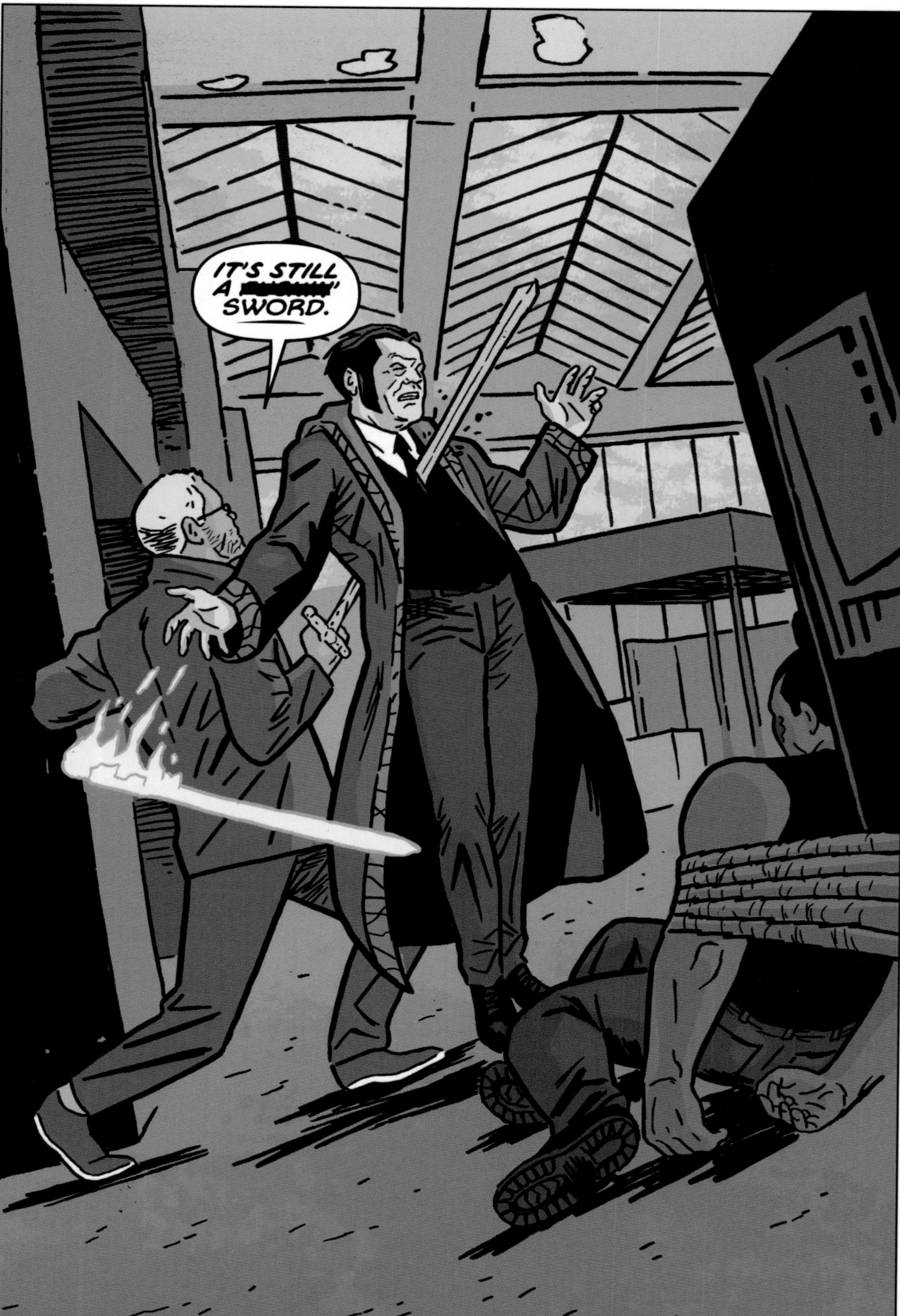
IT'S STILL A [redacted]' SWORD.

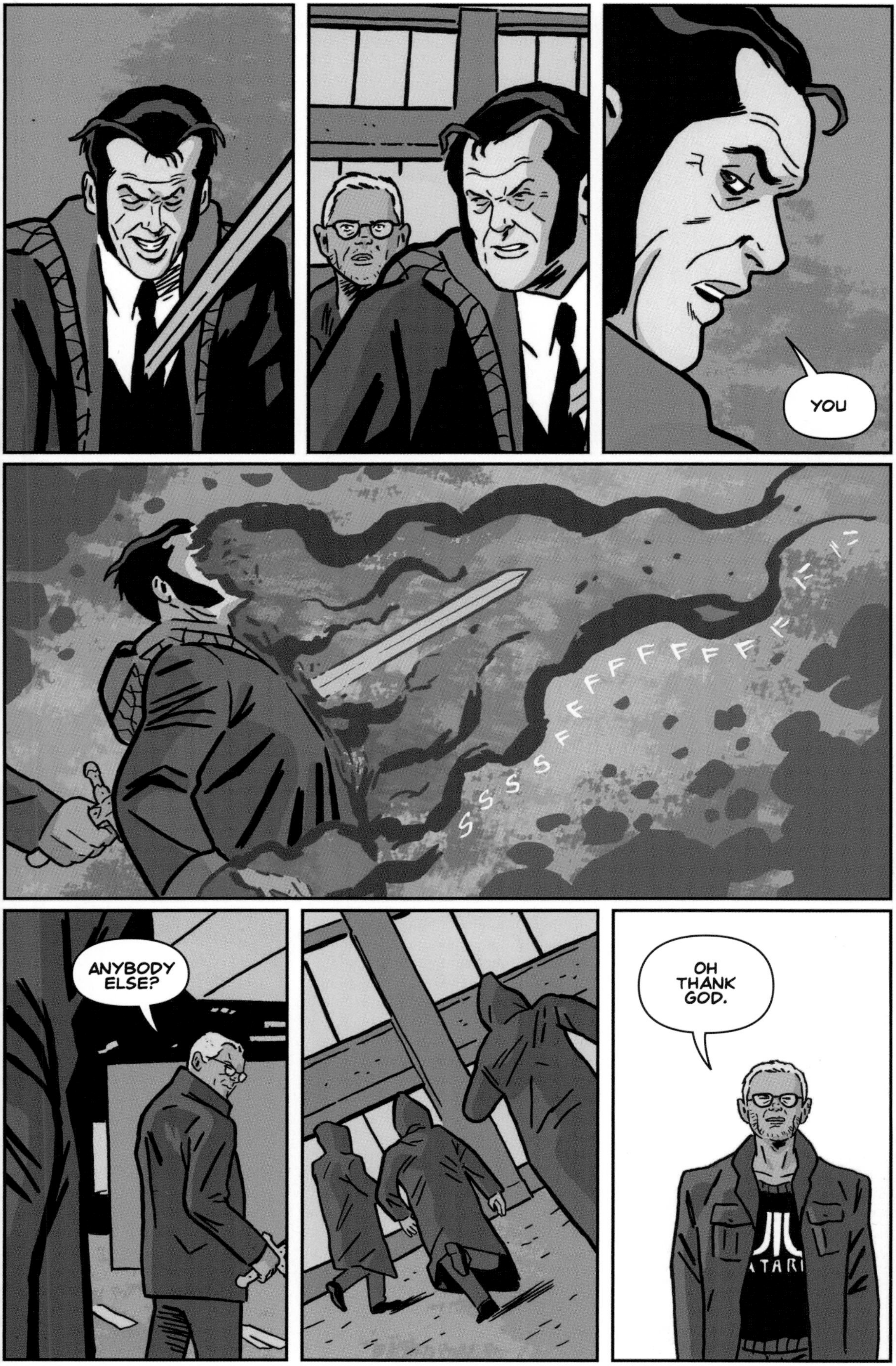
YOU
SSSSFFFFFFFFFFFF
ANYBODY ELSE?
OH THANK GOD.
ATARI

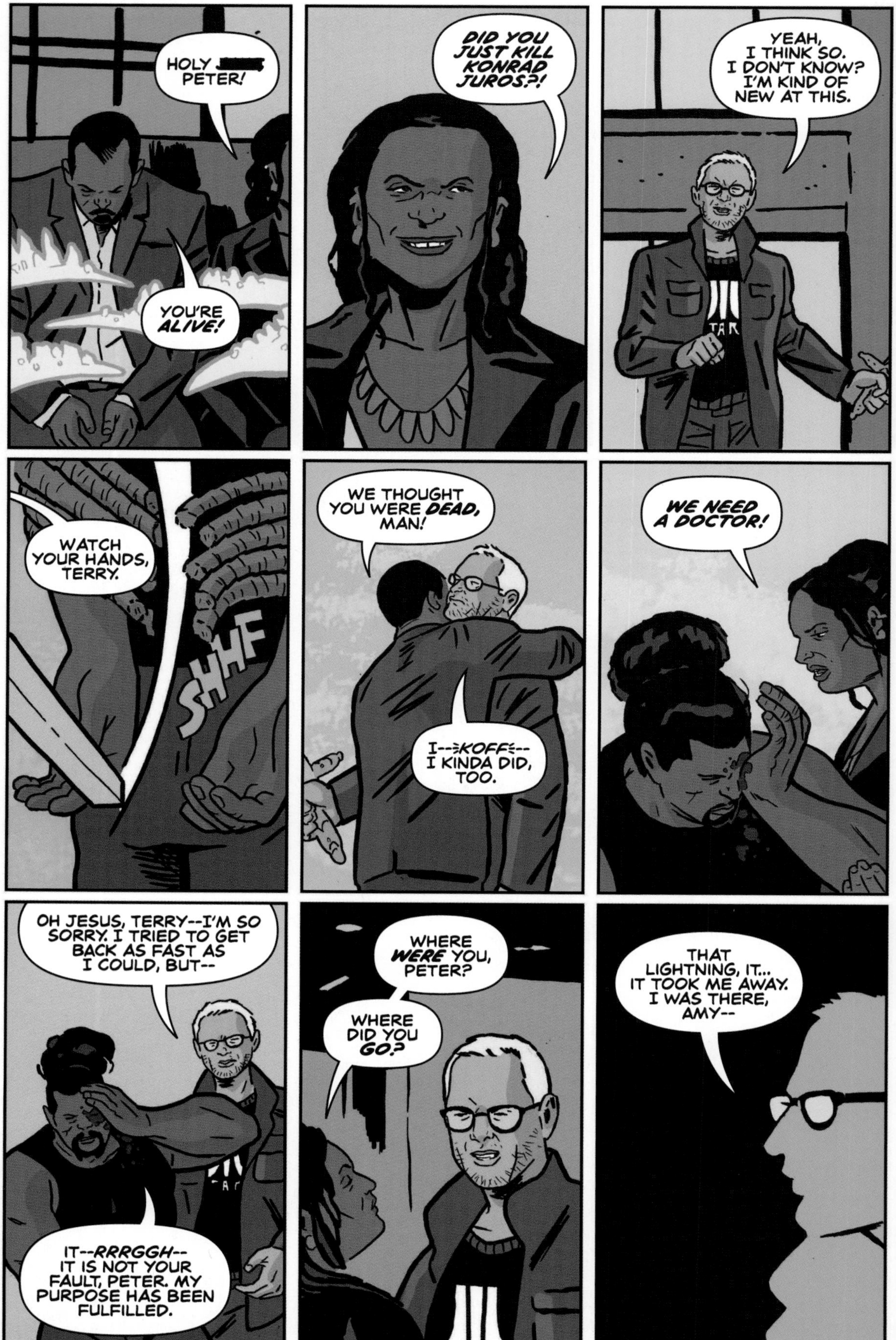
HOLY [redacted] PETER!
YOU'RE ALIVE!
DID YOU JUST KILL KONRAD JUROS?!
YEAH, I THINK SO. I DON'T KNOW? I'M KIND OF NEW AT THIS.
WATCH YOUR HANDS, TERRY.
SHHF
WE THOUGHT YOU WERE DEAD, MAN!
I--KOFF-- I KINDA DID, TOO.
WE NEED A DOCTOR!
OH JESUS, TERRY--I'M SO SORRY. I TRIED TO GET BACK AS FAST AS I COULD, BUT--
IT--RRRGGH-- IT IS NOT YOUR FAULT, PETER. MY PURPOSE HAS BEEN FULFILLED.
WHERE WERE YOU, PETER?
WHERE DID YOU GO?
THAT LIGHTNING, IT... IT TOOK ME AWAY. I WAS THERE, AMY--

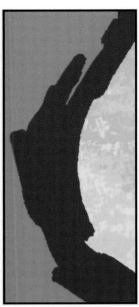

I WAS ON *ATARA*.

WHERE THE HELL...?

WELCOME HOME, GRAND UNITER.

IT TOOK ME TO THE LAST OF THE HOODED ONES, THE ARCHITECTS WHO MADE THAT UNIVERSE FROM THE ELEMENTAL WORLDS. AND WHAT HE TOLD ME...

WELL, IT WAS PRETTY WEIRD.

GAH!

WHAT-- WHERE AM I?

YOU ARE ON *ATARA*, YOUR MAJESTY. THE WORLD THAT CREATED YOU...

THE WORLD YOU CREATED, WHEN YOU *WALKED* UPON IT--

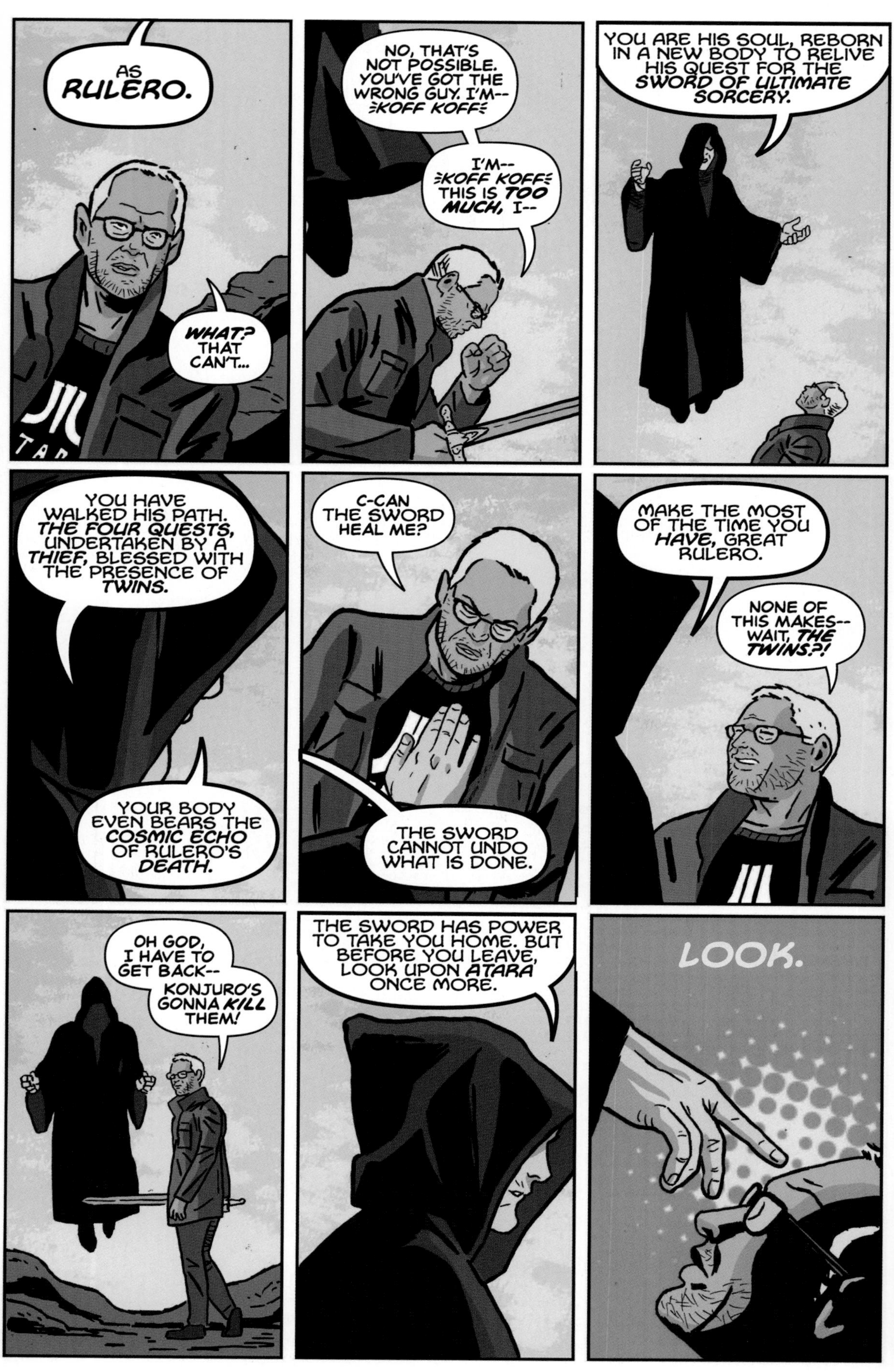
AS RULERO.
WHAT? THAT CAN'T...
NO, THAT'S NOT POSSIBLE. YOU'VE GOT THE WRONG GUY. I'M-- KOFF KOFF
I'M-- KOFF KOFF THIS IS TOO MUCH, I--
YOU ARE HIS SOUL, REBORN IN A NEW BODY TO RELIVE HIS QUEST FOR THE SWORD OF ULTIMATE SORCERY.
TAR
YOU HAVE WALKED HIS PATH. THE FOUR QUESTS, UNDERTAKEN BY A THIEF, BLESSED WITH THE PRESENCE OF TWINS.
YOUR BODY EVEN BEARS THE COSMIC ECHO OF RULERO'S DEATH.
C-CAN THE SWORD HEAL ME?
THE SWORD CANNOT UNDO WHAT IS DONE.
MAKE THE MOST OF THE TIME YOU HAVE, GREAT RULERO.
NONE OF THIS MAKES-- WAIT, THE TWINS?!
OH GOD, I HAVE TO GET BACK--
KONJURO'S GONNA KILL THEM!
THE SWORD HAS POWER TO TAKE YOU HOME. BUT BEFORE YOU LEAVE, LOOK UPON ATARA ONCE MORE.
LOOK.

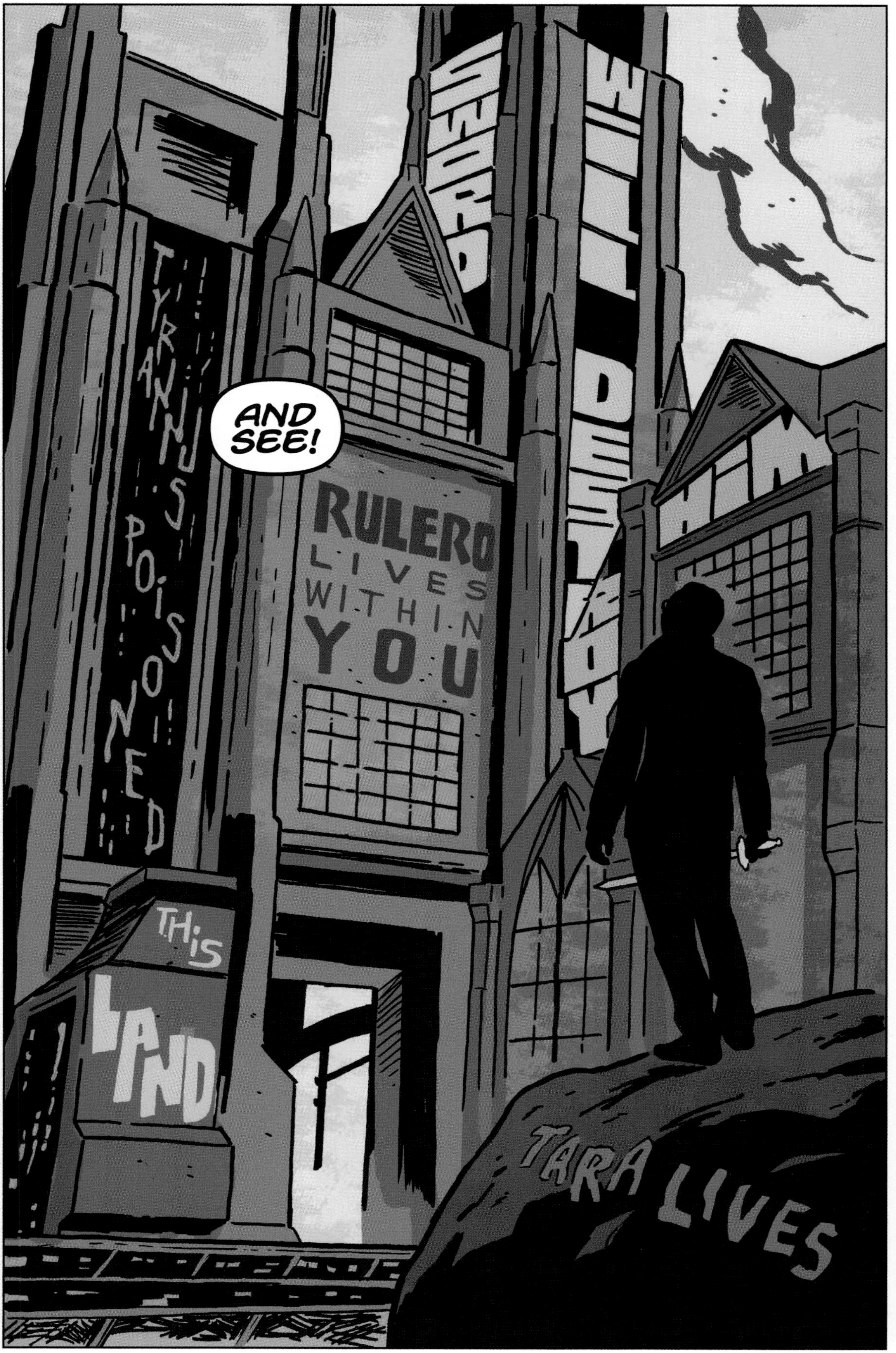

AND SEE!
TYRANNUS POISONED
RULERO LIVES WITHIN YOU
THIS LAND
TARA LIVES

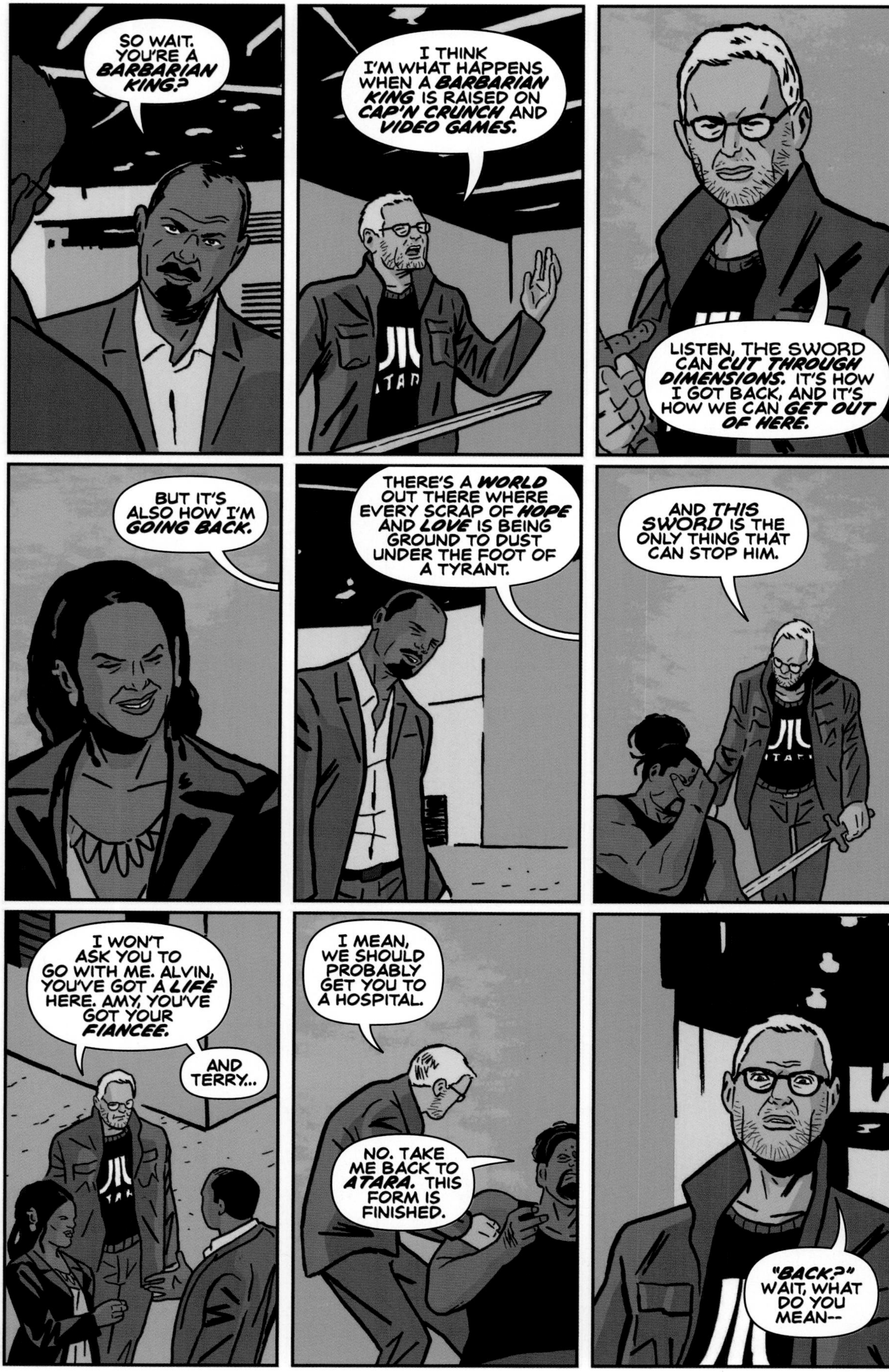
SO WAIT. YOU'RE A BARBARIAN KING?
I THINK I'M WHAT HAPPENS WHEN A BARBARIAN KING IS RAISED ON CAP'N CRUNCH AND VIDEO GAMES.
LISTEN, THE SWORD CAN CUT THROUGH DIMENSIONS. IT'S HOW I GOT BACK, AND IT'S HOW WE CAN GET OUT OF HERE.
BUT IT'S ALSO HOW I'M GOING BACK.
THERE'S A WORLD OUT THERE WHERE EVERY SCRAP OF HOPE AND LOVE IS BEING GROUND TO DUST UNDER THE FOOT OF A TYRANT.
AND THIS SWORD IS THE ONLY THING THAT CAN STOP HIM.
I WON'T ASK YOU TO GO WITH ME. ALVIN, YOU'VE GOT A LIFE HERE. AMY, YOU'VE GOT YOUR FIANCEE.
AND TERRY...
I MEAN, WE SHOULD PROBABLY GET YOU TO A HOSPITAL.
NO. TAKE ME BACK TO ATARA. THIS FORM IS FINISHED.
"BACK?" WAIT, WHAT DO YOU MEAN--

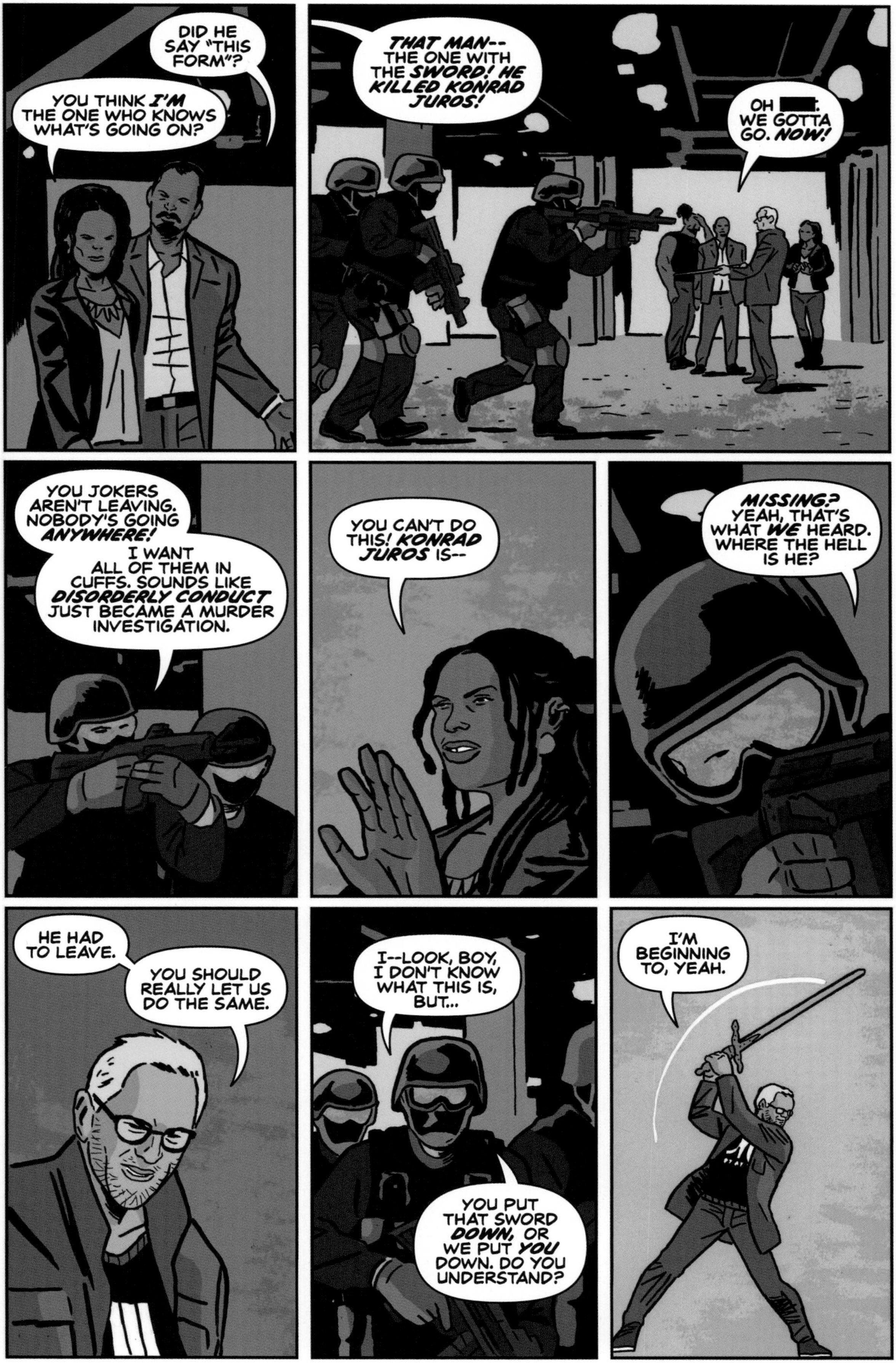
DID HE SAY "THIS FORM"?
YOU THINK *I'M* THE ONE WHO KNOWS WHAT'S GOING ON?
THAT MAN-- THE ONE WITH THE *SWORD! HE KILLED KONRAD JUROS!*
OH [redacted]. WE GOTTA GO. *NOW!*
YOU JOKERS AREN'T LEAVING. NOBODY'S GOING *ANYWHERE!*
I WANT ALL OF THEM IN CUFFS. SOUNDS LIKE *DISORDERLY CONDUCT* JUST BECAME A MURDER INVESTIGATION.
YOU CAN'T DO THIS! *KONRAD JUROS* IS--
MISSING? YEAH, THAT'S WHAT *WE* HEARD. WHERE THE HELL IS HE?
HE HAD TO LEAVE.
YOU SHOULD REALLY LET US DO THE SAME.
I--LOOK, BOY, I DON'T KNOW WHAT THIS IS, BUT...
YOU PUT THAT SWORD *DOWN,* OR WE PUT *YOU* DOWN. DO YOU UNDERSTAND?
I'M BEGINNING TO, YEAH.

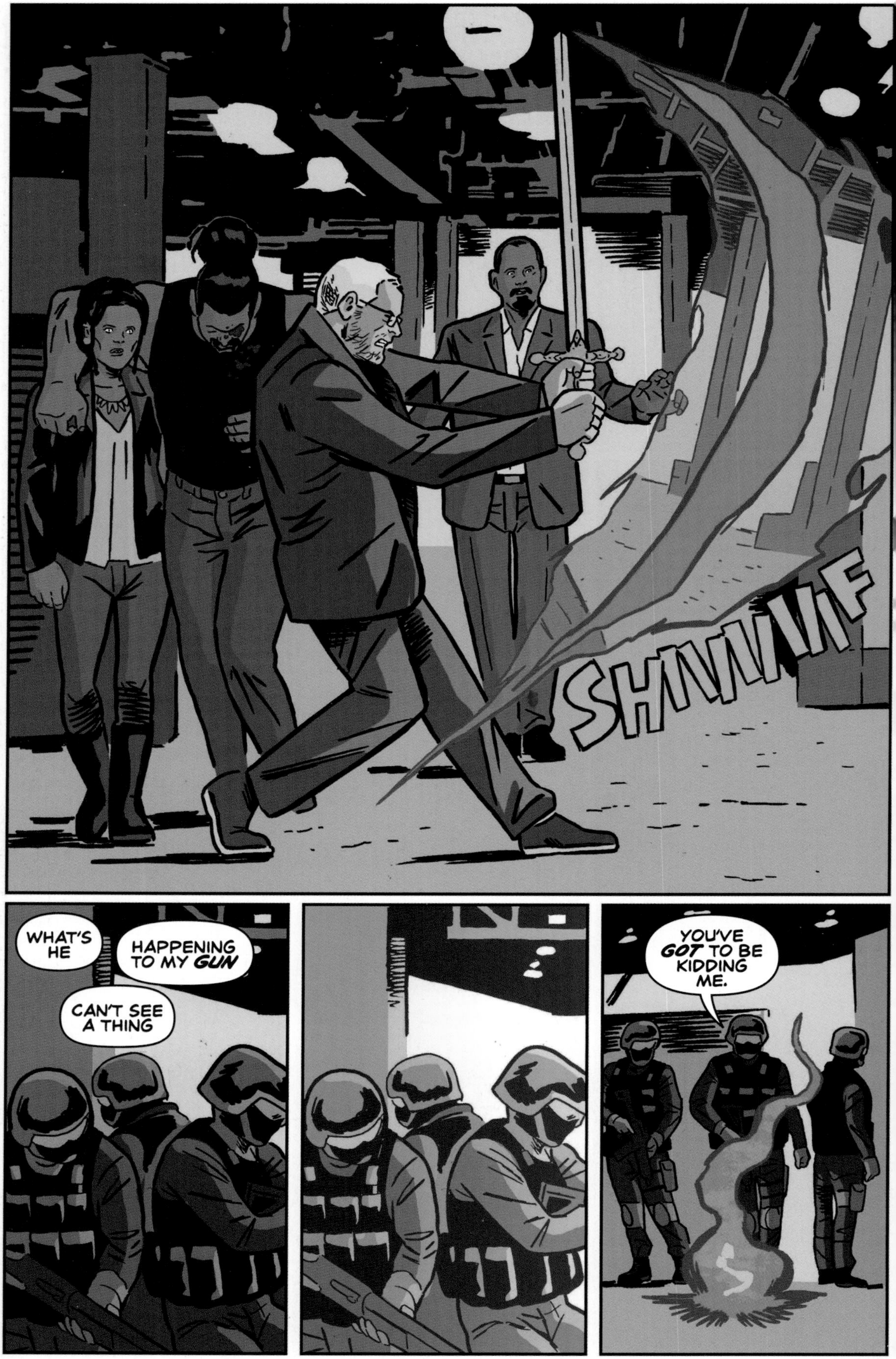

SHWWWF
WHAT'S HE
HAPPENING TO MY GUN
CAN'T SEE A THING
YOU'VE GOT TO BE KIDDING ME.

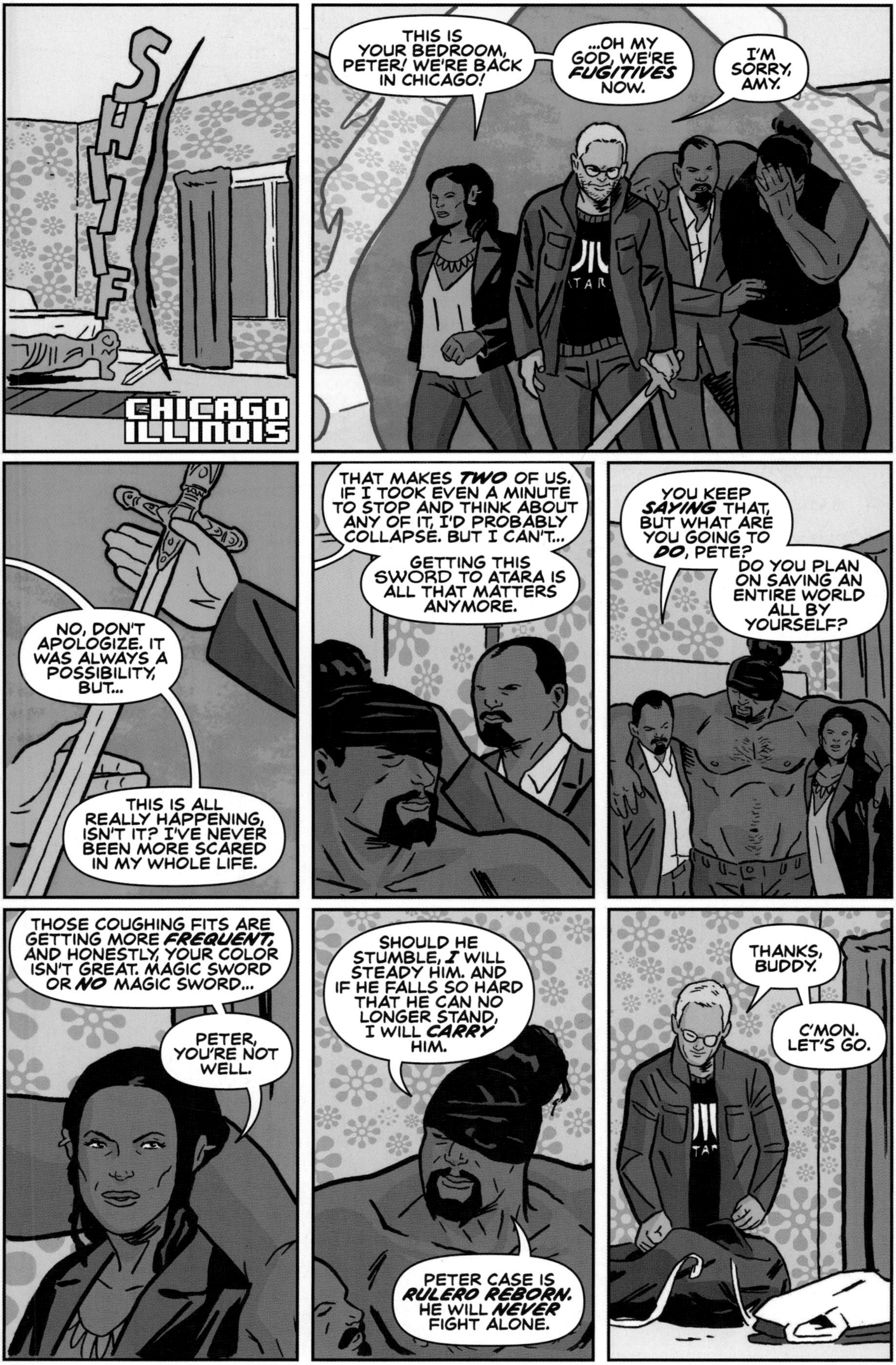
SHHIIF
CHICAGO ILLINOIS
THIS IS YOUR BEDROOM, PETER! WE'RE BACK IN CHICAGO!
...OH MY GOD, WE'RE FUGITIVES NOW.
I'M SORRY, AMY.
NO, DON'T APOLOGIZE. IT WAS ALWAYS A POSSIBILITY, BUT...
THIS IS ALL REALLY HAPPENING, ISN'T IT? I'VE NEVER BEEN MORE SCARED IN MY WHOLE LIFE.
THAT MAKES TWO OF US. IF I TOOK EVEN A MINUTE TO STOP AND THINK ABOUT ANY OF IT, I'D PROBABLY COLLAPSE. BUT I CAN'T...
GETTING THIS SWORD TO ATARA IS ALL THAT MATTERS ANYMORE.
YOU KEEP SAYING THAT, BUT WHAT ARE YOU GOING TO DO, PETE?
DO YOU PLAN ON SAVING AN ENTIRE WORLD ALL BY YOURSELF?
THOSE COUGHING FITS ARE GETTING MORE FREQUENT, AND HONESTLY, YOUR COLOR ISN'T GREAT. MAGIC SWORD OR NO MAGIC SWORD...
PETER, YOU'RE NOT WELL.
SHOULD HE STUMBLE, I WILL STEADY HIM. AND IF HE FALLS SO HARD THAT HE CAN NO LONGER STAND, I WILL CARRY HIM.
PETER CASE IS RULERO REBORN. HE WILL NEVER FIGHT ALONE.
THANKS, BUDDY.
C'MON. LET'S GO.

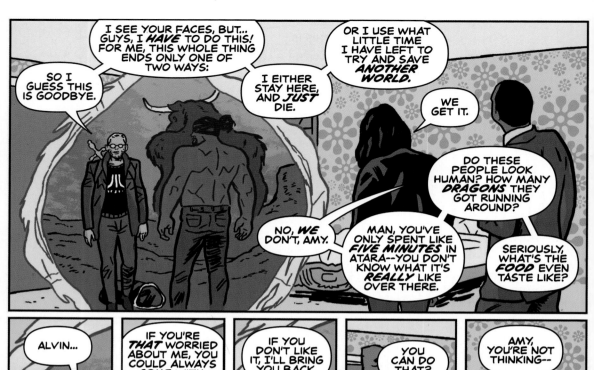

I SEE YOUR FACES, BUT... GUYS, I *HAVE* TO DO THIS! FOR ME, THIS WHOLE THING ENDS ONLY ONE OF TWO WAYS:

OR I USE WHAT LITTLE TIME I HAVE LEFT TO TRY AND SAVE *ANOTHER WORLD.*

SO I GUESS THIS IS GOODBYE.

I EITHER STAY HERE, AND *JUST* DIE.

WE GET IT.

DO THESE PEOPLE LOOK HUMAN? HOW MANY *DRAGONS* THEY GOT RUNNING AROUND?

NO, *WE* DON'T, AMY.

MAN, YOU'VE ONLY SPENT LIKE *FIVE MINUTES* IN ATARA--YOU DON'T KNOW WHAT IT'S *REALLY* LIKE OVER THERE.

SERIOUSLY, WHAT'S THE *FOOD* EVEN TASTE LIKE?

ALVIN...

IF YOU'RE *THAT* WORRIED ABOUT ME, YOU COULD ALWAYS COME WITH.

MAYBE TRY COOKING UP A DRAGON YOURSELF.

IF YOU DON'T LIKE IT, I'LL BRING YOU BACK.

YOU CAN DO THAT?

AMY, YOU'RE NOT THINKING--

...

ARE YOU *SURE* YOU CAN BRING US BACK?

HONESTLY? NO. I'VE ONLY DONE IT ONCE, BUT...

I'M NOT SURE ABOUT *ANYTHING* AT THE MOMENT. STEPPING THROUGH THIS DOOR WITH ME IS A HUGE RISK. AND YOU GUYS HAVE ALREADY RISKED SO MUCH.

OH, I KNOW. MY FREEDOM, MY *FIANCEE,* MY CAREER... MY *CREDIT.*

COMPANY'S GOING TO BE *PISSED* WHEN MY RENTAL CAR'S NOT BACK ON MONDAY.

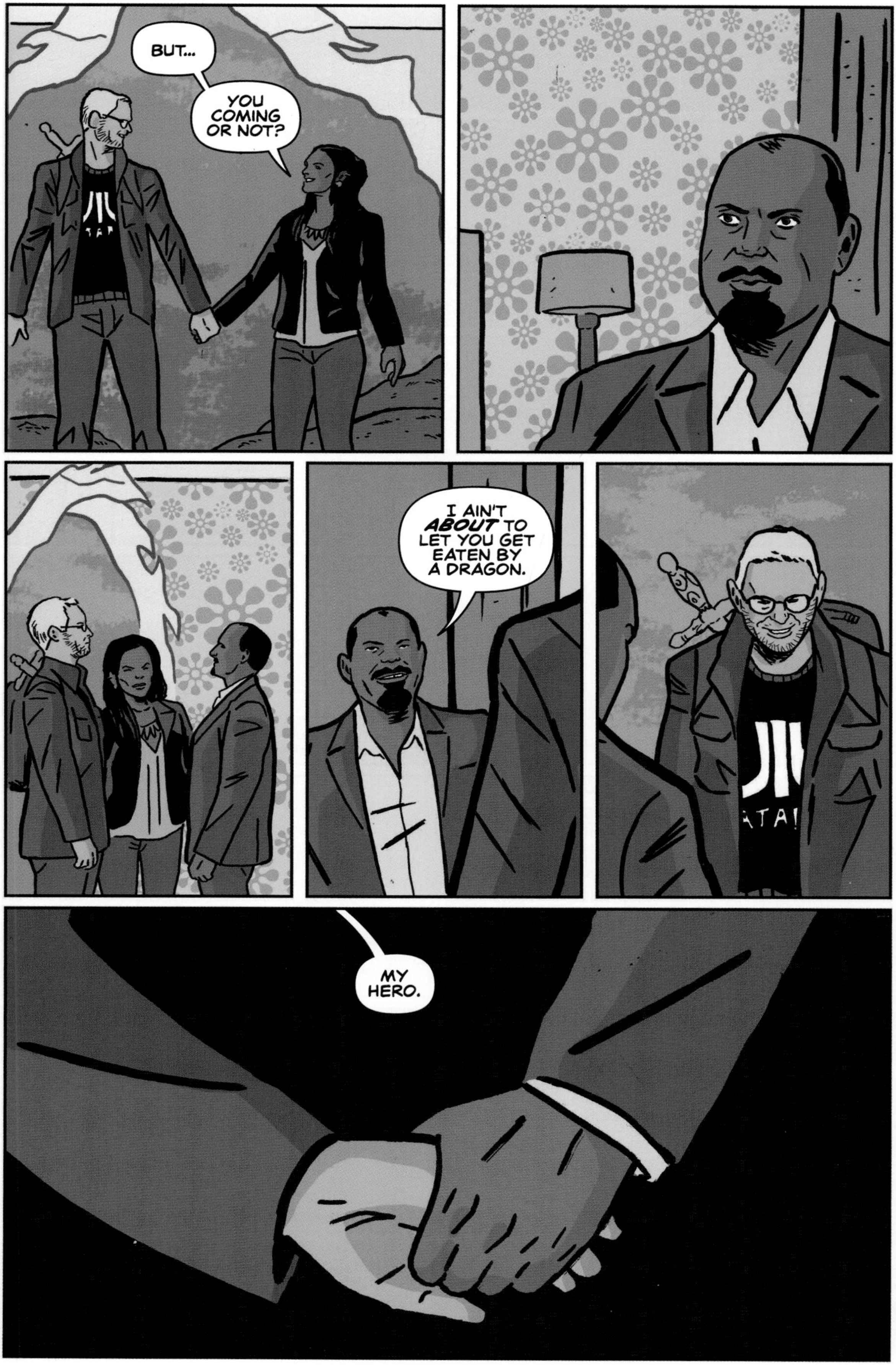
BUT...
YOU COMING OR NOT?
I AIN'T *ABOUT* TO LET YOU GET EATEN BY A DRAGON.
MY HERO.

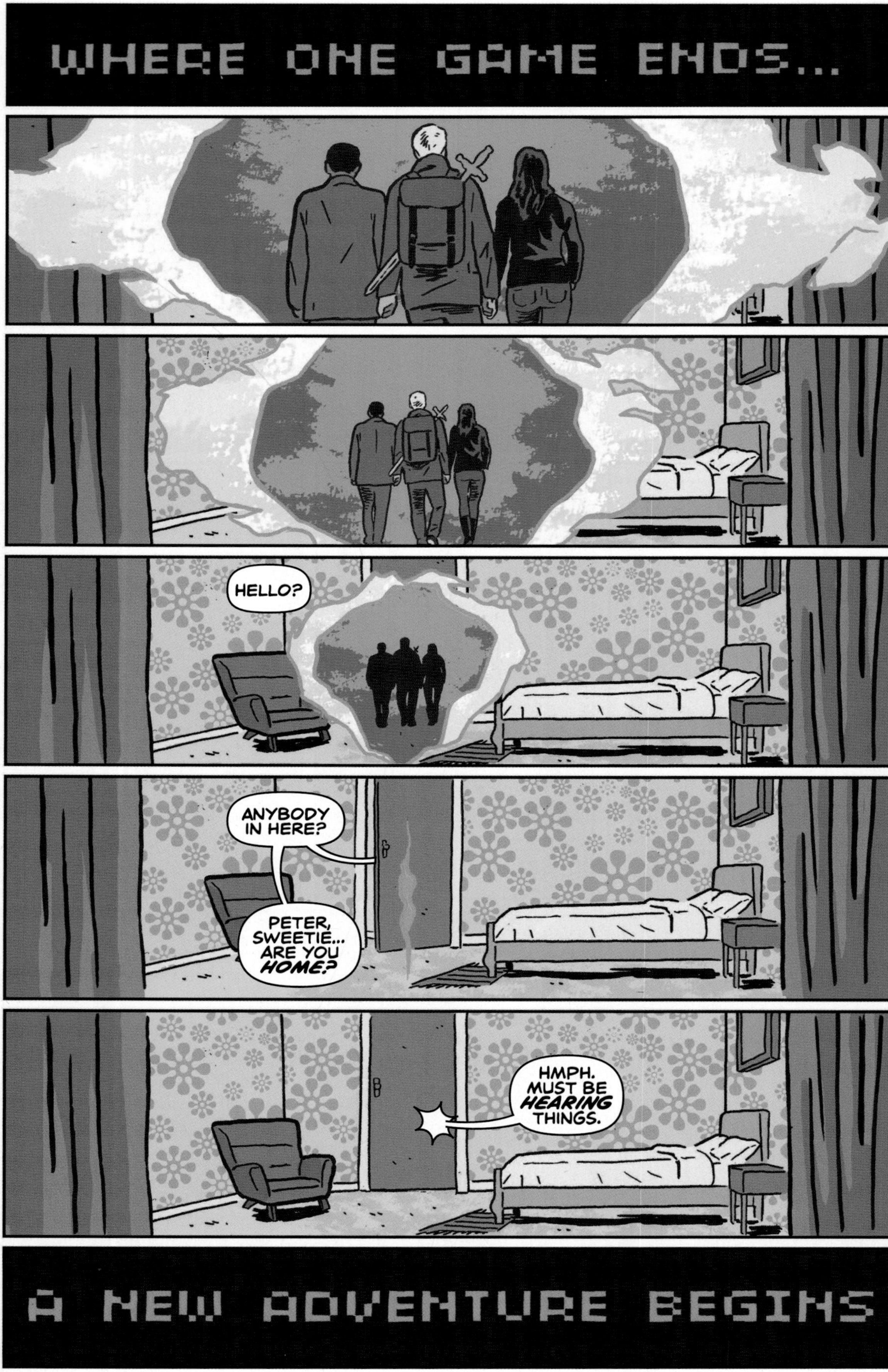
WHERE ONE GAME ENDS...
HELLO?
ANYBODY IN HERE?
PETER, SWEETIE... ARE YOU *HOME?*
HMPH. MUST BE *HEARING* THINGS.
A NEW ADVENTURE BEGINS

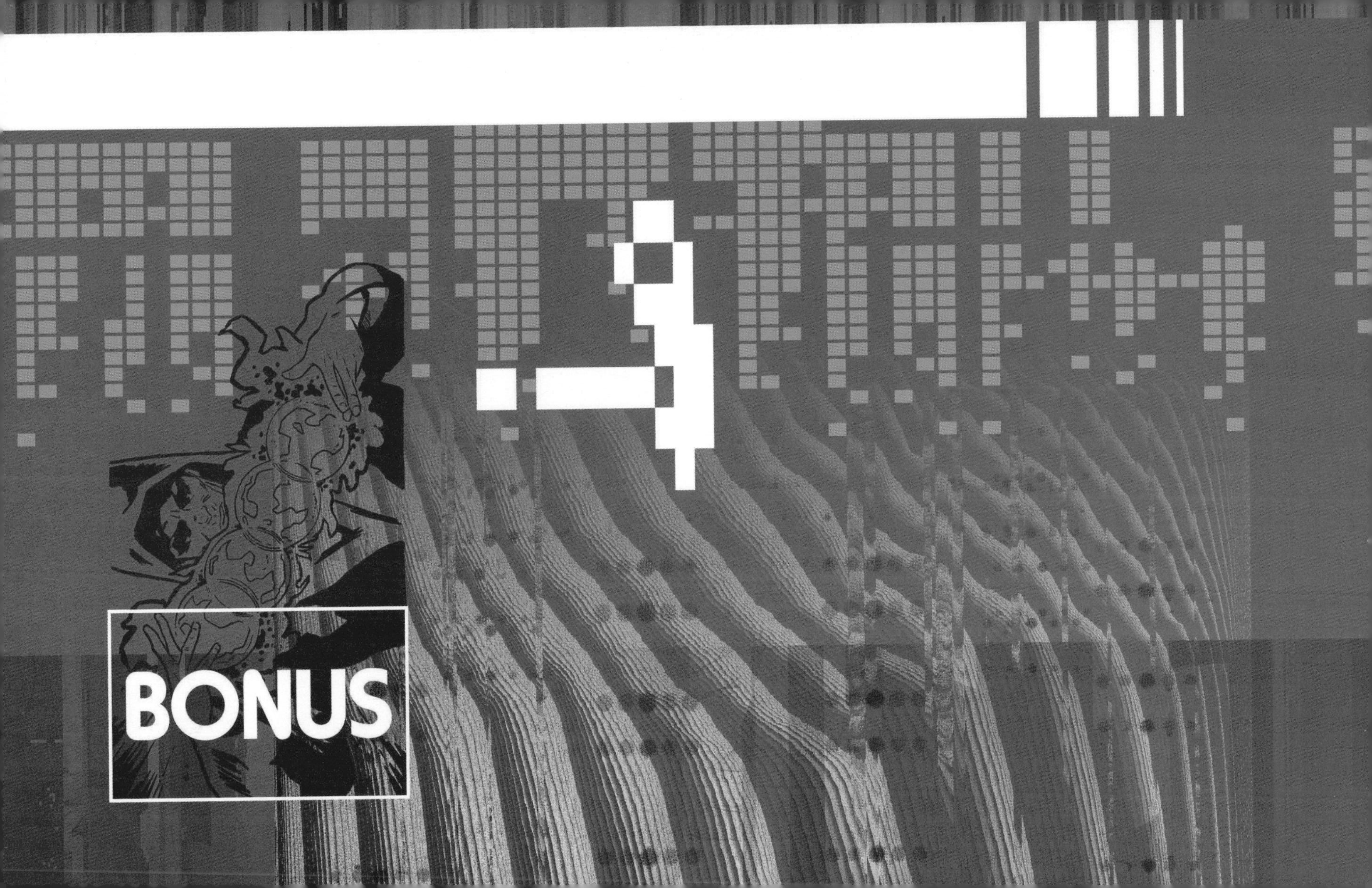
BONUS

ATARI
DYNAMITE

Swordquest™

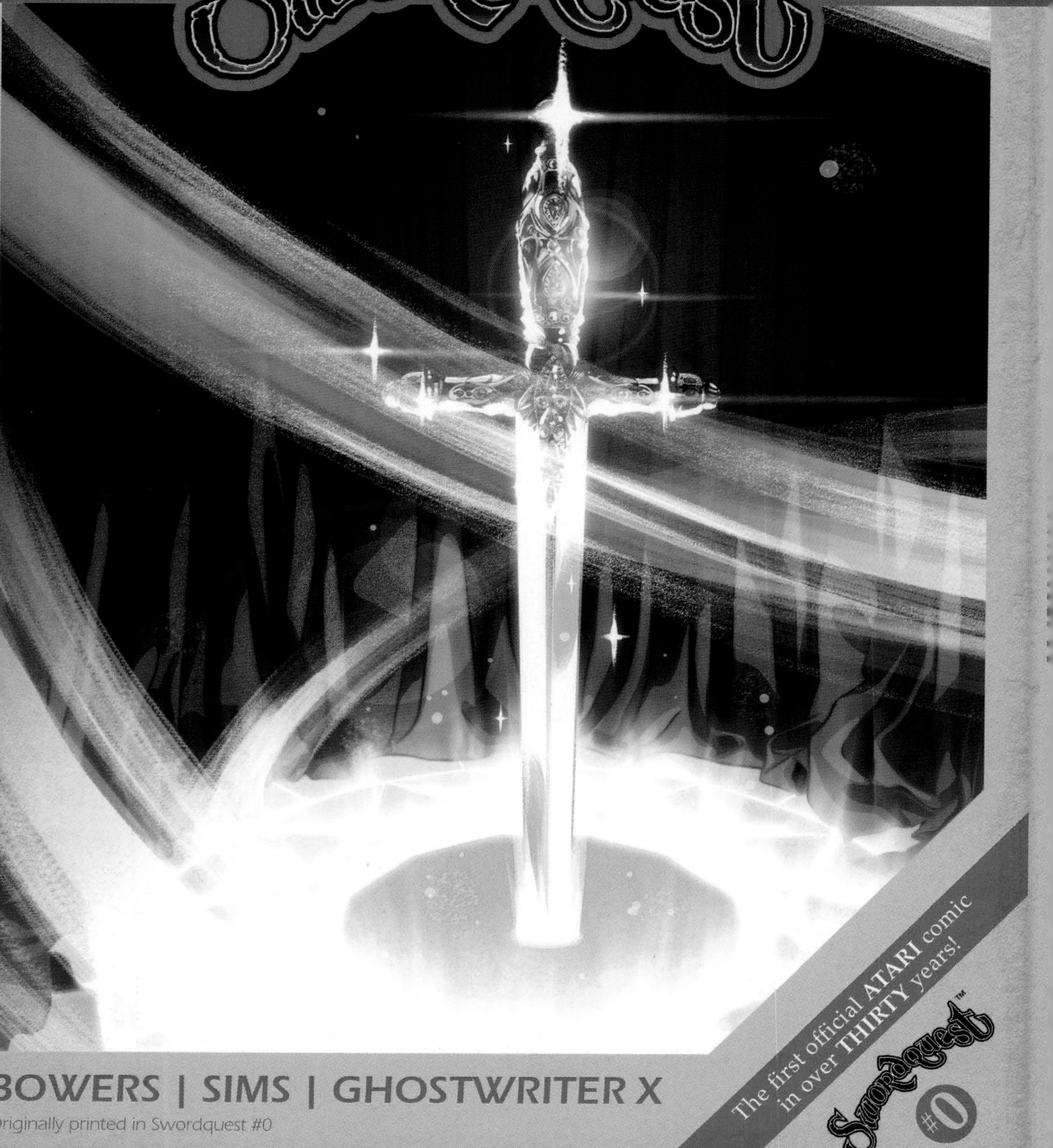

The first official ATARI comic in over THIRTY years!
Swordquest™
#0

BOWERS | SIMS | GHOSTWRITER X

Originally printed in Swordquest #0

PETE
SWORD
STRATEG
GUIDE

ATARI

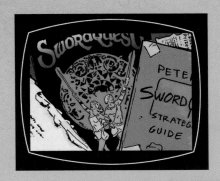

DYNAMITE
www.DYNAMITE.com
/DynamiteComics
@DynamiteComics

SWORDQUEST™ REALWORLD

AN INTERVIEW WITH CHAD BOWERS AND CHRIS SIMS

You're launching the first *ATARI* comic book project from Dynamite, the first *ATARI* comics in thirty years. What are your thoughts on this landmark, and contributing to the legacy of ATARI?

CHAD BOWERS: It's exciting, for sure. We definitely had a 2600 growing up, and I can remember playing a few games like *Jaws* and *Tank Commander*, but I was really too young to catch ATARI fever, which is kind of a shame. For that reason, though, ATARI's always been much more of a pop culture touchstone for me than a video game system, and that's what probably influences our storytelling on *Swordquest* more than anything else – the overall ATARI aesthetic, and its impact on American popular culture as a whole.

CHRIS SIMS: Chad can confirm this, but when I was a teenager, I had this ATARI shirt that I would wear pretty much every day. I've been obsessed with that stuff forever, and getting to kick the door open for comics is a pretty amazing opportunity.

Fans love your recent work on the *X-Men '92* comic book series. How did working on this Marvel project influence the way that you approached *Swordquest* in terms of its retro revival?

CHAD: Working on *X-Men '92* was a tremendous experience and I still can't believe we got to do half of what we did on that book! I loved every minute of it, and with *Swordquest*, yeah, there's the temptation to just fall face first into the same kind of retro-tinged comfort food, for sure, but I'd hesitate to say we're doing another retro book. You'll definitely see some stuff set in the 80s and maybe even the 90s, but beyond that, really the only thing we're reviving with *Swordquest* is the name.

CHRIS: I think the thing we learned on '92 that's really coming through here is how fun it is to take an existing property and go wild with it in ways that people might not expect. We always tried to push the envelope in that book in terms of the stakes we were creating, and with *Swordquest*, we're looking to do the same thing – just maybe not in the way that people expect.

There's a very meta context to this new series, incorporating the infamous real-world *Swordquest* contest into the story. What inspired this innovative take?

CHRIS: I mean, have you read the history of that stuff? Actual golden chalices and swords that gamers had to take a quest for? How could we not go right for that stuff?

CHAD: It's funny, but as we were brainstorming, Chris and I just kept coming across aspects of this game and the contest stuff that was even more bizarre than anything we were trying to come up with. Finally, when we found out the winner of *Fireworld* was from South Carolina and we were getting to work with our *Down Set Fight!* collaborator Ghostwriter X again, I think we knew it was meant to be!

Without giving too much away, what can you tell us about the heroes of *Swordquest*, Peter Case and the Perez siblings? Who are they, and what drives them?

CHRIS: Did you ever have those friends when you were a kid that you bonded over playing video games? They had the console but you had the magazines, and maybe you had another friend with the skills to actually play the game? That was Peter, Alvin, and Amy back in '83. In the years since, they've drifted apart, but when Peter... well, you'll have to read it to see.

Why should fans of the classic ATARI games pick up the comic? What's the appeal for newcomers that, perhaps, are unfamiliar with the *Swordquest* game?

CHRIS: One of the great things about those early video games is how much they relied on players to create their own stories. It was a limit of the technology, sure, but even if you were reading the original pack-in comics next to the video game, you had to create that bridge between them in your mind. That's the idea that we want to really explore here, getting into what it meant to put yourself into those blank-slate games, and how much it meant to get invested in them.

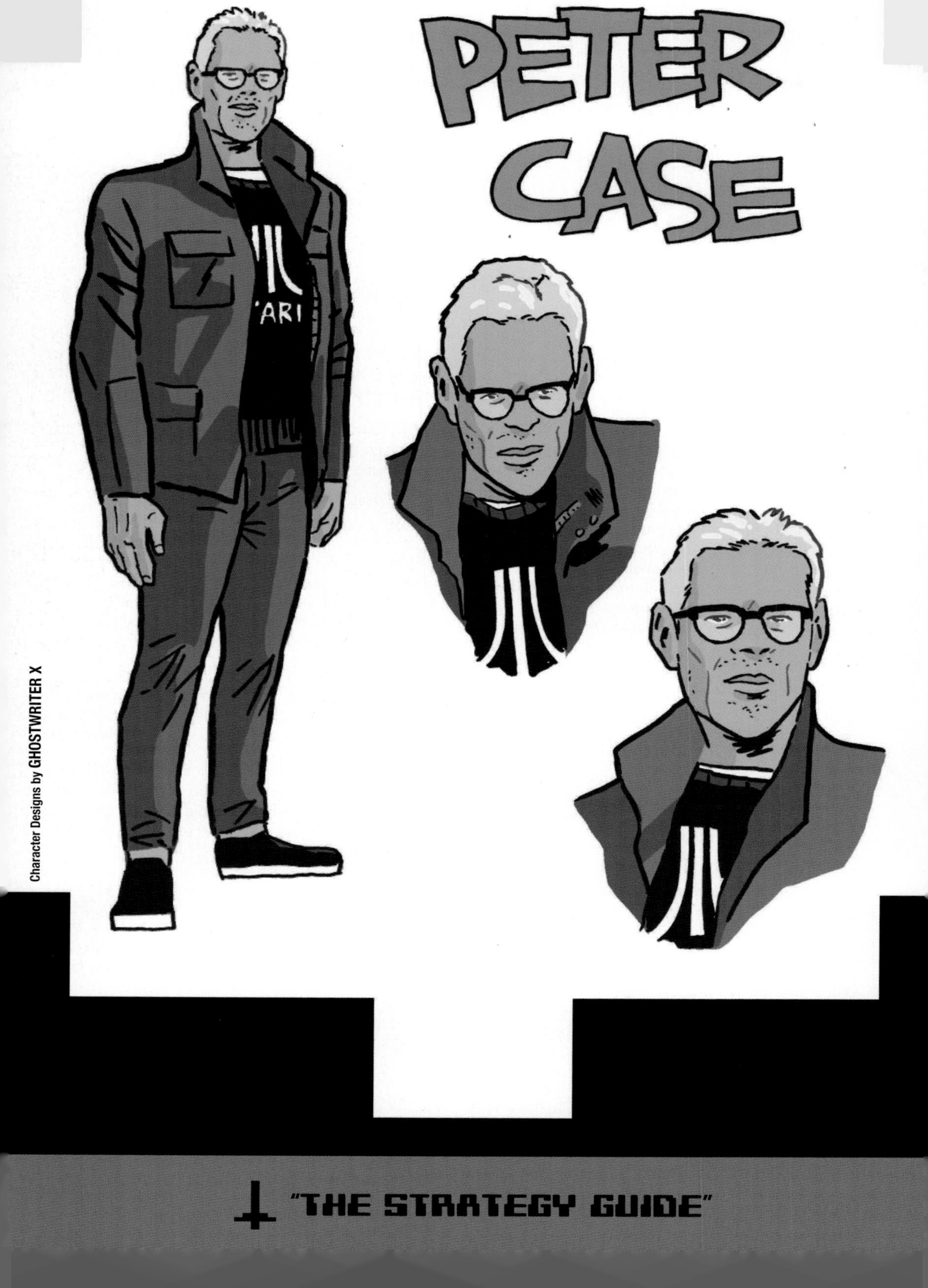
PETER
CASE

Character Designs by GHOSTWRITER X

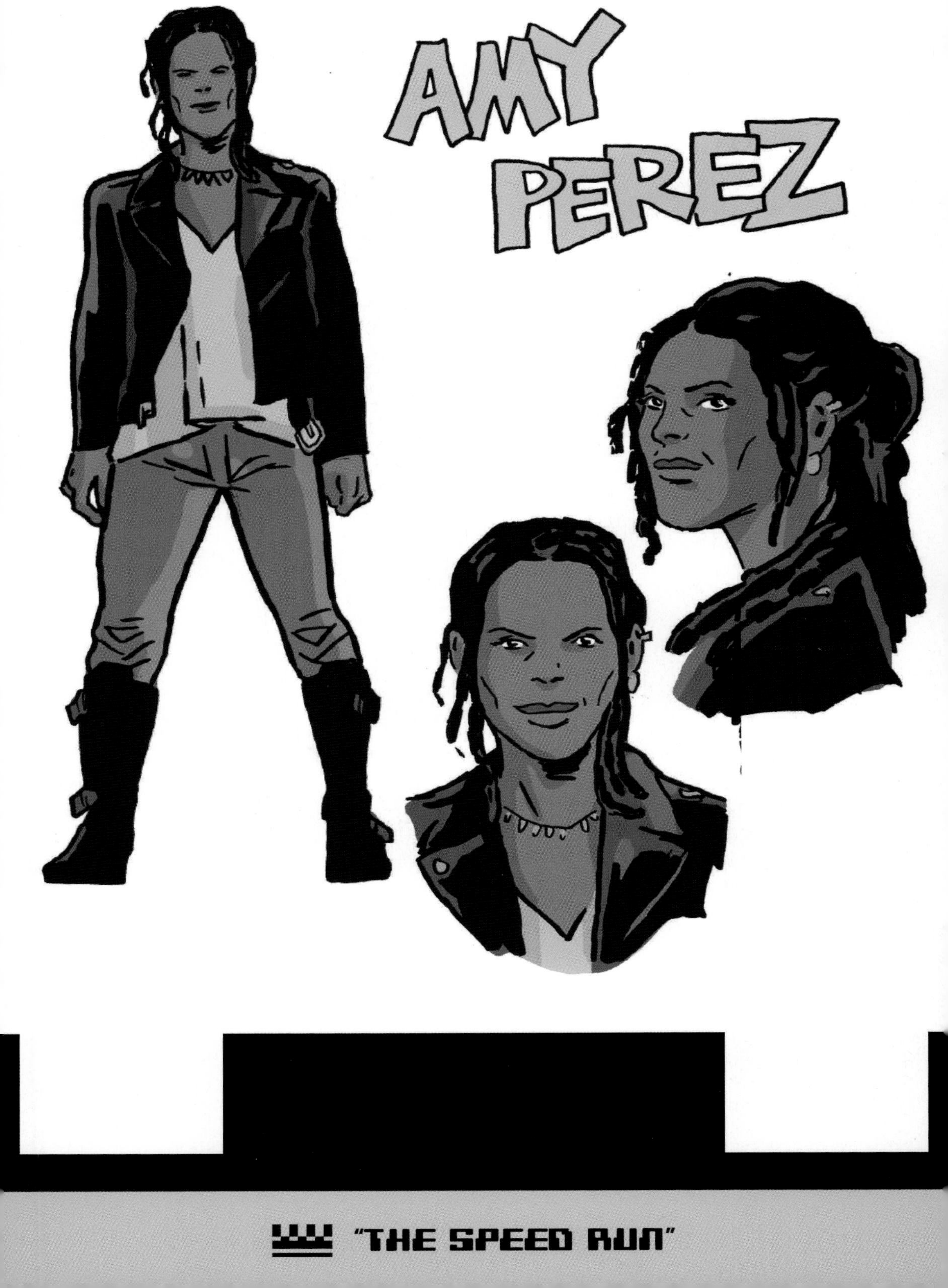
AMY PEREZ

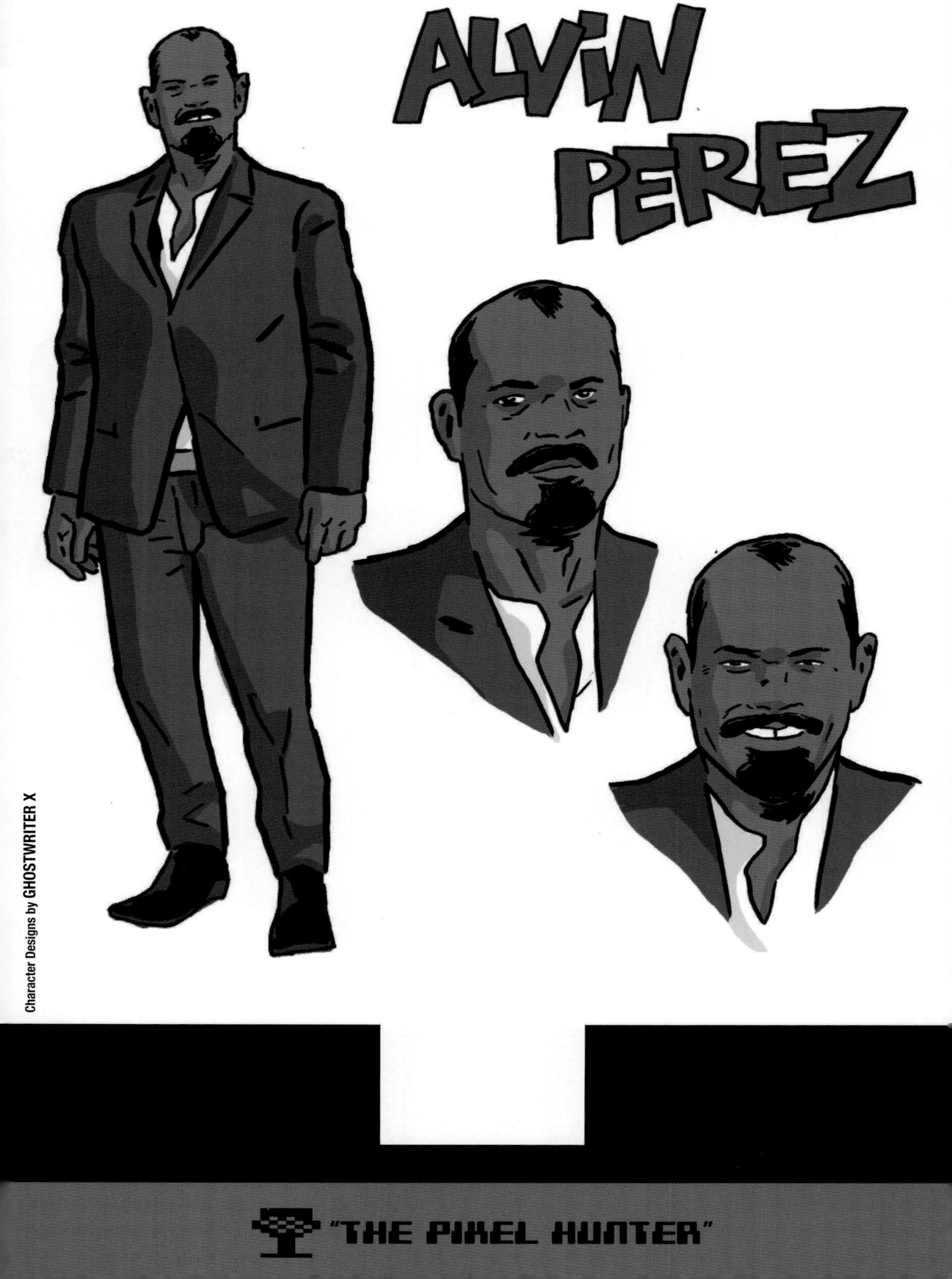
ALVIN
PEREZ

Character Designs by GHOSTWRITER X

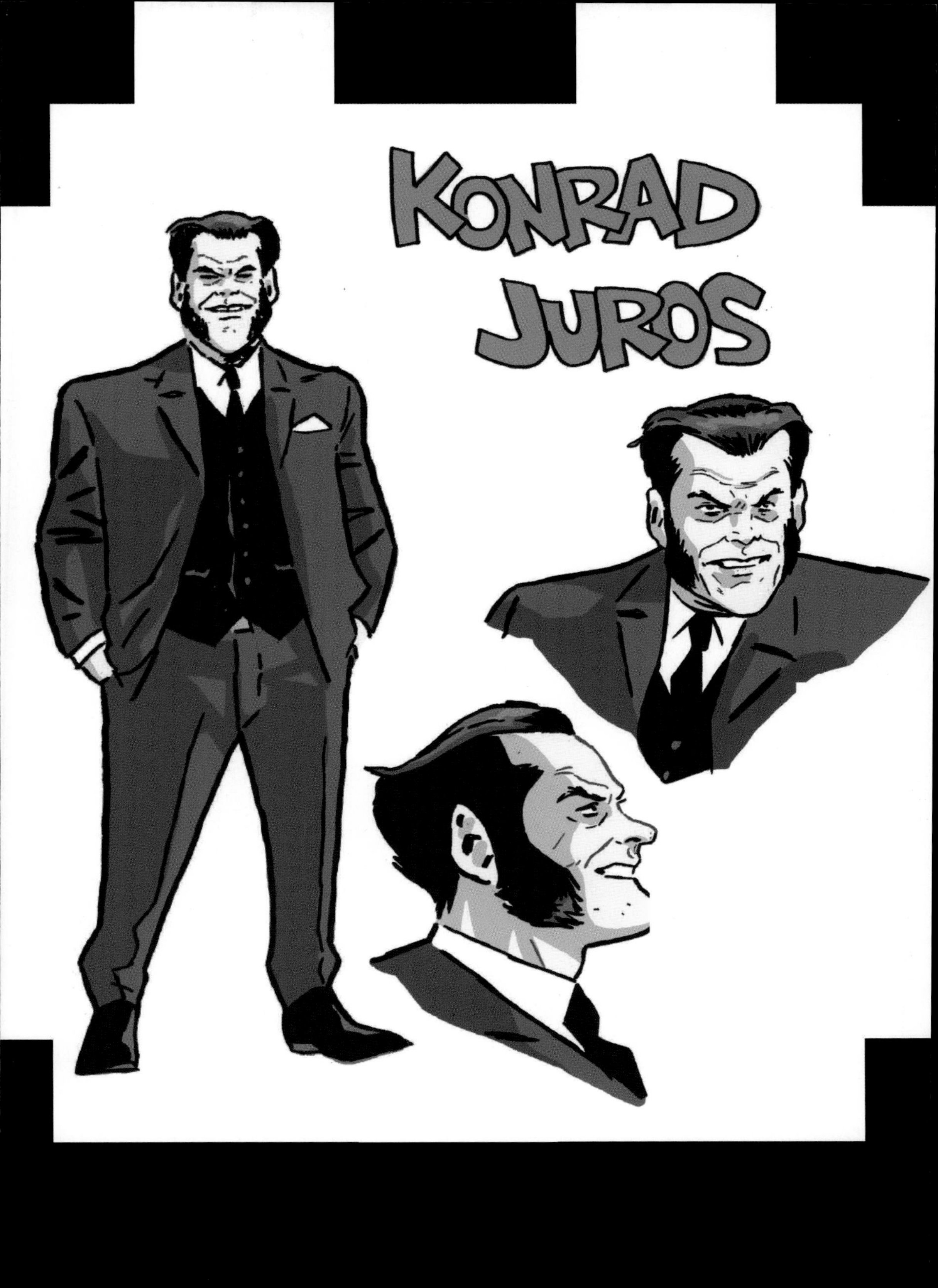
KONRAD
JUROS

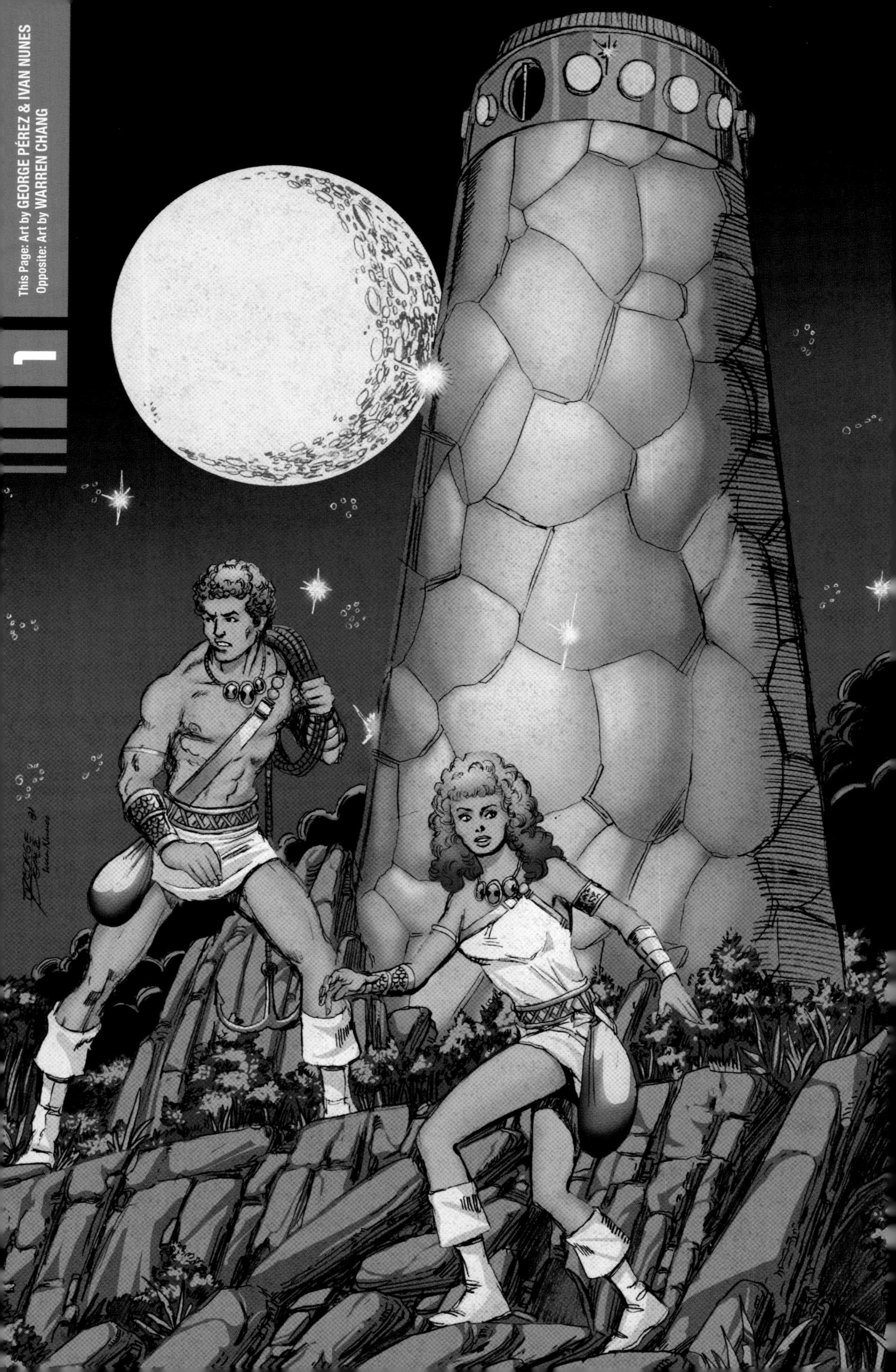

1

This Page: Art by GEORGE PÉREZ & IVAN NUNES
Opposite: Art by WARREN CHANG

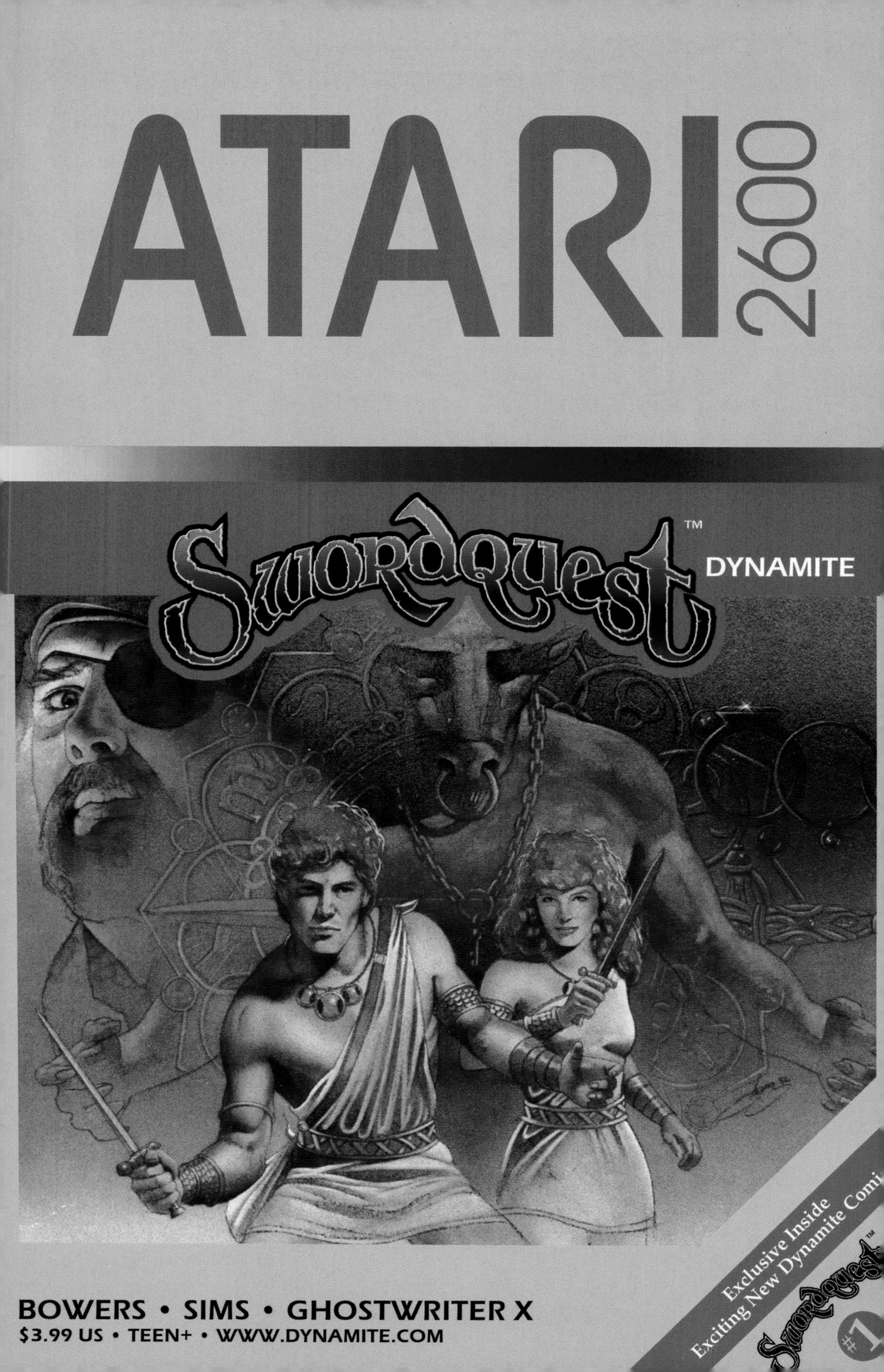
ATARI 2600
Swordquest™
DYNAMITE
BOWERS • SIMS • GHOSTWRITER X
$3.99 US • TEEN+ • WWW.DYNAMITE.COM
Exclusive Inside
Exciting New Dynamite
Swordquest™ #1

This Page: Art by MEL RUBI & OMI REMALANTE
Opposite: LIMITED EDITION RETRO COVER,
Art by GEORGE PÉREZ & ADRIENNE ROY

1

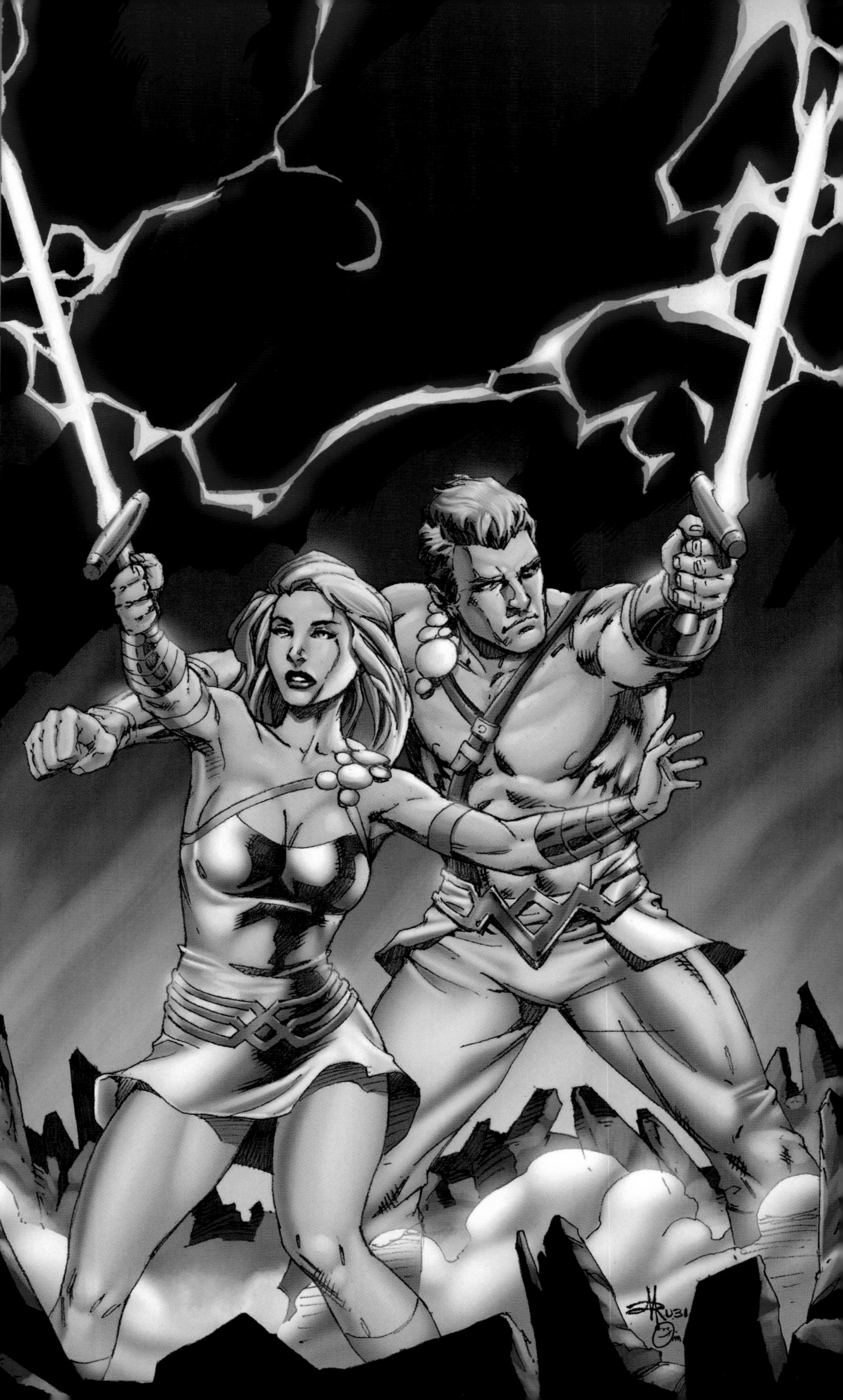

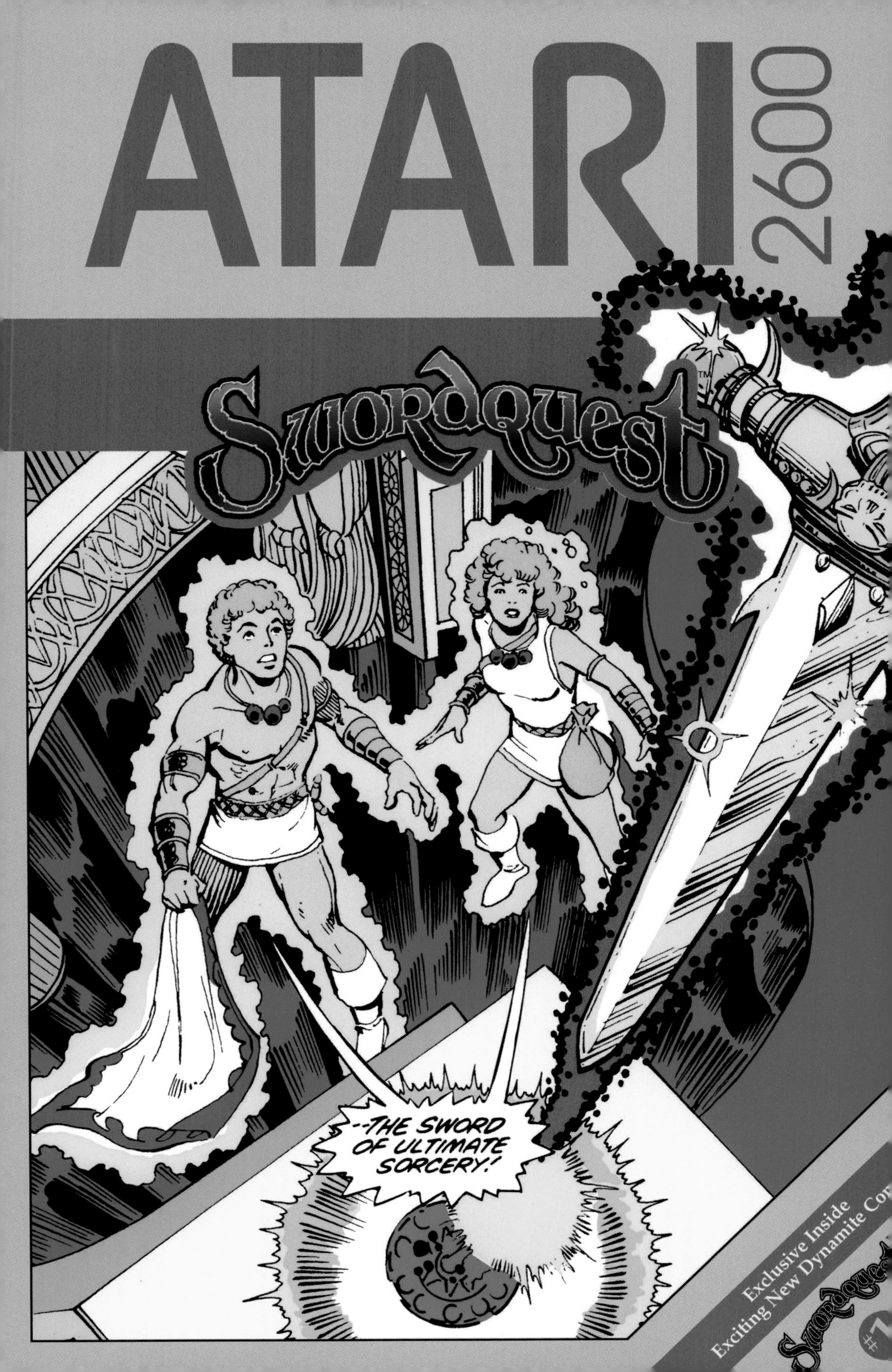
ATARI 2600
Swordquest
--THE SWORD OF ULTIMATE SORCERY!
Exclusive Inside
Exciting New Dynamite

Art by GEORGE PÉREZ & IVAN NUNES

2

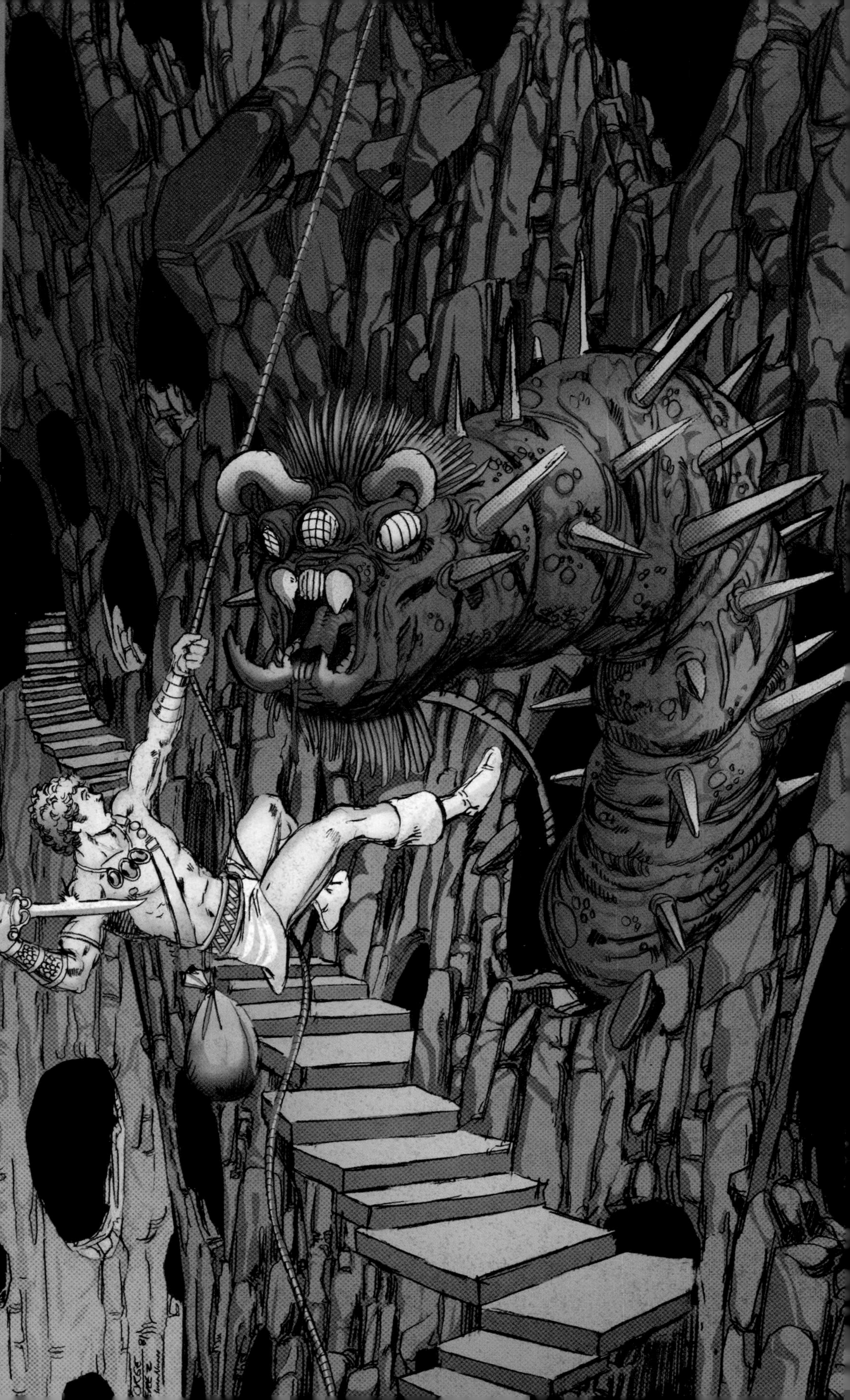

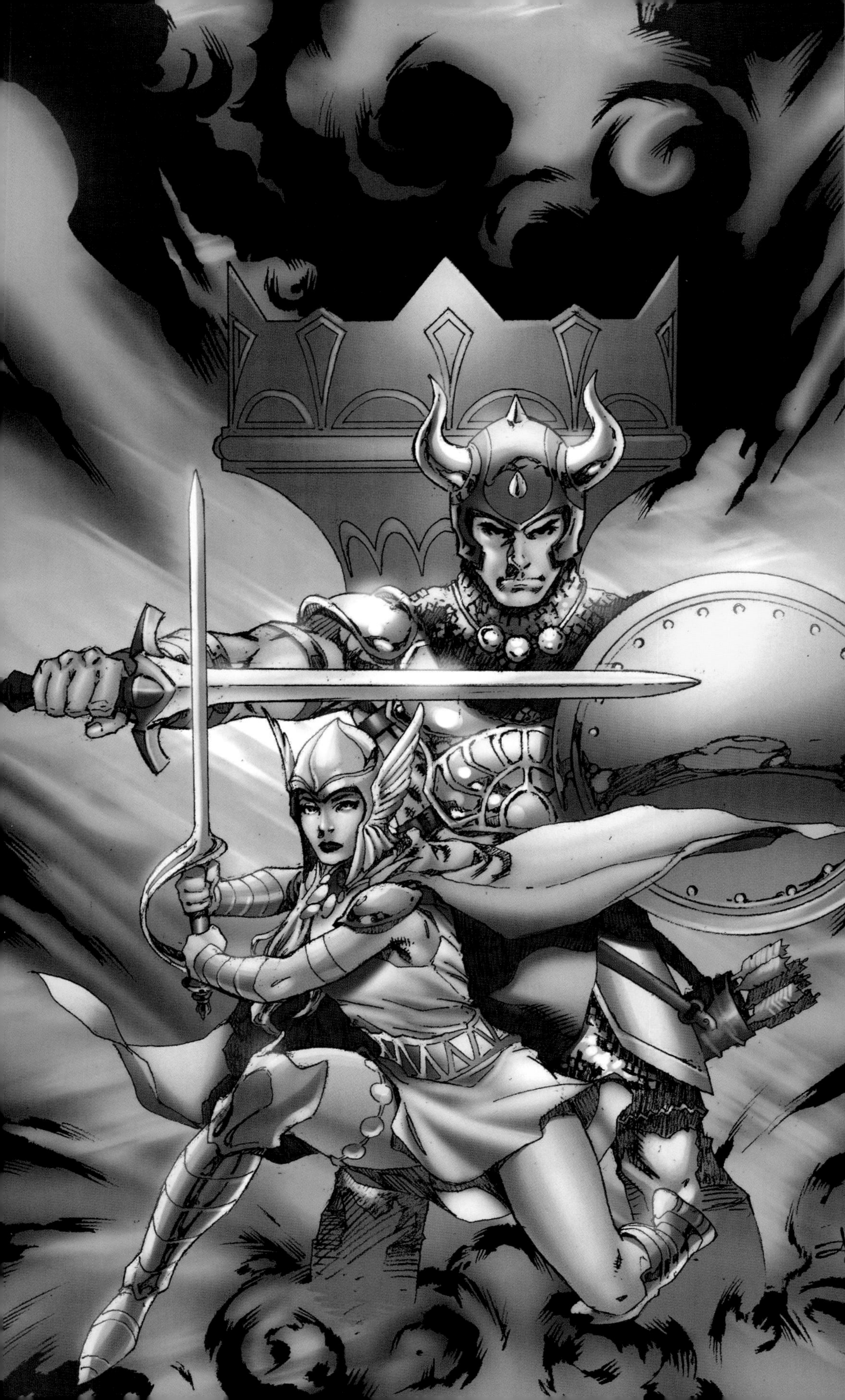

2

Art by MEL RUBI & OMI REMALANTE

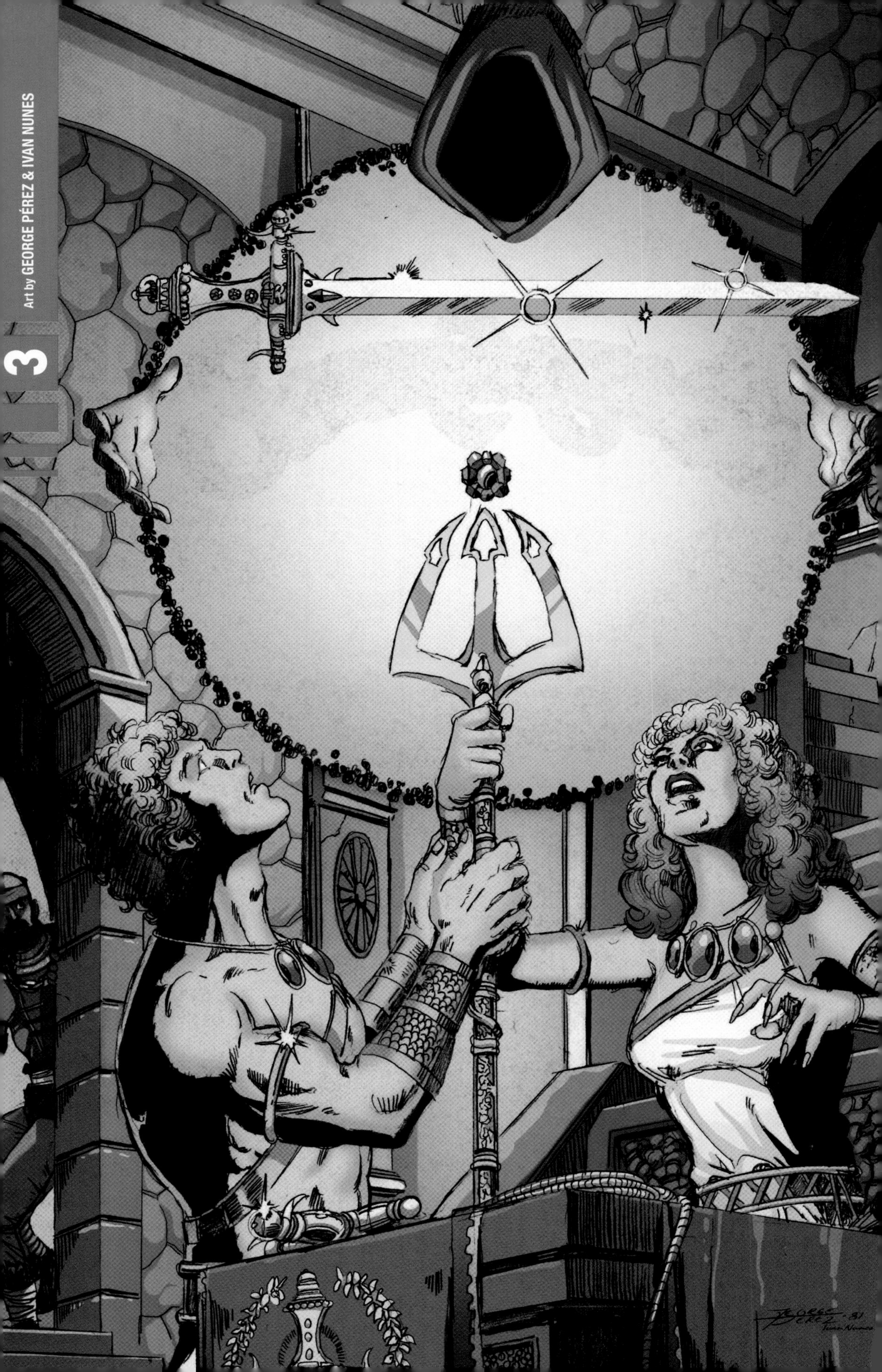

3 Art by GEORGE PÉREZ & IVAN NUNES

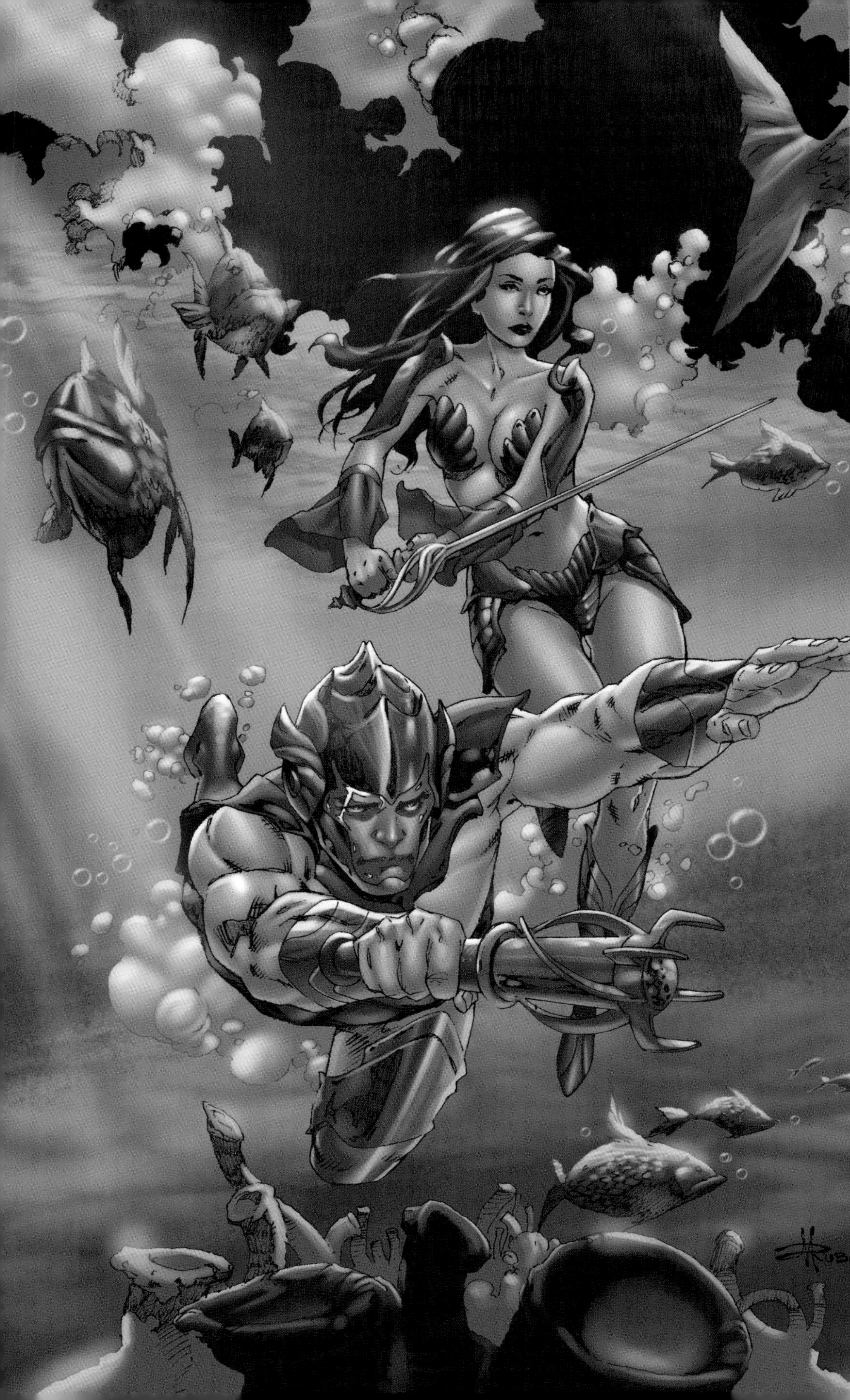

3

Art by MEL RUBI & OMI REMALANTE

4

Art by GEORGE PÉREZ & IVAN NUNES

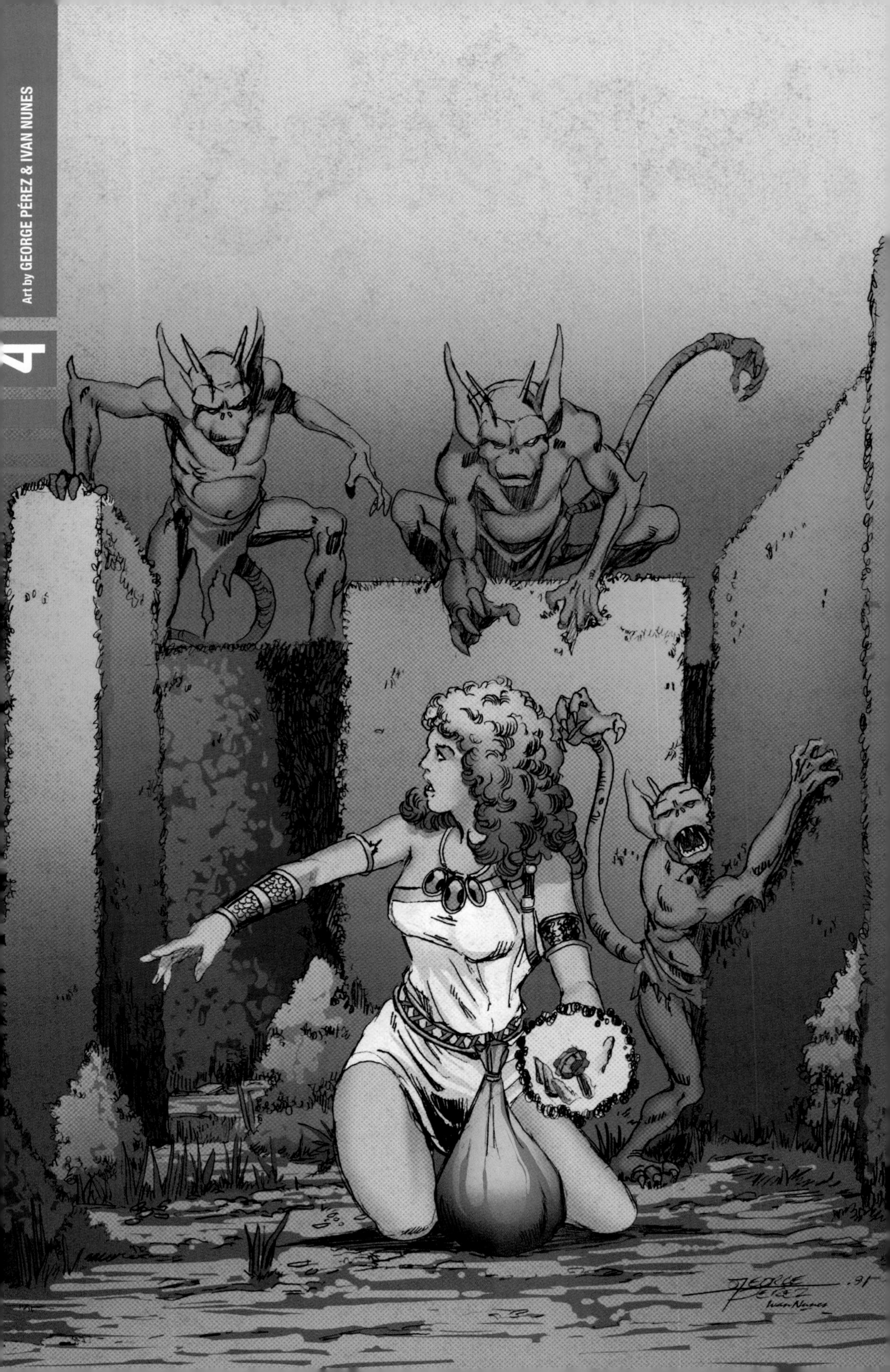

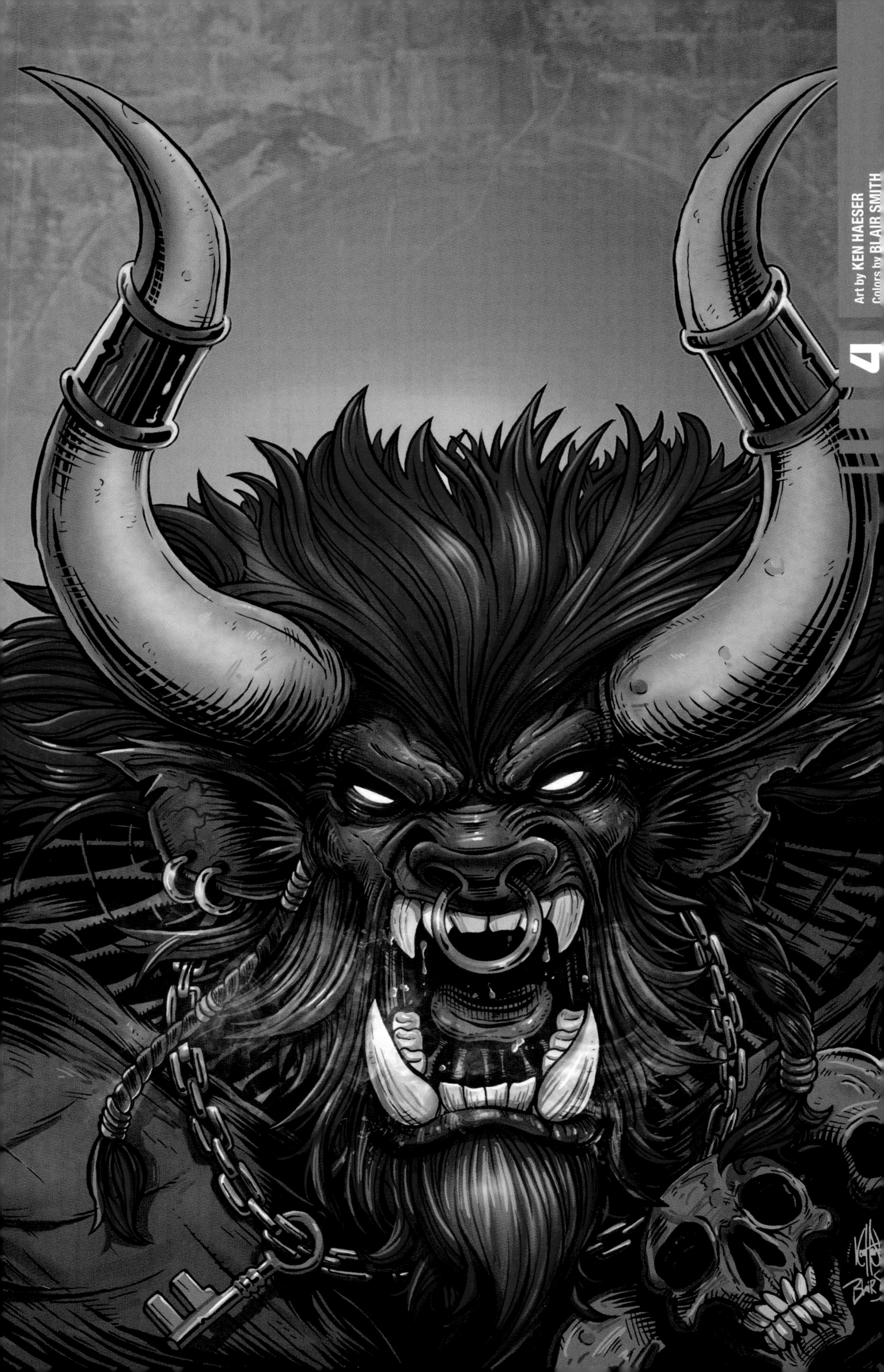
4
Art by KEN HAESER
Colors by BLAIR SMITH

5

Art by JONATHAN LAU & OMI REMALANTE

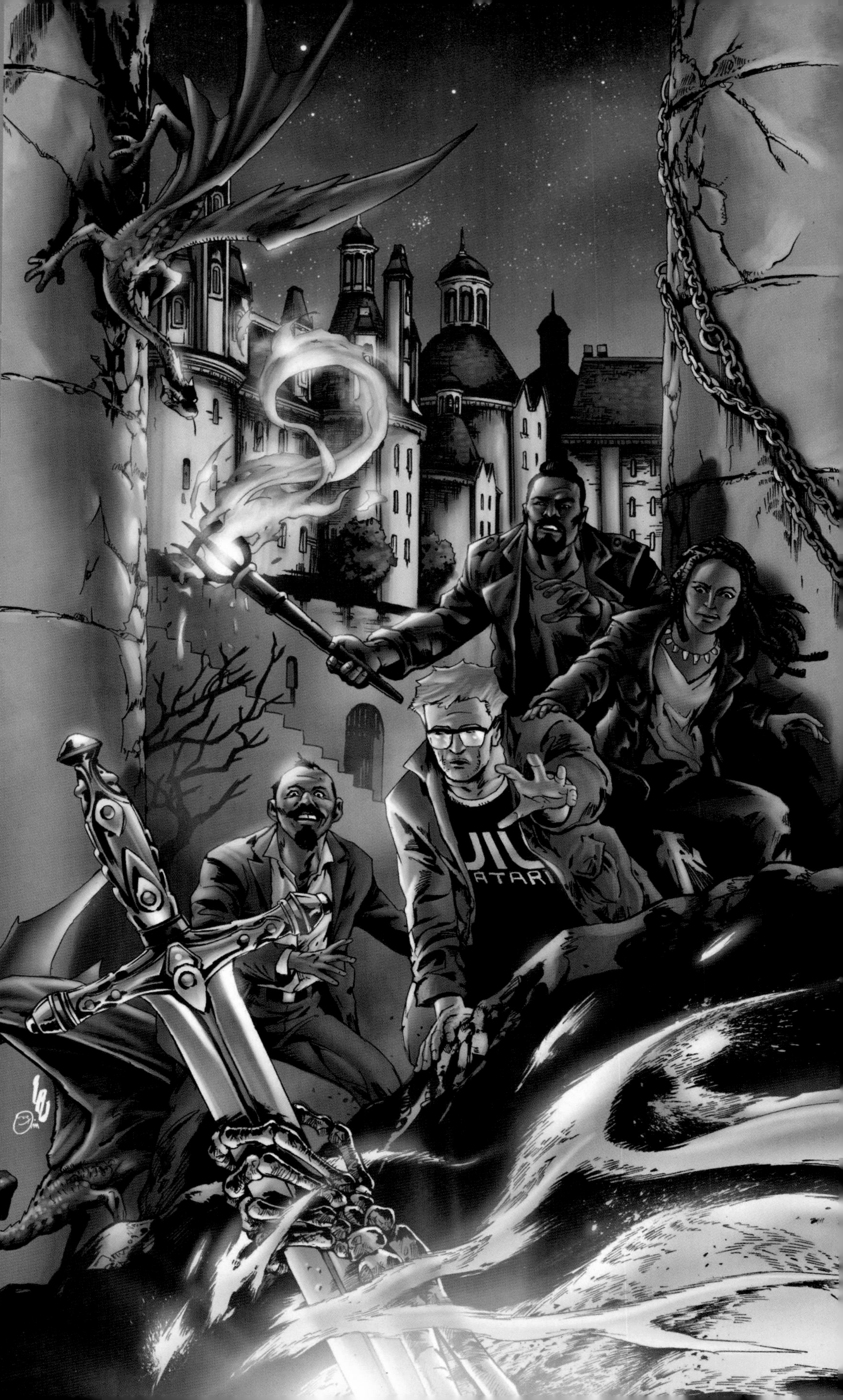
ATARI

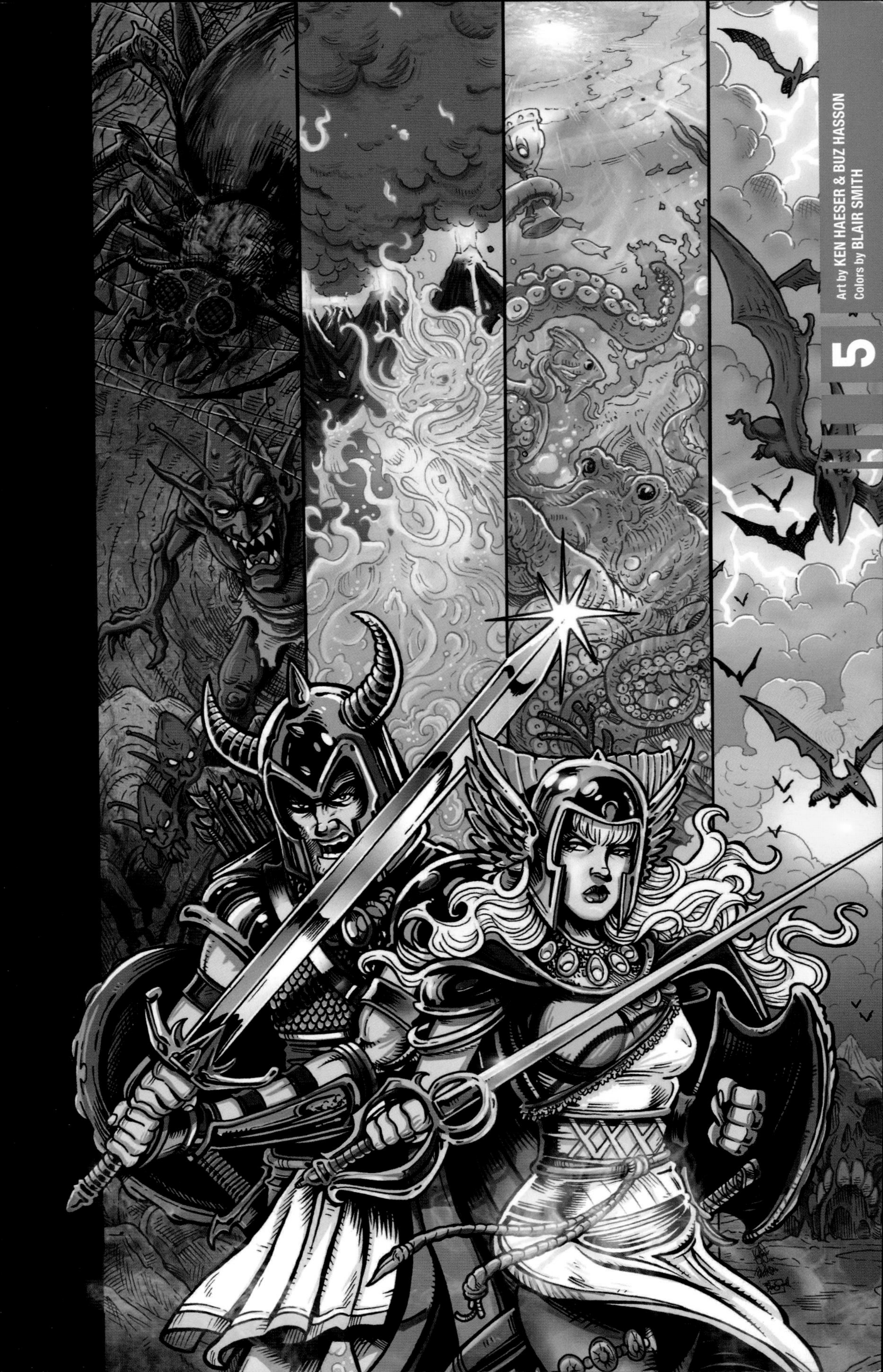
Art by KEN HAESER & BUZ HASSON
Colors by BLAIR SMITH
5

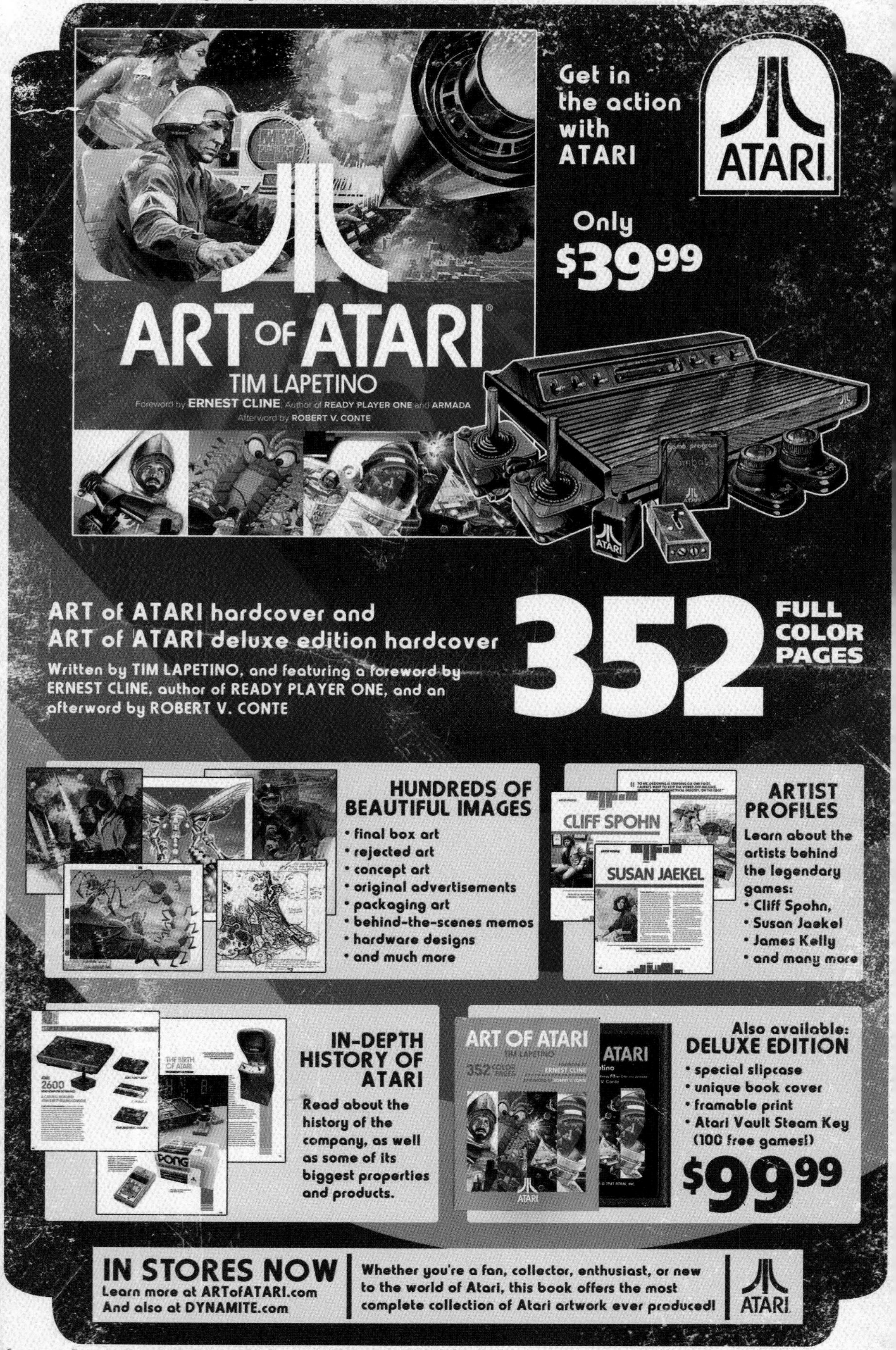
ART OF ATARI
TIM LAPETINO
Foreword by ERNEST CLINE, Author of READY PLAYER ONE and ARMADA
Afterword by ROBERT V. CONTE
Get in the action with ATARI
ATARI
Only $39.99
ART of ATARI hardcover and
ART of ATARI deluxe edition hardcover
Written by TIM LAPETINO, and featuring a foreword by ERNEST CLINE, author of READY PLAYER ONE, and an afterword by ROBERT V. CONTE
352 FULL COLOR PAGES
HUNDREDS OF BEAUTIFUL IMAGES
• final box art
• rejected art
• concept art
• original advertisements
• packaging art
• behind-the-scenes memos
• hardware designs
• and much more
CLIFF SPOHN
SUSAN JAEKEL
ARTIST PROFILES
Learn about the artists behind the legendary games:
• Cliff Spohn,
• Susan Jaekel
• James Kelly
• and many more
THE BIRTH OF ATARI
2600
PONG
IN-DEPTH HISTORY OF ATARI
Read about the history of the company, as well as some of its biggest properties and products.
ART OF ATARI
TIM LAPETINO
352 COLOR PAGES
ERNEST CLINE
Also available:
DELUXE EDITION
• special slipcase
• unique book cover
• framable print
• Atari Vault Steam Key (100 free games!)
$99.99
IN STORES NOW
Learn more at ARTofATARI.com
And also at DYNAMITE.com
Whether you're a fan, collector, enthusiast, or new to the world of Atari, this book offers the most complete collection of Atari artwork ever produced!
ATARI